APPLYING COMPLEXITY THEORY

Whole systems approaches to criminal justice and social work

Edited by Aaron Pycroft and Clemens Bartollas

First published in Great Britain in 2014 by

Policy Press
University of Bristol
6th Floor
Howard House
Queen's Avenue
Clifton
Bristol BS8 1SD
UK
Tel +44 (0)117 331 5020
Fax +44 (0)117 331 5367
e-mail pp-info@bristol.ac.uk
www.policypress.co.uk

North American office:
Policy Press
c/o The University of Chicago Press
1427 East 60th Street
Chicago, IL 60637, USA
t: +1 773 702 7700
f: +1 773-702-9756
e:sales@press.uchicago.edu
www.press.uchicago.edu

British Library Cataloguing in Publication Data
A catalogue record for this book is available from the British Library

Library of Congress Cataloging-in-Publication Data
A catalog record for this book has been requested

ISBN 978 1 44731 140 9 hardcover

Cover design by Policy Press
Front cover image: Billy Alexander
Printed and bound in Great Britain by CPI Group (UK) Ltd, Croydon, CR0 4YY
Policy Press uses environmentally responsible print partners

With love from Aaron to Nicky on our
25th Wedding Anniversary

Contents

List of tables and figures   vii

Notes on contributors   viii

Introduction   1
Aaron Pycroft and Clemens Bartollas

one   Complexity theory: an overview   15
            Aaron Pycroft

two   Risk, attractors and organisational behaviour   39
            Paul Jennings

three   Why do people commit crime? An integrated   59
            systems perspective
            Matthew Robinson

four   Complexity and the emergence of social work   79
            and criminal justice programmes
            Michael Wolf-Branigin

five   Child protection practice and complexity   97
            Peter Hassett and Irene Stevens

six   Youth justice: from linear risk paradigm to complexity   113
            Stephen Case and Kevin Haines

seven   The Stephen Lawrence Inquiry: a case study in   141
            policing and complexity
            John G.D. Grieve

eight   Intersecting contexts of oppression within   159
            complex public systems
            Charmaine McPherson and Elizabeth McGibbon

nine   Complexity theory, trans-disciplinary working   181
            and reflective practice
            Fiona McDermott

ten   Probation practice and creativity in England and   199
            Wales: a complex systems analysis
            Aaron Pycroft

eleven   Responding to domestic abuse: multi-agented systems,   221
            probation programmes and emergent outcomes
            Sarah Lewis

twelve   Complexity, law and ethics: on drug addiction, natural   247
            recovery and the diagnostics of psychological jurisprudence
            Bruce Arrigo and Christopher Williams

thirteen Constituting the system: radical developments in   269
post-Newtonian society
Clemens Bartollas

Conclusion   287
Clemens Bartollas and Aaron Pycroft

Index   295

List of tables and figures

Tables

6.1	The crude, measurement of risk in Risk Factor Research	121
7.1	Stephen Lawrence Inquiry recommendations compared with cognitive dissonance-based and possible complexity applications	153
10.1	Tiering of offenders under the Offender Management Model	201
10.2	Comparing paradigms	205

Figures

i.1	Non-linearity	3
i.2	Contextualising complexity	5
1.1	Cellular Automata	27
3.1	Integrated systems	60
3.2	Numbered relationships in the Integrated Systems Theory of antisocial behaviour	63
3.3	Integrated Systems Theory restated	68
3.4	Development of antisocial behaviour in Integrated Systems Theory	69
6.1	The assessment and planning interventions framework	131
8.1	Intersections of the social determinants of health	164
8.2	Intersecting contexts of oppression within complex public systems	169
10.1	Multiple needs and their approximation to a strange attractor	210
11.1	The 'whole system' context of domestic abuse intervention within probation practice	231
12.1	Psychological jurisprudence, drug addiction and natural recovery: the society of captives, the criminological shadow and spontaneous order	257
c.1	Rethinking relationships between epistemological traditions in relation to complexity	289

Notes on contributors

Bruce Arrigo PhD is Professor of Criminology, Law and Society within the Department of Criminal Justice and Criminology at the University of North Carolina, USA, and holds additional faculty appointments in the Public Policy Program College of Liberal Arts and Sciences, the College of Health and Human Services and the Department of Public Health Sciences. Professor Arrigo is also a Faculty Associate in the Center for Professional and Applied Ethics and a senior member of the University Honors College, and a Faculty Affiliate of Wake Forest University's Bioethics, Health, and Society Program. He is (co-)author of more than 175 peer-reviewed journal articles, law reviews, chapters in books and academic essays and is also (co-)author or (co-)editor of more than 30 monographs, textbooks, reference works and/or edited volumes, with his research and scholarship focusing on the relationship between the possibility of human justice and the problem of social welfare, emphasising the role of praxis and critique in theory, research and pedagogy. His recent monograph-length collaborative work is *The ethics of total confinement: a critique of madness, citizenship, and social justice* (Oxford University Press, 2011). Among his numerous awards and recognitions, Dr Arrigo was the 2012 recipient of the Lifetime Achievement Award from the Crime and Juvenile Delinquency Division of the Society for the Study of Social Problems.

Clemens Bartollas received his PhD from the Ohio State University in sociology, with an emphasis on criminology. He is a full Professor of Sociology at the University of Northern Iowa, USA, where he has taught for the past 33 years. He has written/contributed to many articles, as well as this, his 50th, book, in the areas of juvenile delinquency, juvenile justice, adult corrections and correctional leadership, as well as a number of biographies, including a forthcoming one on Richard Quinney, who developed peacemaking criminology and other paradigm shifts in criminology.

Stephen Case, PhD is an Associate Professor in the Centre for Criminal Justice and Criminology at Swansea University, UK. His research interests include the application of complexity theory to the field of youth justice and the development of children's rights-based, anti-risk approaches to assessment and intervention with young people in conflict with the law. Stephen co-wrote the book *Understanding youth offending: risk factor research, policy and practice* (Willan, 2009) with

Professor Kevin Haines and has published articles in academic journals such as *Youth Justice, Children and Society, British Journal of Social Work* and the *Journal of Substance Use.*

John G.D. Grieve, CBE, QPM, BA(Hons), MPhil has served as a police officer and detective in the Metropolitan Police in every role from undercover officer to policy chair for over 37 years. His duties involved the Drugs Squad, Flying Squad, Robbery Squad and Murder Squad as senior investigator. He was also the borough commander at Bethnal Green and head of training at Hendon Police College and was the first Director of Intelligence for the Metropolitan Police. He led the UK Anti-Terrorist Squad as National Co-ordinator during the 1996–98 Irish Republican Army (IRA) bombing campaigns and created the Race and Violent Crime Task Force. In the latter role, he was responsible with others for the creation and development of the Cultural Change, Critical Incident and Community Impact models for strategic crisis management. He retired in May 2002. He was appointed as one of four Commissioners of the International Independent Monitoring Commission for some aspects of the peace process in Northern Ireland in 2003 by the UK government until 2011. He is a Senior Research Fellow at the University of Portsmouth and Professor Emeritus at London Metropolitan University and has taught in Europe, the US, Russia, China, Japan, Africa, the Caribbean and Australia. He currently chairs the Ministry of Justice/Home Office Independent Advisory Group on Hate Crime and advises a number of policing bodies, including on cultural matters.

Kevin Haines, PhD is a Professor and Director of the Centre for Criminal Justice and Criminology at Swansea University, UK. His research interests lie in the fields of youth justice and social inclusion, including applying complexity theory, developing children's rights approaches and promoting positive behaviour through inclusionary models of prevention. Kevin co-authored the seminal text *Young people and youth justice* (Palgrave Macmillan, 1998) with Professor Mark Drakeford and *Understanding youth offending: risk factor research, policy and practice* (Willan, 2009) with Dr Stephen Case, alongside a wide range of international peer-reviewed journal articles.

Peter Hassett qualified as a social worker in 1972 and worked as a practitioner, trainer and service manager. His last two posts in social work were as Head of Central Council for Education and Training in Social Work in Scotland and Director of Services for Phoenix

House, a national drug services agency. From, 2002, he worked as a freelance consultant, as well as being Clerk to the Board for the Scottish Environment Protections Agency. He came across complexity theory in 2003 and recognised its value in providing a robust framework for the analysis of risk, both at a corporate level and as a practical tool for evaluating specific risks in social work and social care. He retired in 2007 and became active as a writer and presenter on complexity.

Paul Jennings has over 25 years' experience in commercial security and risk management. In June 2013, he became the European Vice President of the Enterprise Security, Risk and Compliance division of First Data, a major credit card and payments processor. Prior to that, he was a Distinguished Engineer at IBM in the Security Specialty Services Area. In both of these roles, he has focused on ensuring that systems are in place to ensure security and risk management at an appropriate level, in the face of commercial and other 'real-world' pressures. Paul has a degree in Mathematics from Southampton University, and is an enthusiastic advocate of applying risk-based methods for large organisations, particularly in facing the challenges that occur when the digital world of systems and processes meets the analogue world of humans and their different drives and motivations, and has been working with Aaron Pycroft in developing understandings of risk within complex systems.

Sarah Lewis, BSc, MSc is a Senior Lecturer at the ICJS (Institute of Criminal Justice Studies at the University of Portsmouth) in Criminal Psychology, and Course Leader for the undergraduate degree Criminology with Psychology. Up until 2012, she worked for Hampshire Probation Trust for six years, starting her career in prisons and then moving into the community as a programme facilitator, delivering cognitive behavioural programmes to probationers. Her academic and research interests include: correctional relationships, convict criminology, offender rehabilitation, domestic abuse, prisons and participatory research with offenders. In 2012 Sarah received the Sir Graham Smith Award from the National Offender Management Service for her research into probationer-supervisor relationships and desistance from crime.

Fiona McDermott, BA, Dip Soc Studs, MUP PhD (Melb) is an Associate Professor and holds a joint appointment in the Departments of Social Work at Monash University and Monash Health, Melbourne, Australia. Her teaching and research is in the areas of multiple and complex needs, health, mental health, and working with groups. She maintains a clinical practice in group work, co-facilitating two long-term groups. Fiona has a particular interest in the development, mentoring and support of practitioner researchers, and in qualitative and action research approaches. She has published in these areas.

Dr Elizabeth McGibbon is an Associate Professor in the Faculty of Science, School of Nursing, St Francis Xavier University, Nova Scotia, Canada. Her research programme is in the area of critical health studies, with a specific emphasis on social justice and health. Her focus is on the structural determinants of health – the economic, social and political structures of society, and the moral and cultural systems that underpin them. Her books include *Oppression: a social determinant of health* (Fernwood Publishing, 2013) and, with Dr J. Etowa, *Anti-racist health care practice* (Canadian Scholars Press, 2009). Dr McGibbon's international journal publications are focused primarily on colonisation and decolonisation, anti-racist practice, complexity theory, the political economy of health inequities, and oppression and mental health. Her research is based in over 20 years of clinical practice in large institutions and in the community.

Charmaine McPherson, RN, PhD is an Associate Professor in the School of Nursing, St Francis Xavier University, Nova Scotia, Canada. Her teaching and programme of research focus on health system strengthening, health in all policy, inter-sectoral and inter-professional collaboration, and social justice for health equity at local, national and international levels. Her publications and technical advisory work use critical social science and complexity science frames to analyse these issues and propose innovative system and societal responses. Dr McPherson's programme of research and teaching expertise are informed by practice as a family therapist, community mental health manager, therapeutic residential care facility owner and governmental policy analyst.

Aaron Pycroft MA, Dip Soc Admin, FHEA [twitter: @aaronpycroft] is Senior Lecturer in Addiction Studies at the Institute of Criminal Justice Studies at the University of Portsmouth, UK, where he teaches, researches and writes on issues related to addiction, rehabilitation, social work and the criminal justice system. His main interests are related to addiction as a complex adaptive system and the implications of this for practice; his previous books include *Understanding and working with substance misusers* (Sage, 2010); *Multi agency working in criminal justice:*

care and control in contemporary correctional practice (Policy Press, 2010), co-edited with Dennis Gough; and *Risk and rehabilitation: management and treatment of substance misuse and mental health problems in the criminal justice system* (Policy Press, 2012) co-edited with Suzie Clift.

Matthew Robinson is Professor of Government and Justice Studies at Appalachian State University in Boone, NC, USA, where he is also Coordinator of the undergraduate programme in Criminal Justice. He received his PhD in Criminology and Criminal Justice from the Florida State University. His research interests include criminological theory, crime prevention, capital punishment, national drug control policy and relationships between social justice and criminal justice. He is the author of scores of articles and chapters as well as 14 books, including *Why crime? An interdisciplinary approach to explaining criminal behavior* (Prentice Hall, 2009), with Kevin Beaver. He is also Past President of the North Carolina Criminal Justice Association and Past President of the Southern Criminal Justice Association.

Dr Irene Stevens qualified as a social worker in 1982. Most of her practice was in residential child care. In 2001, she joined the Scottish Institute for Residential Child Care based at Strathclyde University in Glasgow, UK, where she carried out research, training and consultancy in residential child care. She developed an interest in complexity from 2004, and saw the relevance of its concepts to residential child care. Since then, she has published and presented papers on complexity and its application to children at risk. In 2012, she left Strathclyde University and worked for a time as an independent consultant on a variety of projects. She has recently joined Edinburgh University as a research fellow, where she is examining how to promote practice across inter-professional boundaries.

Christopher Williams, PhD is Professor and Chairman of the Department of Criminal Justice Studies at Bradley University, USA, and has created, developed and taught a wide range of courses within criminology and criminal justice on topics such as criminological theory, ethics and criminal justice, criminal profiling, psychology and the legal system, crime and music, drugs and culture, and social justice. He has published four books, over 25 academic journal articles and book chapters, and numerous essays and reviews, most confronting issues and controversies in social and criminological theory, the sociology of deviance, the philosophical foundations of crime, law, and justice, and the sociological and legal dimensions of mental health and illness. His books include: *Law, psychology, and justice: chaos theory and the new (dis)order* (SUNY Press, 2002); *Theory, justice, and social change: theoretical integrations and critical applications* (Kluwer, 2004); the edited volume *Philosophy, crime, and criminology* (University of Illinois Press, 2006); and *Ethics, crime, and criminal justice* (Prentice Hall, 2007).

Michael Wolf-Branigin, PhD is Interim Chair and Associate Professor of Social Work at George Mason University in Fairfax Virginia, USA, where he teaches research and evaluation methods and social policy. His substantive areas include intellectual/developmental disabilities and addictions. His current research interest focuses on applications of complex systems theory in social service delivery and he has published *Using complexity theory for research and program evaluation* (Oxford University Press, 2013). Dr Wolf-Branigin has published over 40 peer-reviewed articles and serves on a variety of editorial boards. Before coming to George Mason University, he held a variety of positions in human service administration, governmental and non-governmental consulting, and academia.

Introduction

Aaron Pycroft and Clemens Bartollas

> The point about complexity is that it is useful − it helps
> us to understand the things we are trying to understand.
> (Byrne, 1998, p 7)

This book is about challenge, stimulation and intellectual inquiry; in
it, we provide a range of examples from criminal justice, social work
and other public systems settings, which are written by people who
have extensive experience, both academic and practice-based. We argue
that these examples (and they are not exhaustive) demonstrate the
importance of understanding the necessity of whole-systems approaches
based upon understandings of non-linearity. Most of us in our daily
lives, both personal and professional, realise that despite our best efforts,
things do not always work out in the way that we planned, sometimes
with minor consequences and sometimes with dire consequences.
Furthermore, these consequences can sometimes become locked into
patterns and regularities that appear difficult to change despite best
efforts and outside interventions. These consequences can become
evident in criminal justice and social work in relation to reoffending,
addiction and child protection for example, with similar problems
and mistakes seeming to repeat themselves. It is our contention that
interdisciplinary approaches based upon the study of complexity theory
and non-linearity helps us both to understand and to act in just and
ethical ways to respond to these problems.

The study of non-linear dynamical systems (NDS) through the
development of chaos and complexity theory has become increasingly
influential in both the physical and social sciences, having been
proclaimed as the third revolution in human thinking after relativity and
quantum mechanics. The NDS approach views the world as comprising
a series of interacting systems and subsystems, where change in any
part of those systems or their subsystems can change the context for
all of the other elements. Increasingly, approaches based around ideas
of complexity theory are being used in the study of organisations and
the delivery of services, social work, psychology, medicine, and mental
health and addiction studies. Importantly, complexity theory addresses
issues of self organisation, evolution and emergence within whole

systems and fractal (nested system) relationships. The interrelated nature of these systems can work from the genetic and cellular foundations of life through to the 'whole systems' of individuals, society and the state, thus having profound implications for our understanding of cause and effect.

Complexity theory is primarily concerned with non-linearity and the findings from a range of inquiries in both the human and physical sciences that change in any given complex system is not (necessarily) proportional to inputs. For example, within the social sphere, politicians want to allocate a certain amount of money to address social problems and demand specific performance measures allied with proportionate outcomes. This is described in the words of Kernick (2006, p 385) as 'the confident assumption … that a simple relationship exists between cause and effect in a system that can be understood by reducing it into its component parts'. However, these assumptions, which underestimate the complexity of the environments in which social policy objectives are delivered, are being challenged by developments in the field of NDS that help to explain what are often called 'unintended consequences'.

Figure i.1 demonstrates in a simple way that outputs from any system, whether it is a probation or social work intervention, are not necessarily proportionate to inputs and are, in fact, unpredictable due to the interaction effects within the system, its subsystems and wider environmental demands. In the social policy field, these outcomes often indicate the existence of apparently intractable problems of the types covered in this book, which are a central feature of debate and research within both the academic and political landscapes. There is a recognition that to address these problems, there need to be new and innovative approaches that move beyond either wildly and overly engineered solutions on the one hand, or laissez-faire approaches on the other; so, for example, both the Munro Review of child protection in the UK (Department for Education, 2011) and the Drug Strategy for England (Home Office, 2010) stress the importance of taking a 'whole-systems' approach to addressing complex problems. However, much of the thinking contained in these examples is still based on general systems theory, an approach from which complexity marks a major development. There have been an increasing number of articles and books (some by contributors to this volume) written on complexity theory in the social work literature but this is the first to look at the interfaces between criminal justice and social work from a complex systems perspective. This book also comes at an important time for both criminal justice and social work, as practice is being re-evaluated, with the need for a reinvigorated search for new (and not so new) ways of

Figure i.1: Non-linearity

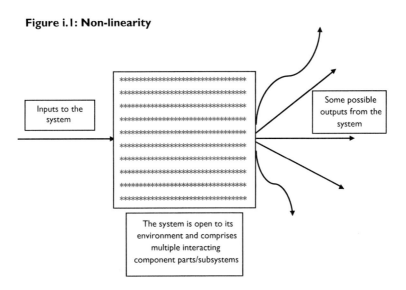

Inputs to the system

Some possible outputs from the system

The system is open to its environment and comprises multiple interacting component parts/subsystems

creative working and less prescriptive practices within the context of financial austerity.

This book is unique in that it will for the first time bring together an international range of experts who are teaching, writing, researching and applying complexity theory in areas that are relevant to the theory and practice of criminal justice and social work (and beyond). This book will be at the forefront of research in these areas by providing a detailed but accessible discussion of some of the key issues presented by complexity, including the efficacy and ethics of criminal justice and social work interventions, notions of change, emergence, and personal responsibility. One of the features of this book is that we have invited a range of perspectives, from positivist, to post–positivist (realist) and to constructivist. The book is ordered so that there is a logical progression from the former to the latter to allow for an appreciation of continuities and discontinuities between the different approaches. However we would not want to give the impression that the development of complexity theory is linear and that one approach follows from another; it does not and we will be returning to this issue in the Conclusion for discussion within the context of teaching and research.

Chapter One, through introducing the key concepts that are foundational to an understanding of complexity theory and its relevance to criminal justice and social work, will provide important contextual information for the following chapters in the book. The chapter will aim to familiarise readers with the vocabulary of complexity theory as a branch of the study of NDS, including notions of complex deterministic systems, attractors, non-linearity, chaos, self-organisation, emergent properties and adaptation.

The chapter will explore the background to key debates in the study of complexity by considering, for example, the highly contested relevance of mathematically derived notions of chaos to the reality of being human. For example, the relevance of the relationship between mathematically derived notions of chaos and complexity and human reality is a contested area. Different approaches to these areas of study are (broadly) defined by positivism, post-positivism and constructivism, although it has also been argued that the study of complexity requires 'doublethink' to avoid polarisation between approaches of contingency and randomness and the search for regularities and patterns. To make sense of these debates, Morin's conceptualisation of 'restricted' and 'general' complexity will be utilised to clarify these different approaches.

To examine the concept of restricted complexity, Cellular Automata will be used as an accessible model to demonstrate the complex outcomes of simple rules of interaction. General complexity will be examined through, for example, looking at Cilliers' (among others) argument that, in part, the postmodern philosophies are sensitive to complexity, and thus he makes a clear distinction between (but does not dismiss) the relationship between chaos theory derived from mathematics and complexity. Also within this categorisation, David Byrne's arguments for a realist (post-positivist) perspective on researching complexity will be examined, allied with the work of Pawson and Tilley.

In Figure i.2, we have given a representation/contextualisation of where the other chapters in this book fit within debates on chaos, complexity and non-linearity. This is not always easy to do, as there are no clear cut-off points that clearly delineate one approach from another, and so the use of fuzzy logic is always required; however, we also invite the reader to look at the possibilities of using complexity theory to bridge ontological and epistemological divides, which is a theme that we return to in the Conclusion.

Chapter Two outlines from a positivist position the mathematical roots of complexity by applying these principles to the study of risk in organisations, and argues that complex causation is inherent in organisations due to the interaction of a variety of factors, ranging from direct constraints imposed externally to implicit constraints that involve operational factors such as resource management and the personal incentives of the people involved. In conjunction, these factors will produce interaction effects and 'unexpected' behaviour, which from a complexity perspective, is emergent in nature. This

Figure i.2: Contextualising complexity

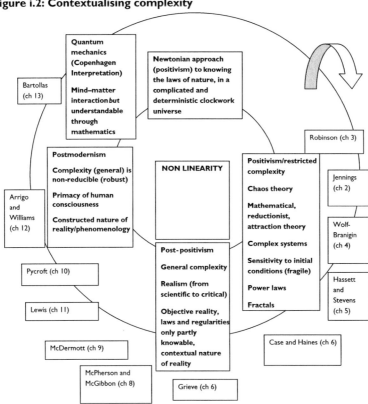

emerge is brought about by being attracted through the reinforcing of, or discouraging of, particular actions within the organisation and its constituent members. While these scenarios are by their nature complex and unpredictable, there are, nonetheless, basic mathematical principles that underpin them, and an understanding of these leads to insights into the behaviour of these chaotic attractors. The chapter critically analyses those underlying principles and the ways in which they shape complexity, and discusses operational approaches to managing the risks that they present. By asserting mathematical concepts including attractor theory and some fundamental principles of probability and statistics in our everyday lives, Jennings is arguing in the Newtonian tradition that these principles are knowable and that we are becoming mathematically and statistically more adept at managing risk in the workplace and beyond. Those who work in criminal justice and social work, for whom risk assessment and management has come to dominate much of their working lives, will want to examine whether becoming more sophisticated in our assessment tools makes us more effective workers in the light of what Jennings argues about the ways in which the human brain has evolved to deal with such situations.

In terms of the layout of the book, Chapter Two is positioned to complement the discussions in the first chapter by outlining in detail attractor theory and some of the mathematical and statistical concepts available to us. In reality, Robinson's discussion on Integrated Systems Theory in Chapter Three could (as per Figure i.1) come before Jennings's chapter as it provides a highly positivistic account of the causes of crime in a way that challenges notions of free will, choice and, ultimately, personal responsibility. The chapter makes an important link between General Systems Theory and understandings of complexity found in the rest of the book through an exposition of positivistic and complicated factors that are probabilistic in leading to crime. This approach assumes that risk factors at all levels of analysis – from cell to organ, to individual, to group, to community and organization, all the way to society – interact to produce behaviour. Integrated Systems Theory identifies many of those risk factors and establishes how they come together to interact and produce behaviour. The chapter also focuses on the most recent developments in theory that relate to these approaches, with the author specifically introducing and summarising what we know about the emerging approach at the cellular level called *epigenetics* and recent efforts to integrate such approaches with higher-level factors as potential explanations of aggressive and violent behaviours. Finally, in relating Integrated Systems Theory to complexity theory, Robinson is suggesting that concepts like complexity, interaction and even chaos hold much promise for understanding and, ultimately, preventing crime. Again, in making links with organisational and practice issues, readers will want to examine the extent to which multiple factors of deprivation limit the extent to which individuals can/should be held responsible for their own actions and what the implications of Robinson's thinking are for public services.

In Chapter Four, Wolf-Branigin makes the case for social work and criminal justice programmes as examples of complex adaptive systems evolving from the efforts of individuals working at the grassroots level. He outlines several properties of these systems, which are to be found in positivist accounts of complexity, including being agent-based, being dynamic, being self-organising, having boundaries, using feedback and producing an emergent behaviour. Wolf-Branigin explains these properties and presents a positivist framework for envisioning these programmes as complex systems and the various states in which they can exist. However, given the linkages between participants, treatment staff, funding sources and other key stakeholders, the chapter develops a post-positivist account of complexity based upon an understanding of the person in environment perspective and its relevance to social work and criminal justice. Importantly, his approach does not break with the positivist tradition, but, through using the example of Gödel's *Incompleteness Theorems*, demonstrates that from a positivistic perspective, there is an acceptance that not all aspects of a system or its rules are necessarily knowable.

The reader, if working in or the user of an organisation and its services, may want to think through what the nature of that system is and what its complex and adaptive features might be, for example: what scope is there for innovation and creative thinking and practice? Is there an emphasis on bureaucracy and standardisation, and how does the organisation compare with, for example, Alcoholics or Narcotics Anonymous? Is it possible to influence how organisations develop and evolve or are there processes that govern this behaviour beyond the control of individuals?

In Chapter Five, the area of child protection is considered by using an explicitly positivist approach to the existence of power laws within complex adaptive systems that explains repeated failures to protect children from serious harm and death. Hassett and Stevens argue that, historically, reports and inquiries that have examined these failures have taken a linear approach in the analysis of the chronology of service failure, with the result that their recommendations have failed to take account of the dynamic nature of the complex adaptive systems within which children are embedded. They further argue that an approach based upon complexity suggests that there will be unintended and unpredictable consequences as the tightening of procedures leads to defensive practice and a 'tick-box' approach to assessment of risk in the future. Building upon the previous chapters, this, then, raises serious questions about how practitioners use their judgements in managing risk, and also what our understanding of complex adaptive systems says about the inevitability of child deaths in the future. Again, in a move away from determinism towards post-positivism, the final proposition of the chapter is not one of defeatism, but one of empowerment of professionals to balance procedural dictates with professional judgement. A key question, then, is the extent to which we need to recognise and understand the existence of power laws in changing judgements and practices in our professional lives.

In Chapter Six, Case and Haines address the issue of developing risk assessment tools from a post-positivist complexity perspective and, in so doing, challenge the dominance of positivist, reductionist, deterministic and linear, risk-based models of understanding and responding to young people's offending behaviour within the field of youth justice in England and Wales. The positivist risk paradigm is contrasted with evolving arguments to integrate more complexity, contextuality and multidimensionality into youth justice theory, research, policy and practice.

Case and Haines examine the risk factor paradigm in contemporary youth justice practice, and particularly the notion that the risk of future offending by young people can be accurately assessed/measured/predicted and then targeted via preventive intervention. By arguing from a post-positivist perspective, the reductionist nature of risk-based youth justice is dissected and the chapter advances an alternative approach using two central elements of Complex Systems Science: the use of more sensitive and thus accurate measurement instruments (fractal theory); and closer consideration of the impact of the origins of specific behaviours in different individuals based upon path sensitivity. They argue for the reorientation of youth justice in England and Wales through assessment and intervention practices that are more sensitive to socio-structural, historical and localised contexts and their impact on psychological and immediate social circumstances, with particular emphasis on accessing the views of young people. This last point is crucial in moving away from positivism because it allows us to develop the idea that observers of a system are, in fact, interacting with that system and are not separated from it. This foundational view of observer positionality within post-positivism, then, allows for the development of these ideas with links between scientific realism, critical realism, postmodern views on constructivism and quantum mechanics. The reader might want to consider the extent to which the use of both quantitative and qualitative approaches to risk assessment enhance that process and what methods might be used and, ultimately, to what end for both the service user, the organisation and wider society.

In Chapter Seven, Grieve addresses the issue of the Metropolitan Police as a complex adaptive system and develops the theme of path dependence identified by Case and Haines in Chapter Six. Grieve does this by examining the inquiry and responses to that inquiry into the racist murder of Stephen Lawrence. By using a complex systems analysis (realist), the chapter addresses the important issue of 'order for free' as a key component of complex systems and the ways in which features and behaviours such as racism can become 'locked in' despite efforts to change these features. One of the key features of a complex adaptive system is that it has a history and by being adaptive, is a learning system, but one that operates at the level of the whole system. Grieve's chapter finds that the original investigation into the murder was overly reductionist and that the response to the inquiry relied on reductionist approaches to critical incident analysis, whereas Grieve contends that complexity thinking about learning and adaptation of policies and practices could have improved the progress made in the 15 years since the Stephen Lawrence Inquiry and, in particular, the finding of institutional racism. Readers might want to reflect on the idea of 'order for free' and the ways in which organisational behaviours become 'locked in' and what the evidence for these is. This chapter also demonstrates the robustness of systems based around initial conditions and the ways in which the system is able to adapt to external threats and pressures; hence the argument that despite some progress over the 15 years, the Metropolitan Police is still open to accusations of being institutionally racist.

Whereas Grieve's chapter focuses on path dependence, in Chapter Eight, McPherson and McGibbon develop the whole-system context of oppression for traditionally marginalised people from an intersectionality perspective. They argue that this approach, based on a critical social science (realist) perspective, might be used to better understand the conflating relationships among the social determinants of health and well-being, social/public service access, and identities such as race and gender. They argue that our analytical gaze should be at the macro-systems level, with emphasis on the unjust structural policy and practice factors that contribute to the development and maintenance of systemic oppression, and that we should specifically interrogate equity issues of exclusion from services. This approach moves us away from scientific realism to an approach grounded in critical realism, which argues that exclusion arises from entrenched structural oppression based on race and gender such that vulnerable populations are systematically denied appropriate access to key social services. McPherson and McGibbon argue that this approach to complexity science helps to explain the non-linear synergy at play across multiple contextual, situational and identity factors, which often amounts to system-based oppression, and provides an explanation for the context of this oppression. Importantly, this chapter argues for understanding the contribution of the individual actor to the behaviour of the whole system (and so is in the realist tradition) and the reader might want to think about their own experiences of oppression, either within or by organisations that they are involved with. Important questions include the extent to which complexity theory can help us to develop our own anti-oppressive practice and the impact that this might have on the overall system/s in which we work and operate.

These themes are further developed by McDermott in Chapter Nine, who makes the argument from a realist perspective that it is at the level of *practice/intervention* that the interconnectedness and interdependency of systems are revealed with particular clarity, confronting practitioners with the reality of what complexity is and means, and its potentially overwhelming impact. The classic argument of realists is that the task for human service workers at the service delivery level is to deconstruct complexity both to make action possible and to enable creative and innovative responses to problems. As the delivery of public services becomes more complicated and complex, with partnership (formal and informal) arrangements and multi-agency working being the norm, the focus for an interdisciplinary team might, for example, be on disentangling knowledge, values and interests in order to find common ground for action. For McDermott, this highlights the importance of reflective practice and the need to develop this in line with complexity theory and she argues that what emerges from the interaction of the team itself is a source of insight for reflection-on-practice and reflection-in-practice. McDermott makes an argument for a 'new' type of human service provider, one who is a specialist or expert in working across systems, and the reader might want to consider the ways in which this is applicable to their own role, and what the implications are of this for service users, for example: does this trans-disciplinary working aid the flow of information or is it hindered by an increase in bureaucracy? Importantly, does the reflective practice lend itself to working within a complexity framework, not just within the approach taken by the chapter, but by any of the theoretical orientations outlined in this book?

Both Chapters Ten and Eleven focus on probation practice in England and Wales, with Chapter Ten exploring the changing nature of probation practice through a critical analysis of the multiple and complex roles of practitioners, who are required to be agents of public protection and enforcement, and rehabilitation. This develops the theme of trans-disciplinary working and asks the question of whether it is possible for practitioners to maintain these roles in a state of 'superposition' or whether they give rise to unintended and damaging consequences. In this chapter, Pycroft argues that the work of the Probation Service needs to be identified at three levels of a complex adaptive system (while acknowledging from a realist and general complexity perspective that all complex systems are nested in nature, and that the boundaries of any system are unclear, and also that any system or subsystem has influence beyond what the boundaries may be): the policy system, the organisational system of the probation trust and the individual practitioner–probationer relationship. Pycroft focuses on the importance of the individual practitioner as a key network member who can either help or hinder the flow of information to help probationers and why the human aspects of the professional relationship, ethically founded, are fundamental in bringing about positive change. Within the context of complexity theory, arguments are made for the importance of creativity at all levels of the system and the need for positive feedback within those systems that allows organisations and practice to exist at the 'edge of chaos', which allows novel solutions to apparently intractable problems. The reader might want to think about the implications of facilitating key work sessions with service users at the edge of chaos and what the implications for this might be at the service user, organisational and policy level.

In Chapter Eleven, Lewis continues the exploration of the multi-agented context for the delivery of probation programme group interventions for people who have been convicted of domestic violence. The chapter examines these programmes and identifies their contexts as being constituted by the legal requirements of the programme, the programme tutors, the probationers, the offender manager, the victim and the women's support workers and others and as an example of a complex adaptive system. It argues from a realist perspective that any changes in probationers' attitudes and behaviour constitute a form of emergence that can be positively or negatively distorted by changes in any part of the overall system. Lewis argues for the necessity of reducing particularly bureaucratic complexity in programme delivery settings and focusing on relationships at the human level to improve outcomes and reduce reoffending. Importantly, Lewis uses a complexity perspective to explore the reasons for poor outcomes from domestic abuse interventions to date through highlighting the importance of an approach that recognises the practitioner as a complex adaptive system in their own right, who is given opportunities to be responsive to individual needs rather than adhere to a manual for the running of programmes. Readers might want to consider the nature of emergence within their own practice and the ways in which different styles of intervention effect different types of outcomes, and whether these are predictable. For example, are their advantages to delivering programmes within group work rather than one-to-one settings, and how do the interaction effects increase or decrease complexity?

In Chapter Twelve, Arrigo and Williams argue from a general complexity (constructivist) perspective that humans are complex adaptive systems whose capacities include self-organisation, especially when human/social conditions are in place that maximise the potential for spontaneous order (ie natural recovery from drug addiction). Importantly, these conditions include symbolic, linguistic, material and cultural forces whose flows and intensities are interdependent and co-productive. Ultimately, for Arrigo and Williams, this is an ethical project and they use an approach based on psychological jurisprudence to analyse the ways in which current conditions set limits on this potential for self-organisation in humans and their overcoming of problems. In Chapter Ten, Pycroft discusses the importance of virtue ethics and this chapter also recommends that a virtue-based approach be used when setting policy on the matter of drug addiction and recovery as it advances citizenship and excellence in ways that dignify and affirm being human (the humanness of being a recovering subject/addict) and that celebrate and honour the transformations to be found in recovery. Readers could think about the ways in which individuals are able to construct pathways out of crime and/or problematic behaviours and lifestyles and the ways in which current interventions aid or hinder those processes. In particular, what does it mean to affirm the humanness of the other, who may well be seen as deviant or undesirable due to their behaviour or lifestyle, and what ethical resources do we use to do that?

In Chapter Thirteen, Bartollas examines the limits of our knowledge by examining the possibility of quantum mechanics, especially the Copenhagen Interpretation, to develop a paradigm shift in criminological theory and practice. Along with other chapters in the book, the argument is made that positivism's causation model (cause and effect) is unable to explain the complexity of the multidimensional nature of human behaviour. In contrast, it is postulated that quantum mechanics' theory is better able to understand the emergence and persistence of delinquent and criminal behaviours. It is also postulated that religious beliefs – which have been separated from science since the time of Isaac Newton – have a role to play in post-positivism generally and quantum mechanics particularly. Bartollas uses Peacemaking Criminology as an example of a non-positivistic approach that shows how an openness to religious principles can lead the way to a more humane society based on equality, justice and compassion. This approach is an expression of the ability of humanity to create and invest in new approaches to society and inclusivity through the recognition and embracing of the fundamental interrelatedness of all things. The reader might want to consider the study of criminology as 'spiritual' and the practice of criminal justice as contributing to peacemaking and lasting change in society.

In the conclusion, we draw together and reflect upon the key themes and messages from the book and suggest future developments in the study, research and practice of complexity theory in criminal justice and social work. We also offer guidance on using the chapters in the book as a teaching tool and the kinds of issues that can be addressed, and provide some additional resources for those interested.

Acknowledgements and thanks

In the conclusion, we reflect on the challenges of completing this book, from initial ideas through to completion, and there are a number of people that we need to thank: first, the team at The Policy Press and, in particular, our Commissioning Editor Karen Bowler for her support for the project and latterly Emily Watt for seeing the project through to completion when Karen started a family (and we wish her well); second, the constructive comments and advice of the peer reviewers, from the initial proposal through to comments on the manuscript; and, third, colleagues, and especially Sarah Lewis, Dennis Gough and Madeline Petrillo, from the Institute of Criminal Justice Studies at the University of Portsmouth, who have responded to unreasonable demands to read drafts of chapters or sections of chapters and who have responded with constructive feedback and good humour.

References

Byrne, D. (1998) *Complexity theory and the social sciences: an introduction*, London: Routledge.

Department of Education (2011) *The Munro Review of child protection: final report, a child-centred system*, London: Stationary Office.

Home Office (2010) *Drug Strategy 2010, reducing demand, restricting supply, building recovery: supporting people to live a drug free life*, London: Stationery Office.

Kernick, D. (2006) 'Wanted – new methodologies for health service research. Is complexity theory the answer?', *Family Practice*, vol 23, no 3, pp 385–90.

ONE

Complexity theory: an overview

Aaron Pycroft

Introduction

A whole range of physical, biological, psychological and social systems constitute our lives, largely influencing how, when and where we are born, what the quality of our lives and lived experiences will be, and ultimately how we will die, and what we leave behind. Of course, in our efforts to survive and flourish, we have a tendency to try and reduce uncertainty to provide us with at least the illusion of control as we try to navigate the multitude of systems in which we live, leading to an innately reductionist approach (see Jennings, Chapter Two).

The same applies if we work in public services such as criminal justice or social work, when we are probably more used to thinking about systems in the formal sense of partnership/multi-agency working, or team work for example; but, even then, what is the extent of our observation and understanding of what constitutes systems or the contribution that we make to the overarching, under-arching or whole systems of criminal justice or social work? What is the totality of our contribution to the outcomes from those systems, not just for the people that we directly work with, but for those from whom we are further removed or who are unknown to us, and, indeed, how would we know what our impact has been, and could it be measured in any meaningful way? In asking these questions and in attempting to provide a framework for answering them, one of the key arguments of complexity theory is that we need to understand that, as individuals, we are constitutive components of the various systems (as individual human beings, we are also a system) that we live and work in, whether we are conscious of it or not; furthermore, we need to understand that we impact upon the behaviour of that whole system, including that which lies beyond our immediate and observable environs.

In this chapter, to help to understand this idea of being constitutive components of systems, the key tenets of complexity theory from differing perspectives will be introduced and examined. Initially, this will involve a discussion of its mathematical beginnings, but the good news (for non-mathematicians at least) is that you do not have to be a mathematician to work with complexity; rather, we can work with mathematics by analogy or metaphor, and the way that we can do this is through the philosophy of mathematics and the use of logical argument. These understandings are foundational to our project as they make clear the links between differing traditions in mathematics, philosophy and the ontology, epistemology and methodology of social research and how these might relate to complexity theory. In particular, it is useful to highlight the importance of understanding complex systems as entities that are non-linear and uncertain precisely to help us to analyse and intervene more effectively with, for example, criminals who pose a high risk of serious harm or to protect children from abuse.

The purpose of this chapter is to introduce and explore these key concepts and to provide important contextual information for the following chapters in the book. We will explore the background to the key debates in the study of complexity, which, in the words of Paul Cilliers (2010, p 41), 'is a house divided'. As with other areas of study in social research, approaches to the study of complexity are (broadly) defined by positivism, post-positivism and constructivism, although it has also been argued that the study of complexity requires 'doublethink' to avoid a polarisation of the approaches of contingency and randomness (constructivism) and the search for regularities and patterns (positivism and post-positivism).

To help to make sense of these debates, we can utilise Morin's (2005) conceptualisation of 'restricted' and 'general' complexity to clarify these different approaches. The notion of 'restricted' complexity is used by Morin to denote the type of complex systems theory that has developed within, rather than representing a break from, the Newtonian paradigm of the classical scientific method (see later). This paradigm has seen great advances in our understanding of the universe in which we live but has also led to the discovery of Einstein's theory of relativity, quantum-level mechanics, chaos, fractals and disorder. Studies of complexity within this framework acknowledge that complexity exists within and is allowed for within the Newtonian paradigm and searche for the laws of complexity (the work of Stuart Kauffman and the Santa Fe Institute fall within this framework – for a discussion of agent-based modelling, see Wolf-Branigin, Chapter Four). Morin (2005) argues that this approach is still taking an essentially reductionist approach to complexity by trying to reduce complexity to its component parts (see the example of Cellular Automata later).

For Morin (2005), rather than seeking to understand through simplifying and reducing systems to their basic rules, 'general' complexity is more concerned with the relationships between the parts and the whole, and suggests that it is not possible to make a distinction between the two (a principle of conjunction rather than distinction). The principles of general complexity have also been useful in linking studies from both Byrne's (1998) arguments for a realist (post-positivist) perspective on researching complexity and Cilliers' arguments for linking complexity with postmodernism (constructivism). Within these debates, one of the key points of contention is the relationship between mathematically derived notions of chaos and the nature of complexity.

The mathematical background to complexity

The issue of complexity arising from mathematical study is an important one and one that initiated ontological and epistemological understandings of complexity. It is important to note that there are also different philosophies of mathematics based around two central questions that are of relevance to researching and understanding not just complexity, but studies in 'physical', 'biological' and 'social' research generally. It is suggested by Avigad (2007) that these two questions are: first, what are mathematical objects; and, second, how do we have knowledge of them? These questions come back to differences between Plato and Aristotle, with Plato stating that mathematical objects such as triangles or spheres have an objective a priori existence whose imperfect shadows we see in this world (Plato's Theory of Forms).[1] In contrast, Aristotelian accounts of mathematics argue that objects such as triangles and circles are objects that we abstract from our experiences. So, Avigad (2007) says 'that from our interactions with various roughly spherical objects, we form the concept of a perfect sphere. Reasoning about spheres in general boils down to reasoning about specific spheres that we have encountered'. So, on the one hand, we have the Platonic idea of mathematical objects as having an independent existence, in which case, we have to understand how we can have knowledge of them (That is, is our methodology accurate in discovering these 'truths'?), and then we have the Aristotelian idea of abstracting from experience, which raises the question of whether these are then mathematical certainties. There is a third approach associated with the 19th-century Bishop Berkeley, known as 'nominalism', which sees mathematics as a science of governing the use of relatively concrete signs, that is, that mathematical symbols such as numbers are a kind of linguistic convention. This again fits with constructivist arguments and again begs the question of the nature and validity of knowledge or the importance of it.

Chaos

Complexity theory has developed from the mathematics of chaos theory and especially (but not entirely) the work of Edward Lorenz and his study of weather patterns (see Jennings, and also Case and Haines, Chapter Six). The term 'chaos' comes from the ancient Greek word 'kaos', meaning a wide-open abyss or confusion. In its etymological development, it is also associated with the Greek word 'pan', meaning 'every' or 'all', and Pan is the ancient Greek god of violent crowds, who creates panic, terror and chaos from everyone blindly imitating the desires of others (see Girard, 2001).

Byrne (1998) cites the work of Hayles (1990, 1991) to suggest that popularly chaos is a synonym for anti-order, but in chaos theory, 'chaos' is not randomness, but, in fact, quite the opposite. In chaos theory, 'chaos' is the natural output (or interaction effects) of deterministic systems; however, determinism cannot be reduced to simplistic causation, but rather to the increased/decreased probability of an outcome/event based upon a configuration of factors. So, while such systems appear random when they are initially studied, order and patterning are, in fact, observable. To make this clearer, Kernick (2004) distinguishes between two other types of behaviour, namely, random and periodic. Random behaviour never repeats itself, although the average behaviour of the system can be statistically predicted, and periodic behaviour is highly predictable because it always repeats itself, with a pendulum as an example. A pendulum is a deterministic system because by knowing the point of the pendulum at any one point, we can predict its position at any other point in time. The key to understanding the sensitivity, determinism and non-linearity of chaotic systems are the properties of predictability, extreme sensitivity to initial conditions (see Case and Haines, Chapter Six; but also see Cilliers' arguments for the primacy of the robustness of systems in the section on constructivism later) and the presence of an attractor or pattern of behaviour (see Jennings, Chapter Two).

This language of chaos and complexity is relatively new in both the 'natural' and 'social' sciences and is a useful way to understand developments in systems-level thinking (ie looking at the whole system rather than its individual component parts). To understand this approach, it is useful to understand and contrast it with the work of Sir Isaac Newton and the concept of the 'clockwork universe'. We will discuss this to set the scene for developments in our understanding, particularly of the social world, and developments in methodological approaches to social research.

The clockwork universe and the positivist tradition

Newton developed the work of philosophers such as René Descartes, who sought to understand the world and the universe through adopting a general and mechanistic world view; this is still very much the basis of the scientific method and experimental design today, which seeks to test and retest hypotheses until the 'truth' is revealed through consistent replication of findings. This approach requires that complex phenomena be reduced (atomised) to their smallest component parts to make them intelligible; in fact, to simplify the complex. The Newtonian approach is materialistic in nature and assumes that the permanent substance that is called matter constitutes all physical, biological, mental or social phenomena. The only thing that distinguishes the elementary particles (atoms) that make up this material universe are their positions in space; so all phenomena are simply different arrangements in space brought about by the movement of those atoms. This approach argued that the movement of atoms brought about by deterministic laws of cause and effect are entirely predictable through understanding the absolute space and time in which the matter moves and the forces that determine that movement (Heylighen et al, 2007).

The 19th-century scientist Pierre-Simon Laplace gave this determinism a key place in science by arguing that (as with a pendulum) a world is deterministic if its current state defines its future (Smith, 2007). The scientific method, then, seeks to reduce the system to its component parts and, through observation, to identify and make sense of how it works as if it were an engine or a clock for example, that is, mechanical. All knowledge, then, is essentially Platonic in that what we have gained is an understanding of the pre-existent order of things; so, in this sense, the scientific method is not creative or innovative, merely a discovery of what is, and what will always be, albeit in differing configurations over time. This is best expressed under the guise of Laplace's 'Daemon', an 'intellect' that he conceived of that could: know all past events and predict all future events; understand any composite entity through only knowing the constituent parts; and, through applying the principle of disjunction, isolate and separate intellectual and cognitive difficulties from each other, thus hermetically sealing academic disciplines from each other (Morin, 2005).

Positivism and human agency

So far, we have been discussing a range of issues and using evidence from the domain of natural science, but a key question then becomes: what is the relevance of this for being human? Does this tell us anything, for example, about human society, or crime and punishment, or helping people? The answer to those questions and the message of this book is 'yes', and that the traditional scientific approach taken by Newton and his disciples has also fundamentally influenced the ways in which we understand human agency, carry out research and provide interventions to address social problems.

To put it bluntly, in the Newtonian paradigm of a deterministic universe, there is absolutely no scope for notions of free will or human purposive action. Heylighen et al (2007) argue that this provides the explanation for the idea of value-free methodology in classical science (positivism), but also, of necessity, leads to the philosophical innovation of Descartes, who saw the mind as an independent category separate from the mechanical laws of nature;[2] hence his famous dictum, 'I think therefore I am'.

Heylighen et al (2007) argue that the development of rational choice, particularly in economic theory and based on the concept of utility, was one of the ways in which classical scientific principles have sought to get around the problem of determinism and free will. Philosophers such as Jeremy Bentham and John Stuart Mill argued that people always choose an option that maximises their utility. Utility is defined as 'happiness' or 'goodness', and it is assumed that if the actor has complete knowledge of utility or options (similar to Laplace's Daemon), then the actions of minds are as predictable as the laws of nature; approaches to rational choice also underpin classical jurisprudence and legal systems, with the basic premise of personal responsibility being based upon the fact that one could have done otherwise (Frankfurt, 2006).

The 'scientific method' and its positivist underpinning is also the basis of modern medicine, and has a strong tradition in the social sciences. Particularly in the development of evidence-based medicine, the randomised controlled trial (RCT), which seeks to demonstrate causality, has been the gold standard of research. The way that the RCT operates is explained by Pawson and Tilley (1997): 'identical' subjects are randomly allocated to either an experimental group or a control group, and only the experimental group is exposed to the experimental treatment. The same pre- and post-treatment measures are applied to both groups to compare the changes in both groups. The logic of this approach is that any changes in behavioural outcomes are explained by the action of the treatment, and thus it is possible to infer that cause and effect are linked in a linear fashion.

But if we take the examples of working in healthcare, social work or criminal justice, life is rarely simple and linear precisely because of the biological, psychological and social context in which problems arise. Within this complex framework, it can be said that most issues neither have a single cause nor cure (Wilson et al, 2001). It is argued by Plsek and Greenhalgh (2001, p 625) that 'across all disciplines, at all levels and throughout the world, healthcare is becoming more complex', not just in terms of the problems that people are presenting with, but also in clinical and organisational practice. This is also reflected, for example, in dealing with substance misuse problems, with the recognition of multiple needs as the norm within the 'clinical' population and the argued need for multi-agency responses to address these issues. In 1990, the Institute of Medicine in the US, for example, called into question whether the gold standard of scientific inquiry, the RCT, was really the way forward in helping to address substance misuse problems, and called for a different approach to the methodology used to determine outcomes from treatment (Pycroft, 2010). The same challenges apply to any system that involves drivers that are bio-psychosocial in nature.

Differences between complex and complicated

Despite (or perhaps because of) widespread interest in complexity, there is a lack of consensus or a unified theory or agreement as to what complexity actually is; if we take complexity to mean *complexus* (that which is woven, enmeshed), in the sense of a system with multiple and enmeshed components, then we would want to distinguish it from that which is complicated. Complex systems have relationships between the component parts of the system (variables), which are non-linear in nature in the sense that, for example, outputs from the system are not necessarily proportional to inputs. As an example, we can think of the fact that commissioners of social or criminal justice services usually expect that in return for funding, particular objectives and outcomes are met, such as reductions in reoffending, the number of children taken into care or waiting times for assessment, and these desired outcomes are not always met.

Merely (but, nonetheless, often impressively) 'complicated' engines, for example, are complicated in that they can be understood by identifying and describing their component parts, which follow a linear process from ignition through to cruise control; however, complex systems and the interaction between the component parts and their openness to their environments mean that they cannot be fully understood by identifying their components (see Cilliers, 1998), making it very difficult to predict how they will act (but, importantly, not futile, as a part of the argument of this book is that an understanding of complexity allows us to better understand systemic behaviour). In this sense, complicated systems are actually quite simple once you understand how they work and you have a manual that describes their interactions.

A good example that highlights what is complicated and what is complex comes from one of my favourite films, *Apollo 13*, which is based upon the real-life scenario of the manned spaceflight to the moon in 1970. An explosion on the spacecraft two days into the flight caused serious problems to the functioning of the ship, threatening the lives of the astronauts and raising serious questions as to whether they would be able to safely return to earth.

Some of the complicated factors were in the functioning of the ship itself and the need to conserve energy through closing down electrical functions, including the onboard computer and heating system. Essentially, for a successful re-entry into the earth's atmosphere, there needed to be a 'power up' of energy from scratch, for which there was not a procedure in the flight manual, as this was never intended to happen in flight. However, this was achieved through great skill and ingenuity by engineers on earth working with the manual on an exact replica of the spaceship to create a procedure that was then implemented by the astronauts, with a happy ending.

What develops from a complicated to a complex scenario involves the fact that this was a space flight with people on board and, despite being thousands of miles away in space, the interactions between the flight team, the backup crew and the National Aeronautics and Space Administration (NASA) itself, including the ways in which decisions were made in a critical scenario that was being watched live on TV across the globe and had the potential for uncertain and potentially unknowable outcomes. To focus on one aspect of uncertainty: the loss of heating, problems with carbon dioxide levels and the shortage of rations meant that these extremes of environment could have impaired the crew's performance or ability to respond, especially their ability to manually fly the vessel and make the necessary judgements.

Complex adaptive systems

A complex adaptive system is defined as 'a collection of individual agents with freedom to act in ways that are not always totally predictable, and whose actions are interconnected so that the action of one part changes the context for other agents' (Wilson et al, 2001, p 685). Human beings, communities, families, ecosystems and governments are all examples of complex systems, and Bar-Yam (1997) outlines the elements that distinguish them from simple systems. These include: the number of elements involved and the subsequent interactions between those elements and their strength; the formation and operation of the system and the timescales involved; the diversity and variability of the system; the environment in which it exists and the demands that it places upon the system; and the activities and objectives of the system (Pycroft, 2010).

There is a consensus about the key features of complex systems, which are as follows (the following is an amalgamation of Byrne, 1998; Cilliers, 1998; Wilson et al, 2001):

- Complex systems consist of multiple elements: when the number of elements is relatively small, the system can be described and analysed through mathematics; however, when the number of elements is larger, this becomes far more difficult and impractical. In fact, we can say that the system becomes more than the sum of its parts and so interactions between the elements generate emergent behaviours/ properties that cannot be predicted or explained through studying the individual elements of the system. This is the basis of a whole-systems approach: that it is the behaviour of the overall system rather than the individual parts of the system that needs to be the focus of inquiry. For example, the human body is composed of multiple interacting and self-regulating physiological systems that operate within a process of homeostasis.
- For a system to be complex, there needs to be a large number of elements, although this is not sufficient in itself to distinguish between what is complex and what is complicated. The interaction of the elements needs to be dynamic and have the capacity to change over time. Cilliers (1998) also makes the point that these interactions do not have to be physical as they can also be thought of as the transfer of information within a network.
- The exact behaviour of the system is not quantifiable to the precise amount of interactions allocated to individual elements. Different elements in the system can be connected to a greater or lesser degree to other elements and a number of loosely connected elements can have the same effect as one strongly connected element.
- These interactions are non-linear in nature and can produce unpredictable (chaotic) behaviour or outcomes that are not proportionate to inputs into the system. It is this non-linearity that defines the behaviours of complex systems and also determines that small changes in the system can have disproportionate effects.
- The environmental impact on a system and its inputs is mediated by the elements in the system to either strengthen or weaken those

inputs, but, essentially, the behaviours of the elements are usually most influenced by the elements that are closest to them (see Cellular Automata later). The web of relationships in which individuals exist may powerfully determine beliefs, expectations and behaviours (consider the role of social context and peer pressure in relation to substance use).

- The interactions of the elements can be recurrent in that they can have feedback loops that are either direct or indirect (mediated through a number of stages). This feedback is either negative or positive, with the former helping to enhance and stimulate a system and the latter doing the opposite.

- Complex systems are open systems that interact with their environment, which, in turn, is usually populated by other systems. It is often not possible to identify the boundaries of systems as they are also often nested within other systems (known as fractals; see Case and Haines, Chapter Six). Cilliers (1998) argues from a postmodern (constructivist) perspective (see later) that what is seen as the system is usually dependent upon the position of the observer,[3] who is able to frame or bracket (construct) boundaries. However, knowing what is a discrete system or what constitutes a subsystem is difficult, notwithstanding the fact that dynamic outputs from one system (or subsystem) provide the inputs for another. For individuals, immediate social circumstances are further embedded in wider social, political and cultural systems, which can influence outcomes in unpredictable ways (consider the way that the supply and availability of psychoactive substances are legislated for).

- Interacting systems are dynamic and fluid (eg it would appear that some people may move in and out of problematic substance use and crime). Complex systems are engaged in a process of self-organisation, which 'occurs when the system is in a state of high entropy, or far from equilibrium conditions, and takes on a structure that allows the system to operate in a more energy-efficient manner' (Guastello and Liebovitch, 2009, p 23). Far from equilibrium is also referred to as the 'edge of chaos', where novel and innovative solutions to systemic problems can be found. What this means is that the structuring of a system is not dependent upon an external designer or architect; it is what Kauffman (1993, 1995) describes as 'order for free'. The process of self-organisation allows the system to adapt, evolve and survive and, for this to happen, needs to operate under conditions far from equilibrium. Systems in equilibrium are static and non-creative and, ultimately, atrophy (for a discussion on system states, see Wolf-Branigin, Chapter Four).

- This principle of 'order for free' also allows us to understand the nature of emergent properties. We have already identified these as outputs or interaction effects from a system but it is important to remember that emergent properties cannot simply be reduced to their component parts as they are more than the sum of these parts. So, for example, in a therapeutic group, the outcomes from the group cannot simply be reduced to individual contributions to the group, or a musical symphony to the notes, or a painting to brush strokes and so on.
- Complex systems have a history, evolve through time and are sensitive to initial conditions so that small changes in one part of the system, can lead to much larger changes in another part of the system (one drink or use of a drug can lead to a major relapse or not).

A recapping of complex adaptive systems

A complex adaptive system, then, has the following characteristics: it is a multi-agented system that is connected through local agent–agent interactions that tend to be non-linear and feedback on each other; the boundaries between the internal agents and the system and its environment are indistinct and dynamic; energy and other resources are taken from the environment and are continuously dissipated, keeping the system far from equilibrium, and although there is a turnover of components, structures and information are preserved over time; importantly, the system can adapt to changes in the internal and external environment and there is an overlap between subcategories of agent in the system so that an individual may belong to more than one subcategory; because of this connectivity, the existence of fuzzy boundaries and overlap, it is difficult to simply remove a part of the system and to replace it; the system has a history, which determines its current structure, internal organisation and behaviour, so that it is capable of learning; finally, emergent properties may arise through the lower-level interactions between agents and such properties cannot be understood at the level of the agents themselves (ie the sum is more than the total of the parts).

Thus, an understanding of complexity requires a move away from the idea of linear relationships with singular causes, to a focus on decentralised interactions and feedback loops, which emerge from simple interactions. Importantly, complex adaptive systems are modular in nature and are made up of subsystems or modules (similar to modern computers), so that there is no overall control mechanism, which means that if one part of the system fails, then another part compensates for it, meaning that there is not a wholesale incapacitation of the system. It can be seen that within an evolutionary context, these systems are dynamic and adaptable in nature and demonstrate emergent properties.

Within complex adaptive systems: 'complexity' refers to the multiple elements, levels, interactions and subsystems that are continually operating within the system; 'adaptation' refers to the system's ability to accommodate perturbations (threats) from within or outside the system and is a feature that is fundamental to all living organisms and social structures; 'dynamic' refers to a system's inherent drive to change (and survive) through the constant interactions of its lower-order components; 'emergent properties' demonstrate that the whole is greater than the sum of its parts; and 'homeostasis' shows that the system may exist at a suboptimal level, and is 'locked in' through a variety of feedback loops.

Positivism, cellular automata and rule-based complexity

To demonstrate positivist and rule-based approaches to complex systems, we can use the relatively simple example of Cellular Automata. I have used the following example in Pycroft (2010) as a useful and straightforward way to model the behaviour of these interaction effects (Guastello and Liebovitch, 2009). The rules of Cellular Automata can either be deterministic or random and the following are examples of deterministic rules. Cellular Automata are a collection of cells (normally coloured) placed on a grid that evolve through a series of time steps. In addition to having a position on a grid, the cell has a 'neighbourhood' that it affects, and it is itself affected by other cells depending upon some basic rules of 'engagement'. Figure 1.1 is a simplified use of Cellular Automata that demonstrates the key qualities of a complex system emerging from simple interactions, which demonstrates evolutionary (emergent), dynamic and adaptable behaviour.

In this model, the rules of interaction are as follows:

- a cell remains alive with two to three contiguous neighbours;
- a cell dies of overcrowding with more than three neighbours;
- a cell dies of exposure if it has less than two live neighbours;
- an empty cell becomes alive if three neighbouring cells are alive; and
- most importantly all of the moves are synchronous rather than asynchronous and so every component of the system interacts with every other component of the system in each time step and as

directed by the rules of interaction. This is the process of conjunction rather than distinction in action.

In this example, the number of elements and the original position on the graph was completely chosen at random, and has produced a system that has developed from 'order for free' to becoming 'locked in'. From Time Step Three, it will simply continue to cycle through each time step infinitely. One of the key points here is that a slight change to the configuration of the system, that is, a change to one of the cells, would change the system as a whole, with different outcomes.

Figure 1.1: Cellular Automata

The system

	1	2	3	4	5	6	7	8
2								
3			X		X			
4			X	X				
5					X			
6								

Time Step One

	1	2	3	4	5	6	7	8
2								
3				X	X			
4				X	X			
5								
6								

Time Step Two

	1	2	3	4	5	6	7	8
2								
3			X	X	X			
4			X		X			
5								
6								

Time Step Three

	1	2	3	4	5	6	7	8
2				X				
3			X	X	X			
4			X	X	X			
5								
6								

Time Step Four

	1	2	3	4	5	6	7	8
2			X	X	X			
3			X		X			
4					X	X		
5								
6								

Time Step Five

	1	2	3	4	5	6	7	8
2								
3								
4			X	X	X			
5			X		X			
6								

Time Step Six

	1	2	3	4	5	6	7	8
2								
3				X				
4			X	X	X			
5			X	X	X			
6								

Cellular Automata are deterministic in that the dynamism and emergent changes in the whole system (its phase state, see Jennings, Chapter Two, and Wolf-Branigin, Chapter Four) are entirely determined by the rules of interaction. This mathematically based determinism has been challenged by both post-positivist and postmodern (constructivist) versions of complexity.

Post-positivism (realism)

Having outlined the Newtonian paradigm and some of the broad areas of agreement about what constitutes complex as opposed to merely complicated systems, we are now in a position to look at and develop some of the ontological and epistemological approaches to understanding these systems from post-positivist and also constructivist perspectives.

In the 'natural sciences', and through the analogy of the machine, Mikulecky (2001) argues that Cartesian reductionism does not work in making models of complex systems because it merely reduces them to an aspect of the overall system; so in reducing the complexity through abstracting from the whole to understand it, we cannot understand it because we only have a part and not the whole (but for a discussion of Gödel's *Incompleteness Theorems*, which provide an interesting link between positivism and post-positivism, also see Wolf-Branigin, Chapter Four). This is a major paradox that runs throughout the study of complexity, with realists arguing that to work effectively within complex systems, we need to reduce that complexity to make it manageable (see McDermott, Chapter Nine). However, this then begs the question of what is a reasonable level of abstraction that provides for an understanding of the whole system?

This issue is addressed by Mikulecky (2001) as a process of observing the world around us and using mental activity to makes sense of and interpret that sensory information. He refers to this as the 'modelling relation', in that the 'natural system' and the events of causality are our objects of study, which we then, however, translate or encode into another system that we cognitively construct and call a 'formal system'. We then use this system in various ways to identify and copy the changes in the natural system (ie Apollo 13 having an exact replica that engineers could work on). The real world is complex and, in reality, simple systems do not exist (Mandelbrot sets are an indication of this; for explanations and images of fractals, see eg http://mathworld. wolfram.com/Fractal.html; see also Case and Haines, Chapter Six), and, in fact, Mikulecky argues that simple systems are fictitious, created by

---

reductionists to model the real world. However, critically, the modelling relation is forgotten because the formal system has become reality. This is an example of what critical realists call the epistemic fallacy (see later) or the ontic fallacy, with the model being seen as reality rather than the reality itself.[4]

In 'social science', it is argued by Byrne (1998) that the realist tradition arises from the work of Bhaskar and also Sayer, who provide a metatheoretical account that is neither phenomenological nor positivist and reductionist, and seeks an understanding of *contingent* causation. Philosophically, realism continues in the Platonic tradition by taking 'the view that entities exist independently of being perceived, or independently of our theories about them' (Phillips, 1987, cited in Maxwell, 2012, p 3). Scientific realism refers to 'the view that theories refer to real features of the world. "Reality" here refers to whatever is in the universe (i.e. forces, structures and so on) that causes the phenomena we perceive with our senses' (Phillips, 1987, cited in Maxwell, 2012, p 3).

Although not writing in the complexity tradition per se, it has been argued (eg by Byrne, 1998) that the work of Pawson and Tilley is useful in developing methodologies for studying complexity. Pawson and Tilley (1997, p 64, emphasis in original) highlight the key principles of scientific realism as, first, 'the *embeddedness* of all human action within a wider range of social processes as the *stratified nature of social reality*'. They argue that causality does not reside in individual persons or objects, but within *social relations*, which are formed by these individuals and objects. This embeddedness is fundamental to understanding the kinds of social programmes that are delivered within criminal justice or social work and the links to the wider system or systems that they inhabit. Second, Pawson and Tilley refer to the principle of *mechanism* (or, more precisely, *social mechanisms*), which look for explanation in the relationship between the part and the whole (or the individual and the group). This is a key reference to the importance of agency and structure, with rule-based complexity (such as in Cellular Automata) arguing that the rules are the structure (or the attractor) that drives the agency (decisions and choices that individuals make). The principle of *mechanism*, then, highlights the importance of *contexts*, with the proposition that 'the relationship between causal mechanisms and their effects is not fixed, but contingent' (Pawson and Tilley, 1997, p 69), and from a complexity perspective, any programme is an open system that is influenced by the wider system (for a discussion of domestic violence programmes, see Lewis, Chapter Eleven). Within scientific realism, the goal of these principles is to identify *regularities*, patterns and outcomes from, for example, the delivery of programmes, which can be generalised from to inform other programme delivery; the aim is then to be able to measure *change* that can be attributed to the programme. However, as a programme is an open system, Pawson and Tilley (1997, pp 72–3) argue:

> People are often aware of the patterns and regularities into which their lives are shaped, are aware of the choices which channel their activities, and are aware too of the broader social forces that limit their opportunities. This awareness will result, in some people at least, in a desire to change the pattern. This may or may not happen because the people desiring the change may or may not have the resources to bring it about, or their efforts may be countermanded by other groups with more resources. Further unpredictability is introduced because people have imperfect knowledge of the contextual conditions which limits their actions and the proposed change mechanism itself may have unanticipated consequences. So, whilst the exact path cannot be foreseen, we know social regularities have a habit of transforming themselves…. [This] gives social explanation a distinctly more complex task.

There are various disagreements within and consequent strands to philosophical realism, and our focus here is on *critical realism* and its key components. First, critical realists argue that mental states, meanings and intentions, although not directly observable, are a part of the real world, a position denied by logical positivists (Cartesian dualism) and constructivists (see later). Second, critical realists argue that *causality* is a real phenomenon and that in the social sciences, *process* is central to understanding causality. Third, it has been argued by constructivists that the term 'reality' is, in itself, a form of meta-narrative, as it denotes one overarching version of reality whereas it has been claimed that we construct multiple realities. Byrne (1998, p 8) had argued that the combination of critical realism as a philosophical ontology and chaos/complexity as a scientific ontology 'should be fatal to post modernism as an intellectual project'. After making this claim, and on reading Cilliers (1998), Byrne (1999) did concede that there was much to be contributed to the debate on complexity from a postmodern/constructivist perspective (see later). Critical realism, while rejecting multiple realities, would argue the validity of multiple perspectives on reality, and Maxwell (2012) also argues that some versions of critical realism are compatible with some versions of constructivism, with both having a scepticism towards general laws and a relativist methodology; the key difference is in the realist commitment to an objective although not entirely knowable world. Within debates on complexity, Byrne (1999), while acknowledging the importance of Cilliers' work, also argued for the importance and reality of *bifurcation* in systems and attractor states, which stem from chaos theory and underlying rules of interaction. A bifurcation 'is a pattern of instability in which a system attains greater complexity by accessing new types of dynamical states' (Guasetello and Liebovitch, 2009, p 14) and can be a change in the type of attractor from simple to strange, thus driving the system through states of being chaotic, complex, cyclic and in equilibrium (see Wolf-Branigin, Chapter Four; see also Jennings, Chapter Two).

Constructivism (postmodernism)

The scope of postmodernism and the eschewing of a meta-narrative of Platonic reality takes many forms. In developing a postmodern narrative, Paul Cilliers (2007, p 4) agrees with Morin (2005) in saying 'that we should resist an unreflective use of scientific discourse which reinstates an essential, if disguised reductionism', and that rule-based and analytic approaches to complex systems are flawed. In terms of understanding some of the differences with Platonism, it is worth recapping the Aristotelian view of understanding based upon what we derive from our experiences rather than a life of recollection of and return to 'Platonic perfection'. The work of Cilliers is concerned with an understanding of some postmodern approaches having an implicit sensitivity to the complexity of the phenomena that they are dealing with. However, it is also important to include the caveat that Cilliers is avoiding any approach that can be described as entirely relativistic; what he is arguing is that rather than trying to reduce complexity to laws or principles, 'it is not possible to tell a single and exclusive story about something that is really complex' (Cilliers, 1998, p viii). Some of the key features of a postmodern agenda in studying complexity are suggested by Heylighen, Cilliers and Gershenson (2007, p 129ff):

- *Boundaries and limits.* Due to systems being open to their environments, it is often not clear where the boundary of the system is, which itself is not the same as the limit (or influence) of the system. They argue that context and system mutually reinforce each other and that the postmodern principle of the positionality of the observer and the way in which they frame (bracket) what they see/understand can help to understand these problems.

- *The problem of difference.* They argue that for the postmodernist, the diversity of the system is the most important resource for a complex system, rather than it being a problem to be solved (reduced to its component parts under the positivist paradigm).
- *The idea of subject.* They argue that the self-contained, atomised subject (as in agent-based modelling [see Wolf-Branigin, Chapter Four] or Cellular Automata [see earlier]) is undermined by complexity theory based on postmodernism. This is not to say that ideas of agency and responsibility are not important, but that they need to be informed by notions of self-organisation and social construction.
- *Complexity and ethics.* Cilliers (2010) argues that we have to accept our limitations in understanding complexity, and as these can only ever be provisional, we need to move beyond the scientific discourse of objectivity and neutrality and, in fact, find a new language to do this. So, for Cilliers, it is not the rightness or wrongness of general or restricted complexity, but an acceptance that the methods are different, which leads to the necessity of discussing the importance of human action, values and ethics (the issue of *praxis* is discussed by Arrigo and Williams, Chapter Twelve), which cannot be reduced to calculation alone (this is what I would define as utilitarian ethics), especially as there is no objective or neutral framework for understanding reality – 'we cannot escape the moment of choice, and *thus* we are never free of normative considerations'[5] (Heylighen et al, 2007, p 130, emphasis in original).

It is argued from this constructivist perspective that we need to think in terms of relationships rather than deterministic rules. Cilliers (1998, p 35) uses the examples of quantum mechanical descriptions of subatomic particles as being essentially relational and that 'the significance of each atom is ... not determined by its basic nature, but is a result of a large number of relationships between itself and other atoms'. He argues for the importance of developing neural network approaches (connectionist model), rather than relying on rule-based models. These networks have similar characteristics to Cellular Automata, but, it is argued, are more flexible in that they do not seek to reduce the complexity, but rather reflect it in the following ways:

- They conserve the complexity of the systems that they model because they have complex structures themselves.
- They encode information about their environment in a distributed (modular) form.

- They have the capacity to self-organise their internal structure (eg Cellular Automata cannot change the rules of interaction).

The most sophisticated neural network that we know of is the human brain, which is comprised of neurons that are richly and extensively related to each other by synapses. The brain is modular in nature and through neuroplasticity is able to survive, developing new neural pathways when presented by severe challenges, such as strokes:

> Patients are able to regain function due to the principle of neuroplasticity, or the brain's ability to change, especially when patients continue therapy long after their injuries. Therapists once believed the brain doesn't develop new neurons; but, now they know neurons change their shape and create new branches to connect with other neurons, rewiring the brain following an injury or trauma.[6]

Quantum mechanics

The final area for consideration in our discussion of complexity picks up on the issue of quantum mechanics raised by Cilliers (1998), which is discussed by Bartollas (Chapter Thirteen) in relation to chaos and complexity theory (and by Pycroft through the use of metaphor in Chapter Ten). Quantum theory is a difficult and problematic area of physics that is not entirely understood, but is of growing importance in our understanding of not just the nature of causality, but the nature of consciousness and the relationship between the two. Quantum theory is becoming of increasing significance in relation to the study of the brain and the resolution of the problem of the relationship between brain and mind (Penrose, 1999), and also in a range of applications including healthcare, finance and economics (see Bartollas, Chapter Thirteen). Schwartz et al (2005) discuss how the connection between human knowledge and the physical world has never been resolved in classical physics following the Cartesian divide. However, they go on to argue that quantum theory is essentially a theory of mind–matter interaction that the early founders of quantum theory sought to develop. It is argued that the quantum approach has turned inside out the whole concept of what science is. As Schwartz et al (2005, p 7, emphases in original) argue:

> the core idea of quantum mechanics is to describe both *our activities as knowledge seeking and knowledge-acquiring agents,*

and *the knowledge that we thereby acquire*. Thus quantum theory involves, essentially what is 'in here,' not just what is 'out there.'

From the point of view of the scientific method, humans are no longer objective, passive observers, but constitutive agents in the process. In this respect, conscious-free choices affect the physically described world in a way that the determinism of the Newtonian paradigm cannot grasp, precisely because it seeks to reduce the human brain to a computer-style algorithm machine.

Conclusion

The study of complexity covers a broad spectrum, with rapid developments in applications, research studies and the consequent literature. This has not yet had an impact upon human services such as criminal justice and social work, which may, in part, reflect (unfounded) concerns with physics envy or abstract empiricism. However, as we have seen, there are debates ranging from classical positivist mechanics, mathematics and physics (including quantum mechanics) through to postmodernism (and perhaps full circle back into quantum mechanics) which demonstrate that these approaches all have in common an interest in the system and its behaviour as a whole, rather than simple and sterile approaches to reductionism.

Notes

[1] It is interesting to note that this Platonic thinking exercised great influence on Christian thought, particularly through Plotinus, for whom contemplation (about which both Plato and Aristotle had described as the height of human endeavour) is a return to the One from which people emanated (see Underhill, 1960). Contemplation is, of course, also very much evident in other religious traditions, such as Buddhism, Islam and Hinduism, the commonalities of which have contributed to interfaith movements (see the work of Thomas Merton, http://merton.org/ITMS/).

[2] Importantly, this Cartesian dualism also separates mind from body and so is also referred to as 'ghost in the machine' consciousness, or the mind–body problem. Quantum mechanics addresses the further problem of brain and mind and relationships with 'reality' (see later).

[3] The issue of positionality is also central to Einstein's theory of relativity, which marks a major development in the Newtonian model (see Penrose, 1999), with the understanding of it being rule-based.

[4] In Arrigo and Williams (Chapter Twelve), the issue of ontological reality free of 'shadow' is discussed through the concept of 'being in itself' and 'being for itself'. This existential tradition (which Tillich [1969, p 136] describes as rebelling 'in the name of personality against the depersonalizing forces of technical society') is explored as a way of reinvigorating ethics and rediscovering virtue through the discovery of the wholly constituted self (for a realist perspective on virtue, see also Pycroft, Chapter Ten).

[5] I am reminded of Camus's (1992) observation on Nietzsche that having proclaimed the death of God, he now had to act.

[6] From: http://www.sciencedaily.com/releases/2009/11/091117161118.htm

References

Avigad, J. (2007) 'Philosophy of mathematics', Department of Philosophy, Paper 34. Available at: http://repository.cmu.edu/philosophy/34

Bar-Yam, Y. (1997) *Dynamics of complex systems*, Cambridge, MA: Perseus.

Burton, C. (2002) 'Introduction to complexity', in K. Sweeney and F. Griffiths (eds) *Complexity and healthcare: an introduction*, Oxford: Radcliffe.

Byrne, D. (1998) *Complexity theory and the social sciences: an introduction*, London: Routledge.

Byrne, D. (1999) 'Complexity and postmodernism reviewed by David Byrne'. Available at: http://jasss.soc.surrey.ac.uk/2/2/review1.html (accessed 4 June 2013).

Camus, A. (1992) *The rebel: an essay on man in revolt*, London: Vintage.

Cilliers, P. (1998) *Complexity and postmodernism: understanding complex systems*, London and New York, NY: Routledge.

Cilliers, P. (2007) 'The philosophical importance of thinking complexity', in P. Cilliers (ed) *Complexity and philosophy volume 1*, Mansfield: ISCE Publishing, pp 3–5.

Cilliers, P. (2010) 'The value of complexity: a response to Elizabeth Mowat and Brent Davis', *Complicity: An International Journal of Complexity and Education*, no 1, pp 39–42.

Frankfurt, H. (2006) 'Alternate possibilities and moral responsibility', in D. Widerker and M. McKenna (eds) *Moral responsibility and alternate possibilities: essays on the importance of alternate possibilities*, Aldershot: Ashgate, pp 17–26.

Girard, R. (2001) *I see Satan fall like lightening*, Leominster: Gracewing.

Gleick, J. (1987) *Chaos: making a new science*, New York, NY: Penguin.

Guastello, S. and Liebovitch, L. (2009) 'Introduction to nonlinear dynamics and complexity', in S. Guastello, M. Koopmans and D. Pincus (eds) *Chaos and complexity in psychology: the theory of nonlinear dynamical systems*, Cambridge: Cambridge University Press, pp 1–40.

Heylighen, F., Cilliers, P. and Gershenson, C. (2007) 'Philosophy and complexity', in J. Bogg and R. Geyer (eds) *Complexity science and society*, Oxford: Radcliffe, pp 117–34.

Institute of Medicine (1990) *Broadening the base for the treatment of alcohol problems*, Washington, DC: National Academy Press.

Kauffman, S. (1993) *The origins of order: self-organization and selection in evolution*, Oxford: Oxford University Press.

Kauffman, S. (1995) *At home in the universe: the search for laws of complexity*, London: Penguin.

Kernick, D. (ed) (2004) *Complexity and healthcare organization: a view from the street*, Oxford: Radcliffe.

Maxwell, J. (2012) *A realist approach to qualitative research*, Thousand Oaks, CA: Sage.

Mikulecky, D. (2001) 'The emergence of complexity: science coming of age or science growing old?', *Computers and Chemistry*, vol 25, pp 341–8.

Morin, E. (2005) 'Restricted complexity, general complexity', paper presented at the Colloquium 'Intelligence de la complexité: épistémologie et pragmatique', Cerisy-La-Salle, France, 26 June.

Pawson, R. and Tilley, N. (1997) *Realistic evaluation*, London: Sage.

Penrose, R. (1999) *The emperor's new mind*, Oxford: Oxford University Press.

Plsek, P. and Greenhalgh, T. (2001) 'The challenge of complexity in healthcare', *British Medical Journal*, vol 323, pp 625–8.

Pycroft, A. (2010) *Understanding and working with substance misusers*, London: Sage.

Schwartz, J.M., Stapp, H.P. and Beauregard, M. (2005) 'Quantum theory in neuroscience and psychology: A neurophysical model of mind/brain interaction', *Philosophical Transcript of the Royal Society*, vol 360, pp 1309–927.

Smith, L. (2007) *Chaos, a very short introduction*, Oxford: Oxford University Press.

Stapp, H. (2001) 'Quantum theory and the role of mind in nature' in *Foundations of Physics*, vol 31(10), pp 1465-99.

Tillich, P. (1969) 'The person in a technical society', in W. O'Neil (ed) *Selected educational heresies: some unorthodox views concerning the nature and purposes of contemporary education*, Illinois, IL: Scott, Foresman and Company, pp 136–47.

Underhill, E. (1960) *Mysticism*, London: Vantage Books.

Wilson, T., Holt, T. and Greenhalgh, T. (2001) 'Complexity and clinical care', *British Medical Journal*, vol 323, pp 685–8.

TWO

Risk, attractors and organisational behaviour

Paul Jennings

This chapter aims to consider the behaviour of organisations in the light of complexity theory. Some of the basic mathematical principles behind complexity and chaotic behaviour will be discussed, and the effect of these principles on organisations will be analysed through case studies from different areas of society.

The behaviour of all living creatures is influenced by many factors (Goodenough et al, 1993), including external pressures such as temperature and presence of food, and internal factors such as electrochemical balances. The interaction of these factors is complex enough to lead to a wide spectrum of actions in any single creature, which in themselves can lead to chaotic and complex behaviour (Sumpter, 2010). When the effects of human thoughts, incentives and society are taken into account, the potential for complexity is increased by many orders of magnitude (Stewart, 2000).

From a mathematical perspective, the roots of complexity lie in the interaction between classical mechanical behaviour (positivist) and chaotic behaviour in systems (Kellert, 1993). Complexity arises in systems that, from a mathematical perspective, are typically considered as dynamic – that is, systems in which a number of fixed rules determine how they vary in time and space. It is generally not feasible to treat organisations as dynamical systems with full mathematical rigour, as the fixed rules governing their behaviour are almost certain to have too many variables for a complete analysis to be carried out. Approximations can be made, however, based on observation and underlying mathematical principles, and can be used to develop predictions of organisational behaviour (Burt, 2010).

Classical mechanics is concerned with the behaviour of bodies under the influence of a set of forces, described by a set of physical laws. This approach is one of the oldest human scientific theories, with evidence of some understanding of classical mechanics as far back as Neolithic times. The body of knowledge was formalised in Newton's time, building on the theories of natural philosophers such as Galileo and Kepler, and the extremely accurate observations of astronomers such as Brahe. The underlying principle of classical mechanics is that given a complete understanding of the physical laws determining the behaviour of each component of a system, and the forces acting upon each component, the future state of that system can be determined with complete accuracy. The relevance to complex systems is clear: given knowledge of the laws governing the behaviour of each element of the system, and the pressures acting on each element, the behaviour of the system as a whole should be predictable. This approach has been explored by many philosophers and writers over the centuries (Morin, 2008).

Classical mechanics gives extremely accurate predictions, but is dependent not only on the accuracy of the parameters of the physical laws, but also on the measurement of the forces involved (Tél and Gruiz, 2006), with the effect of these caveats being extremely significant. Chaos theory developed from the realisation that the behaviour of complicated (for a discussion of complicated and complex, see Chapter One) systems is extremely sensitive to its initial conditions. In a chaotic system, an arbitrarily small change in the initial conditions will lead to large variations in the eventual state of the system. Newton himself explored this when trying to predict the positions of the sun, earth and moon when moving under the laws of gravity. He found that even in a system as apparently straightforward as three bodies moving under one simple rule, their predicted positions varied wildly for arbitrarily small changes in initial position and velocity. Even though the system is fully deterministic – that is, defined by its initial conditions, with no randomness – it is inherently unpredictable (Chandrasekhar, 1995). This is the underlying principle of chaos theory, described by Lorenz (one of the formulators of chaos theory) as 'Chaos: when the present determines the future, but the approximate present does not approximately determine the future' (Danforth, 2013).

Despite the chaotic nature of complicated systems, it is obvious that chaos is not the only factor at work. Although the moon's position may be uncertain a million years hence, it is possible to predict the position of the moon with practical accuracy. Lorenz's work as a meteorologist trying to predict weather patterns led him to chaos theory, and although weather prediction is clearly an imprecise science, its predictions are significantly better than chance in the short term, although they rapidly decline in specific local accuracy as the term of the prediction increases. Systems of sufficient complexity demonstrate some tendency towards self-organisation, and this is where the study of complex systems is focused (Green, 2000).

From a purely positivist, mathematical perspective, complex systems are systems that have some drive or energy forcing behaviour, and some retardant to 'dampen' behaviour, in which the drive is energetic enough to exceed the conditions for classical mechanical behaviour, but are not so energetic as to lead to complete chaos. Although there may be a very large set of possible states that the complex system can exist in, known as the 'phase space', over time, the interaction of the drives and dampeners can lead the behaviour of a complex system to evolve towards the equilibrium of a single steady state, or set of states (Yolles, 2006). This set of states is known as the 'attractor' for a chaotic system, and may be unlike the behaviour of the individual components. Attractors (ie end-states towards which the equilibrium tends) are classified into general types. Simple attractors are typically single points such as the final 'at rest' position of a pendulum – a static equilibrium – or the dynamic equilibrium of limit cycles, where a system cycles through a set of states, such as the regular orbits of planets (Three-Body Problem aside). Attractors with a more complex, fractal structure are known as 'strange attractors' (see Pycroft, Chapter Ten). These are useful in dealing with complex systems in science as, given enough quantifiable information about the structure of the phase space, the attractor may be calculable through advanced mathematics. Although the attractors governing the behaviour of complex organisations may be strange, the qualitative nature of the information surrounding them is likely to mean that direct calculation is not possible, although approximations may be made (Cutler, 1993).

Attractors do not have to be positive in effect. An attractor that acts as a negative, repulsive force on the evolution of a complex system is often referred to as a 'rejector', but for the purposes of this discussion, the term 'attractor' will be used throughout.

When considering organisational behaviour, the drivers that give momentum to the system can include numerous factors, such as the goals of that organisation, the aims of the people within it, its customers and stakeholders. The dampening behaviour may be due to the restrictions under which the organisation operates: its internal policies, regulations governing its behaviour or economic conditions. The drives putting energy into the system may not be separated from the dampeners – some elements may dampen one type of activity while driving another. As previously discussed, the specific state that a complex organisation will evolve towards may be unpredictable. The attractor set may be definable either quantitatively or qualitatively, and can provide useful insights into organisational behaviour when trying to understand why organisations behave in a particular way given particular inputs, and how to tailor interventions in order to achieve the required goals. It is clear that there are strange attractors governing organisational behaviour, although these may not be directly susceptible to quantitative methods. Organisations are robust to a certain extent, often surviving for many years, with a complex pattern of attractors governing their behaviour. The stakeholders within an organisation are themselves part of this pattern, changing their attractive behaviour in response to external and internal pressures and motivations (Rahim, 2011).

The critical factor governing the behaviour of most, if not all, organisations is the attempt to manage outcomes (Lewis, 2011). All organisations exist to achieve goals; otherwise, the organisation has no reason to exist in the first place. In order to manage outcomes, some form of measurement of progress and achievement is critical. The outcomes can be considered as attractors, driving the behaviour of that organisation. The challenge is that in a complex organisation, the causal link between the desired outcomes and the actions that individuals or subgroups can take are not clear. Measurement of actions can only help if there is some understanding of the causal link; otherwise, an organisation is replacing knowledge with metrics – which is often observed in organisations trying to deal with uncertainty. As organisational complexity grows, the gap between knowledge and measurement increases, and can only be addressed through risk analysis and management (Savolo, 2011).

Each complex system will have a different set of factors that govern the behaviour of its components. The factors governing organisational behaviour are particularly complex, as they are primarily driven by the interactions of uniquely complex components – human beings. Each human is a complex system in him/herself, and, as humans, we have evolved our own attractors to cope with the phase space we operate in (the set of conditions we are likely to experience) in order to achieve the outcomes we desire (Stewart and Cohen, 1997). The immediate challenge is that the phase space in which we operate is massively larger than we can handle. The total set of outcomes that might occur is unmanageable, and any creature that spent its time trying to navigate through every possible outcome would be unlikely to survive, let alone flourish (Boccara, 2010).

One of the ways in which every animal deals with the effectively infinite phase space in which it operates is to prioritise the likeliest scenarios, based on some risk criteria. So, for instance, birds may limit the phase space they have to deal with by flying away if something large moves to close to them. This behaviour will become honed over evolutionary time – birds that fly away too early waste time and energy that could be spent on feeding and breeding, whereas birds that fly away too late may not survive to breed. So, eventually, the complex interaction between predator and prey leads to a particular attractor within the phase space.

Humans have developed a particular attractor response to the phase space we operate in (Stewart and Cohen, 1997, p 173). In particular, we have developed an instinctive response to risk, and an instinctive understanding of probability and statistics. Both of these areas of instinct are calibrated for the prioritised phase space mentioned earlier, however. The instincts we have developed are predicated on the fact that for most of our history, we lived in small family groups, surrounded by predators, interacting with only a small number of individuals. When living in a largely hostile environment, a very risk-averse attitude is likely to be the safest course, and a sophisticated understanding of probability and statistics was likely to be a waste of effort and energy. The subtleties of group dynamics were limited by the shared goal of survival. Large organisations present humans with a phase space for which we are not prepared. The behaviour of many other individuals with widely varying motivations must be considered, and the risks of those interactions must be analysed and understood. Probability and statistics need to be taken into account in order to try to make reasonable predictions of the behaviour of the complex system, and also in order to identify the likely effect of interventions (Schneier, 2007).

As previously discussed, for complex organisations (including animals and humans), the approach to risk is a major part of any phase space prioritisation. Animals tend to respond to risk in a deterministic way – any animal that does not take the optimal response to any given risk is likely to lose out to other animals that do happen to take the optimal response. Over time, this evolutionary arms race leads to animals developing a sophisticated risk response with an optimised reaction to the probabilities of harm and reward in their environment (Thompson, 2013). Human culture, organisation and communication capability gives an additional dimension to the approach to risk. Although there is evidence of limited communication of hazard among animals, human cultural communication of risk, or the information allowing the individual to manage risk, is of a very different qualitative nature. The strategy of using the abstract communicated experience of others in order to simplify the risk analysis of the phase space in which we operate has been developed to a unique extent by humans (Koné and Mullet, 1994). The manner in which the event information is analysed for risk, however, can be based on simplifications that, when taken in conjunction with other attractors, such as the drive towards loss aversion, can lead to a significant intuitive miscalculation.

Human calculation of risk takes into account two sets of experiences: the personal experiences of the risk calculator; and the received experiences from other sources. For most of human history, interaction was limited to a small, localised social group, so the received experiences were strongly correlated with the risks that an individual him/herself was likely to face, and the inclination would develop to accept those communicated experiences as very similar in significance to personal experience. Over time, this could even become strongly selected for, culturally or biologically. Risky events would be communicated through a group very quickly, and risks with memorable consequences, such as shark attacks, would rapidly change the behaviour of the social group. Risks with unresolvable consequences lead to immediate and extreme loss aversion because a small group may not have the resources to withstand those consequences – the death of a child, for instance. The rapid growth of communication networks and mass media means that we have access to a much wider source of received risk experiences (Koné and Mullet, 1994). The human brain's intuitive risk analysis engine is not calibrated for such a wide source of experiences. So, when extremely rare events with dramatic consequences are reported in the mass media, particularly if done as part of a human interest story, our intuition leads us to evaluate the event as if it happened nearby. The natural inclination is to vastly overestimate the risk these events represent, even more so if those risks include an unresolvable element. Our intuition effectively calculates that 'If I heard about this risk, it must have happened nearby, and is therefore something I must take extreme measures to avoid' (Bernstein, 1996). This tendency has a huge impact on the risk perception of society at large, leading to moral panics and knee-jerk reactions against threats that are dramatic, but which may not present a major hazard compared with other, more prosaic risks.

The tendency to overestimate dramatic risks with unresolvable consequences can have a dramatic effect on organisational thinking – particularly in complex organisations that have to deal with life-changing events. The organisational approach to risk will be strongly influenced by the stakeholders' personal reactions to these dramatic risks and their attempts to avoid the perceived loss, rather than by an objective view of the actual quantification of the risk – even when that quantification may be quite straightforward (Lawson, 2008).

Quantification in cases like these may be rejected out of hand due to an unfamiliarity and mistrust of statistics and probability. For example, in the UK, legal defence based on Bayes' Theorem as an explanation of the improbability that the suspect had actually committed a crime has been thrown out of court.[1] In fact, attempts to even quantify risks that involve unresolvable elements may be considered as ethically and morally unacceptable, even though proper quantification would be in the greater interests of society at large. This tendency can be seen at work whenever decision-makers consider topical risks based on single instances or smaller samples rather than broader risks that are widespread throughout a population. It is also a predictable part of any organisational structure where risk responsibility is clear (Lawson, 2008). When this set of behaviours is taken together, it has a profound impact on the risk response of the stakeholders. Risk is fundamentally a function of probability and impact, and risk analysis can be considered in its most fundamental form as a review over the phase space of the probabilities of events happening, multiplied by the likely gain or loss associated with each of those events. A view of impact based on non-quantifiable measures, together with an innate tendency for intuition to handle probability incorrectly, can lead to a significant miscalculation of risk.

As an example, if two fair dice are rolled, the probability of rolling a double six is 1 in 36. If a gambler bets £1 on a double six being rolled, then the bet will be lost 35 times out of 36, and won once out of 36 times. So, to make the bet worthwhile, the reward for the gamble needs to be greater than £35 (assuming the stake is also returned). If the gambler is offered, say, £30 for each double six, he will lose on average £5 over each 36 times he plays, and will eventually go bankrupt. If he is offered, say, £40 for each double six, he will gain £5 for each 36 plays, and will eventually break the bank. In this trivial example, it would appear that the appropriate response is obvious. Simple risk analysis says that if the odds are obviously not in the gambler's favour, then the game should not be played. Economic and risk theory has, until recently, worked primarily on the principle that humans will make rational choices. But many gambling establishments make huge profits on the fact that humans continue to gamble despite the fact that the odds are not in their favour. The approach to risk and reward is not as straightforward as a purely reductionist view of risk would suggest, and there is a dichotomy between the simple mathematical view of probability and impact, and the decision-making and risk-taking behaviour of people faced with choices in these areas.

At the basis of this dichotomy is the human inability to deal rationally with numerical data and processes. Human methods tend to rely on short cuts and approximations, which are effective in many circumstances, but become less effective when applied to more complex situations. Furthermore, risk analysis relies on objectivity, information and a fully rational approach to the risks and probabilities. Human emotion interferes with that entirely rational approach – gamblers may feel lucky or unlucky, and unintentionally recalibrate their approach to risk based on that feeling (Bernstein, 1996). Faced with different degrees of desperation, humans may see a risk as worth taking if the reward is high enough, even if a purely mathematical analysis shows that the probability of a successful outcome is vanishingly small. Lotteries work on the principle that the payout is less than the money taken in – so, on average, everyone is a loser. But people still buy lottery tickets. In many cases, when faced with risk, humans often do not take into account all the factors relating to that risk – they simplify based on a limited sample of outcomes (typically, their own experience), or on their simplified phase space of how they feel the world *should* work (Kahneman and Tversky, 1984). There are even complex instinctive processes within the brain to reduce the complexity of the phase space by handling many of these calculations intuitively, and often wrongly (Kahneman, 2011). Even supposedly rational approaches to risk vary. Trimpop notes that even the definition of risk and the approach to risk analysis appear to be influenced by the personal values of the researchers involved (Trimpop, 1994).

There are a number of mathematical principles that are useful in considering risk, and attempting to understand and influence organisational behaviour. One of the most important is 'regression to the mean'. This is the tendency for variable random factors that are outside the normal range to return to the normal range. Examples are rife – tall parents tend to have children that are still tall, but less tall than they are. Athletes and sports teams that do exceptionally well in one season tend to do less well the season after. This has been referred to as the 'Sports Illustrated Jinx'. Teams or people featured in magazines often seem to suffer a reverse in their career soon afterwards. Regression to the mean explains this: magazine coverage tends to come with performance above the mean, so a trend towards the mean should not be unexpected thereafter (Ross, 2009, pp 368–71).

In any intervention-based approach, regression to the mean must be taken into account. If a population subset shows a change after an intervention, this can be seen as evidence that the intervention was effective. But, in many cases, the population change is actually within statistical norms and is unrelated to the intervention taken. Another example is that, in the UK, speed cameras are often placed at accident black spots after a bad year for accidents. In the following years, a reduction in accidents is heralded as a success for speed camera usage, when, in fact, it is another example of regression to the mean: bad years are typically followed by less-bad years (Blastland and Dilnot, 2007).

Regression to the mean is a well-understood statistical effect, and the degree of impact it has in most situations can be analysed through a variety of statistical methods. In a trial of treatment or other interventions, the use of a control group of exactly the same statistical make-up as the group undergoing the treatment is a typical method. As long as the members of both the control group and the treatment group are fairly sampled from the same underlying population, and are treated in exactly the same way, both sample populations will be subject to a similar degree of regression to the mean, so the average effect on the treated population minus the average effect on the control population can be a reasonable estimate of the effect after correcting for regression to the mean.

Organisational culture, particularly in the Western world, often operates in a manner that does not take regression to the mean into account. It is a fundamental part of management theory that rewarding good performance and punishing bad performance act as attractors to drive the organisation in the direction required (Shields, 2007), but regression to the mean indicates that this may not be the case. There are obviously many factors that govern success, some of which may be affected by positive and negative incentives, but many of which may not be. Unless regression to the mean is considered, an organisation runs the risk of building an ineffective incentive system, which actually reduces the incentive for desirable behaviour. The earlier example of the gambler could be extended to a team. If the team of gamblers is big enough, then it is likely that one of them will be lucky, and will do significantly better than average over a given period. Another of them is likely to do significantly worse than average. But the performance of both gamblers is likely to regress to the mean over the next period, as their success or failure is totally down to the luck of the dice. If their appraisal rating at the end of the period was purely based on their success in the game, it would have no effect on future performance – and would probably have a negative effect on the rest of the team. Again, this seems obvious, but studies have shown that industries that reward performance based on purely financial considerations are misunderstanding the underlying statistics, and the effect of regression to the mean (Pfannkuch and Wild, 2004).

A complex organisation needs to consider which, if any, methods of addressing regression to the mean will most closely match the goals of the organisation. A broader historical view of performance may be valuable, or feedback from a wider range of peers. Some organisations may be happy to remain insensitive to the entire subject, arguing that even a completely arbitrary set of rewards that appears to be correlated with performance will incentivise an uninformed workforce and act as an attractor for the desired behaviour. This may be an example of the next failure of probabilistic thinking – the Gambler's Fallacy.

Humans have a well-documented inclination to attribute causation to events that appear to be correlated but, in fact, have no scientifically detectable causal relationship (Jung, 1955). Examples range from the trivial ('Step on a crack, break your mother's back'), through casual risk-aversion ('Better not to say I disbelieve in ghosts, just in case I annoy them'), to quite strongly held belief systems, such as astrology. These are examples of the general principle of apophenia – the experience of seeing meaningful patterns or connections in random, meaningless data. Apophenia may be another example of algorithms that have evolved in the human brain to simplify the risk phase space. If causal connections can be detected between events, then the chain of causation can be manipulated in the direction of the desired attractor. This appears to be strongly selected for in human evolution, not only because it is such a widespread cultural phenomenon, but also because it appears to regularly overreact, leading us to spot patterns where none exist (spotting shapes in clouds or faces in random patterns – an effect known as pareidolia) (Bednarik, 2011). The negative attractor of the cost of overreaction does not cancel out the positive benefit of apophenia overall as an evolutionary attractor, so a risk-optimised phase space includes a significant degree of apophenial behaviour.

In terms of probabilistic thinking, the tendency to apophenia leads humans to believe that random events in some way have a memory of previous random events and act to balance things out. To revisit the gambling analogy, consider the toss of a fair coin. The result can be either 'heads' or 'tails', with the equal likelihood of 50%. So, the probability of each occurrence is 0.5. If the coin is tossed 10 times, then the expected outcome would be five heads, and five tails. There is no guarantee of this outcome, and we would not be surprised to have a result of six heads and four tails, or four heads and six tails. In fact, if we performed sets of 10 coin tosses 500 times, statistics tells us we are very likely to get one run of 10 heads or 10 tails. Runs of five heads or tails will be quite common. This also demonstrates a statistical principle known as the Law of Large Numbers. As the number of events in a trial increases, the average of the results will get closer and closer to the expected value, even if the variation of any single result can be larger.

Imagine that a gambler is betting on the outcome of the tossing of a fair coin. After a run of 10 heads, he is very likely to start betting more heavily on tails, because, after so many heads, he feels it is 'time' for more tails, in line with an intuitive feel for 'the law of averages'. But the coin has no memory, and there is no cosmic hand guiding the result. The chance of a tail next toss is still 50/50, as is the chance of a head – the distribution of results has incorrectly led the gambler to feel that there is some rectifying force in the universe that will balance things out. This is the Gambler's Fallacy – that if repeated independent trials of a random process show deviations from expected behaviour in a particular direction, then deviations in the opposite direction are in some way more likely (Blastland and Dilnot, 2007; Ross, 2009).

This behaviour can be observed in complex organisations, at many different levels. If an event has not happened for some time, the Gambler's Fallacy can lead to either of a pair of false assumptions: 'If an event hasn't happened for some time, it's bound to happen soon'; or 'If an event hasn't happened for some time, then it's never going to happen'. Both of these can be seen to be attractive in terms of phase space simplification, in conjunction with misfiring of the attractor algorithms that have evolved in the human brain when faced with modern culture and communication. The global reach of reporting, coupled with the natural tendency for media to focus on unusual occurrences with dramatic consequences, leads to an unrepresentative number of reports that appear to support the first case – people winning lotteries or suffering events with an element of ironic payback – while actually just being a statistical artefact (Kahneman and Tversky, 1984; Koné and Mullet, 1994). The tendency of the human phase space simplification mechanisms to give undue credence to third-party experiences exacerbates this trend. In the other case, the phase space simplification mechanism is informed by our evolutionary history: if, in a small group, a risk has not happened for some time, then it has probably gone away. With enough small groups in a population, one or two may suffer due to this approach, but in the longer term, the behaviour is likely to be attractive in evolutionary and chaotic terms. But complex organisations are not small groups, the fact that a risk has not happened for some time has no influence on whether it will occur in the near future, and the Law of Large Numbers indicates that the period of time without an occurrence of the risk may just be a statistical artefact. Extreme cases of where events with very high impact are ignored because of their very low probability have become known as 'The Black Swan' effect (Taleb, 2007).

Taken together, this set of problems with probabilistic thinking are challenging for organisations to deal with, because the effects can be contradictory, and the thought processes necessary run counter to so many human phase space simplification mechanisms and intuitions. Stakeholders do not have the time or inclination to develop the mathematical skills necessary to address these elements directly, arguments based on statistics and probability are unlikely to be compelling, so even discussing the issues can be problematic. Risk is an expression of both probability and impact, however, and, many times, a misunderstanding of the probability is matched with a converse misunderstanding of the impact in order to match experience. In trying to encourage an organisation to take an appropriate view of risk, a detailed exposition of statistical principles can often be avoided through a more careful discussion of the impact. For instance, in organisations responsible for public health and safety, the stakeholders may become very focused on completely avoiding any incident for which they may be considered liable. In general, risk avoidance is not just impractical, but the measures necessary to resolve smaller and smaller risks rapidly become increasingly expensive. There is always a point where it becomes more valuable to an organisation to discuss and evaluate the real impact of an occurrence of a risk, and to investigate measures to reduce that impact. Reduction of the impact of a risk may be just as effective as reduction of the probability of the risk, and may be much more cost-effective and understandable to stakeholders, particularly if the impact has been overestimated, as can often be the case when discussing unlikely, but dramatic, events.

The Gambler's Fallacy and the Law of Large Numbers are relevant in situations where events in the phase space are effectively independent from each other – the occurrence of one event does not alter the probability of the other. This statistical independence can be mathematically defined – events A and B are statistically independent if the probability of both A and B occurring together is equal to the probability of A occurring, multiplied by the probability of B occurring. So, for instance, in the event of the gambler rolling dice, the probability of a one being rolled on the second die, or the third die, or any subsequent die remains the same – 1/6 – despite what the Gambler's Fallacy tells the gambler. Knowing the result of the first die-roll does not help to predict subsequent ones. Conditional probability considers the situation in which the results are linked in some way. So, for instance, the gambler rolls a first die and the result is revealed to be a three. The croupier rolls a second die without revealing the result to the gambler directly – but the sum of the two dice is revealed to be six or less. In that case, what is the probability of a one being rolled on the second die? If the first die roll is a three, then the second die can roll can only have been a one, two or three; otherwise, the sum of the rolls would be greater than six. The probability of each of these can be shown to be equal – so, given that the sum of two dice is six or less, and the first die is a three, the conditional probability of the second die being a one is 1/3, different from the independent probability of rolling a one on the die in isolation.

Conditional probability is one of the most important, subtle and misunderstood elements of probability and risk analysis. It is easy to mistake statistically independent events for events with a causal connection, and vice versa. As might be expected, there are many mathematical approaches to identifying and evaluating conditional probability, which go beyond the scope of this treatment, but one useful and relatively simple tool is Bayes' Theorem. If there are two events with known probabilities, Bayes' Theorem shows the mathematical link between the probability of each event happening and the probability of either event happening, given that the other has happened. One common expression of Bayes' Theorem is that for two events A and B, their probabilities are written as $P(A)$ and $P(B)$, the probability of A happening given that B has happened is $P(A|B)$ while the probability of B happening given that A has happened is $P(B|A)$. Then:

$$P(A|B) = P(B|A) \times P(A) \text{ divided by } P(B).$$

This is not exactly intuitive, or even easily understood, but it is very valuable in allowing one conditional probability to be calculated from the opposite one. For example, after an intervention strategy has taken place, a sample can be drawn from the affected population in order to try to measure the effect of that intervention. But, for the reasons discussed earlier, the sample may not be truly representative of the real population. However, Bayes' Theorem allows the tester to relate the chance that an event happened given that the sample indicates it with the chance that the sample would indicate it if the event happened. One classic exposition of this is in the case of a medical test, where a small number of a large population suffers from a condition, and the medical test is not always correct. Bayes' Theorem enables calculation of the probability that given a positive result, the tested person actually does have cancer.

For example, a population could have the following parameters:

- A particular cancer affects 1% of people.
- The test for this cancer is 90% accurate if the cancer is there (ie in 10% of cases, the test will miss the cancer).

- The test is 95% accurate if the cancer is not there (ie in 5% of cases, the test will report cancer where it does not exist).

If the population consists of 10,000 people, then 1% of them actually have cancer – 100 people. The test will correctly report that 90 of those 100 people have cancer. It will incorrectly report that 10 of those 100 cancer sufferers are cancer-free – a 'false negative'.

Considering the 9,900 people who do not have cancer, 95% of them will be correctly reported as cancer-free – 9,405 people. But 595 people will be incorrectly reported as having cancer – a 'false positive'. So, for every 90 people correctly reported with cancer, there are 595 false positives and 10 false negatives. So, not only should anyone reported by the test as suffering from cancer remain optimistic as their chance of actually having it is less than 15%, but any stakeholder who advocates the test should prepare for a significant number of unhappy patients.

When faced with this level of mathematical complexity, it is easy to see why organisations shy away from a rational consideration of conditional probability. As the example demonstrates, even handling two variables that depend on each other can be taxing, and organisational behaviour will typically involve management of many interdependent variables. But the effect of incorrectly handling conditional probability, or misunderstanding whether elements are statistically independent, can be significant.

The pragmatic use of Bayes' Theorem is most effective when the phase space is reduced – typically, at the point where decisions are being made. For instance, when considering intervention-based strategies, Bayes' Theorem can be used to identify the most likely balance of outcomes, and can be used as an attractor towards the appropriate strategy. To do this, it is necessary to identify how the strategy will be tested, and what the likelihood of a false positive and a false negative in the test could be. As discussed previously, the informed risk analyst will avoid a discussion of the detail of the mathematics by presenting the often surprising difference in scale between false positives and false negatives, and should consider relating the risk to both the scale and the impact. In the preceding medical test example, there may be a vast difference in the impact of 10 false negatives on the tested parties and to the organisation, from the impact of 595 false positives, and leading a discussion in this direction can have significant effect on the organisational appetite for risk. It is worth remembering, however, that correlation does not imply causation, as is illustrated by the old quip from a nervous traveller: 'I always take a bomb onto the plane – because what are the chances of there being two bombs on the same plane?' The conditional probability calculation in this case is left to the reader.

No discussion of the human perception of probability and risk in terms of chaos and complexity can afford to ignore the rapidly developing work on the behaviour patterns surrounding decision-making that has grown out of a diverse set of academic disciplines, including both economics and psychology. Classical economics is generally based on the principle that humans are rational, and make rational choices when faced with situations including risk. Human populations act in ways that run counter to economic theory, and the study of this behaviour and the reasons behind it is grouped together under Prospect Theory.

Prospect Theory throws another light on the risk phase space reduction strategies developed by the brain, and has produced, and continues to produce, fundamental breakthroughs in the understanding of decision-making, intuition and rationality as a whole. Kahneman and Tversky, who won a Nobel Prize for their work on Prospect Theory, consider that when faced with the need to make rational decisions in the face of overwhelming complexity, humans try to generalise, often using inappropriate short cuts, misleading samples or spurious but compelling evidence, leading to incorrect conclusions.

Prospect Theory points out that the human response to risk is asymmetric – if a risk is represented as a potential gain, then the human response to it will be very different than if the same risk is represented as a potential loss. In one of their examples (Kahneman and Tversky, 1984; McKean, 1985), they consider a rare disease that is expected to kill 600 people. There are two different treatment regimes available. Regime A will save 200 people, and Regime B has a 33% chance of saving everyone, but a 67% chance of everyone dying. When faced with a choice between these two regimes, 72% of respondents choose Regime A and the certainty of saving 200 people. But the example can be phrased differently. Imagine Regimes C and D. Under Regime C, 400 of the 600 sufferers will die, whereas under Regime D, there is a 33% chance of all 600 surviving. When phrased in that way, 78% of respondents preferred Regime D. But obviously, Regimes A and C are identical, as are Regimes B and D. The only thing necessary to cause a huge swing in respondents' behaviour is to rephrase the risks in terms of gains and losses. This principle is known as the Failure of Invariance, the tendency to make a different decision simply because the question has been asked in a different way. A purely rational, risk-based decision should not vary just because a different 'spin' has been put on it.

In terms of the human brain's efforts to simplify the risk analysis phase space, the attractiveness of Prospect Theory as a strategy is clear. Simple tendencies leading to loss-aversion in some cases and risk-seeking in others depending on phrasing may be short cuts to a decision based on the decisions of others, moderated by the brain's own intuitive systems. If other people phrase the risk as a loss, that implies they have already performed the calculation, and have decided to be risk-averse. There is an evolutionary attractiveness in acting on the basis of that risk calculation, instead of wasting the energy of a repeat calculation.

Even this one conclusion from among the many that Prospect Theory develops can be seen to have the potential for huge effects in complex organisations. Something as simple as phrasing a risk in terms of loss or gain can lead to a completely different approach towards the same risk, from enthusiastic acceptance of one alternative over another, to enthusiastic rejection of the same alternative. This can be of profound significance when considering life-changing interventions. Consider the hypothetical case of a surgical team advising cancer patients on the choice between a radiation treatment and surgery. Patients treated with radiation never die while undergoing the treatment, while patients sometimes die under surgery. But patients who have radiation therapy have a shorter life expectancy than those who survive surgery. Prospect Theory shows that the surgical team can cause a significant difference in the treatment choices that patients make depending on whether they highlight the risk of the treatment or the effect on life expectancy.

Our understanding of how human risk analysis and decision-making evolved in response to the pressures of chaos and complexity is increasing rapidly. The effects of this on the behaviour of complex organisations are also becoming clearer. But it is becoming increasingly apparent that risk experts need to understand the mathematical principles underneath risk, the pitfalls they can lead to and how the human response to risk is both informed and confused by our efforts to navigate complexity and chaotic systems in search of the desired outcomes. The risk expert is his/herself a part of the risk phase space, and Prospect Theory shows that their conclusions and guidance has the opportunity to be one of the most critical factors in decision-making processes for complex organisations.

Complex organisations need to develop robust strategies for dealing with risk in the light of their stakeholders' variable views on probability and impact, the difficulties of identifying cause, and the challenges of measuring the effect of actions on outcomes. There are many other areas of human endeavour where risk must be handled properly, and in many of those, an actuarial, evidence-based approach to risk analysis has been implemented, despite the initial organisational and social issues this may have caused. Population risks of mortality are calculated from real data, and are used in many areas such as social healthcare and life insurance, without it being seen as ethically dubious. A more positivist view of risk analysis based on a statistical treatment of outcomes may be challenging initially, but may lead to the possibility of simplifying the organisational phase space to the extent that the effect of individual stakeholder misunderstandings of probability and impact can be, if not removed, at least reduced.

Note

[1] See: http://www.theguardian.com/law/2011/oct/02/formula-justice-bayes-theorem-miscarriage

References

Bednarik, R.G. (2011) *The human condition*, New York, NY: Springer Science+Business Media.

Bernstein, P.L. (1996) *Against the gods: the remarkable story of risk*, New York, NY: John Wiley & Sons Ltd, pp 270–5.

Blastland, M. and Dilnot, A. (2007) *The tiger that isn't: seeing through a world of numbers* (2nd edn), London: Profile Books, p 64.

Boccara, N. (2010) *Modelling complex systems* (2nd edn), New York, NY: Springer, pp 30–48.

Burt, G. (2010) *Conflict, complexity and mathematical social science*, Bingley: Emerald Group, pp 6–10.

Chandrasekhar, S. (1995) *Newton's principia for the common reader* (3rd edn), Oxford: Oxford University Press, pp 265–8.

Cutler, Colleen D. (1993) 'A review of the theory and estimation of fractal dimension', in H. Tong (ed) *Dimension estimation and models*, Singapore: World Scientific Publishing Co, pp 35–40.

Danforth, C.M. (2013) 'Chaos in an atmosphere hanging on a wall', *Mathematics of Planet Earth*, June. Available at: http://mpe2013. org/2013/03/17/chaos-in-an-atmosphere-hanging-on-a-wall (accessed 1 June 2013).

Goodenough, J., McGuire, B. and Jakob, E. (1993) 'Genetic analysis of behavior', in J. Goodenough, B. McGuire and E. Jakob (eds) *Perspectives on animal behavior*, New York, NY: Wiley and Sons, p 186.

Green, D. (2000) 'Self-organisation in complex systems', in T. Bossomeier and D. Green (eds) *Complex systems*, Cambridge: Cambridge University Press, pp 12–46.

Jung, C.G. (1955) *Synchronicity: an acausal connecting principle*, London: ARK.

Kahneman, D. (2011) *Thinking, fast and slow*, London: The Penguin Group.

Kahneman, D. and Tversky, A. (1984) 'Choices, values and frames', *American Psychologist*, vol 39, no 4, pp 342–7.

Kellert, S.H. (1993) *In the wake of chaos: unpredictable order in dynamical systems*, Chicago, IL: University of Chicago Press, p 32.

Koné, D. and Mullet, E. (1994) 'Societal risk perception and media coverage', *Risk Analysis*, vol 14, pp 21–4.

Lawson, A.B. (2008) 'Stakeholder participation in risk management decision making', in E.L. Melnick and B.S. Everitt (eds) *Encyclopedia of quantitative risk analysis and assessment, volume 4*, Chichester: John Wiley & Sons Ltd, pp 1668–9.

Lewis, L.K. (2011) *Organizational change: creating change through strategic communication*, Chichester: John Wiley & Sons Ltd, pp 52–84.

McKean, K. (1985) 'Decisions', *Discover*, June, pp 22–31.

Morin, D. (2008) *Introduction to classical mechanics: with problems and solutions* (1st edn), Cambridge: Cambridge University Press.

Pfannkuch, M. and Wild, C. (2004) 'Towards an understanding of statistical thinking', in D. Ben-Zvi and J.B. Garfield (eds) *The challenge of developing statistical literacy, reasoning and thinking*, Netherlands: Kluwer Academic Publishing, pp 64–6.

Rahim, M.A. (2011) *Managing conflict in organizations* (4th edn), New Jersey, NJ: Transaction Publishers.

Ross, S.M. (2009) *Introduction to probability and statistics for engineers and scientists* (4th edn), London: Elsevier Academic Press.

Savolo, P.P. (2011) 'Knowledge, complexity and networks', in C. Antonelli (ed) *Handbook on the economic complexity of technological change*, Northampton, MA: Edward Elgar Publishing Group Ltd, p 177.

Schneier, B. (2007) 'Why the human brain is a poor judge of risk'. Available at: http://www.schneier.com/essay-162.html (accessed 1 June 2013).

Shields, J. (2007) *Managing employee performance and reward*, Cambridge: Cambridge University Press, pp 37–42.

Stewart, I. and Cohen, J. (1997) *Figments of reality: the evolution of the curious mind*, Cambridge: Cambridge University Press, pp 177–85.

Stewart, J. (2000) *Evolution's arrow: the direction of evolution and the future of humanity*, Canberra: The Chapman Press, pp 50–5.

Sumpter, D.J. (2010) *Collective animal behavior*, New Jersey, NJ: Princeton University Press, pp 1–56.

Taleb, N.N. (2007) *The black swan: the impact of the highly improbable*, Harlow: Allen Lane.

Tél, T. and Gruiz, M. (2006) *Chaotic dynamics: an introduction based on classical mechanics*, Cambridge: Cambridge University Press, pp 158–62.

Thompson, J.N. (2013) *Relentless evolution*, Chicago, IL: University of Chicago Press, p 348.

Trimpop, R.M. (1994) *The psychology of risk-taking behaviour*, Amsterdam: Elsevier Science.

Yolles, M. (2006) *Organizations as complex systems: an introduction to knowledge cybernetics*, Charlotte, NC: Information Age Publishing, pp 37–41.

THREE

Why do people commit crime? An integrated systems perspective

Matthew Robinson

Introduction

Integrated Systems Theory (IST) has been referred to as 'the most ambitious, comprehensive interdisciplinary attempt so far to move integration of criminological theory to new heights' (Lanier and Henry, 2004, p 351). Yet, most people have never heard of it and the theory has received little attention in criminology, probably because of its complex, systems-based approach.

IST is based on the positivist systems perspectives of Whitehead (1925), Lewin (1935), Murray (1938) and especially Miller (1978). Miller (1978) characterised human behaviour as a product of factors interacting among seven different living systems. This systems approach was first applied to criminological theory by C. Ray Jeffery, in his book *Criminology: an interdisciplinary approach* (Jeffery, 1990), which he called the 'integrated systems perspective' (ISP). ISP is a perspective – a way of looking at or studying crime – that is interdisciplinary in nature, meaning it integrates findings from numerous academic disciplines in order to better understand human behaviour.

In response to the question 'Why do people commit crime?', IST asserts that there is no easy answer. This is because there is no single cause of crime, or any *cause* at all. Instead, lots of different things impact the likelihood of antisocial and criminal behaviour, and these things can be found at several *levels of analysis*.

A level of analysis (see Figure 3.1) refers simply to a living system that survives on its own and that can be studied independently of the others (eg biologists study cells, neurologists study organs, psychologists study individual organisms, sociologists study groups, etc). ISP assumes that there are things (factors, concepts or variables) at each of these levels of analysis that influence the likelihood of antisocial behaviour. Most criminologists examine one or two levels of analysis across the course of their careers and very few make efforts to cross disciplinary boundaries to develop a more complete understanding of criminal behaviour.

Figure 3.1: Integrated systems

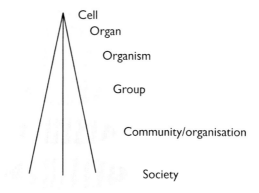

The levels are connected, meaning that each system above is part of the systems below it and each system below is made up of all the systems above it (eg cells make up organs, which make up organisms, which make up groups, etc). This means that a change in one level or system leads to a change in all levels or systems. For example, a genetic abnormality can produce chemical imbalances of the brain (organ level) and lead to mental illnesses such as depression or schizophrenia (organism level), as well as antisocial behaviour that is likely to strain families (group level), which can impact neighbourhoods and hospitals (community/organisation level), and ultimately affect the entire country in which individuals with mental illnesses live (society level) (for examples of how this works, see Robinson and Beaver, 2009).

IST is a theory based on this perspective offered in the book, *Why crime? An integrated systems theory of antisocial behavior* (Robinson, 2004). The text and theory were updated in *Why crime? An interdisciplinary approach to explaining criminal behavior* (Robinson and Beaver, 2009). No one has yet tested the theory in its entirety, although individual parts of the theory enjoy wide empirical support given that it is based on a wide literature that confirms various parts of the theory to be true. In this chapter, I summarise IST and then relate it to complexity theory, focusing on some of the most recent studies that have examined claims made in the theory.

Integrated Systems Theory: the main argument

IST is built around a summary of known risk factors that have been identified by scholars in numerous academic disciplines (eg sociology, psychology, biology, behavioural genetics, neurology, anthropology, economics, etc). *Risk factors* are things in the real world that increase one's risk of committing antisocial behaviour upon exposure, especially when exposure is frequent (*frequency*), regular (*regularity*), intense (*intensity*) and occurs early in life (*priority*). IST is thus similar to what Bernard (2001, p 337) called the *risk factor approach*, whereby 'risk factors associated with an increased or decreased likelihood of crime' are identified. Since there 'are many such risk factors', every academic discipline can potentially add something to our understanding of the aetiology of human behaviour, including criminality.

IST does not just restate the known risk factors for criminal behaviour in proposition form, but also specifies how the various risk factors likely interact to produce antisocial behaviour in individuals, including interactive and intervening effects between the numerous risk factors. According to Bernard (2001, p 343), '[t]he essential questions should be: which variables are related to crime, and in which ways?'. Vila (1994) concurs, asserting that the most important question for theorists to answer now is which variables or factors at what level of analysis interact in what ways to produce criminality? 'What relationships and processes tend to be fundamentally important for understanding changes over time in the ... behaviors of any social organism?' (Vila, 1994, p 313). Miller (1978, p 1) himself predicted that a systems explanation of behaviour would 'select, from among different and sometimes opposing viewpoints, fundamental ideas already worked out by others, and fit them into a mosaic, an organized picture of previously unrelated areas'. This was one of the goals of IST.

IST is thus very different from most mainstream criminological theories. The great bulk of theories present a single factor or handful of factors that are intended to explain why crime occurs. Their answer to the question 'Why do people commit crime?' is often simple and parsimonious, but so simple that they are inconsistent with the great bulk of evidence showing that the sources of human behaviour are numerous and complex.

Of the scores of theories of crime currently in existence, virtually all of them enjoy at least some empirical support. Yet, none of them can fully account for criminal behaviour. Further, the sheer volume of theories, as well as the division between criminologists, is harmful to society because we are unable to explain crime, as well as effectively prevent it (Agnew, 2011; Robinson, 2012). Since IST embraces factors from numerous academic disciplines, it is potentially capable of explaining more crime and will thus be more useful for crime prevention.

IST asserts that:

- people have a choice as to whether or not to commit crime (but choice cannot explain why people behave because choosing is a behaviour, ie, if people choose to commit crime, what must be explained is their choice: why do they choose crime?);
- people's choices are influenced by factors beyond their control, and, thus, free will is a myth (ie people may choose to behave in one way or another but their choice is not a free one, it is influenced by factors beyond their control);
- the factors that influence people's choices (and hence their behaviours) are *risk factors* and *protective factors*;
- these risk and protective factors exist among six different levels of analysis, including cells, organs, organisms, groups, communities/ organisations and society;
- exposure to risk factors generally increases the risk of antisocial and criminal behaviour, especially when exposure is frequent, regular, intense and occurs early in life;
- exposure to protective factors generally decreases the risk of antisocial and criminal behaviour, especially when exposure is frequent, regular, intense and occurs early in life; and
- risk and protective factors are not *causes* of behaviour; human behaviour is not caused by, but instead is made more or less likely based on, exposure to factors at six different levels of analysis.

Integrated Systems Theory: major propositions

Figure 3.2 visually illustrates IST in its original form. Each numbered arrow depicts relationships between risk factors and antisocial behaviour. Notice that the figure includes early antisocial behaviour and continued antisocial behaviour, meaning that the theory explains both why people start committing antisocial behaviour and why they continue. What follows is a very brief summary of each arrow, identifying its meaning for understanding criminal behaviour. There are literally hundreds of studies supporting each of the relationships depicted in the theory (for summaries of each of these relationships and affiliated citations, see Robinson and Beaver, 2009).

Figure 3.2: Numbered relationships in the Integrated Systems Theory of antisocial behaviour

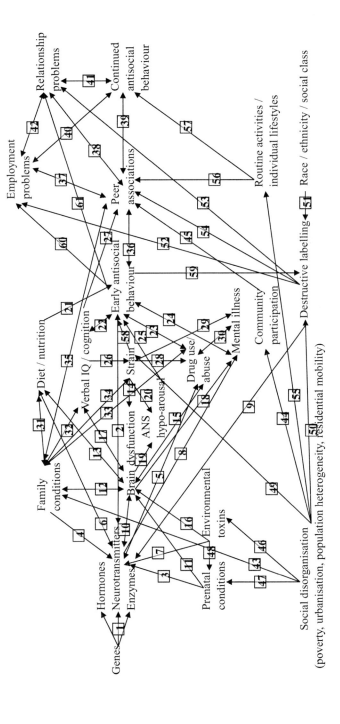

Note: ANS – autonomic system; IQ – intelligence quotient

Propensities for antisocial behaviour begin at the moment of conception, when genes are passed down from parent to child. Genes influence levels of brain chemistry (neurotransmitters and enzymes) and influence levels of hormones in the body (arrow 1). High levels of the neurotransmitters dopamine and low levels of serotonin and norepinephrine increase the risk of antisocial behaviour. Furthermore, low levels of the enzyme Monoamine oxidase (MAO) increase the risk of antisocial behaviour, as do high levels of the hormone testosterone and low levels of the stress hormone cortisol (arrow 2). Levels of these substances are also affected by prenatal conditions, including drug use/abuse during pregnancy, unhealthy diet/nutrition during pregnancy and stress during pregnancy (arrow 3). Some forms of aggression will also increase testosterone levels and likely affect brain chemistry, suggesting that the relationships will be reciprocal.

Once a child is born, these chemicals are affected by family conditions such as inconsistent discipline, harsh discipline and unaffectionate parenting (arrow 4), as well as by consumption of drugs (arrow 5), level of nutrition (arrow 6) and exposure to environmental toxins (arrow 7). Relationships between brain chemistry and drugs and nutrition are likely reciprocal, since once brain chemistry is changed, it will increase cravings for certain drugs and foods. Abnormal levels of neurotransmitters produce severe mental illnesses (arrow 8).

Whether or not early antisocial behaviour results from abnormal levels of neurotransmitters, destructive labelling can also affect these substances (arrow 9). Levels of neurotransmitters, enzymes and hormones can increase the risk of early antisocial behaviour, but it is likely that they will not produce antisocial behaviour without the influence of other factors.

Since brain dysfunction suggests abnormal brain activity, logic suggests that forms of it such as head injury will affect levels of these substance as well (arrow 10). Six sources of brain dysfunction are identified, including harmful prenatal conditions (arrow 11), harmful family conditions (arrow 12), abnormal diet/nutrition (arrow 13), perceptions of strain (arrow 14), drug abuse (arrow 15) and exposure to environmental toxins (arrow 16). Relationships between brain dysfunction and the following factors are reciprocal: harmful family conditions, abnormal diet/nutrition and drug abuse. This means that once brain dysfunction is experienced, it is likely that family conditions will worsen as parents struggle to deal with the outcomes, and individuals with brain dysfunctions will be more susceptible to abnormal diets and drug abuse because people experiencing brain dysfunction will be more likely to consume things that make them feel better (as a form of self-medication).

As shown in the figure, outcomes of brain dysfunction include many individual-level outcomes, including increased risks for family disruption (arrow 12), abnormal diet (arrow 13) and drug abuse (arrow 15), as well as a lower verbal intelligence quotient (IQ)/cognitive deficits (arrow 17) and mental illness (arrow 18). Another result of brain dysfunction is autonomic system (ANS) hypoarousal (arrow 19), which is also produced by stress or perceptions of strain (arrow 20). Several of these organism-level risk factors increase the likelihood of early antisocial behaviour, including abnormal diet/nutrition (arrow 21), low verbal IQ/cognitive dysfunction (arrow 22), drug use/abuse (arrow 23), mental illness under certain circumstances such as in the presence of delusions and drug abuse (arrow 24), and ANS hypoarousal (arrow 25). It is likely that the relationships between antisocial behaviour and verbal IQ/cognitive dysfunction, drug use/abuse and mental illness are reciprocal, because once antisocial behaviour begins, individuals are at greater risk of experiences that will impair cognition and of situations where drug use and abuse are prevalent, and of being diagnosed with minor if not serious mental illnesses. Low verbal IQ/cognitive problems also lead to perceptions of strain (arrow 26) and likely increase the risk of associating with others with similar problems (arrow 27).

Both drug use/abuse (arrow 28) and mental illness (arrow 29) can result from experiences of general strain; each can be considered a means of coping with negative or noxious stimuli. There is also a reciprocal relationship between drug use/abuse and mental illness (arrow 30). Drug use often serves as a trigger for major brain disorders such as manic depression and people with major mental illnesses often use/ abuse drugs as a form of self-medication.

At the group level, both family conditions and peer associations are important for antisocial behaviour. Family conditions obviously affect the diet/nutrition of children since parents largely determine what children eat (arrow 31). Family conditions also affect IQ level/ cognition (arrow 32), the likelihood of drug use/abuse in adolescents (arrow 33) and experiences of general strain (arrow 34). Each of these relationships is thought to be reciprocal given that what affects a child will affect all the groups he or she is part of, including the family. Finally, family conditions also affect peer associations (arrow 35), and peer associations affect family conditions; thus, the relationship is reciprocal. Specifically, failure to supervise children and monitor their behaviour increases the likelihood that children will associate with deviant peers, and associations with deviant peers interferes with the ability of families to correct the behaviour of their children.

Peer associations are often preceded by early antisocial behaviour (arrow 36), so that people with like outlooks on life and certain characteristics flock together. Yet, peer associations are also reinforced by antisocial behaviour, so that the relationship is reciprocal. Associations with deviant peers often interfere with employment opportunities and experiences (arrow 37) and with other relationships (arrow 38). Each of these relationships is reciprocal because problems in employment and other interpersonal relationships can increase the importance of peer associations. As associations with deviant peers typically follow early antisocial behaviour, reinforcement of antisocial behaviour occurs in the group context, making continued antisocial behaviour more likely (arrow 39) – a relationship that is also reciprocal. Both employment problems (arrow 40) and relationship problems (arrow 41) increase the risk of antisocial behaviour, and antisocial behaviour will likely increase these problems. Employment problems and relationship problems also feed off each other, meaning that there is a reciprocal relationship between these factors (arrow 42).

Such group-level factors are also affected by community- and organisation-level factors. For example, conditions of social disorganisation such as poverty, population heterogeneity and residential mobility make it harder for families to regulate the behaviour of their children and peers (arrow 43). These conditions also make it more difficult for residents to participate in community organisations (arrow 44). Low levels of community participation increase the ability of deviant peers to congregate without adequate supervision (arrow 45). Conditions of social disorganisation, such as poverty and urbanisation, increase the likelihood of exposure to environmental toxins (arrow 46), as it is in poor, inner-city neighbourhoods that these toxins are at their highest levels. Poverty is also detrimental to healthy pregnancies (arrow 47), as is exposure to environmental toxins (arrow 48). Living in poverty (especially in a society as rich as the US) increases perceptions of strain (arrow 49).

Living in conditions of social disorganisation increases the risk that an individual will be labelled in a destructive manner by agencies of social control, largely because socially disorganised areas are the most heavily patrolled areas by the police (arrow 50). Being a member of a racial or ethnic minority (ie black or Hispanic) and/or being a member of the lower class also increases the risk of destructive labelling (arrow 51). Being labelled as a delinquent, criminal or deviant increases the likelihood of employment problems (arrow 52), relationship problems (arrow 53) and associations with deviant peers (arrow 54). Such problems with employment, relationships and associating with other antisocial people will increase the risk of continued antisocial behaviour.

Social disorganisation is also related to patterns of routine activities in a community as a result of the lifestyles of residents and space users (arrow 55), which thus affect peer associations (arrow 56) and the likelihood that one will engage in antisocial behaviour. The effect of lifestyle patterns on antisocial behaviour is through the creation of suitable opportunities for antisocial behaviour (arrow 57).

Strain, historically treated as a society-level factor because of its relationship with anomie theory, is important in this model. It is general strain (really, an individual-level factor) that increases the risk of early antisocial behaviour (arrow 58). Early antisocial behaviour increases the risk of being labelled in a harmful way (arrow 59), and when committed in adolescence or later, will likely lead to employment problems (arrow 60) and relationship problems (arrow 61).

This is obviously a very complex account of criminal behaviour. And it should surprise no one that a fuller account of criminality will inevitably be complex given the enormous breadth of criminology and contributing fields. Yet, IST may be so complex that testing it is impossible.

Integrated Systems Theory: a restatement

As noted earlier, IST was thus revised and updated (Robinson and Beaver, 2009). Figure 3.3 is the new version of the theory, revised to make it more parsimonious and easier to test. This version of the theory posits the same basic relationships between risk factors and crime as the original version, yet leaves out some of the specific variables from the original theory to make theory-testing easier. This version of the theory focuses on the impact of community characteristics (ie social disorganisation) on parenting and the impacts of parenting on the brains of children through the factors of attachment, discipline, nutritional intake and peer influences.

One example of a well-established relationship between community characteristics and crime depicted in the figure is that *social disorganisation* (eg poverty and residential turnover) strains good parenting by making it more difficult to: spend time with and love one's children (ie attachment); effectively discipline children; provide proper nutrition for children; and regulate peer relationships. A poor, single parent has a much harder time supervising his or her children, spending time

Figure 3.3: Integrated Systems Theory restated

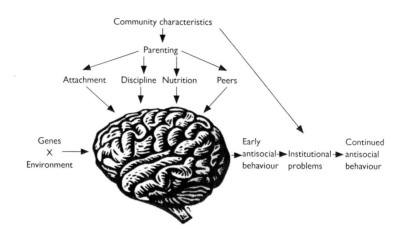

with them, and affording proper nutritional intake. When living in a place inhabited with other, similar parents, it is much more difficult to supervise children and regulate with whom they associate.

All of this impacts the brains of children, which interact with genetic factors to increase the odds of antisocial behaviour (Walsh, 2001). Early antisocial behaviour (in young children) can heighten institutional problems (eg peer relationships, romantic relationships and work relationships), each of which can thereby reinforce criminality or make further criminality more likely (Robinson and Beaver, 2009). That is, when children misbehave, they are more likely to have problems in their relationships, including with friends, boyfriends and girlfriends, and even with bosses at work; this leads to additional strain, thereby increasing the odds of further misbehaviour.

IST posits these kinds of relationships as potential explanations of criminality. To test the theory, one must still have access to a database with information on genetics, parenting styles and numerous other variables. It is now possible to test IST using longitudinal databases that contain measures of not only social factors like those depicted in the theory, but also genetic factors. Although this version of IST retains its focus on numerous risk factors for crime, as well as a recognition that there are complex relationships between variables, the theory was simplified in the hopes that criminologists would begin to test it. This is occurring now under the direction of one of the authors of the theory.

Integrated Systems Theory: developmental aspects

IST incorporates the risk factors into a developmental timeline, suggesting greater or lesser import for some factors at different times over the life-course. Figure 3.4 shows this timeline. Although research shows that there may be more than one path to antisocial behaviour, the figure depicts when risk factors from IST are likely to first influence a person's behaviour. This is based on the growing literature of developmental criminology (see, eg, Kelley et al, 1997; Huizinga et al, 1998; Kumpfer and Alvarado, 1998; Piquero and Mazerolle, 2001; Benson, 2002).

Figure 3.4: Development of antisocial behaviour in Integrated Systems Theory

Pre-birth/Birth	Early childhood	Adolescence	Early adulthood

Genetics ⟶
Maternal drug use/abuse ⟶
Maternal diet/nutrition ⟶
Stress during pregnancy ⟶
Exposure to environmental toxins ⟶

Diet/nutrition ⟶
Family influences ⟶
Neurotransmitters/enzymes ⟶
Brain dysfunction ⟶
Environmental toxins ⟶
Verbal IQ/Cognition ⟶

Hormones ⟶
Drug use/abuse ⟶
Mentall illness ⟶
Peer influences ⟶
Strain ⟶
Destructive labelling ⟶

Employment problems ⟶
Relationship problems ⟶

Therefore, criminal behaviour is obviously not static, nor are the risk factors and protecting factors that increase and decrease it, respectively. Several of the risk factors begin before birth, such as inheriting genetic propensities, maternal drug use/abuse during pregnancy, maternal diet/ nutrition during pregnancy, stress during pregnancy and exposure to environmental toxins during pregnancy. The effects of diet/nutrition, family influences, chemical imbalances in neurotransmitter and enzyme levels, brain dysfunction, environmental toxins, hypoarousal of the ANS, and low verbal IQ/cognitive problems are likely to begin in early childhood. Given the unique demands of adolescence, the risk factors of hormones, drug use/abuse, mental illness, peer influences, general strain and destructive labelling are most likely to occur during this time period. Finally, employment problems and relationship problems are most likely to occur in early adulthood.

This developmental timeline is not meant as an absolute, it is simply a way of visualising when certain risk factors are most likely to begin to have deleterious effects on individuals. Generally, the earlier that risk factors begin to influence people (priority), the greater the likelihood that individuals will commit acts of antisocial behaviour. Also, the more risk factors a person is exposed to during any stage of life, the more likely it is that antisocial behaviour will occur.

What is unique about Integrated Systems Theory?

IST is unique in criminology because it is:

- *Interdisciplinary*: Numerous academic disciplines have important contributions to make to understanding behaviour. Historically, criminological theory has been dominated by sociological and psychological theories of crime, but biology has also been prominent and has resurged in importance over the past two decades, with accounts of criminal behaviour rooted in genetic and neurological sciences (Bernard et al, 2009). IST uses the works of various academic disciplines in an effort to more fully explain criminal behaviour.
- *Scientific not philosophical*: IST is positivistic in the sense that it is based on the assumption that empirical evidence is vital to verifying or falsifying theories of crime. Philosophical explanations that cannot be tested cannot advance our understanding of human behaviour and are thus excluded. This is the primary reason why free will is abandoned in IST.
- *Consistent with empirical evidence about the nature and sources of behaviour*: Human behaviour (including criminality) is remarkably complex rather than simple. Thus, our explanations of it must also be complex, although as parsimonious as possible. There is no single-factor theory that can fully account for criminality, nor can any multi-factor theory currently in existence (Agnew, 2011). Any person committing a crime is under the simultaneous influence of numerous factors, both inside him or her and outside him or her, and some of these are factors in the present while others are from the past or even anticipated in the future.
- *Not deterministic but probabilistic*: Criminal behaviour is not *caused* by factors beyond our control (Wilson et al, 2001). Further, there is no empirical evidence that we possess free will and are thus in complete control of our own behaviour. Instead, human behaviour results from scores of factors at several different levels of analysis in a non-linear, interactive and sometimes random and chaotic way (Agnew, 2011).

These risk factors and protective factors increase or decrease the likelihood or probability of criminal behaviour, respectively.

- *Systemic*: A human being is a living system comprised of smaller living systems (ie cells, organs) and comprising larger living systems (ie groups, communities, society). Within each system, there are numerous risk factors for criminality, as well as protective factors to help prevent it. It is not possible to fully understand criminal behaviour without taking into account all these unique systems, as well as how they interact with and impact upon one another.
- *Contextual or circumstantial*: Even if a person is exposed to numerous risk factors, whether criminal behaviour occurs depends upon the context or circumstances of the situation. Risk factors are thought to be more likely to produce criminality when people are exposed to them frequently and regularly, and when the risk factors are numerous and intense. Similarly, exposure to protective factors will be more likely to reduce criminality when people are exposed to them frequently and regularly, and when the protective factors are numerous and intense.
- *Chaotic or at least not entirely predictable*: While it is possible to identify risk and protective factors at various levels of analysis in different living systems, there is still no way to know with certainty which individuals exposed to them will respond with criminality or conformity, respectively. This is because human behaviour can be chaotic and even unpredictable. For this reason, it is quite difficult to predict which individuals will commit serious crimes and/or recidivate after punishment (Walker, 2010). Yet, it is possible to identify risk factors that tend to produce criminality and utilise them to prevent crime (Robinson, 2013).
- *Developmental*: Different factors influence people differently at different times in their lives. As they develop, some risk and protective factors are more relevant early in early childhood, whereas others are more relevant in later childhood, adolescence, early adulthood and late adulthood.

Although most criminological theories are scientific and aim to be consistent with the empirical evidence on criminal behaviour, most of them are not interdisciplinary, probabilistic, systemic, contextual, chaotic or developmental. Instead, they tend to be rooted in one or two academic disciplines, they are generally deterministic, and they often ignore many of the various systems and contexts that promote criminal behaviour. According to Agnew (2011, p 73), 'criminologists are selective in their focus, considering certain potential causes but ignoring others ... based on the academic disciplines in which criminologists were trained'. This is problematic because criminal behaviour does not belong to one or two disciplines and it cannot fit neatly into one or two theoretical approaches.

Criminologists also tend to see crime as an orderly and very predictable outcome that is relatively easy to explain and understand using only a few variables (hence the popularity of approaches such as low self-control theory, one of the most popular theories in criminology). Finally, they are often static, ignoring the fact that the variables that impact behaviour are *variables*, meaning they change over time, depending on the context or circumstances, and thus can have unpredictable impacts, as well as varying impacts over time.

It is understandable that criminologists desire to neatly explain criminal behaviour with only a handful of variables that they can adequately measure and even manipulate. Yet, the variables that impact behaviour – from genes, to the brain, to conditions and systems within the living body, to group dynamics (including at a minimum friends and families), to a wide range of community characteristics, to organisational arrangements within and outside of criminal justice agencies, to the incredible variety of structures and processes within larger society – are each complex in themselves. Furthermore, each of these variables constantly interacts with the others over time, making relationships between variables and behaviour even more complex. One example is the relationship between sexual victimisation in childhood and brain structure and function; suffering victimisation changes the brains of victims (Briken et al, 2010). Another example is that approximately 25% of the variance in measures of the family environment, including parenting, owes itself to genetic factors. That is, genes influence how people parent (Jaffee et al, 2012a). As of today, it is impossible to collect data and measure the impact of all of these variables at one time and assess their impact on human behaviour; therefore, it is impossible to fully explain criminality. Given this, every study in existence is partial and incomplete and, thus, any resulting conclusions from these studies are, at best, partial and incomplete.

To better explain crime, criminological theory must, at the least, acknowledge and embrace the reality of the complexity of crime. Complexity refers to the fact that behaviour stems from multiple factors interacting with each other across time in chaotic and even random, non-linear ways (see Pycroft, Chapter One).

Examples of complexity and crime

Examples from recent research illustrate clearly how complexity is involved in criminal behaviour. In the following, several examples are provided, focusing only on interactions between genes, the brain and environmental factors. Research shows that each of these factors highly impacts aggressive, violent and criminal behaviours (Taylor and Kim-Cohen, 2007, 2008; Beaver et al, 2011; Vaske et al, 2011). Yet, they also interact in complex ways to produce outcomes of interest to criminologists.

First, consider a study examining the effects of the monoamine oxidase A (MAOA) genotype (a gene that influences the levels of the MAO enzyme in our bodies) and childhood maltreatment on antisocial behaviour in a sample of males from the Dunedin Multidisciplinary Health and Development Study (Caspi et al, 2002). The authors hypothesised that the low MAOA activity alleles would only have an effect on antisocial phenotypes for males who had been maltreated as children. Analysis of the data substantiated their propositions – specifically, the low MAOA activity alleles were unrelated to antisocial behaviour for the full sample. However, when this association was examined in greater detail, the data revealed that the low MAOA activity alleles were strongly related to antisocial behaviour among males who were maltreated as children. The effect size for this finding was quite impressive: although only about 12% of the sample had been maltreated and possessed the low MAOA activity alleles, they accounted for 44% of all violent convictions. The importance of this study is that a measured gene (ie MAOA) was found to interact with a putative environmental risk factor (ie childhood maltreatment) to predict a behavioural phenotype (ie antisocial behaviour). Such results draw attention to the fact that antisocial behaviours emerge when genetic factors and environmental factors work interactively. Importantly, a recent meta-analysis confirmed that the low MAOA activity alleles work in tandem with adverse environments to produce maladaptive outcomes (Kim-Cohen et al, 2006).

Second, a similar study of 627 maltreated and non-maltreated low-income children found that child maltreatment and its parameters demonstrated strong main effects on early antisocial behaviour according to self-, peer and adult reports. That is, regardless of how antisocial behaviour was measured, maltreatment was correlated with antisocial behaviour. Genetic effects moderated the impact of child maltreatment on antisocial behaviour, and among maltreated children, specific polymorphisms of three genes were related to increased antisocial behaviour (Cicchetti et al, 2012). Specifically, children with genetic risks of aggression who were exposed to maltreatment were found to be the most likely to become aggressive.

Third, a study of 506 six-year-old twins examined possible gene–environment interactions concerning peer victimisation and genetic risk for aggressive behaviour. The study found a gene–environment interaction between peer victimisation and children's genetic risk for aggressive behaviour in girls, whereas in boys, peer victimisation was related to aggression regardless of genetic risk for such behaviour (Brengden et al, 2008). This is another study showing that the impact of genes on behaviour depends upon specific environmental conditions, a relationship that, in some cases, also depends on gender.

Fourth, another study examined possible relationships between three genes of the dopaminergic system in the brain and found that they are associated with measures of maternal negativity, paternal negativity and childhood maltreatment, at least for Caucasian males (Jaffee et al, 2012b). Thus, parenting quality is associated with genetic variation as well as neurotransmitter levels in the brain. This study is important because it best demonstrates the limitations of traditional studies of parenting and crime, which tend to ignore the biological bases of behaviour.

Fifth, a study of 12,098 children found that child saturation (the proportion of the population consisting of children under the age of 15 years in a given area) was associated with increases in aggression. And the relation of child saturation to adolescent aggression was moderated by the MAOA gene (Jaffee et al, 2009). Thus, the impact of opportunity factors is also impacted by genetic factors.

These five examples demonstrate the incredible complexity involved in criminal behaviour, and yet each of these examples is itself limited in that it focuses on only a handful of factors. With each passing day as criminology continues to evolve, it moves inevitably to the realisation that the degree to which we understand criminal behaviour is directly related to the degree to which our theoretical endeavours are interdisciplinary, probabilistic, systemic, contextual, chaotic and developmental. That is, to more fully understand the sources of crime, we must: utilise the tools and knowledge of numerous academic disciplines; abandon our belief that crime is caused by factors beyond people's control and instead embrace the reality that behaviours are made more or less likely based on exposure to risk and protective factors found within many different living systems and contexts; and accept that the interactions between hundreds of factors can logically be expected to oftentimes be chaotic.

Conclusions

The next step is for criminologists to continue to embrace, test and evaluate theories such as IST. Tests of such theories should be conducted using longitudinal data that are sensitive to trajectories, like the one laid out within this chapter. Scholars must test for reciprocal relationships and interactive effects. The theory does not require that all the risk factors in the model be present for antisocial behaviour to occur; rather, the more factors that are present, the greater the likelihood that antisocial behaviour will occur. The theory is probabilistic, meaning that the presence of these risk factors increases the likelihood of antisocial behaviour.

Because all individuals are different in their biological make-up and social experiences, factors will affect people differently – that lies at the heart of chaos theory. The effects of the risk factors on behaviour will also depend on the frequency, regularity, intensity and priority of a person's exposure, so that the more times a person is exposed (frequency), the more consistently one is exposed (regularity), the earlier a person is exposed (priority) and the stronger the factor (intensity), then the more likely antisocial behaviour will occur. Finally, the presence of protective factors will counteract the effects of risk factors, especially if exposure to them is frequent, regular and begins early in life, and if the protective factors are many.

Given all this, it should be abundantly clear that explanations of criminal behaviour that do not take into account complexity are doomed to under-explain crime. As recently explained by Agnew (2011, pp 193–4):

> In brief, we live in a complex and variable world. The assumptions that underlie particular crime theories and perspectives are overly simplistic, each reflecting only a part of this world. As a result, each theory or perspective typically has some support, but falls far short of providing a complete explanation of crime.

References

Agnew, R. (2011) *Toward a unified criminology: integrating assumptions about crime, people, and society*, New York, NY: NYU Press.

Beaver, K.M., Mancini, C., DeLisi, M. and Vaughn, M.G. (2011) 'Resiliency to victimization: the role of genetic factors', *Journal of Interpersonal Violence*, vol 26, no 5, p 874.

Benson, M. (2002) *Crime and the life course: an introduction*, Los Angeles, CA: Roxbury.

Bernard, T. (2001) 'Integrating theories in criminology', in R., Paternoster and R. Bachman (eds) *Explaining crime and criminals*, Los Angeles, CA: Roxbury Publishing Company.

Bernard, T., Snipes, J. and Gerould, A. (2009) *Vold's theoretical criminology*, New York, NY: Oxford University Press.

Brendgen, M., Boivin, M., Vitaro, F., Girard, A., Dionne, G. and Pérusse, D. (2008) 'Gene–environment interaction between peer victimization and child aggression', *Development and Psychopathology*, vol 20, no 2, pp 455–71.

Briken, P., Habermann, N., Berner, W. and Hill, A. (2010) 'The impact of childhood sexual abuse on activation of immunological and neuroendocrine response', *Aggression and Violent Behavior*, vol 15, no 6, p 440.

Caspi, A., McClay, J., Moffitt, T., Mill, J., Martin, J., Craig, I., Taylor, A., and Poulton, R. (2002) 'Role of genotype in the cycle of violence in maltreated children', *Science*, vol 297, pp 851–4.

Cicchetti, D., Rogosch, F. and Thibodeau, E. (2012) 'The effects of child maltreatment on early signs of antisocial behavior: genetic moderation by tryptophan hydroxylase, serotonin transporter, and monoamine oxidase A genes', *Developmental Psychopathology*, vol 24, no 3, pp 907–28.

Huizinga, D., Weiher, A., Menard, S., Espiritu, R. and Esbensen, F. (1998) 'Some not so boring findings from the Denver Youth Survey', paper presented to the annual meeting of the American Society of Criminology.

Jaffee, S., Caspi, A., Moffitt, T., Dodge, K., Rutter, M., Taylor, A. and Tully, L. (2009) 'Neighborhoods and genes and everything in between: understanding adolescent aggression in social and biological contexts', *Development and Psychopathology, suppl. Precursors and Diverse Pathways to Personality Disorder*, vol 21, no 3, pp 961–73.

Jaffee, S., Caspi, A., Moffitt, T., Dodge, K., Rutter, M., Taylor, A. and Tully, L. (2012a) 'Genetic influences on measures of parental negativity and childhood maltreatment: an exploratory study testing for gene × environment correlations', *Journal of Contemporary Criminal Justice*, vol 28, no 3, p 273.

Jaffee, S., Caspi, A., Moffitt, T., Dodge, K., Rutter, M., Taylor, A. and Tully, L. (2012b) 'The effects of child maltreatment on early signs of antisocial behavior: genetic moderation by tryptophan hydroxylase, serotonin transporter, and monoamine oxidase A genes', *Development and Psychopathology, suppl. Multilevel Approaches Toward Understanding Antisocial*, vol 24, no 3, pp 907–28.

Jeffery, C. (1990) *Criminology: an interdisciplinary approach*, Englewood Cliffs, CA: Prentice-Hall.

Kelley, B., Loeber, R., Keenan, K. and DeLamatre, M. (1997) 'Developmental pathways in boys' disruptive and delinquent behavior', *OJJDP: Juvenile Justice Bulletin*, Washington DC, US Department of Justice.

Kim-Cohen, J., Caspi, A., Taylor, A., Williams, B., Newcombe, R., Craig, I. and Moffitt, T. (2006) 'MAOA, maltreatment, and gene-environment interaction predicting children's mental health: new evidence and a meta-analysis', *Molecular Psychiatry*, vol 11, no 10, pp 903–13.

Kumpfer, K. and Alvarado, R. (1998) 'Effective family strengthening interventions', *OJJDP: Juvenile Justice Bulletin*, November, Washington DC, US Department of Justice.

Lanier, M. and Henry, S. (2004) *Essential criminology*, Boulder, CO: Westview Press.

Lewin, K. (1935) *A dynamic theory of personality*, New York, NY: McGraw-Hill.

Miller, J. (1978) *Living systems*, New York, NY: McGraw-Hill.

Murray, H. (1938) *Explorations in personality*, New York, NY: Oxford University Press.

Piquero, A. and Mazerolle, P. (2001) *Life-course criminology: contemporary and classic readings*, Belmont, CA: Wadsworth.

Robinson, M. (2004) *Why crime? An integrated systems theory of antisocial behavior*, Upper Saddle River, NJ: Prentice-Hall.

Robinson, M. (2012) 'The perversion of criminology', *The Journal of Theoretical and Philosophical Criminology*, vol 4, no 2, pp 27–39.

Robinson, M. (2013) *Crime prevention: the essentials*, San Diego, CA: Bridgepoint Education.

Robinson, M. and Beaver, K. (2009) *Why crime? An interdisciplinary approach to explaining criminal behavior*, Durham, NC: Carolina Academic Press.

Taylor, A. and Kim-Cohen, J. (2007) 'Meta-analysis of gene–environment interactions in developmental psychopathology', *Development and Psychopathology*, vol 19, no 4, pp 1029–37.

Taylor, A. and Kim-Cohen, J. (2008) 'Gene–environment interaction between peer victimization and child aggression', *Development and Psychopathology*, vol 20, no 2, pp 455–71.

Vaske, J., Wright, J.P. and Beaver, K.M. (2011) 'A dopamine gene (DRD2) distinguishes between offenders who have and have not been violently victimized', *International Journal of Offender Therapy and Comparative Criminology*, vol 55, no 2, p 251.

Vila, B. (1994) 'A general paradigm for understanding criminal behavior: extending evolutionary ecological theory', *Criminology*, vol 32, pp 311–60.

Walker, S. (2010) *Sense and nonsense about crime, drugs, and communities*, Belmont, CA: Cengage.

Walsh, A. (2001) *Biosocial criminology: introduction and integration*, Cincinnati, OH: Anderson.

Whitehead, A. (1925) *Science and the modern world*, New York, NY: MacMillan.

Wilson, T., Holt, T. and Greenhalgh, T. (2001) 'Complexity science: complexity and clinical care', *British Medical Journal*, vol 22, pp 685–8.

FOUR

Complexity and the emergence of social work and criminal justice programmes

Michael Wolf-Branigin

As professionals or students, you may wonder how the social work and criminal justice services in which you are working came to exist. We readily grasp that the programmes are delivered within organisations, and funding from both governmental and private sources support our efforts; however, what were the initial mechanisms that led to these programmes becoming established and later sustained? Whether you are new to these fields or have a wealth of experience, knowing how services evolve and improve provides vital skills in shaping future service delivery. Becoming an agent of change in these fields, rather than simply conforming to established protocols, is how individuals contribute to developing robust services. This chapter explores and explains the mechanisms – from the lens of complexity theory – behind the evolution of such programmes. This involves, first, discussing the four states in which systems exist; second, explaining the components of a complex system in order to frame inquiry; third, delving into the evolution, maintenance and sustaining programmes; and, lastly, concluding with a discussion of other considerations.

Social service organisations in the US, for example, typically consist of several programmes, each with their own funding mechanisms and expectations. These programmes address social problems identified by individuals advocating at the grassroots level for the creation of an intervention to address the social need they identified. These advocates typically have a deeper knowledge and purpose of mission concerning the issues than do others. They were motivated to find or develop their own schemes to address them because they have a friend or family member who has experienced a problem. Addictions-related criminal justice programmes are no different.

Given that the social work discipline has been grounded for decades in a person-in-environment perspective that highly values interconnectedness with others that are supportive, it is argued that using complexity theory as an undergirding approach provides the potential for developing a more informed and humane approach. This chapter assumes a post-positivist orientation (Morin, 2008) because those involved in identifying need, planning to address it, implementing the plan and then evaluating the plan apply an iterative process that continually modifies the programmes created.

Whereas positivists view the researcher and the research as independent of one another, post-positivists accept that the theories, background, knowledge and values of the researcher influence what is observed, and account for such bias and the effects of observers and participants in the evolution of programmes. Thomas Kuhn (1962) brought the idea of paradigm shifts into focus by suggesting a critique of logical positivism: that major shifts in thought occur in response to overwhelming evidence. From a complex systems perspective, we realise this as meaning that programmes addressing substance misuse and criminal justice issues emerge in response to changing societal needs and expectations.

Complex systems in criminal justice and social work intersect and overlap because the participants (agents) in these complementary programmes often have problems with substance misuse that may lead to criminal activity. Complexity occurs at many levels, for example, the participant's level may be chaotic and that person's family or probation officer may request that the person seek substance misuse treatment. This same situation may occur with many others who have substance misuse issues, which leads families and the probation officers of others to begin building a critical mass to initiate new treatment services. This may be one level of self-organisation. Unlike other social services, persons in correctional and/or addictions treatment are often coerced into participating. Initially, this may appear to contradict the concept of the person's ability to make individual choices or to self-organise; however, the participant retains these abilities as s/he may decide to continue and complete treatment, or choose to opt out. From a post-positivist perspective, the participant's decision to remain involved is not deterministic. They may have additional limits or constraints (eg family concerns), but the participant retains the ability to make individual choices by either conforming to the rules set upon them (eg remaining abstinent) or not. A person rarely enters substance misuse treatment willingly. Often, it is on a court order, or strong encouragement from a family member or employer.

The efforts of individuals, their families, probation officers and others advocating to secure additional programmes and resources both represent and are possessive of several properties typically found in complex systems. These properties include being agent-based, being dynamic, self-organising, having boundaries, using feedback and producing an emergent behaviour. Complex systems theory provides the ontological perspective to explain complexity. From this framework, we can envision how programmes emerge based upon the self-organising behaviour of concerned individuals, with the programmes representing the emergent behaviour resulting from the advocates' initial efforts.

We begin with an overview of how a system may operate and then explain that these properties present a framework for envisioning social programmes as complex systems. Given the linkages between participants, treatment staff, funding sources and other key stakeholders, a discussion of a complexity perspective facilitates understanding of the history and factors influencing the development, evaluation and sustainability of such programmes. An application of complexity theory offers insight into the value of strengthening individuals' social networks within substance misuse treatment. This lends support to efforts by social care and community corrections services, who were early adopters in understanding and applying the influences that networks, the interconnectedness of individuals and ecosystems have on individuals, their families and communities.

One of the advantages of a complexity perspective is in recognising the importance of the whole system and the understanding that the system arises from the interactions of agents that comprise its component parts. These interactions can include both competitive and cooperative tendencies. Complex systems (from a positivist/ post-positivist perspective) develop from the operation of simple rules, where complex patterns emerge from these simple interactions of the agents (see Chapters One and Two) and can exist in a large number of possible states. The emergence of criminal justice and social work programmes shares several attributes found in complex systems theory. These include that: decisions come from the grassroots; attractors maintain an agent's interest in participating and completing interventions; rules set the boundaries; feedback is vital to improving outcomes; and self-organisation of these agents creates an emergent behaviour (see also Chapter Ten).

Antecedents to the formulation of complexity theory, particularly in the social and economic sciences, include Adam Smith's (1776) concept of the 'invisible hand', which focused on the self-regulating behaviour of the marketplace and Friedrich Hayek's (1948) work on individual decisions and the organisation of individuals. In these works, individual (agent) decisions lead to an emergent behaviour for the collective of agents. Understanding the importance of how individuals (agents) within a social system influence the entire system is paramount in understanding the use of complex systems. It is from these interactions and the interconnectedness of the individual agents that an emergent behaviour for the entire system originates.

Other antecedents in the development of complexity theory include those from the fields of physics, ecology, computational sciences and linguistics. For the sake of clarity, I will use Mitchell's (2009, p 13) definition of a complex system to define complexity as 'a network of components with no central control and simple rules of operation that give rise to complex collective behavior, sophisticated information processing, and adaption via learning or evolution'.

Emergence identifies patterns that result from a chain of events. This emergence is guided not by an assigned leader, nor simply by being dissected into interactions; reather, it is 'order for free' (see Pycroft, Chapter One). Emergence in social care applications involves non-linear relationships between factors that may be chaotic and dynamic, and includes an iterative process of participants and their eventual choices (Waldrop, 1993). Non-linearity, as used in this chapter, refers to change in one variable leading to disproportionate changes in another variable. On a larger organisational scale, this may include the maintenance of an organisation or system improvement given the vast diversity of consumers, their demographic and functional characteristics, and services provided. Whether applied to the participant or organisational level, non-linearity involves pattern recognition of an emergent behaviour. Emergence concerns the self-organising of participants or consumers of human services. Measuring emergence, represented by various temporal and spatial autocorrelation indices, plays a vital role. Applying an emergence approach, or an emergent phenomenon, provides a promising paradigm for organisational-level inquiry because of the psychosocial and physical attributes and patterns resulting from human service interventions.

The four states of systems

Studying complex systems begins with understanding the states in which any system can be as a consequence of the attractor and phase space that it is moving through (see Jennings, Chapter Two). I will focus on four possible states of systems; being in equilibrium, cyclic, chaotic and complex (Wolfram, 2002; Smith, 2007). I then focus on the patterns found in systems that are in a complex state by working through an example of the interconnectedness found in strengthening social networks for persons in substance misuse treatment. Throughout, this chapter assumes a post-positivist orientation because complex systems are non-linear, dynamic and evolving, as feedback continually informs the system's next iteration.

Systems in equilibrium operate routinely, which may appear healthy and beneficial upon first glance, but, while often the case, in reality, frequently represents a system in status quo. As such, the components of the system may lack innovation and exist more to support the workers rather than those seeking to receive and those receiving services. While such systems may be stable, they lack innovation in the long term, which may lead to its eventual decline.

Systems in a cyclic state can be healthy. Think of the intake patterns at a residential addictions treatment programme. For example, the annual onset of colder weather will lead to an increase in the number of individuals seeking admission. In this type of state, the managers of the programme can anticipate this pattern and make appropriate accommodations to handle the forecasted increased seasonal demand. From a different angle, advocates for programmes within a community may recognise the need to advocate for more resources from local and regional governments to address social problems such as substance misuse. This self-organising of advocates creates the emergence of the developing programmes.

Systems operating in a chaotic state have a high degree of what appears to be randomness occurring within them (Smith, 2007). This apparent randomness may make it difficult for the system to operate efficiently, as individuals providing and receiving services within such systems are likely confused about what is occurring and how the system relates to other components of an organisation. Systems that have been operating in equilibrium or a cyclic state can enter a state of chaos if threats are made to the systems that make their operation less predictable. Given the fluctuations in private and public funding of programmes over recent years, this may throw a treatment system into chaos.

Finally, systems that are complex may first appear to be chaotic, but are actually operating with a distinct, though sometimes hidden, pattern. The difficulty rests in finding this pattern. Systems may appear to operate in a chaotic state; however, when they are complex, approaches leading to social change emerge because of a present underlying structure. Consistent with the overall intent of this book, we need to recognise that to address social problems such as criminality and substance misuse, innovative approaches need to emerge that are flexible to the diverse needs, skills and abilities of the intended participants.

The advocates develop and implement programmes because the larger system, beyond the treatment services, likely resided in a chaotic state. These advocates therefore perceived the need to create an intervention in order to address and alleviate the problems associated with this chaos. In essence, these advocates sought to reduce risk to the person, family or the community (Jennings and Pycroft, 2012).

To illustrate, examples of complexity found in the emergence of criminal justice and addictions may include drug courts, training schemes to support adolescents with disabilities as they may experience brief moments of delinquency and the evolution of Alcoholics Anonymous (AA) and similar self-help groups. The following three examples simply introduce how complexity theory (or complex systems) occurs across various situations. A more detailed example discusses sustainability and innovation later in this chapter.

In the first example, the emergence of drug courts in the US responded to the mandatory sentencing guidelines put into effect during the 1970s and 1980s in several states. Progressive judges understood the benefit of referring cases to drug courts when the accused primarily had a substance misuse problem that led him/her to non-violent criminal activity (Van Wormer and Starks, 2012). These judges organised at different locations throughout the country to begin their approach and used feedback mechanisms regarding both how the corrections system operates and how the offender can be better served by community placement in order to continually inform their decisions.

The second example is the 'Sit Down, Shut Up, and Call an Attorney Curriculum' for adolescents with intellectual and or developmental disabilities. The training curriculum – developed by lawyers, social workers and parents – was in response to adolescents with intellectual and developmental disabilities acquiring the natural supports (eg friendships) of their adolescent peers without disabilities. This programme, initiated in the Detroit area, sought a means to provide a legal protection to adolescents who were fully included in their communities. Realising that these adolescents may occasionally participate in delinquent behaviours as they became friends with their peers without disabilities, they realised that they were the ones most likely to be caught by law enforcement officers. Parents and advocates of persons with intellectual and developmental disabilities self-organised the project in order to minimise the negative situations and impacts that could result from involvement in the juvenile justice system. While the adolescents were instructed to respect the authority of the law and police officers, the programme was designed to ensure that their legal safeguards were protected.

   The final of the three brief examples involves the development of AA and other self-help groups, and provides one of the clearer examples of complex adaptive systems as they began with a few developers, but then expanded rapidly. In this example, the originators of the groups were two individuals who self-organised in the 1930s and expanded their services worldwide (Alcoholics Anonymous, 2001). Within the self-help movement, people with similar concerns or problems are interconnected to support one another through creating mentoring relationships with sponsors. These sponsors are individuals who have also had a history of alcoholism, but who have remained sober for a significant length of time.

   Governments tend not to be the creators of ideas, but instead the funders and regulators of the ideas proposed by advocates. In a funding or regulatory manner, the governments serve to create boundaries for their respective complex system. Governments' ability to regulate and constrain systems aids in justifying the use of complexity theory to examine the key links between criminal justice and social work, with particular reference to coercion as a basis for understanding the consequences in these areas of work.

   Weaver (1948) described three levels of inquiry for solving problems. The first, problems of simplicity, originating in the 19th century, investigated how a few variables relate to one another. During most of the 20th century, we entered into a period focusing on problems of disorganised complexity, defined as a large number of variables summarised with averages and other statistical methods. The third phase includes the study of complexity and emergence, which inquired into problems of organised complexity. The focus is on what we are seeking to generate, factors interrelated within an organic whole, through using a moderate number of variables. The study of organised complexity relies initially on four disciplines: dynamics, information, computation and evolution.

Components of complex systems

The discussion and use of chaos and complexity in human services began in the late 1990s with Warren, Franklin and Streeter (1998). Since then, we have experienced an increase in scholarly output discussing its application (Bolland and Atherton, 1999; Trevillon, 2000; Hudson, 2004; Wolf-Branigin, 2009a). As practical applications received scant attention, recent evaluation publications demonstrate a growing interest (Westley et al, 2006; Stevens and Hassett, 2007; Stevens and Cox, 2008).

This framework provides an overarching structure for investigating processes, outcomes and the collective behaviour of groups.

Because complex systems continually adapt, I use the term complex adaptive systems (CAS) interchangeably throughout this chapter. The first component of a CAS involves being agent-based, whereby individuals or small groups become the evaluands (the individuals or groups who are the units of analysis within an evaluation) in social service organisations. They are the *agents* within a CAS framework. They make decisions from their available and perceived options. With roots in economic game theory (Wolf-Branigin, 2013), CAS emphasises the importance of unintended consequences arising from the interactions of heterogeneous agents as they apply simple rules to their behaviour. These agents decide whether it is in their best interest to act alone or to work cooperatively in order to maximise benefits (Axelrod, 1997; Mankiewicz, 2001). The component of being agent-based builds upon social work's person–in–environment perspective by developing and encouraging the interdependencies and interconnectedness of individuals and their environments (Germain and Gitterman, 1980). Complex systems emphasise the value and importance that human relationships serve as a condition to ensure that the evaluand's ecosystem receives a sufficient understanding.

The second component, attraction, represents the participants' initial and continued programme participation. Attraction is what facilitates an agent's initial interest. It reflects consumer empowerment, and concerns itself with the complete set of variables affecting participant behaviours (Halmi, 2003). Complexity advances the concept of ecosystems by using an open systems approach to explain more than the simple causal explanations of behaviour (Bolland and Atherton, 1999). Within social service programmes, participants (agents) may have different levels of functioning, attributes and other characteristics when initiating a social intervention. The person's level of functioning affects the type, intensity and duration of intervention the participant receives. For example, within social work's core values, competence and integrity are vital. This assumes that individuals have access to services that address their strengths, preferences and immediate needs (National Association of Social Workers, 2008).

Self-organisation, the third component of CAS, provides the magnet that draws agents together and encourages them to initiate and continue their participation. It identifies how agents or participants with similar interests, strengths or needs will group together (Hudson, 2000). Examples may include self-help groups or a local neighbourhood's efforts to combat gang violence. Building a robust social network in a complex system parallels well with the social service concept of resiliency. Through formal and informal networks, the self-organising of agents encourages interdependencies. It promotes dignity and the worth of human relationships by striving to encourage future cooperation by creating network of agents involved in: (1) enlarging future impacts; (2) changing the payoffs; (3) teaching people to care about each other; and (4) encouraging reciprocity (Axelrod, 1984).

In social service and criminal justice contexts, boundaries represent the fourth component. Boundaries are often determined by legislation, court decisions or administrative rules supporting policies, funding or incentives. Boundaries play an essential role in understanding and developing a CAS approach in studying the emergence of programmes. For example, Critical Systems Heuristics (Ulrich and Reynolds, 2010) aids in setting the limits of understanding and inquiry. Boundaries set the limits and define the evaluation targets that agents follow, which lead to an emergent behaviour.

Feedback, the fifth component, informs decision-making. Positive feedback includes information from outside the system and is used to continually adapt to sources of external instability. Negative feedback maintains organisational equilibrium through monitoring or quality assurance and improvement processes (Miller and Page, 2007). Failing to use positive feedback increases the likelihood that an organisation maintains the status quo by not responding to new challenges. Organisations that fail to use a wide range of positive feedback affect the dignity and worth of the participants. This limits empowerment and reduces the possibility of improved service provision by restricting the collective wisdom provided by the diverse perspectives of current and future participants (Surowiecki, 2004; see also Grieve, Chapter Seven). Organisations that fail to use this feedback self-perpetuate and tend to focus on their own survival by maintaining the status quo. This discourages innovation and the emergence of new ideas to alleviate social problems.

Emergent behaviour, the final component of a complex system, represents the outcomes of interventions given the changing context of policy, economic or cultural conditions. Evaluators using complexity seek to identify non-linear patterns within outcomes. As conditions change, so different patterns may emerge. For example, the movement to community-based services in the 1970s affected the societal desire for persons with intellectual and developmental disabilities to be increasingly included in their communities. To measure this inclusion, we may geographically plot the self-organising that occurs in housing patterns as individuals with disabilities strive for social inclusion. A random pattern may represent inclusion.

For decades, criminal justice professionals and social workers have applied schemes similar to those used in the current term *social innovation* when confronting human need. These innovations occur within both the public and private sectors, or a combination of the two, in order to alleviate social issues arising from rapid urbanisation in Western industrialised countries. These innovations can occur in several situations, and self-organise to create organisations that emerge from the grassroots (Wolf-Branigin, 2009b) to support the emergence and evolution of improved criminal justice and social work programmes.

Complexity arises from the interactions of competitive and cooperative tendencies of agents. Such systems are in a continual state of dynamic equilibrium; these systems navigate between being in rigid order and chaos. Such systems operate according to a set of simple rules, yet patterns emerge from these simple interactions without a predetermined template (Mankiewicz, 2001). Contemporary social service practice shares several attributes found in complex systems theory. These include: (1) decisions come from the participant or grassroots level; (2) attractors are instrumental in participants maintaining interest and completing interventions; (3) limits, laws and rules set boundaries; (4) participant and organisational feedback are vital to improving outcomes; and (5) self-organisation leads to emergent outcomes. In addition to these attributes, related CAS issues include: using conflict to develop cooperation (Axelrod, 1984); having threats to a social network to improve that network's robustness and resiliency; and using the wisdom of crowds, represented by diverse characteristics of group members, to improve decision-making (Surowiecki, 2004; Page, 2007). To begin a dialogue with the evaluation community, this chapter also suggests that evaluation prompts us to consider each component of complexity.

Self-similarity suggests that phenomena occur consistently on smaller scales. For example, on a smaller scale, social networking tools are beneficial in monitoring individual progress in increasing the robustness of individual participant systems. These instruments can forecast the likelihood of sustaining improvements. One example is the Orientation of Social Support (OSS), which measures the strength of egocentric social networks of participants in substance misuse treatment. The OSS consists of three functional areas where participants list their social network members by frequency of contact, importance of contact and whether the network member has a positive or negative attitude towards substance use. Also, with small-world networks, add a few random connections and the robustness of the systems increase as clusters can more readily self-organise (Watts and Strogatz, 1998).These small-world networks increase the robustness of social systems because each agent has additional and closer contacts from which they can seek and receive support (Braun et al, 2006). Increasing an individual's small-world network improves that person's ability to establish positive relationships and contacts for items such as employment because the person has more direct contacts.

Developing strong social networks remains paramount to successful addictions treatment (Greenfield and Wolf-Branigin, 2009).Whether at the macro-level (Tenkasi and Chesmore, 2003) or micro-level (Hudson, 2004), creating robust social support systems that encourage substance-free living aids individuals in becoming resilient to ecosystem threats (Riley, 2002; Mitchell, 2009; Wolf-Branigin and Duke, 2007).Applying social networks to problem-solving has evolved in less than a decade from theory to applications (Trevillon, 2000; Halmi, 2003).

Innovation, maintenance and evaluation

The discussion of innovation, maintenance and evaluation of complex systems begins with a detailed example. The agents in this study of a residential substance misuse treatment centre were primarily referred from criminal justice settings from whom the organisation has service contracts. The remaining participants were referred from the central assessment and intake of the single-state authority in Washington, DC. Before admission, referral sources used the Additions Severity Index (ASI) to evaluate functional levels on several domains, including medical status, substance use, social relations and psychological status (McLellan et al, 1992). These assessment and placement tools served as simple rules or boundaries for the system. Programme placements were consistent with the American Society of Addiction Medicine (ASAM, 2001) criteria.

Rigorous tools measuring the degree to which participants receive support from persons in their lives and providing valuable insights into delivering successful substance misuse treatment were included in the treatment protocol. Instruments typically used for determining the effectiveness of substance misuse treatment rely primarily on participant functioning and quality of life measures.While these provide valuable measures of individual functioning, they indicate little of what occurs within the participant's ecosystem.The objective within this complex systems approach was to strengthen the robustness of the participants' ecosystems.While numerous substance misuse treatment interventions use an ecosystems approach (Szapocznik and Williams, 2000; Tapia et al, 2006), rarely are the strengths of social networks that support these individuals measured. In keeping with the intent of viewing their treatment approach as a complex system, the organisation used an additional instrument – the OSS – to measure the strength and positive interconnectedness of persons involved in the lives of those receiving substance misuse treatment services. A reliability analysis indicated strong test–retest reliability (r^2 = .976; p = .000; n = 21) and appeared to sufficiently identify the strength of small-world social network supports, which include random contacts that may strengthen the participant's robustness to threats of returning to substance misuse or criminal activity (Watts and Strogatz, 1998) because supports with more positive influences are in closer proximity.

A Bayesian group comparison approach was used to measure how participating in different activities affected treatment completion after eliminating other predictor variables. This Bayesian analysis investigated the use of these activities as an attractor to treatment completion (Wolf-Branigin and Duke, 2007). Probabilities of treatment programme completion for participants active in the activities versus similar participants not involved in these activities were calculated. The results indicate that participation provided a valuable attractor leading to treatment completion.

The complex systems perspective informed the participants and managers, while increasing the likelihood of completion because the approach facilitated the interconnectedness between the participant and their larger system of support. Participants exchanged both negative and positive feedback to improve their likelihood of success. Attraction via the spirituality component provided the agents with simple rules to follow in conforming to programme expectations.

While coming from a vast range of referral sources, agents who completed treatment organised around a simple set of rules, leading to an emergent behaviour. They learned to avoid or reduce conflict with those who contributed to their substance-abusing behaviour and used the wisdom of their fellow group members to complete treatment. The study used a simple probability function to derive the likelihood of treatment completion. These agents encountered exigencies inhibiting their continued participation. Future research can expand the set of predictor variables in order to increase the likelihood that future agents are resilient to negative external forces. Agents who accessed information to make their decisions demonstrated cooperation as they benefited from the wisdom of their respective group members.

The advantages and disadvantages of applying a complexity framework are numerous. Among its advantages, a complexity framework builds upon Patton's developmental evaluation (Patton, 2011) and utilisation-focused evaluation approaches (Patton, 2008). From these approaches, it is realised that a complexity model performs best when empowered agents select services from programme options based on information they receive about their expectations, and that fit with their preferences and effectiveness. This suggests that the planners and staff do not simply follow the status quo when designing services, but instead encourage innovation and cooperation to address their participants' continually changing strengths, needs, abilities and preferences. This returns to the idea of the microstates of the individual agents, and how their decisions collectively result in a macrostate or emergent behaviour.

As the next advance in our fields, innovators in criminal justice and social work may use agent-based modelling (ABM) for creating predictive simulations to forecast social service phenomena. ABM applies a bottom-up approach that accounts for individual agent behaviour, rather than the traditional top-down testing of models. It provides a sensitive method for investigating and forecasting individuals' responses to social interventions. Investigating the properties of robustness (resiliency), scalability in generalist social work practice (eg use of goals and objectives at both the individual participant and programme levels) and the diversity of agents (Miller and Page, 2007) appears to be a key research focus for social work researchers to develop.

The primary disadvantages include having difficulty creating multi-agent models for simulating phenomena, which will be a vital line of work for future researchers. Given the problems social programme managers encounter when adopting simple inferential statistics, applying ABM will be a difficult task. Applications of ABM have appeared in public health (Gorman et al, 2006), racial segregation (Schelling, 1978), behavioural and ecological interactions (Epstein and Axtell, 1996), drug epidemics (Agar, 1999), and the evaluation of social science literature (Epstein, 1999).

Challenges exist when applying a complex systems approach to measure the collective behaviour of agents rather than the simple aggregated outcomes. Because the study of complexity assumes non-linearity, unintended consequences will likely occur. This concept returns us to the idea of chaos and the apparent randomness within a system. These problems must address defining the boundaries of models, verifying the reliability and validity of models, keeping the model agent-based, and deciding when a complex systems approach best fits (Epstein, 2007). The innovators and evaluators of these programmes should integrate available statistical and mathematical tools (eg social network analysis, game theory) and the new media into a cohesive toolbox and model. New media methods (eg social networking) provide promising platforms for evaluation communities to self-organise, problem-solve and facilitate multidisciplinary collaboration (Hollingshead and Contractor, 2006). As complexity becomes more familiar to social programme evaluators, Miller and Page (2007) remind us of the Buddhist *Eightfold Path* of right view, right intention, right speech, right action, right livelihood, right effort, right mindfulness and right concentration. This suggests a useful mindset when applying the concepts of complexity to evaluation efforts.

Considerations for social programmes

Given the increasing availability of evaluation tools and computing power, adopting a complex systems framework provides a promising framework, as new modelling forecasting methods are available. A complex systems perspective has a widening appeal for analysing quantitative (numerical) and qualitative (non-numerical) data. Complexity can appear at several levels within criminal justice and social work and it provides a promising approach for conducting programme evaluations. When considering the influence of complexity theory in corrections and social service delivery, we can look towards the renowned Santa Fe Institute (SFI) and their recent endeavours into the complexity of cities by seeking the simple rules guiding life in urban environments and societies.

Further support for the post-positivist approach used in this chapter can be found in Kurt Gödel's 'Incompleteness Theorems', proven in 1931. These theorems demonstrate that it is not possible to find a complete and consistent axiomatic set across all of mathematics (Casti and DePauli, 2000). The first of Gödel's theorems states that there is not a consistent system of axioms whose theorems can be listed by an effective procedure that is capable of proving all truths about the relations of numbers. For any such system, there must be statements about the natural numbers that are true, but are not provable within the system. The second incompleteness theorem expands upon the first to demonstrate that such a system cannot demonstrate its own consistency. As such, all cannot be known about criminal justice and substance misuse programmes; however, the overall trends occurring within these systems can be understood.

In conclusion, this chapter introduced the reader to four concerns in the creation of criminal justice and social work programmes. These included: the four states of systems (equilibrium, cyclic, chaotic and complex); the components of complex systems and how this leads to self-organising; an example demonstrating how to measure what a complex system intends to accomplish (greater interconnectedness); and how these assist in explaining the emergence of social programmes to meet the diverse perspectives of substance misuse and criminal justice. This emergence does not represent a static situation, but rather a fluid environment that requires continual monitoring, leading to improvements. While innovations and new programmes emerge from any of the four states in which a system may be, systems in a chaotic state will most likely experience such change. A key point to realise from this discussion is that, typically, an individual (or small group of advocates) realises an unmet need. These agents of change, who often are social workers or criminal justice professionals, then organise additional people and resources to address the identified problem or need. Just as complexity theory can guide us in understanding the emergence of programmes, so too can it be used to identify the chaotic environments that may lead to substance misuse.

References

Agar, M. (1999) 'Complexity theory: an exploration and overview', *Field Methods*, vol 11, pp 99–120.

Alcoholics Anonymous (2001) *Alcoholics Anonymous* (4th edn), New York, NY: Alcoholics Anonymous World Services, Inc.

Alemi, F., Stephens, R., Llorens, S., Schaefer, D., Nemes, S. and Arendt, R. (2003) 'The orientation of social support measure', *Addictive Behaviours*, vol 28, pp 1285–98.

ASAM (American Society of Addiction Medicine) (2001) *Patient placement criteria – revised* (2nd edn), Annapolis Junction, MD: American Society of Addiction Medicine.

Axelrod, R. (1984) *The evolution of cooperation*, Jackson, TN: Basic Books.

Axelrod, R. (1997) *The complexity of cooperation: agent-based models of competition and collaboration*, Princeton, NJ: Princeton University Press.

Bolland, K. and Atherton, C. (1999) 'Chaos theory: an alternative approach to social work practice and research', *Families in Society: The Journal of Contemporary Human Services*, vol 80, no 4, pp 367–73.

Braun, R.J., Wilson, R.A., Pelesko, J.A., Buchanan, J.R. and Gleeson, J.P. (2006) 'Applications of small-world network theory in alcohol epidemiology', *Journal of Studies in Alcohol*, vol 67, pp 591–9.

Casti, J. and DePauli, W. (2000) *Gödel: a life of logic*, Cambridge, MA: Perseus Publishing.

Epstein, J.M. (1999) 'Agent-based computational models and generative social science', *Complexity*, vol 4, no 5, pp 41–60.

Epstein, J.M. (2007) *Generative social science: studies in agent-based computational modeling*, Princeton, NJ: Princeton University Press.

Epstein, J.M. and Axtell, R.L. (1996) *Growing artificial societies: social science from the bottom up*, Cambridge, MA: MIT Press.

Germain, C. and Gitterman, A. (1980) *The life model of social work practice*, New York, NY: Columbia University Press.

Gorman, D., Mezic, J., Mezic, I. and Gruenewald, P. (2006) 'Agent-based modeling of drinking behaviour: a preliminary model and potential applications to theory and practice', *American Journal of Public Health*, vol 96, no 11, pp 2055–60.

Greenfield, L. and Wolf-Branigin, M. (2009) 'Mental health indicator interaction in predicting substance abuse treatment outcomes in Nevada', *American Journal of Drug and Alcohol Abuse*, vol 35, no 5, pp 350–57. doi: 10.1080/00952990903108223.

Halmi, A. (2003) 'Chaos and non-linear dynamics: new methodological approaches in the social sciences and social work practice', *International Social Work*, vol 46, no 1, pp 83–101.

Hayek, F. (1948) *Individualism and economic order*, London: Routledge.

Hollingshead, A. and Contractor, N. (2006) 'New media and small group organizing', in L. Lievrouw and S. Livingstone (eds) *The handbook of new media*, London: Sage, pp 114–33.

Hudson, C.G. (2000) 'From social Darwinism to self-organization: implications for social change theories', *Social Service Review*, vol 74, no 4, pp 533–59.

Hudson, C.G. (2004) 'The dynamics of self-organization: neglected dimensions', *Journal of Human Behaviour in the Social Environment*, vol 10, no 4, pp 17–37.

Jennings, P. and Pycroft, A. (2012) 'The numbers game: a systems perspective on risk', in A. Pycroft and S. Clift (eds) *Risk and rehabilitation: management and treatment of substance misuse and mental health problems in the criminal justice system*, Bristol: The Policy Press, pp 7–20.

Kuhn, T.S. (1962) *The structure of scientific revolutions*, Chicago, IL: University of Chicago Press.

Mankiewicz, R. (2001) *The story of mathematics*, Princeton, NJ: Princeton University Press.

McLellan, A., Cacciola, J., Kushner, H., Peters, R., Smith, I. and Pettinati, H. (1992) 'The fifth edition of the Addiction Severity Index: cautions, additions and normative data', *Journal of Substance Abuse Treatment*, vol 9, pp 461–80.

Miller, J.H. and Page, S.E. (2007) *Complex adaptive systems: an introduction to computational models of social life*, Princeton, NJ: Princeton University Press.

Mitchell, M. (2009) *Complexity: a guided tour*, New York, NY: Oxford Press.

Morin, E. (2008) *On complexity*, Cresskill, NJ: Hampton.

National Association of Social Workers (2008) *Code of ethics*, Washington: NASW Press.

Page, S.E. (2007) *The difference: how the power of diversity creates better groups, firms, schools, and societies*, Princeton, NJ: Princeton University Press.

Patton, M.Q. (2008) *Utilization-focused evaluation* (4th edn), Los Angeles, CA: Sage.

Patton, M.Q. (2011) *Developmental evaluation: applying complexity concepts to enhance innovation and use*, New York, NY: Guilford.

Riley, J.G. (2002) 'Physical health', in R.R. Greene (eds) *Resiliency: an integrated approach to practice, policy, and research*, Washington, DC: NASW Press, pp 171–93.

Schelling, T. (1978) *Micromotives and macrobehaviour*, New York, NY: Norton.

Smith, A. (1776) *An inquiry into the nature and causes of the wealth of nations*, London: Strahan & Cadell.

Smith, L. (2007) *Chaos: a short introduction*, Oxford: Oxford University Press.

Stevens, I. and Cox, P. (2008) 'Complexity theory: developing new understandings of child protection in field settings and in residential child care', *British Journal of Social Work*, vol 38, no 7, pp 1320–36.

Stevens, I. and Hassett, P. (2007) 'Applying complexity theory to risk in child protection practice', *Childhood*, vol 14, no 1, pp 129–46.

Surowiecki, J. (2004) *The wisdom of crowds*, New York, NY: Random House.

Szapocznik, J. and Williams, R.A. (2000) 'Brief strategic family therapy: twenty-five years of interplay among theory, research and practice in adolescent behaviour problems and drug abuse', *Clinical Child and Family Psychology Review*, vol 3, no 2, pp 117–35.

Tapia, M.I., Schwartz, S.J., Prado, G., Lopez, B. and Pantin, H. (2006) 'Parent-centered intervention: a practical approach to preventing drug abuse', *Research on Social Work Practice*, vol 16, no 2, pp 146–65.

Tenkasi, R.V. and Chesmore, M.C. (2003) 'Social networks and planned organizational change: the impact of strong network ties on effective change implementation and use', *The Journal of Applied Behavioural Science*, vol 39, no 3, pp 281–300.

Trevillon, S. (2000) 'Social work, social networks, and network knowledge', *British Journal of Social Work*, vol 30, pp 505–17.

Ulrich, M. and Reynolds, M. (2010) 'Critical systems heuristics', in M. Ulrich and S. Howell (eds) *Systems approaches to managing change: a practical guide*, New York, NY: Springer, pp 243–92.

Van Wormer, K. and Starks, S. (2012) 'Therapeutic jurisprudence, drug courts and mental health courts: the US experience', in A. Pycroft and S. Clift (eds) *Risk and rehabilitation: management and treatment of substance misuse and mental health problems in the criminal justice system*, Bristol: The Policy Press, pp 153–74.

Waldrop, M.M. (1993) *Complexity: the emerging science at the edge of chaos*, New York, NY: Simon & Schuster.

Warren, K., Franklin, C. and Streeter, C.L. (1998) 'New directions in systems theory: chaos and complexity', *Social Work*, vol 43, no 4, pp 357–72.

Watts, P.J. and Strogatz, S.H. (1998) 'Collective dynamics of "small world" networks', *Nature*, vol 393, pp 440–2.

Weaver, W. (1948) 'Science and complexity', *American Scientist*, vol 36, pp 536–44.

Westley, F., Zimmerman, B. and Patton, M. (2006) *Getting to maybe: how the world is changed*, Toronto: Random House Canada.

Wolf-Branigin, M. (2009a) 'Applying complexity and emergence in social work education', *Social Work Education: The International Journal*, vol 28, no 2, pp 115–27.

Wolf-Branigin, M. (2009b) 'The emergence of formalized Salvation Army addictions treatment', *Journal of Religion and Spirituality in Social Work: Social Thought*, vol 28, no 3, pp 327–37.

Wolf-Branigin, M. (2013) *Using complexity theory in research and program evaluation*, New York, NY: Oxford University Press.

Wolf-Branigin, M. and Duke, J. (2007) 'Spiritual involvement as a predictor to completing a Salvation Army substance abuse treatment program', *Research on Social Work Practice*, vol 17, no 2, pp 239–45.

Wolfram, S. (2002) *A new kind of science*, Champaign, IL: Wolfram Media.

FIVE

Child protection practice and complexity

Peter Hassett and Irene Stevens

Introduction

This chapter looks at the relevance of complexity theory to understanding child protection. It is argued that over the past 50 years, approaches to the understanding of and practice of dealing with child protection issues have been guided by a largely linear approach, with an increasing emphasis on controls and proceduralised responses. Despite this, children continue to be abused and regularly die. The National Society for the Prevention of Cruelty to Children (NSPCC) gathers together statistics from a range of different sources about child deaths in England and Wales. In their recent briefing paper (NSPCC, 2013), they estimate that there is at least one death per week attributable to child abuse; official statistics from the US put the number of deaths from child abuse at around five per day (United States Government Accountability Office, 2011). This chapter seeks to critique existing responses to child protection using concepts from complexity theory.

Data from casualty departments show unexplained causes of injury to children as a significant feature in admissions of children to hospital. Evidence would suggest that there has been very little significant change to these data in the last 20 years (Louwers et al, 2010; ROSPA, 2012). Privately, many professionals accept that child protection systems will never stop or detect all child abuse. Indeed, this was acknowledged by Munro in her comprehensive review of child protection (Munro, 2011). Nevertheless, huge amounts of time and money are going into structures for intervention with very little empirical evidence of success, cost-effectiveness or finding the 'holy grail' of child protection: a diagnostic tool that will predict the degree of risk to any given child.

So, why do we believe that complexity theory has something to contribute to this area? Both of the authors come from social work practice backgrounds within different settings, yet they also have an abiding interest and background in the natural and life sciences. In

2003, one of the authors missed a train and had an hour to wait for the next one. The author was attracted to a book while browsing, called *Ubiquity: the science of history or why the world is simpler than we think* (Buchanan, 2001). The author bought it and read it on the train. The ideas contained within the book made huge sense when applied to child protection issues in social work. From that point, we read as much as we could about concepts from complexity theory. For us, it created a perspective within which to provide a clear theoretical base for why some things happen over and over again in practice. Our discovery of this powerful set of concepts was, in itself, an example of complexity in action: how a small action (ie a train being late) can lead to unintended consequences that take life and ideas in a different direction.

In presenting this chapter, we work from a stance of scientific realism/post-positivism. We believe that social work happens within complex adaptive systems. The laws governing the systems within which we work, be they families, groups, organisations or communities, actually exist. At the moment, these laws can only be imperfectly known given the number of agents that impact upon any complex adaptive system. However, scientific realism would assert that we can ultimately discover the agents that exist and that we can find out the truth of the laws that govern the systems within which agents interact. For us, complexity concepts are not metaphors, they are real. We suggest that an understanding of the concepts will lead to better-informed practice in this important area.

The development of child protection practice as a linear process

Understandings of child protection in its modern form began in the mid-1960s with the work of Kempe, a US paediatrician (Kempe et al, 1962). He collected together signs and symptoms of unexplained injuries to children and after eliminating virtually all possible accidental causes, suggested that certain injuries, in particular, in babies, are almost certainly as a result of abuse. Kemp defined the phenomenon as 'non-accidental injury' (NAI). By the late 1960s and early 1970s, paediatric inventories of collections of physical signs and symptoms that indicated NAI were developed. The focus on physical harm was then expanded to take into account psychological factors, such as the concept of 'frozen watchfulness' (where very young children learn that it is unsafe to show any manifestation of physical or emotional pain). The rapidly expanding profession of social work then widened the theoretical understanding to include social factors (parents with low self-esteem, those who themselves had been abused, poor educational attainment, etc) (Chu et al, 2011; Davies and Ward, 2012).

This led in the 1970s and 1980s to the development of ever-widening diagnostic tools. The realm of application moved out of the paediatric hospital into the wider network of social agencies involved in protecting children. Social workers and other professionals were trained in how to recognise child abuse and what immediate action to take. This led to further refinement of the tools. What started as an evidence-based exercise with Kempe (he suggested the probability of NAI based on the age of the child and the nature of the injuries) rapidly moved beyond the scientific to the quasi-scientific and into the realm of social judgement described in apparently factual terms but essentially impressionistic.

The professionalisation of child protection comes from the childcare and welfare legislation of the post-war period. In the 1960s, local Case Co-ordination Committees brought together all those involved in working with families with complex social needs. The committees lacked the authority and systematic approach of the modern statutory multidisciplinary child protection structures, but, nevertheless, provided an early experience of the complex nature of child protection and how it is not the 'property' of any single profession or agency. In the 1960s, community intervention with children was a specialist area of work undertaken by childcare officers, health visitors and charities such as the NSPCC. Social work experienced exponential growth in the 1970s, together with serial reorganisations (as discussed in Harris, 2003), and local authority social services became the lead agency in child protection.

Generic working, the influx of vast numbers of new social workers and the movement away from social work as an individual 'professional' activity to being part of a bureaucratic department with a growing emphasis on management controls changed the nature of child protection work (Cree, 2009; Munro, 2011). This is a statement of fact, not a suggestion that the new way was any better or worse; the fact is that child protection was approached differently after 1972. There is very little data on child protection surviving this era of expansion, the emphasis being on 'doing' not understanding. The notion of evidence-based practice was still some 25 years away.

For anyone working in child protection at the time, the emphasis was on the trees and not the wood. The only concrete fact was that a significant numbers of children were subject to NAI. As described, professionals were being equipped with a range of diagnostic tools to enable them to identify those who had been harmed and those at risk of being harmed. The scale of the problem appeared to be increasing but there were strong suspicions that this was as a result of intervention rather than a reflection of society becoming less safe for children. This reinforced the focus on linear approaches, as manifested by the growing use of linear diagnostic tools based on cause and effect. Everything changed with the publication of the Colwell report (Field-Fisher, 1974).

Marie Colwell was a seven-year-old who died in 1973 as a result of abuse and neglect. An official inquiry found that factors directly contributing to Maria's death were failure of communication between those involved, a lack of training of professionals and changes in social structures resulting in families such as these becoming socially isolated. Whilst Field-Fisher (1974) made it clear that Maria died at the hands of the perpetrators, his findings in relation to the structures that should have helped her have been echoed in subsequent reports into the deaths of children. For example, inquiries into the deaths of Victoria Climbié in 2000 and Baby P (Peter Connelly) in 2007 still identified communication between agencies and failure to ensure regular face-to-face contact with families as contributory factors in the deaths. Laming's (2009) review of progress on improving structures to protect children lamented 'a failure to learn from experience' (p 3). *Every child matters* (Department for Education and Skills, 2003) draws Laming's conclusions together and gives guidance on how to protect children better. Again, though, the emphasis is on structures and procedures, with an implicit suggestion that getting these right will make life safer for children.

So, serious case reviews and investigations reveal familiar themes, with subsequent professional, political and public exasperation at how the same failings can be repeated time after time. Recommendations lead to yet more refinement of structures and procedures but still deaths of children at the hands of adults occur. By looking at child protection in terms of complex adaptive systems rather than the fault of dysfunctional structures, a better understanding can be acquired of why children continue to die, and always will.

The role of complexity theory in understanding child protection

Complexity theory looks at complex adaptive systems and provides a useful way of understanding why the same things appear to go wrong time and again in failures to protect children (see Pycroft, Chapter One). It has to be recognised, however, that as long as children are in families, they will be harmed. This is because families and their environments are a complex adaptive system. Byrne (1998) provides a definition of a complex adaptive system as being 'the domain between linearly determined order and indeterminate chaos' (Byrne, 1998, p 1). We will now explore some of the principles that apply to complex adaptive systems and that may help in our understandings of how to manage risk in child protection.

Complex adaptive systems do not follow linear models. Mathematically, they follow power laws. Injuries to children can be expressed as a power law. Stevens and Hassett (2007) stated that the majority of these injuries will be trivial (eg bruises, small cuts, etc). However, inevitably, a small number will be of a more serious nature (eg broken bones, concussions, etc). Of these more serious injuries, one or two may be fatal. This is a power law, so unless minor injuries can be prevented from occurring, an event leading to a fatality will eventually happen. Most child protection procedures are set up to prevent the worst-case scenario from happening. But, as injuries to children follow a power law, such procedures are based on the fallacy of mechanistic linear thinking. While there is a place for understanding the pathology of participants in child protection situations, the mechanistic adding up of risk factors will not act as a predictor as to whether or not things will go wrong. Jennings and Pycroft (2012, p 15), in their exploration of risk in complex systems, support this when they state that 'within complex environments populated by multi-agented systems, it is not possible to map all of the potential risk interactions'. Risk assessment attempts to be predictive, but good risk assessment no more changes the systemic factors than poor risk assessment or no risk assessment at all. Risk assessment is a means to an end not an end in itself and is only relevant when viewed as part of complex social situations. We conclude that until policy and strategy in the field of child protection moves away from a linear focus on structures and procedures, basic mistakes will continue to be made. Child protection is an area that cries out for an approach based on a dynamic understanding and judgement of complex adaptive systems; a judgement and understanding that is informed and not driven by procedures.

Three other principles that apply to complex adaptive systems are attractors, bifurcation and emergence. Attractors are agents within the system that cause this dynamic entity to shift and change (see Jennings, Chapter Two). Attractors pull aspects of the system towards them. Bifurcation is the cusp at which the system changes; things can go one way or another. This dynamic point is often referred to as 'the edge of chaos'. Emergence has been defined by Mihata (1997, p 31, emphasis in original) as 'the process by which patterns or global-level structures arise from interactive local-level processes. *This structure or pattern cannot be understood or predicted from the behaviour or properties of the component units alone'*. The emergent complex adaptive system, responding to the action of agents within, strives for order. However, the order for which it strives cannot be predicted. As Stevens and Cox (2008, p 1325) comment in their discussion on complexity and child protection, 'emergence itself cannot be controlled or predicted'. We will now use a case example to illustrate the operation of these principles.

Case example

Samuel McLaren was sentenced to life imprisonment for the abduction and sexual assault of an eight-year-old boy. He is of limited intelligence and ability. He had been subject to serial sexual abuse as a child and commenced offending against young boys when about 14. Since then, he has been convicted of over 30 offences – from indecent exposure to serious sexual assaults. The sequence of events that led to his conviction is as follows.

McLaren was released on licence 13 months prior to the offence. He had just completed a five-year sentence for sexual assault on a number of young boys. While in prison, he attended a sexual offender's programme. He was risk-assessed on release and judged to present a serious risk to young boys. He was placed in a hostel that provided a high level of supervision and he was subject to electronic monitoring. He continued to attend groups run by the probation service. An employment project run by a voluntary organisation placed and supported him in a community recycling project, where he was closely supervised and had no opportunities to come into contact with children. A review a month prior to the offence showed that he was making progress: his life had stabilised, he seemed more open about his offending behaviour and there were no indications of failing to meet the conditions of his licence or curfew in the hostel.

A major plank of McLaren's management was the establishment and maintenance of routines. This was considered important; when he had structure, he tended to keep to it. On the day in question, he got up at 7.30 and came down for breakfast. He always had cereal, a boiled egg and toast. However, there were no eggs. There was also trouble in the dining room between two of the other residents (not involving McLaren). He would normally walk to work. On this occasion, he was annoyed because there were no eggs and upset by the trouble. He asked if he could go to work early and get some breakfast at a local cafe, which would involve a detour from his normal route to work. In the daily log, the staff member noted that McLaren was outside his curfew hours, was allowed to go to work on his own, was allowed to go to the cafe and had just had a positive review. The worker was also concerned that McLaren might become involved in the trouble with the other residents. So he agreed and McLaren left the hostel and went to the cafe without incident. He left the cafe at 8.40 and took a short cut across a busy park to get to his work.

His victim lived in a flat beside the park. He was eight years old. The household had overslept that morning. Normally, the victim left his house at 7.30 (when his mother left for work) and went to his aunt, who lived around the corner. However, because it was 8.40 his mother told him to go straight to school, using the short cut across the park. He was crossing the park and was seen by McLaren. McLaren intercepted him and persuaded him to go into some bushes, where the assault took place. Fortunately, a person out with a dog heard a commotion and intervened, finding the boy semi-naked and traumatised. McLaren ran off and was later found drunk in the bus station, and the connection was made. He admitted the offence and pleaded guilty.

The subsequent serious case review found that all relevant policies and procedures had been followed. The risk assessment was thorough and comprehensive – and none of the risk controls had been breached. Staff were not criticised for the decision to allow him to get his breakfast at the cafe and the episode was put down to an unfortunate combination of unforeseen circumstances.

The conclusions reached have a slight air of bemusement about them. This arises from the assessment of risk focusing on the pathology of the individual. It was always known that McLaren posed a risk to children, so the controls put in place focused on him. That is not to say that this was inappropriate; however, it missed the dynamic situation that was presented here. The fallacious linear analysis undertaken in the serious case review presented a hierarchical picture of the factors in this situation. This led to a disproportionate emphasis on the pathology of the individual, with the sequence of events following on. The line of questioning went something like:

1. Was the risk of McLaren offending properly assessed? Yes; he was always seen as presenting a high risk to children.
2. Were inadequate controls in place? No; the controls (electronic monitoring, a strict routine, curfew, sheltered working conditions, etc) were all relevant, appropriate and proportionate.
3. Did the decision to allow him to go out for breakfast breach any of the controls? No; it was a reasonable judgement in the circumstances.

4. Could his contact with the child have been foreseen? No; any other day, this would not have been a problem.

One function of serious case reviews is to learn lessons, both specific and general, about what would have prevented an incident from occurring and how to avoid future problems. The weakness of this is that it addresses only those matters that would have prevented the occurrence of the specific incident. So, as the relevant factors are listed in this case, the absence of eggs could be seen as the starting off point of what followed. If there had been eggs in the hostel, McLaren would have left later, not taken the same route and so not have had any contact with the boy. Another factor was that the family overslept, so the boy's normal routine was disturbed. If the family had a properly functioning alarm clock, problems of punctuality in the mornings would be addressed. So, in this scenario, the boy and McLaren would not have crossed paths.

Clearly, it is ludicrous to suggest that if hostels do not run out of eggs or families are given good alarm clocks, then the community would be safer. A wider analysis of the systems involved is much more fruitful in understanding the issues of risk posed by this scenario. An analysis of the complex adaptive system highlights agents such as nested social situations, time and social geography as significant. The pathology of McLaren in this picture is only one agent. He is part of the complex adaptive system that comprises the hostel and its various nested social subsystems (the staff, the other residents and any number of combinations therein). The family is a social system that is nested within other social systems, in particular, the mother's work (her imperative was not to be late) and the school. The cafe and people in the park also constitute overlapping complex systems, leading to an image that looks more like a web. The serious incident review was flawed because it only looked at one strand of the web. The problems actually resulted from complex interactions within and between these systems, setting off a dynamic process that resulted in the boy being harmed. Complexity theory is relevant to this approach. Complex adaptive systems are dynamic and move from stability to instability and back again, depending on the actions of the agents within it. In this case, a bifurcation point was reached within the system that resulted in a situation where individual pathology became highly significant. That suggests the problem arose primarily as a result of the newly emergent system rather than because McLaren conspired to assault a child.

This case can best be understood through relating it to the systems of social interaction, the use of space and the intersection of timelines.

These are dynamic systems in a constant state of change and with overlapping margins. The morning in question was not a unique event in general terms. People got up, went out and travelled to a place to be occupied through the day. The specific and detailed course the events took, though, was unique. It just so happened that there was a catastrophic outcome. Tantalisingly, minute changes in any of the systems would almost certainly have resulted in a different, unpredictable outcome.

Discussion

Applying a complexity lens to child protection provides a valid way through the two extremes of avoiding oversimplification and fatalism. It also puts structures and procedures into perspective as a means to an end rather than as an end in themselves. Attending case conferences, visiting families, writing case records and a myriad of other professional activities do not in themselves stop children from being harmed. Much of child protection is based on the wisdom of hindsight applied to current events. Complexity theory suggests that this is not valid. As has been illustrated by the McLaren case, it is the concatenation of seemingly random events that is significant, not what professional workers plan and do. Good practice does not stop children being harmed any more than bad practice does the converse. This is illustrated with an example coming from one of the authors helping a group of staff in a residential unit for children to assess the risks of different activities.

One activity under consideration was horse-riding. Recently, there had been a much-publicised event in the locality where an eight-year-old girl had fallen off a horse and died. The manager of the unit agreed that horse-riding should be considered as an activity for their residents, but only if it could be made 100% safe. This led to a lengthy discussion about the need for docile horses, trained staff, protective equipment, careful selection of where to go and so on. It rather missed the manager's point, though, who said that nothing she had heard gave her the comfort she was looking for. Using the understanding of how power laws work, the staff group and the manager were helped to understand that risk cannot be eliminated:

- Question 1. If people get on horses, no matter how careful they are, will someone eventually fall off? Answer: Yes.
- Question 2. Will the majority of those who fall off suffer no injury? Answer: Yes.

- Question 3. Of those who suffer injury, will the majority not need any treatment and recover without any ill effects? Answer: Yes.
- Question 4. Of those needing treatment, will most go to a casualty unit, have treatment and be sent home with no long-term effects?... And so on until the inevitable fatality is reached.

The understanding of how power laws apply to risk in horse-riding suggests that as long as people get on horses, someone somewhere will lose their life. However, while that is a given fact, predicting who that person is and when it will happen is impossible.

This example is relevant in looking at the wider issue of child protection, in particular, when trying to understand its epidemiology. Inquiry reports usually address the strategic framework within which child protection services are delivered, as well as considering specific cases (for comprehensive reviews and analyses of child protection inquiries, see Corby et al, 2001, 2012). They make recommendations in relation to inter-agency cooperation, respective responsibilities within or between agencies, managing information collection, sharing information, training, intervention protocols, and recording. Assessment processes and data collection have been standardised to address issues of consistency or shortfalls in information. The structures, procedures and protocols have one purpose: to protect children. This leads to a paradox; namely, how can success be measured? In the area of reduction of recorded cases of child abuse, there is no benchmark of what is an 'acceptable' level of child abuse. That probably suggests that, politically, anything other than 'zero' is unacceptable even though child abuse is not like an infectious illness that can be prevented and then eliminated. Also, there is no current way to measure child abuse that has been prevented by structures and procedures. It stands to reason that if child abuse has not happened, it cannot be quantified. Even if it could be quantified, it is not possible to say that increases or reductions in injuries to children are as a result of any specific intervention.

Another issue when trying to measure outcomes of interventions is that there is a tendency to see what is wanted to be seen. In the McLaren case, for example, if shift patterns had been recently changed in the hostel, resulting in reduced supervision in the mornings, then an argument might be put forward that with the previous levels of staffing, things would have happened differently. It could be that a staff member would have gone out and got eggs, or more time would have been spent one to one with McLaren or he would have been escorted to work. As illustrations, these points may or may not be accurate; that is not the issue. The issue is one of reductionist thinking and linear interpretations of a complex process, where complex adaptive systems nest and overlap.

Linear models indicate cause–effect thinking. National statistics in Scotland indicate that there are around 20 deaths per year of children who are looked after by local authorities (Care Inspectorate, 2013). Anecdotally, one social work manager known to the authors confirmed that such a level of deaths of children known to his department was evident in his long-term experience. He based his comment on an observed pattern. He was not making a prediction or suggesting that intervention was working (or not working) or that three to five was a reasonable number of deaths to expect. It reflects the reality of working in complex adaptive systems, where despite the apparent chaos of the systems, patterns appear. This is less of a problem in scientific disciplines. For example, climatology makes a distinction between climate (the long term) and weather (what is happening today). The fact that the weather is consistently hot, cold, wet, dry and so on is not evidence of climate change. Climate change can only be observed through looking at long-term data gathered over decades or centuries. Even when climate change appears to have occurred, there is debate as to why. Is it due to natural cycles occurring over millennia as against recent human activity? So, even in a discipline with a strong scientific base, there are issues of interpretation when it comes to explaining why the climate behaves as it does. This is because the climate is a complex adaptive system, ever changing and subject to abrupt unpredictable shifts.

Another example is road safety, which is perhaps more relevant when looking at child protection. The annual total of road traffic deaths and injuries has decreased slightly in the last 10 years (Department of Transport, 2012). Despite the slight downward trend, the annual number has stayed within a limited range irrespective of changes such as traffic growth, changes in the basic training of drivers, safer vehicles or speed limits. At a micro-level, individual roads can become safer through intervention but the overall numbers of deaths and injuries remain stubbornly consistent (see Jennings, Chapter Two). That is to say, simple linear approaches in very specific circumstances can produce the desired outcome but, overall, the laws that affect the complex adaptive system mean that patterns continue to be evident.

Returning to child protection, the same phenomena between the micro and macro are apparent. Interventions can be successfully targeted in specific circumstances to produce a better outcome for an individual child experiencing a particular set of risks. Generalisation from, or aggregating, the particular will not give a better understanding of child protection at the population level. As with horse-riding, there will be a power law that, when applied, will suggest a fairly narrow range of deaths and injuries to children as a result of abuse. If it is accepted that as long as adults use physical measures to control children, injuries will result, then a logical projection is that at some time, in some place, a child will die.

At a policy level, this is a helpful way of looking at child protection. The initial premise of the power law, that children will be harmed by adults, puts the pathological responsibility back where it belongs. Children die because adults harm them, not because professionals fail to visit or keep adequate records or because of failure in any other element of accepted practice in child protection. This brings the discussion full circle back to Kempe. He started from the point of identifiable injury to children and probable cause. He was able to provide evidence to support his hypothesis but not to explain why NAI occurred or how to prevent it. It was later that presumptions were made about signs and symptoms beyond the measurable physical ones. This became lore (And even law!), which has informed practice ever since.

That is not to say that the wider social assumptions are incorrect, but the lack of population evidence can result in policy driven by well-meaning intentions, public opinion, dogma, impressionistic data presented as fact, professional interests, political pressures and so on. Depending on the overall environment, these can act as attractors pulling the system towards it (see Jennings, Chapter Two; Wolf-Branigin, Chapter Four; Pycroft, Chapter Eleven). For example, political focus on the unacceptability of child deaths leads to risk aversion, which, in turn, changes the way that social workers practice.

The identification of a power law linking trivial chastisement of children, say, and ultimately death would be a significant step forward in understanding the epidemiology of child abuse and in providing a sound evidence base for the reality of complex adaptive systems. In the US, some work has been done in this area. It is estimated that 23.1 in 1,000 presentations of children in emergency rooms are as a result of child abuse (Sedlak et al, 2010). Rather than digressing into a discussion of data-gathering, statistics and epidemiology, the point is that the tools are there to gather and analyse data, the methodology is well tested and, as with road casualty deaths, population studies would give an indication of trends. Such population-based information is a prerequisite for any wider study of effectiveness of policies, procedures and inter-agency structures for delivering services. One of the authors discussed power laws in child protection with a well-known mathematician. He acknowledged that there exists an unhelpful divide between the social sciences and pure mathematics. However, he stated that his business was numbers and that if we could provide the numbers, mathematics would provide the computation and development of the power law.

Having considered the relevance of principles of complexity theory to population-level understanding of child protection, risk in individual cases will be considered. Typically, risk assessment in social and criminal justice services is based on standardised tools. By working through a risk inventory that covers every aspect of an individual's (or family's) life, a profile is produced from which levels of risk are identified. The assessment process compartmentalises different areas, so, overall, the assessment reached is an aggregate of a number of specific factors. Research into risk assessment models (particularly in youth justice – see Case and Haines, Chapter Six) has been extensive and, by and large, researchers have found the assessment tools to be valid (by genuinely measuring risk) and reliable (by predicting the tendency to recidivism). They are used to inform decision-making, especially where that involves restrictions on liberty (such as in mental health or criminal justice work). However, the McLaren case example illustrates the strengths and weaknesses of such a risk assessment. When the case was reviewed, the risk assessment was not criticised and what happened was put down to the fortuitous nature of events. Short of locking McLaren away, it was acknowledged that the community could never have been 100% protected from his proclivities. The level of risk that he presented had been assessed and it had been judged that while there was a high impact as a result of him reoffending, the likelihood was subject to satisfactory controls. This becomes a circular argument. No matter how good a risk assessment, unforeseen or unwanted events happen. When aggregated, linear risk assessments can give indications of probabilities but they can never apply to individual cases. In effect, what is being said is that in all past examples studied and evaluated, there is an x% likelihood of something happening in the future in a specific case. Jennings and Pycroft (2012) are clear about the absurdity of this in criminal justice and other settings.

What is a complicated argument is simple in practice. Child protection structures and procedures as they stand do not encourage wider considerations. Such wider considerations may be taken into account but seldom explicitly and as part of a legitimate decision-making process. Looking at child protection 'failures', patterns emerge. All of the agents contribute, in unpredictable ways, within the complex adaptive system of which the child is part. Assessing risk effectively has to include an appreciation of these agents and how the system is a process and not a structure. Pathology suggests predisposition, but precipitation of action depends on the dynamic nature of the system at any given time.

So, to return to McLaren, a worker understanding the nature of complex systems and patterns will ask a number of questions beyond the simple one of 'Is he allowed to do A, B and C?' It is not difficult to identify what the complex systems are. What is going on in the hostel, how McLaren gets from A to B when there is an intermediate destination, what the patterns are in the community (such as school starting time when there are more children on the streets), the safety of places through which he might pass (the park versus surrounding busy streets), and so on. By sketching in these complex systems as a simple web-like network, and looking for nodes in the web where systems may overlap or bifurcate, potential difficulties can be seen more clearly. In the case of McLaren, the critical bifurcation points were the disruption of his routine, the time of day, the geography of the area and the change in routine of the family. There might be others, such as weather, the movement of other residents or other significant places in the locality. A worker trained to think in a more dynamic way is more likely to arrive at a wider understanding of less tangible risk factors that are the product of the moment. Knowing that McLaren could be in a park and that there could be children there might prompt a worker to change the parameters of his permissions. This might seem self-evident, but child protection inquiries show time and time again that the same issues that appear to be self-evident, obvious points are not considered.

Conclusion

It is socially and politically challenging to suggest inevitability, so any messenger bearing this view is likely to have a short life expectancy. Supporters of structuralism and linear models in tackling child protection see such a view as defeatist, which is to miss the point. The application of principles of complexity to child protection provides a window to view the significance of what happens within the complex adaptive systems that form around the child at risk. It moves understanding beyond cause and effect to a recognition that unpredictable and trivial events can and do result in catastrophic outcomes. Seemingly 'trivial' events could never be incorporated into any professional diagnostic model, nor could procedures anticipate them. This is not a suggestion that children cannot be protected, which is a much misunderstood point in applying principles of complexity to child protection. The authors were giving a presentation on this theme at a conference and the comment of a leading academic in the field could be paraphrased as follows: 'So what you are saying is shit happens, so we might as well not bother ... that's certainly an interesting approach!' Of course, structures and procedures are important in regulating and controlling how professionals intervene. They are, however, a means to an end and not an end in themselves. Having clear procedures or the best interdisciplinary committee in the country do not in themselves mean any given child is safer in any given family. A more constructive approach would be to enable professionals to develop an understanding of how complex adaptive systems work and to envisage the world of children as a web of possibilities.

References

Buchanan, M. (2001) *Ubiquity: the science of history or why the world is simpler than we think*, London: Orion.

Byrne, D. (1998) *Complexity and the social sciences*, London: Routledge.

Care Inspectorate (2013) *A report into the deaths of looked after children in Scotland 2009–2011*, Dundee: Care Inspectorate.

Chu, A.T., Pineda, A.S., DePrince, A.P. and Freyd, J.J. (2011) 'Vulnerability and protective factors for child abuse and maltreatment', in J.W. White, M.P. Koss and A.E. Kazdin (eds) *Violence against women and children, Vol 1: Mapping the terrain*, Washington, DC: American Psychological Association, pp 55–75.

Corby, B., Doig, A. and Roberts, V. (2001) *Public inquiries into abuse of children in residential care*, London: Jessica Kingsley.

Corby, B., Shemmings, D. and Wilkins, D. (2012) *Child abuse: an evidence base for confident practice*, Berkshire: Open University.

Cree, V.E. (2009) 'The changing nature of social work', in R. Adams, L. Dominelli and M. Payne (eds) *Social work. Themes, issues and critical debates* (3rd edn), Basingstoke: Palgrave Macmillan, pp 20–9.

Davies, C. and Ward, H. (2012) *Safeguarding children across services: messages from research*, London: Jessica Kingsley.

Department for Education and Skills (2003) *Every child matters*, London: TSO.

Department of Transport (2012) 'Reported road casualties in Great Britain: quarterly provisional estimates 2012'. Available at: https://www.gov.uk/government/uploads/system/uploads/attachment_data/file/83000/road-accidents-and-safety-quarterly-estimates-q3-2012.pdf (accessed 6 May 2013).

Field-Fisher, T.G. (1974) *Report of the Committee of Inquiry into the care and supervision provided in relation to Maria Colwell*, Department of Health and Social Security, London: TSO.

Harris, J. (2003) *The social work business*, London: Routledge.

Jennings, P. and Pycroft, A. (2012) 'The numbers game: a systems perspective on risk', in A. Pycroft and S. Clift (eds) *Risk and rehabilitation: management and treatment of substance misuse and mental health problems in the criminal justice system*, Bristol: The Policy Press, pp 7–20.

Kempe, C.H., Silverman, F., Steele, B.F., Droegemueller, W. and Silver, H.K. (1962) 'The battered child syndrome', *Journal of the American Medical Association*, vol 181, pp 17–24.

Laming, H. (2009) *The protection of children in England: a progress report*, London: TSO.

Louwers, E.C., Affourtit, M.J., Moll, H.A., De Koning, H.J. and Korfage, I.J. (2010) 'Screening for child abuse at emergency departments: a systematic review', *Archives of the Disabled Child*, vol 95, no 3, pp 214–18.

Mihata, K. (1997) 'The persistence of emergence', in R.A. Eve, S. Horsfall and M.E. Lee (eds) *Chaos, complexity and sociology*, Thousand Oaks, CA: Sage, pp 30–8.

Munro, E. (2011) *The Munro Review of child protection*, London: TSO.

NSPCC (National Society for the Prevention of Cruelty to Children) (2013) 'Child killings in England and Wales: explaining the statistics'. Available at: http://www.nspcc.org.uk/Inform/research/briefings/child_killings_in_england_and_wales_wda67213.html (accessed 6 May 2013).

ROSPA (Royal Society for the Prevention of Accidents) (2012) 'Number of emergency hospital admissions as a result of unintentional injury for children under 5 years old and adults aged 65 and over, by type of injury'. Available at: http://www.rospa.com/homesafety/aroundtheuk/scotland/statistics.aspx (accessed 28 April 2013).

Sedlak, A.J., Mettenburg, J., Basena, M., Petta, I., McPherson, K., Greene, A. and Li, S. (2010) *Fourth National Incidence Study of child abuse and neglect (NIS–4): report to Congress*, Washington, DC: US Department of Health and Human Services, Administration for Children and Families.

Stevens, I. and Cox, P. (2008) 'Complexity theory: developing new understandings of child protection in field settings and in residential child care', *British Journal of Social Work*, vol 38, no 7, pp 1320–36.

Stevens, I. and Hassett, P. (2007) 'Applying complexity theory to risk in child protection practice', *Childhood*, vol 14, pp 128–44.

United States Government Accountability Office (2011) 'Child maltreatment: strengthening national data on child fatalities could aid in prevention (GAO-11-599)'. Available at: http://www.gao.gov/new.items/d11599.pdf (accessed 6 May 2013).

SIX

Youth justice: from linear risk paradigm to complexity

Stephen Case and Kevin Haines

An enormous amount of fiction has been produced, masquerading as rigorous science. (Freedman, 2010, p 16)

This chapter explores and evaluates the underlying principles, delivery and future of youth justice in England and Wales in the emerging context of complexity. A reductionist risk-based approach has attained hegemony in the Youth Justice System (YJS) of England and Wales, perpetuating understandings of offending behaviour by young people as the linear, proportional and deterministic outcome of exposure to 'risk factors'. This simplistic caricature of young people's lives has been derived from positivist 'Risk Factor Research' (RFR) (Case and Haines, 2009), which itself has informed a 'Risk Factor Prevention Paradigm' (RFPP) for youth justice. We evaluate the dominant positivist risk-based model of youth justice in relation to the inherent complexity, unpredictability, context-dependence and multidimensionality of the young people and behaviours targeted by the YJS. We put forward a post-positivist argument (rather than a critical realist stance) that quantitative criminology is both necessary and valuable, but not in the positivist form in which it has come to be applied to youth justice, such as through crude measurement and crude linear statistical tests. We argue for better measurement of social-scientific phenomena (cf Byrne, 1998) and post-positivist statistical analyses.[1] Our posited approach is grounded in the dynamic model inherent to Complex Systems Science and has two basic elements: that the *measurement* of key concepts (eg 'risk', 'offending') in positivist RFR and practice has been too crude and insufficiently 'fractal' (following Mandelbrot, 1967); and that there has been insufficient sensitivity to initial conditions in the linear *analysis* of relationships between risk and offending behaviour (following Lorenz, 1963). Therefore, we are not arguing against measurement, statistical analysis and quantitative methods per se, but arguing that much quantitative criminology and RFR, in particular, has utilised measurement scales and quantitative analyses that are too crude to sustain the conclusions that many have come to. As a consequence, we suggest that the results of RFR are largely artefactual and present inaccurate and misleading accounts of causality and offending behaviour by young people. Finally, we draw on the critique developed here to assess a proposed new framework for understanding and responding to offending behaviour by young people.

The hegemony of positivist criminology

> positivism has long ceased to be a viable option, though the message has still not got through to some researchers. (Robson, 2011, p 163)

Positivism still dominates criminology. Debates and critiques addressing the positivist hegemony within criminological research and theory stretch back over history and have reached another peak in contemporary criminology. This peak is due (at least in part) to the proselytising of experimental methods by high-profile criminologists (eg Farrington, 2003; Sherman, 2009). The 'Positivistic hubris of experimental criminology' (Goldson and Hughes, 2010, p 222) has been endorsed by official funding bodies in the UK (eg the Home Office, Ministry of Justice and Economic and Social Research Council – see Hope, 2009) and the US (eg the Office of Juvenile Justice and Delinquency Prevention – see Sherman, 2009), and positivistic research has had the greatest influence on official criminal and youth justice policy – to the extent that positivism holds the hegemonic high ground.[2]

Positivist criminologists and others heavily influenced by positivist methodology have privileged *empiricism* (the validation of knowledge through the so-called scientific method based on experimentation, survey questionnaire and interview – see Williams, 2006) and *frequentism* (defining an event's probability as the limit of its relative frequency in a large number of trials – Feller, 1957) as the route to the acquisition of criminological knowledge.[3] The positivist belief is that it is both possible and correct to understand, in this context, offending behaviour by measuring variables and combining them in linear statistical analyses.[4] The positivist method remains the gold standard route to purportedly 'evidence-based' knowledge in contemporary criminology; typically animated by 'experimental' criminology, the 'randomised controlled trial' (see Hough, 2010), the privileging of positivist survey research (see Farrington, 2003) and the results of statistical tests of significance. The reductionist simplicity of the experimental (and quasi-experimental) method ideally suits positivist goals to identify stable, predictable, deterministic, replicable relationships in the social world. Each of these relationship features relies heavily on the researcher's ability to control what s/he is measuring and, thus, to construct an ostensible order out of complex behaviours, systems and situations (Hope, 2009). Positivist predilections have shaped and driven understandings of offending behaviour by young people and the delivery of youth justice in the UK for over a decade. The two central tenets of dominant contemporary understandings of offending behaviour by young people (drawn from RFR – see Case and Haines, 2009) are *linearity* and *proportionality* – the belief that incremental increases in supposedly causal, determinant or predictor variables (known as risk factors) produce linear (direct, straight line) and proportional increases in effects/outcomes (defined as 'offending').

Notwithstanding the confidence of positivists, critics have caricatured this narrow pseudo-'scientific', bureaucratic, administrative form of criminology as beset by abstract empiricism, methodological inhibition, reductionism and fragmented representations of reality (cf Wright-Mills, 1959; Goldson and Hughes, 2010; Young, 2011). These critics have often maintained that positivist methods and analysis have a place within criminology, but that it is not the only route to knowledge and that proponents have overstated its general validity and utility (see Walgrave, 2008), particularly within the youth justice arena (eg France and Homel, 2007). Some have castigated positivist criminology for the erroneous presumption of control over a range of dynamic experimental variables (eg risk factors), which, they argue, simply cannot be readily or validly reduced to static, quantitative form (eg Case, 2007; France, 2008; O'Mahony, 2009; Paylor, 2010; Bateman, 2011).[5] Yet, for the most part, positivists and positivist criminology have been unaffected and untroubled by critiques and challenges.[6] Proponents have not felt the need to properly justify or rationalise the hegemony of positivism; often, simply resorting to reasserting their hegemony through rhetoric (see Hope's [2009] criticisms of Sherman), uncritical application and crude replication (see Case and Haines, 2009). Arguably, what looks like 'science' in criminology, with its sampling rules, methodological coherence, use of statistical tests and certainty of conclusions, is, in reality, a social construct of dubious empirical, real-world validity (Salsburg, 2002). In short, we argue, the fallacy of positivist criminology is rooted in poor measurement and in a misplaced faith in the results of statistical tests of significance – and in the outcome of combining the two. This is a fallacy nowhere more prevalent than within the field of youth justice. Assessment and intervention in the YJS of England and Wales have been beset by crude, reductionist measurements (eg of risk factors for offending), analyses (eg of the relationship between risk factors and offending) and conclusions (eg regarding the nature of the risk factor–offending relationship, regarding appropriate intervention) that have served to oversimplify and misinform the way that offending behaviour by young people has been understood and responded to.

The central argument of this chapter, therefore, is that an effective challenge to the positivist foundations of risk assessment in the YJS is to be found in 'Complex Systems Science' – or 'chaos theory' (see Lorenz, 1963; Young, 1991; Gleick, 1997; Elliott and Kiel, 2000). Complex Systems Science provides ideas and mechanisms through which to critique and undermine the hegemony of the positivist method that underpins risk assessment, and to expose its true nature and the weaknesses of its propositions and claims to knowledge. The focus here is on critique: to use Complex Systems Science to dismantle from within the positivist methodology employed in contemporary youth justice research, typically RFR, its translation into youth justice policy, and its animation through the practice of risk assessment. Although a full exposition of the development and tenets of Complex Systems Science is beyond the scope of this chapter (but see Pycroft, Chapter One; see also Gleick, 1997; Young, 1991), two essential components of Complex Systems Science will be fundamental to our critique of positivist RFR and its animation through risk assessment in the YJS: fractal measurement and sensitive dependence on initial conditions (the 'Butterfly Effect').

The rise and dominance of risk-based youth justice in England and Wales

In 1997, the Labour Party came to power in the UK, inheriting a Conservative Party legacy of increasing public concern over crime levels and the (in)ability of government to deal effectively with the perceived youth crime problem. Their response was a clinical root-and-branch reform of the YJS, pushed through in the Crime and Disorder Act 1998, which mercilessly swept aside the concerns for welfare and justice that had traditionally dominated youth justice in favour of a bold refocusing on the prevention and reduction of offending behaviour by young people by identifying and targeting 'risk' (see Audit Commission, 1996). The Crime and Disorder Act privileged the central tenets and methodologies of the RFPP as the hegemonic model of understanding and responding to offending behaviour by young people (see Stephenson et al, 2011), and the central practice of newly formed Youth Offending Teams (YOTs)[7] was to identify and respond to identified 'risk factors' in young people's lives. The RFPP offered a straightforward, practical and simplistic premise: 'Identify the key risk factors for offending and implement prevention methods designed to counteract them' (Farrington, 2000, p 7).

The RFPP draws heavily on a body of positivist RFR (see Case and Haines, 2009) which posits that offending behaviour by young people is the linear and proportional outcome of a range of 'psychosocial' (ie psychological and immediate social – family, school, community and lifestyle-based) 'risk factors' that can be measured/assessed, then targeted and changed through intervention, thus reducing the likelihood of future offending and reoffending (Farrington, 2000). Positivist RFR has evolved by utilising a common methodological core, typically questionnaires measuring/quantifying psychosocial risk factors, with these risk measures then related (statistically) to future offending or reoffending – an approach labelled 'risk factorology' (Kemshall, 2008; see also France, 2008). As a consequence of widespread risk factorology, risk factors have been asserted to be predictive of offending behaviour by young people; implicating a developmental theoretical understanding of risk as emerging in early life (eg childhood and early adolescence) and exerting an increasing influence in, typically, late adolescence.

The RFPP has provided the UK government and youth justice practitioners with a 'scientific', coherent, common-sense, amenable and practical way of conceptualising and responding to offending behaviour by young people (see YJB, 2004). As Farrington (2000, p 7) has confidently asserted:

> A key advantage of the risk factor prevention paradigm is that it links explanation and prevention, fundamental and applied research, and scholars and practitioners. Importantly, the paradigm is easy to understand and to communicate, and it is readily accepted by policy makers, practitioners, and the general public.

However, the implementation of the RFPP has been crude and oversimplistic. The RFPP was operationalised and animated in 2000 through the 'Asset' structured risk assessment instrument (YJB, 2000; see also Baker et al, 2002), which was created to 'identify the risk factors associated with offending behaviour and to inform effective intervention programmes' (YJB, 2004, p 27). Asset is a risk factor questionnaire completed by YOT practitioners during and following interview with a young person who has been referred to them following arrest and entry into the YJS. A series of 12 risk domains[8] contain statements based on 'dynamic' (ie purportedly malleable) risk factors, with exposure to these risk factors rated dichotomously (yes/no). Each domain is then rated based on the perceived likelihood that these risk factors/domains contributed to the young person's offending (0 = no association; 1 = slight/limited indirect association; 2 = moderate direct or indirect association; 3 = quite strong association, normally direct; and 4 = very strong, clear and direct association). Through this process of factorisation, practitioners explain and 'evidence' this risk influence in a small narrative box at the end of each section. Domain scores are aggregated to give a total risk 'score' indicating the likelihood that a risk domain is associated with the young person's offending behaviour.[9] The content and structure of Asset demonstrates the degree of theoretical and practical duress placed on practitioners by the Youth Justice Board (YJB) to record (factorise) and evidence linear, developmental and deterministic relationships between risk factors and offending behaviour by young people – because the expectation is that risk factors are predictive of offending and should therefore be targeted by risk-focused interventions.

The UK government extended its commitment to risk-based youth justice on 30 November 2009, by introducing the 'Scaled Approach' to assessment and intervention. The Scaled Approach dictates that every young person subject to a non-custodial sentence has the frequency (daily, weekly, etc) and intensity (eg number of hours per contact) of the intervention they receive determined by their Asset score. Intervention levels range from low/standard, to medium/enhanced, to high/intensive (YJB, 2009). Furthermore, the Asset scores across the domains determine the type or nature of the intervention delivered to the young. For example, a high risk score in the substance use domain would lead to a substance use treatment programme, while high scores in the emotional/mental health or thinking and behaviour domains are likely to precipitate cognitive-behavioural programmes. Consequently, assessed risk factors are linked explicitly to primarily offence- and offender-focused interventions that are frequently prescriptive, constraining, individualised, pseudo-psychological and adopted from a menu of 'effective' programmes prescribed by the YJB (see Stephenson et al, 2011). Taken together, therefore, Asset risk assessment and the Scaled Approach illustrate the UK government's commitment to the central tenet of positivist RFR (and the RFPP) – that risk factors exert a linear, deterministic influence on offending behaviour that can be effectively addressed through intervention.

However, Asset is based entirely on positivist RFR, and so, consequently, it replicates, exacerbates and extends the problems associated with this form of RFR. We will now illustrate these problems by subjecting positivist RFR and Asset to a critique based on the central principles of Complex Systems Science.

The complexity critique: fractal youth justice

> Smooth shapes are very rare in the wild but extremely important in the ivory tower and the factory.

> A cloud is made of billows upon billows upon billows that look like clouds. As you come closer to a cloud, you don't get something smooth, but irregularities at a smaller scale. (Mandelbrot, 2004)

We contend that Complex Systems Science offers tools that can be employed to challenge the reductionist positivist foundations of risk assessment in the YJS. One such tool is the concept of *fractal measurement*, which was introduced by Benoit Mandelbrot in 1967, who used the example of the problem of the accurate measurement of the length of the British coastline. Mandelbrot argued that the smaller the increment of measurement (eg when using a six-inch ruler compared to a yardstick), the longer the measured length became, because the measure is laid along a more curvilinear route. From this, he concluded that objects in the real world could be conceived of as 'fractals' – reduced size copies of a larger whole – and that an object's dimensions are relative to the observer and can be fractional – sensitive to the scale of measurement employed (Mandelbrot, 1967, 1982). The concept of fractals, therefore, provides a realistic and useful model for understanding the measurement of 'rough' (ie complex) and non-linear phenomena.

The significance of fractal measurement for youth justice research and policy lies in what it tells us about the importance of scale of measurement for the robustness, reliability and validity of the measures employed in understanding offending behaviour by young people (eg through risk assessment in the YJS), the confidence we can have in these understandings/assessments, and the extent to which they sustain different levels of interpretation. Risk assessments in the YJS, for example, are redolent with rudimentary and unsophisticated measurement and analysis that readily pursues understandings of risks as 'smooth shapes' rather than rough phenomena better understood as fractals.

Questions of the nature and validity of the measurement of variables/factors are, therefore, of central importance to any pursuit of a suitably complex form of youth justice. We intend to explore this critique in methodological detail and in the broader context of the tenets of Complex Systems Science. In practice, positivist RFR has often relied on the simplistic factorisation and generalisation of risk, underemphasising the complexity and quality of young people's experiences, circumstances, events and behaviours in favour of applying static Likert-type ratings scales to a restricted group of generic risk categories such as 'family relationships', 'attachment to school' and 'neighbourhood criminality'. It is, however, difficult to offer comprehensive examples of this approach, because so few risk factor researchers have actually provided full details of their instruments. Although in cross-sectional, questionnaire-based RFR, researchers have been more likely to detail the ways in which they conceptualise, operationalise and measure risk factors, longitudinal RFR (particularly where interview-based) is replete with studies neglecting such crucial methodological detail.[10] However, relevant and archetypal examples are available of the crude and simplistic conceptualisation, operationalisation and measurement of risk, notably, those detailed in Table 6.1.

Table 6.1 illustrates the nature and extent of factorisation typical of positivist RFR. Potentially multifaceted, contextualised and dynamic *processes* (eg family conflict, relationship with parents, commitment to school) have been operationalised as simplistic (often composite, conflated), static, decontextualised *factors* based on the crude aggregation of the outputs of limited (dichotomous, Likert) response/ratings scales. The invalidity and unreliability of the factorisation process is exacerbated by a lack of consensus between and within studies regarding how to conceptualise and operationalise risk (eg the number of statements that should be conflated, the nature of these statements). For example, the risk factor 'family conflict' is operationalised by three identical statements in the Youth Audit and On Track studies, alongside broadly equivalent ratings scales, yet the Youth Audit includes two additional statements as part of its composite risk factor.

The insensitive reduction and generalisation of 'risk' to nomothetic, aggregated, psychosocial and static categories (demonstrated in Table 6.1) washes away the idiographic, complex, contextual and dynamic nature of young people's real lives. The more simplified the measurement of risk is, the further away it moves from the reality it seeks to portray. This weakness has been animated by Asset through broad risk categories comprised of broad, static, simplistic and vague risk statements. For example, the domain of 'Family and

Table 6.1: The crude measurement of risk in Risk Factor Research

Study	Composite risk factor	Measurement
Youth Audit (Beinert et al, 2002) (cross-sectional)	**Family conflict** (five statements): People in my family often insult or yell at each other. People in my family have serious arguments. We argue about the same things in my family over and over again. Adults in my home sometimes try to hurt me, for example, by pushing, hitting or kicking me. Adults in my home sometimes try to hurt each other, for example, by pushing, hitting or kicking each other.	**Four-point Likert:** NO!; no; yes; YES!
On Track Youth Lifestyles Survey (Armstrong et al, 2005) (repeated cross-sectional)	**Family conflict** (three statements): People in my family often insult or yell at each other. People in my family have serious arguments. We argue about the same things in my family over and over again.	**Four-point Likert:** YES; yes; no; NO.
International Self-Reported Delinquency Survey (Junger-Tas et al, 2003) (cross-sectional)	**Parental supervision** (two statements): Parents know with whom you are. Parents know where you are.	**Yes/No.**
	Relationship with parents (one statement): Get along with mother/father.	**Three-point Likert:** well; quite well; not very well.
Rochester Youth Delinquency Survey (Thornberry et al, 2003) (longitudinal)	**Attachment to parents** (ten statements): Get along well with, respect, enjoy being with, feel anger, violence, trust, pride towards, lack understanding, too demanding, interfere with child's activities.	**Four-point Likert:** Never; seldom; sometimes; often.
Seattle Social Development Project (Chung et al, 2002; Hawkins et al, 2003) (longitudinal)	**Commitment to school** (two statements): I do extra work on my own in class. When I have an assignment to do, I keep working on it until it is finished.	Yes/No.

personal relationships' is an aggregation of vague risk measures such as 'inconsistent supervision' and 'stable relationship with one parent', while the broad domain of 'Neighbourhood' aggregates responses to similarly broad risk statements focused on, inter alia, 'involvement in reckless activity' and 'antisocial friends'. Each Asset domain aggregates multiple responses into a single risk measure: a five-point Likert scale measuring association between the broad risk domain (not any of the individual risks within it) and a generic, insensitive measure of offending. Both the Asset risk assessment tool and the RFR on which it is based, therefore, rely heavily on crude, overgeneralised measurements of key variables, producing equally crude and overgeneralised answers. Conversely, more sensitive measurement would lead to very different and more precise, reliable and valid answers. The scale of measurement used by youth justice practitioners in their assessments of young people is, therefore, intimately linked to the accuracy and veracity of the conclusions reached. As Mandelbrot (1982, p 1) states: 'On a map an island may appear smooth, but zooming in will reveal jagged edges that add up to a longer coastline'.

Asset does not offer practitioners sufficient scope for 'zooming in' to reveal the fractal qualities and 'jagged edges' of risk, and instead privileges superficial understandings of risk as a 'smooth', generic island of psychosocial, quantifiable factors. For example, the Asset risk assessment tool contains a series of statements related to the young person's self- and practitioner-perceived exposure to risk, with each risk factor rated in a simplistic, dichotomous (yes/no) fashion and each risk domain receiving a single (0–4) rating based on responses to risk factor statements in that domain. Thus, the practitioner rates the influence of simplistic measures of risk factors conflated into a composite, aggregated risk domain score, as opposed to considering the individual influence of specific risk factors. Individually, these risk statements are often crude, insensitive and vague in their wording (and temporal nature – discussed in detail in the 'Sensitive dependence to initial conditions' section). For example, the 'Family' domain asks a series of questions about parents/ carers in an aggregated, generalised manner under the categories of 'family members', 'carers' and 'significant adults', rather than allowing the young person and practitioner to consider the influence of each parent/carer individually. The generalised, imprecise wording and conceptualisation of risk leaves Asset vulnerable to accusations of invalidity and unreliability, as risk statements may be incapable of the accurate and holistic measurement/assessment of the issues, influences, nuances and complexities associated with a particular risk factor or risk domain. This invalidity is even more likely when it is considered that relatively little attention has been paid to the qualitative narratives of practitioners at the conclusion of each risk domain. Practitioners are compelled by the ratings scale to make definitive judgements regarding the influence of risk factors on the basis of poorly measured 'evidence' (often grounded solely in practitioner perception) of actual exposure to that specific risk factor in the young person's life and inadequate information on how the young person constructs, experiences and negotiates that risk factor (eg they may not perceive it as a risk).

An overarching criticism of risk-based youth justice, therefore, has been that of *reductionism*. The conclusions of positivist RFR and the risk assessment in the YJS that it informs have been founded on the certainty of stable, linear, proportional, reliable and definitive relationships between criminological variables (eg risk factors) and offending behaviour by young people. In order to demonstrate these relationships, both the risk assessment process and its underpinning evidence base of positivist RFR have relied on the factorisation of complex and rich experiences, circumstances, interactions, perspectives and behaviour for the purposes of manageability and producing actionable, user-friendly conclusions. Such sweeping reductionism is particularly problematic when the crudity of the measurement tools (eg risk factor questionnaires, risk assessment tools, rating scales) is taken into account (see France and Homel, 2007; Case and Haines, 2009; O'Mahony, 2009). Reductionism has constituted a blunt tool used by statistically minded risk factor researchers to carve out oversimplified, superficial, specious, 'soundbite' understandings of complex, dynamic social (criminological) phenomena.[11] The risk factors measured in risk assessment are, therefore, partial and restricted. This critique is much-rehearsed, yet when viewed afresh through a fractal lens, it becomes even more evident that the sophistication and penetration of positivist RFR (and consequently Asset) into the full complexity of young people's lives has been overly crude and superficial.

The reductionist measurement of risk factors in RFR has reflected and perpetuated an overriding *lack of complexity* in thinking about and trying to understand the lives of young people. In particular, the potential dynamism of risk factors has been neglected (see, eg, Armstrong, 2004; Hine, 2005; France and Homel, 2007; Kemshall, 2008). Risk factors have been measured in a static manner, as one would measure variables in the physical world. But human behaviour is not static and, instead, has a dynamic quality. For example, measurements taken at one (unknown) point in time will be different from measurements taken at different points in time – leading to different conclusions. This *temporal imprecision*, if nothing else, should caution us to the dangers of overdeterminism. In reality, rather than artefact, 'risk' is likely to function as a multifaceted, constructed and negotiated aspect of young people's lives – experienced in a multitude of overlapping dynamic, micro-, meso- and macro-level domains. If the full range of potential forms of (risk factor) influences on a young person's life is not measured and explored by the assessment process, then the result is a partial and misleading 'understanding' of offending behaviour and potentially invalid and ineffective responses (eg inaccurately targeted interventions, social policies, laws, universal programmes, youth justice processes). It is crucial, therefore, that we examine the consequences of (the lack of attention paid to) the dynamic nature of social life.

The complexity critique: sensitive dependence on initial conditions

> Clouds are not spheres, mountains are not cones, coastlines are not circles and bark is not smooth, nor does lightening travel in a straight line. (Mandelbrot, 1982, p 1)

> The inherent nonlinearity of many social phenomena ... must explain, in part, the challenges social scientists face when attempting to understand the complexity of social dynamics ... a simple deterministic equation can generate seemingly random or chaotic behaviour over time. (Elliott and Kiel, 2000, p 4)

While conducting meteorological research in the 1950s, Edward Lorenz discovered that minute variations in the initial values of variables in his model produced significantly different weather patterns/outcomes/ predictions (Lorenz, 1963). Contrary to one of the fundamental assumptions of modern statistical analysis, that small measurement errors are irrelevant (cf the early findings of Poincaré, 1900), Lorenz found that minute differences in the measurement of initial conditions (independent variables) caused points of instability throughout complex systems that could result in unpredictable and fundamentally non-linear 'unpredicted' outcomes – giving rise to notions of complexity and chaos. Lorenz also discovered that the introduction (into a time sequence) of intervening variables could exacerbate the unpredictability (non-linearity), complexity and chaos of a system's outcomes. In short, when using tests of statistical significance, very slight variations in (the initial measurement of) variables produced very large *differences* in the predicted outcomes, and the introduction of intervening variables at different points produced very large *variation* in the predicted outcomes. For Lorenz, therefore, the physical world is constituted by three-dimensional, dynamical systems that can evolve in complex, non-linear ways, which are subject to abrupt, random and unpredictable influences and changes; dynamics that cannot be analysed with validity using established linear statistical tests (Lorenz, 1963). Lorenz concluded that the accurate analysis of any behaviour required 'sensitive dependence on initial conditions'; a phenomenon he dubbed 'The Butterfly Effect'.[12] The possibility of 'chaos' or instability in complex systems indicates that small changes in (the measurement of) initial variables can lead to large differences in outcomes or conclusions. Accordingly, given the dynamic nature of social life, the relationship between risk factors and offending behaviour by young people is likely to be non-linear and not strictly proportional. Consequently, analysing the risk factor–offending relationship in a manner that is sensitive to Complex Systems Science could enable an exploration of criminal behaviour 'in ways not possible in ... [positivist methods] ... and the linear causality they presume' (Young, 1991, p 447).

Our central argument here, therefore, is that the so-called Butterfly Effect has significant implications for the analysis of the risk factor–offending relationship and the linear, deterministic conclusions that flow from positivist RFR. The arguments that we advance in this section are that:

- poorly measured (risk) variables plugged into statistical tests of significance produce facile answers and conclusions regarding the risk factor–offending relationship; and
- temporal sensitivity to the measurement of variables is essential, because of the potential for variability in the outcomes of analysis.

Positivist RFR has analysed the statistical relationship between vague and ill-defined measures of both risk factors and offending, yet promoted supposedly reliable and homogeneous conclusions as to the deterministic and developmental nature of the risk factor–offending relationship (ie that risk factors cause and/or predict offending by young people). The inherently crude, imprecise and overgeneralised measurement/assessment of risk factors, when plugged into tests of statistical significance, readily permit and produce a plurality of facile, easily replicable findings/conclusions, reflecting Mandelbrot's (2004) humorous perception that 'your hammer will always find nails to hit'. However, the findings/conclusions from RFR lack rigour, robustness and reliability. Positivist RFR has imputed the causality and predictive validity of risk factors erroneously from statistical correlations between offending and ill-defined, crude and poorly understood measures of risk.

The principle of sensitive dependence on initial conditions has profound implications for the statistical analyses of quantitative data and presumptions about the (predictable) linearity and proportionality of relationships between risk factors and offending behaviour by young people. Human social relations are rarely, if ever, mechanistic in nature and are more accurately described as open dynamical complex systems. We argue that the notion that human behaviour is amenable to mechanical (experimental) modelling and that cause and effect in human behaviour can be understood in linear, consistent and predictable analyses necessitates a level of abstraction and generalisation as to render any conclusions so distant from the original social reality as to make them worthless artefacts. This criticism is compounded by Lorenz's findings that systems are dynamic, unstable and chaotic, and are influenced significantly by minute changes in initial conditions, which render the outcomes of statistical analysis to be fundamentally unpredictable, non-linear and disproportionate. Nevertheless, the linearity, stability and proportionality of relationships between variables is an assumption at the core of frequentist analysis (Ziliak and McCloskey, 2007; McGrayne, 2011) and at the heart of understandings of the risk factor–offending relationship.

Temporal sensitivity is essential for the accurate, valid analysis of the risk factor–offending relationship. In youth justice, the errors introduced by imprecise measurement and a lack of sensitive dependence on initial conditions are multiplied and compounded because these 'conditions' (eg personal, social and structural characteristics) can vary dramatically in temporal terms. Asset demonstrates very little measurement sensitivity to *temporality* – when exposure to the risk occurred within the measurement period, whether first exposure was experienced prior to the measurement period, when exposure occurred in relation to exposure to other risk factors. The risk assessment measurement period is insensitive to the precise time of initial exposure (or most recent exposure) to a given risk factor, the precise time of offending behaviour and the relative temporal relationship between the two. Therefore, practitioners have little way of linking this exposure to offending in a temporal manner (For example, does the risk pre-date the offending behaviour?), raising doubts as to whether exposure to a given risk factor is, in fact, an initial condition at all (eg the start point in a causal or predictive chain of events leading to offending) and, indeed, whether a variable actually constitutes a 'risk factor' in any predictive sense (eg the notion of 'risk' implies that the variable pre-dates and increases the probability of a future outcome). Furthermore, the conditions that pertain this year are often different to those that pertained last year or will pertain next year; the conditions of this month may not equate to those of last or next month; so it goes in relation to weeks, days and even hours and minutes. That there are, in fact, multiple initial conditions is irrefutable, what is uncertain is the necessary degree of sensitivity to the measurement of subsequent initial conditions over time. For example, is annual, monthly or weekly measurement sufficient to permit robust and generalisable conclusions?

In methodological terms, lack of temporal sensitivity precipitates developmental and deterministic imputations that risk factors predict offending behaviour by young people (and particularly that early life experiences 'determine' adolescent behaviour – following a developmental thesis). However, these conclusions are insensitive to the potential for intervening (unmeasured) variables to influence behavioural outcomes over the temporal period of risk measurement. The conclusion that a risk factor measured at point A exerts a deterministic influence on offending behaviour measured at point B overlooks the possible influence of a multitude of additional variables (eg other risk factors, complex processes of change) to which a young person could have been exposed before, during and after point A and simultaneous to point B. The influence of any of these unmeasured factors could mean that the assessed relationship between a risk factor and offending is nothing more than statistical artefact, rather than the identification of a deterministic risk factor that serves as a valid initial condition from which to trace pathways into offending. While Lorenz's arguments apply to the analysis of relationships between variables separated by a single time period, they are even more powerful when additional, intervening variables (eg unmeasured risk factors) are added in a time sequence – particularly when these time periods can extend to many years. The notion of sensitive dependence on initial conditions alerts us to the significance that additional variables can set off a chain of events that magnify the chaos in complex systems, leading to radically different outcomes.

The chaotic and unstable nature of complex systems, identified by Lorenz, has significant implications for the statistical analysis of behaviour and casts doubt over the ecological validity of results that emerge from inherently linear statistical tests. Lorenz's findings stand in stark contrast to the traditional scientific tenets of approximation and convergence that are employed for mitigating initial small influences and differences in initial conditions within the underpinning statistical models used to establish the risk factor–offending relationship.

Whereas contemporaries such as Smale (1961) had claimed that all dynamical systems tend to settle into stable behaviour and predictable, linear outcomes, Lorenz established that minute variations in initial conditions cause points of instability throughout systems and can result in unpredictable and fundamentally non-linear 'unpredicted' outcomes. In particular, the notion of chaos in systems provides conceptual space to consider 'non-linear equations', whose component parts cannot be broken down into smaller pieces and then re-formed to produce predictable solutions, in contrast to linear equations. An illustration of this point is derived from John Conway's 'Game of Life'.

The Game of Life is a 2D computer simulation in which the player decides a basic linear algorithm that determines the rules that govern how black or white squares on a grid propagate (Conway, in Gardner, 1970; see also the discussion of Cellular Automata in Chapter One). Because these algorithms are linear, the outcome of any game should be predictable and constant for any replication. In practice, however, the outcomes of any game are neither predictable nor constant. If the same game is run twice, different outcomes result. If run 100 or 1,000 times, different outcomes occur each time. Chaos rules and the fundamental principles of linearity, predictability and certainty are shown to be fallacious.

The significance of the notion of non-linear outcomes from linear tests (as illustrated by Conway's Game of Life) for the linear testing of statistical relationships is profound. What it means is that generalisation (from a sample to a wider population) and prediction is basically invalid. This strikes at the heart, the very justification and purpose, of (linear) statistical analysis. The fundamental claim of statistical analysis – that by taking a random sample and applying linear statistical tests to the data, one can generalise from the specific to the wider population or that one can predict future outcomes – is shown to be false, because the outcome of linear statistical tests is inherently non-linear (ie different every time). What this means in practical terms is that the statistical results of the panoply of positivist RFR, which have been used (generalised) to explain the causes of offending behaviour by young people, to predict who will become delinquent and to predict future behaviour, are basically nothing more than statistical artefacts, that is, they are devoid of meaning and value in the real world.

The complexity critique: unfractal measurement and insensitive analysis

Taken together, the concepts of fractal measurement and analysis informed by sensitive dependence on initial conditions pose major problems for extant youth justice practices. Simply put, plugging crudely measured risk factors into ill-conceived statistical models begets insensitive analysis. The outcome is pervasive invalidity and unreliability. Positivist RFR has paid very limited attention to initial conditions, for example, the timing, foci and sensitivity of the measurements of these conditions and how constant recursive interactions following initial measurement may have more impact on outcomes than a predetermined linear pathway. Positivist risk factor researchers (especially developmentalists) have seldom acknowledged the inherent uncertainties in initial conditions – both in terms of when these initial conditions are measured (in time) and how they are measured (in terms of sensitivity) – nor have they acknowledged that iterative interactions between measured (and unmeasured) variables produce the unpredictable.

Notwithstanding these uncertainties and oversights, positivist RFR has produced a large and durable evidence base of ostensibly replicable risk factors, which have been used to populate the Asset risk assessment tool and the Scaled Approach to assessment and intervention in the YJS. As a consequence, the Scaled Approach imputes and prescribes understandings of risk factors (heralded as replicable/reliable) as exerting a temporally specific, deterministic, predictive, linear influence on offending behaviour by young people as the bedrock to informing suitable (largely risk-focused) interventions. However, these allegedly replicable risk factors have been seldom conceptualised or measured in an equivalent manner across RFR studies (see, eg, Table 6.1 and its associated discussion) or with equivalent risk instruments, thus offering the illusion of replicability through repeated links between offending and generic risk measures (see Case and Haines, 2009). Even within the same measurement tool, *inter-rater reliability* can be a highly problematic issue, due to the generic and vague nature of the wording of risk statements, the ratings scales employed and the measurement periods covered. For example, youth justice practitioners do not necessarily conceive or operationalise risk factors in an equivalent, reliable manner. The ordinal ratings scales prescribe that practitioners rate their perceptions of the association between risk factors (measured in a generic, dichotomous manner) and previous and/or future offending (the precise nature of the offending 'dependent variable' is unclear – see earlier) on a five-point scale. However, the points on the scale could mean different things to different practitioners (or to the same practitioner at a different time) as there are no logical, consistent or 'scalable' intervals between these points (ie as the data is ordinal rather than interval). The differences between each measurement point on a scale are not fixed/interval level, but subjective, fluctuating and arbitrary – a '1' measure on a ratings scale does not necessarily mean the same thing to different people, any more than the distance between ratings of '1' and '2' on a scale is necessarily equivalent to the distance between ratings of '4' and '5' for the same and different people.[13] Thus, it is likely that there will be between-practitioner differences in how the ratings scale is operationalised for different young people (or for the same young person if multiple practitioners complete Asset with them at different times).

The potential for between- and within-practitioner differences places serious doubts over the reliability of the processes and outcomes of positivist RFR generally and youth justice risk assessment specifically; doubts that were reflected by the process evaluations of Asset (Baker et al, 2002; Baker, 2005) and the Scaled Approach (YJB, 2009). The process evaluations all highlighted several areas of potential unreliability regarding how Asset and the Scaled Approach were understood and completed, which differed between practitioners and within and between local areas (Baker et al, 2002; Baker, 2005). This revelation magnifies the criticism that risk assessment and intervention in the YJS is hampered by unreliability/inconsistency in the initial measurement of risk, which then feeds into unreliable analyses and invalid conclusions; an ironic outcome for a tool viewed by some as 'necessary for ensuring consistency of assessment practice' (Baker, 2005, p 107).

The complexity critique: where next?

When examined through the lens of complexity, modern youth justice policy and practice falls alarmingly short. Overly simplistic, often crude, quantified measures of risk are used uncritically to populate insensitive analyses of the risk factor–offending relationship, and these unsatisfactory measurement and analyses processes conspire to produce the self-fulfilling, invalid and unreliable conclusions that 'inform' youth justice. The complexities, nuances and qualitative meaningfulness of young people's lives are neglected by existing youth justice policies and practices, which are detached from the everyday realities that they seek to understand and address. But all is not lost. In March 2011, in direct response to growing criticisms of reductionist and invalid youth justice practices (notably, risk assessment), the YJB published a proposal to replace the Scaled Approach with a more complex and contextualised assessment model to be known as 'AssetPlus' (YJB, 2011). The YJB has received ministerial approval to implement the new framework in April 2014, constituting an explicit and deliberate move for youth justice assessment and intervention towards a more holistic strengths- and needs-based approach and away from a model grounded in the assessment of risk factors (YJB, 2011). The new model (outlined in Figure 6.1) proposes a broader assessment process, 'reflecting the complexity of the young person's personal circumstances/behaviour representing a shift away from a one size fits all approach to assessment' (YJB, 2011, p 9).

Figure 6.1: The assessment and planning interventions framework

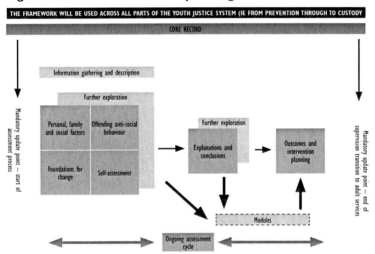

The revised Scaled Approach (AssetPlus) eschews the static, linear, generic determinism of positivist RFR and the psychosocial risk factors in risk assessment tools in favour of more iterative, dynamic and flexible assessments that consider the complex context of the young person's life alongside local contexts, priorities and challenges. The holistic assessment process incorporates more emphasis on young people's voices and their qualitative, dynamic constructions of their life experiences, rather than prioritising adult understanding/prescriptions of quantitative, static, risk-focused 'factors'. The model is intended to be responsive to changes in young people's lives by employing a greater, more sensitive, range of assessments/measurements (eg interactions between different factors), rather than relying on a static, linear and deterministic risk factor paradigm. The YJB proposal makes it very clear that future assessments will employ 'a variety of ratings and measures, not just one score' (YJB, 2011, p 9). As a consequence, the proposed revisions will afford a variety of more 'fractal', sensitive measures and analyses of different aspects of the lives of young people in conflict with the law and the YJS – simultaneously offering a holistic 'bigger picture' of their lives alongside a nuanced, idiographic investigation of the contexts, circumstances, live events and individual and social influences on the behaviours of and outcomes for these young people.

Crucially, the revised assessment process is intended to facilitate greater practitioner discretion in assessment and intervention planning, rather than compelling an uncritical adherence to prescriptions for standardised (risk) assessment. This will allow youth justice practitioners more scope to utilise their expertise, experience and unique relationship with the young person and thus to provide more fractal–aware assessments and recommendations for appropriate interventions. Consequently, these recommendations can be grounded in a sensitive and reflective consideration of the recursive interactions between known and unknown variables (which need not be numerical) and the full range of initial conditions that can influence behavioural and life outcomes for young people. By placing the child at the centre of the new assessment and intervention framework, practitioners will be given a clear focus and touchstone for their interventions. Although the precise nature of interventions may vary, their focus will remain consistent and principled. Therefore, the proposed new AssetPlus framework represents a 180-degree change in orientation from the Scaled Approach, with the focus of assessment/intervention moving from a crude, simplistic, backward-looking and one-dimensional assessment of risk and its developmental and deterministic influence on offending, towards a forward-looking, holistic focus on the young person, their initial and current circumstances/contexts, and how these may influence their futures.'

Conclusion: complex and contextualised youth justice

The crude and imprecise *measurement* of risk in youth justice processes has fed into insensitive *analyses* and produced invalid conclusions that risk factors exert a linear, proportionate and deterministic influence on offending behaviour by young people. The tools of measurement and analyses in research, therefore, are intimately linked to the validity of the research outcomes and conclusions. Following Complex Systems

Science, using an imprecise and insensitive measurement tool and plugging measurements uncritically into statistical analyses results in alchemy: crude, invalid and artefactual results and conclusions that are distanced from individual and social realities. Conversely, utilising different (fractal) measures and attending to minute differences in initial conditions can have significant effects on answers and outcomes. The distinctive contribution of Complex Systems Science to youth justice, therefore, relates to the importance of both *measurement* and *analysis*. Too much measurement sensitivity is lost in the process of turning a yardstick into a milepost. The very use of a yardstick to take initial measurements of variables (rather than using a fractal-sensitive tool) undermines the validity of risk assessment. As we have demonstrated, crude, insensitive and superficial measurement begets equivalently crude analyses and produces invalid conclusions regarding the relationship between risk and offending and how it should be addressed through intervention. When these crudely measured variables, located within a limited range of life domains, are plugged uncritically into similarly crude linear, developmental and deterministic models of statistical analysis, the result is insensitive and invalid conclusions.

Cast in this light, risk assessment in the YJS is potentially flawed in its thinking, method and analysis. This is grossly insufficient in the modern age. We need a revised approach to youth justice assessment set within a new criminology fit for the 21st century. The proposed revisions to the Scaled Approach offer a promising starting point. Complex Systems Science helps us to understand that the quality of measurement is absolutely fundamental to the accuracy of outcomes. The mathematics of linearity were invented for non-human-related research and are not suited to either modelling or predicting human behaviour (eg offending behaviour by young people) because of the impossibility of identifying one temporally fixed initial condition and the reality that the forces acting on human behaviour are not constant – or perhaps, more accurately, that they are constantly changing. These constantly changing forces and their impacts are anything but linear, predictable and proportional. Complex Systems Science offers an incisive weapon with which to dissect the entrenched, narrow, flawed linear positivist paradigm of knowledge production that dominates contemporary criminology.

Notes

[1] This is not the place to develop detailed arguments as to how such analyses may look, nor is this the focus of the chapter. However, we would advocate as promising approaches such techniques as Bayesian analysis (eg Thompson

et al, 2010; Cai et al, forthcoming; see also Jennings, Chapter Two, and Wolf-Branigin, Chapter Four) and data visualisation (eg Viegas and Wattenberg, 2011; Willison, 2008).

[2] Critics will hold that we overstate the hegemony of positivism within criminology. We do not seek to deny or denigrate the breadth of criminology or its value, but our primary response is to place positivist approaches within their social context and to situate their dominance within contemporary systems of thought, particularly in the youth justice arena. We argue that strict adherence to positivist systems of thought (within which we subsume experimentalism and much quantitative criminology) has rendered youth justice practitioners in England and Wales over-reliant on the quantification (factorisation) of variables in their assessments; variables derived from positivist RFR, which has applied statistical tests of significance to these variables as the route to knowledge production.

[3] The arguments for positivist and experimental criminology have been well-rehearsed and set out by others (see Sherman et al, 1997; Farrington and Welsh, 2005; Sherman and Strang, 2007; Sherman, 2009; Weisburd et al, 2011). We do not propose to rehearse these arguments here.

[4] Linear statistical analyses primarily refer to non-hierarchical significance-testing and the p values that dominate positivist criminology, as well as other disciplines (Salsburg, 2002; Gendreau and Smith, 2007; McGrayne, 2011).

[5] When experimental researchers have taken drastic steps to control and restrict human behaviour in the most artificial of research conditions, the (laboratory and field) experiment, in order to maximise internal validity, they are rightly accused of producing results and conclusions that manipulate behaviour and lack external/ecological validity, forcing results that are unrepresentative of everyday behaviour (see Hope, 2009; Hough, 2010). Similar accusations are merited by the post hoc manipulation of statistical data, which has distorted and distanced data from the original 'reality' that the research was attempting to access and represent (see Case and Haines, 2009).

[6] Or even by those who may be sympathetic to quantitative analysis but who argue that the over-reliance on probabilistic statistical tests of significance is misplaced (Salsburg, 2002; Gendreau and Smith, 2007; Ziliac and McCloskey, 2007).

[7] YOTs are multi-agency teams in each local authority area in England and Wales, consisting of representatives from the four statutory agencies of police, local authority, probation and health, along with other voluntary and charitable services (Souhami, 2007). YOTs were established by the Crime and Disorder Act 1998 and came into being in April 2000. Their practice is

monitored and prescribed by a government quango, the Youth Justice Board for England and Wales.

[8] Living arrangements, family and personal relationships, education/training/ employment, neighbourhood, lifestyle, substance use, physical health, emotional/mental health, perception of self and others, thinking and behaviour, attitudes to offending, motivation to change.

[9] Here, we already see an inherent contradiction and ambiguity within Asset relating to the nature of risk factors. It is unclear whether they are understood as retrospective influences on previous offending or prospective predictors of future offending to target through intervention (which is more in keeping with the conclusions of positivist RFR). Indeed, they are employed within the tool uncritically and inconsistently to suit both purposes.

[10] Positivist and experimental criminologists conducting RFR rarely actually publish complete details of their rating scales and measurements (itself a surprising phenomenon for self-proclaimed scientists). However, in-depth analysis of the available methodological detail within the international body of positivist RFR (see later) has shown these rating scales and measurements to be extremely crude and blunt (see Case and Haines, 2009).

[11] Paradoxically, and perversely, these attributes of the positivist approach are seen by advocates (and often users) as highly valued qualities that reinforce the validity and utility of the method in generating useable knowledge.

[12] Taken from the title of his 1972 paper to the American Association for the Advancement of Science, entitled 'Predictability: does the flap of a butterfly's wings in Brazil set off a tornado in Texas?' (Lorenz, 1972).

[13] There is, in fact, a statistical technique designed to mitigate the negative consequences of poorly measured variables – the errors in variables model (see Chesher, 1991). Whether one believes in the validity of this approach is, for present purposes, moot. What is, in some ways, surprising is that positivist RFR has been progressed without reference to this advanced statistical technique – reflecting, perhaps, weaknesses in the knowledge of 'scientific' criminologists or an unflinching faith in the veracity of their research design and empirical abilities.

References

Armstrong, D. (2004) 'A risky business? Research, policy, governmentality and youth offending', *Youth Justice*, vol 4, no 2, pp 100–16.

Armstrong, D., Hine, J., Hacking, S., Remos, S., Jones, R., Klessinger, N, and France, A. (2005) *Children, risk and crime : the On Track Youth Lifestyles Survey*. London : The Home Office

Audit Commission (1996) *Misspent youth: young people and crime*, London: Audit Commission.

Baker, K. (2005) 'Assessment in youth justice: professional discretion and the use of asset', *Youth Justice*, vol 5, no 2, pp 106–22.

Baker, K., Jones, S., Roberts, C. and Merrington, S. (2002) *Validity and reliability of asset*, London: YJB.

Bateman, T. (2011) 'Punishing poverty: the scaled approach and youth justice practice', *The Howard Journal of Criminal Justice*, vol 50, no 2, pp 171–83.

Beinert, S., Anderson, B., Lee, S. and Utting, D. (2002) *Youth at risk? A national survey of risk factors, protective factors and problem behaviour among young people in England, Scotland and Wales*, London: Communities that Care.

Byrne, D. (1998) *Complexity theory and the social sciences*, London: Routledge.

Cai, Y., Stander, J. and Davies, N. (forthcoming) 'A new Bayesian approach to quantile autoregressive time series model estimation and forecasting', *Journal of Time Series Analysis*.

Case, S.P. (2007) 'Questioning the "evidence" of risk that underpins evidence-led youth justice interventions', *Youth Justice*, vol 7, no 2, pp 91–106.

Case, S.P. and Haines, K.R. (2009) *Understanding youth offending: risk factor research, policy and practice*, Cullompton: Willan.

Chesher, A. (1991) 'The effect of measurement error', *Biometrika*, vol 78, no 3, pp 451–62.

Chung, I.-J., Hill, K.G., Hawkins, J.D., Gilchrist, L.D. and Nagin, D. (2002) 'Childhood predictors of offence trajectories', *Journal of Research in Crime & Delinquency*, vol 39, no 1, pp 60–90.

Elliott, E. and Kiel, D. (2000) *Nonlinear dynamics, complexity and public policy*, Commack, NY: Nova Science Publishers.

Farrington, D. (2000) 'Developmental criminology and risk-focussed prevention', in M. Maguire, R. Morgan and R. Reiner (eds) *The Oxford handbook of criminology* (3rd edn), Oxford: Oxford University Press.

Farrington, D. (2003) 'Methodological quality standards for evaluation research', *Annals of the American Academy*, vol 585, pp 49–68.

Farrington, D.P. and Welsh, B.C. (2005) 'Randomized experiments in criminology: what have we learned in the last two decades?', *Journal of Experimental Criminology*, vol 1, pp 9–38.

Feller, W. (1957) *An introduction to probability theory and its applications, vol. 1*, London: Wiley.

France, A. (2008) 'Risk factor analysis and the youth question', *Journal of Youth Studies*, vol 11, no 1, pp 1–15.

France, A. and Homel, R. (2007) *Pathways and crime prevention. Theory, policy and practice*, Cullompton: Willan.

Freedman, D. (2010) *Statistical models and causal inference: a dialogue with the social sciences* (eds D. Collier, J. Sekhon and P. Stark), Cambridge: Cambridge University Press.

Gardner, M. (1970) 'Mathematical games – the fantastic combinations of John Conway's new solitaire game "life"', *Scientific American*, vol 223, pp 120–3.

Gendreau, P. and Smith, P. (2007) 'Influencing the "people who count": some perspectives on the reporting of meta-analytic results for prediction and treatment outcomes with offenders', *Criminal Justice and Behavior*, vol 34, no 12, pp 1536–59.

Gleick, J. (1997) *Chaos: making a new science*, London: Vintage.

Goldson, B. and Hughes, G. (2010) 'Sociological criminology and youth justice: comparative policy analysis and academic intervention', *Criminology and Criminal Justice*, vol 10, no 2, pp 211–30.

Hawkins, J.D., Smith, B.H., Hill, K.G., Kosterman, R., Catalano, R.F. and Abbott, R.D. (2003) 'Understanding and preventing crime and violence. Findings from the Seattle Social Development Project', in T.P. Thornberry and M.D. Krohn (eds) *Taking stock of delinquency: an overview of findings from contemporary longitudinal studies*, New York, NY: Kluwer.

Hine, J. (2005) 'Early intervention: the view from On Track', *Children and Society*, vol 19, no 2, pp 117–30.

Hope, T. (2009) 'The illusion of control: a response to Professor Sherman', *Criminology and Criminal Justice*, vol 9, no 2, pp 125–34.

Hough, M. (2010) 'Gold standard or fool's gold? The pursuit of certainty in experimental criminology', *Criminology and Criminal Justice*, vol 10, no 1, pp 11–22.

Junger-Tas, J., Marshall, I.H. and Ribeaud, D. (2003) *Delinquency in an international perspective: the international self-reported delinquency study*, The Hague: Kugler.

Kemshall, H. (2008) 'Risk, rights and justice: understanding and responding to youth risk', *Youth Justice*, vol 8, no 1, pp 21–38.

Lorenz, E.N. (1963) 'Deterministic nonperiodic flow', *Journal of the Atmospheric Sciences*, vol 20, pp 130–41.

Lorenz, E.N. (1972) 'Predictability: Does the flap of a butterfly's wings in Brazil set off a tornado in Texas?'. Paper presented to the American Association for the Advancement of Science, Sheraton Park Hotel, Anaheim, USA.

Mandelbrot, B. (1967) 'How long is the coast of Britain? Statistical self-similarity and fractional dimension', *Science, New Series*, vol 156, no 3775, pp 636–8.

Mandelbrot, B. (1982) *The fractal geometry of nature*, London: WH Freeman and Co.

Mandelbrot, B. (2004) 'A theory of roughness'. Available at: http://www.edge.org (accessed January 2012).

McGrayne, S. (2011) *The theory that would not die*, New Haven, CT: Yale University Press.

O'Mahony, P. (2009) 'The risk factors prevention paradigm and the causes of youth crime: a deceptively useful analysis?', *Youth Justice*, vol 9, no 2, pp 99–114.

Paylor, I. (2010) 'The scaled approach to youth justice: a risky business', *Criminal Justice Matters*, vol 81, no 1, pp 30–1.

Poincaré, H. (1900) 'Les relations entre la physique expérimentale et la physique mathématique', *Revue générale des sciences pures et appliqués*, vol 11, pp 1163–75.

Robson, C. (2011) *Real world research*, Oxford: Blackwell.

Salsberg, D. (2002) *The lady tasting tea: how statistics revolutionized science in the twentieth century*, New York, NY: Holt.

Sherman, L. (2009) 'Evidence and liberty: the promise of experimental criminology', *Criminology & Criminal Justice*, vol 9, no 1, pp 5–28.

Sherman, L. and Strang, H. (2007) *Restorative justice: the evidence*, London: The Smith Institute.

Sherman, L., Gottfredson, D., MacKenzie, D., Eck, J., Reuter, P. and Bushway, S. (1997) *Preventing crime: what works, what doesn't, what's promising*, Baltimore, MD: Department of Criminology and Criminal Justice, University of Maryland. Available in full at: http://www.ncjrs.gov/works/ or in summary at: http://www.ncjrs.gov/pdffiles/171676.pdf

Smale, S. (1961) 'Generalized Poincaré's conjecture in dimensions greater than four', *Annals of Mathematics, 2nd Series*, vol 74, no 2, pp 391–406.

Stephenson, M., Giller, H. and Brown, S. (2011) *Effective practice in youth justice*, Cullompton: Willan.

Thompson, P., Cai, Y., Moyeed, R., Reeve, D. and Stander, J. (2010) 'Bayesian non-parametric quantile regression using splines', *Computational Statistics and Data Analysis*, vol 54, pp 1138–50.

Thornberry, T.P., Lizotte, A.J., Krohn, M.D., Smith, C.A. and Porter, P.K. (2003) 'Causes and consequences of delinquency. Findings from the Rochester Youth Development Study', in T.P. Thornberry and M.D. Krohn (eds) *Taking stock of delinquency: an overview of findings from contemporary longitudinal studies*, New York, NY: Kluwer.

Viegas, F. and Wattenberg, M. (2011) 'How to make data look sexy', *CNN.com*, 19 April.

Walgrave, L. (2008) 'Criminology, as I see it ideally', *Criminology in Europe*, Newsletter of the European Society of Criminology, November, pp 3, 15–17. Paper presented following the receipt of the European Criminology Award.

Weisburd, D., Mazerolle, L. and Petrosino, A. (2011) 'The academy of experimental criminology: advancing randomized trials in crime and justice'. Available at: http://www.asc41.com/Criminologist/2007/2007_May-June_Criminologist.pdf (accessed 19 May 2011).

Williams, M. (2006) 'Empiricism', in V. Jupp (ed) *The Sage Dictionary of social research methods*, London: Sage.

Willison, B. (2008) *Visualization driven rapid prototyping*, New York, NY: Parsons Institute for Information Mapping.

Wright-Mills, C. (1959) *The sociological imagination*, Oxford: Oxford University Press.

YJB (Youth Justice Board) (2000) *ASSET: explanatory notes*, London: YJB.

YJB (2004) *National standards for youth justice services*, London: YJB.

YJB (2009) *Youth justice: the scaled approach. A framework for assessment and interventions. Post-consultation version two*, London: YJB.

YJB (2011) *Assessment and planning interventions: review and redesign project. Statement of intent – proposed framework*, London: YJB.

Young, K. (2011) *The criminological imagination*, London: Polity.

Young, T.R. (1991) 'Chaos and social change: metaphysics of the postmodern', *The Social Science Journal*, vol 28, no 3, pp 289–305.

Ziliak, S. and McCloskey, D. (2007) *The cult of statistical significance: how the standard error cost us jobs, justice, and lives*, Ann Arbor, MI: The University of Michigan Press.

SEVEN

The Stephen Lawrence Inquiry: a case study in policing and complexity

John G.D. Grieve

Policing is really quite simple. (Chief Constable X to the author, 2004)

The National Crime Agency will deal with serious, organised and/or complex cases. (Press release and draft legislation for National Crime Agency, 2013)

Any fool can complicate the issues, John. (Mary Midgely, philosopher, to the author, circa 1980)

Introduction

This chapter explores two questions 'Is policing a simple or complex task?' and 'Can complexity theory help us answer that first question?' It will use the Stephen Lawrence Public Inquiry (SLI), its transcripts, findings, conclusions, recommendations and practical policing and other outcomes (if any), as a case study. It is essentially a positivist (things can get better) but realist account, with some analytic philosophy elements (recent explorations of the word 'adaptation'). It concludes that the complexity thinking about learning and adaptation of policies and practices could have improved the progress made in the 15 years since the SLI and, in particular, the finding of institutional racism (IR). The chapter is concerned not with challenging that finding or with re-examining the evidence that the SLI considered, nor with the ongoing investigation, but with the learning and adaptation or otherwise that followed the SLI's findings and recommendations. Other findings and related recommendations, besides IR, are examined in respect of leadership, critical incidents, family liaison, stop and search, independent advice, and hate crime investigation, which support the conclusion of the value of complexity thinking. Finally, the chapter suggests that for policing, there are other ways of looking at the fear of change and return to equilibrium besides the dominant narrative of police failure.

Following the findings of the SLI (see later) 15 years ago, the Metropolitan Police Service (MPS) used critical incidents training and management to take an approach based on a psychological theory of cognitive dissonance, which was both reductionist and, to some extent, linear, that is, it essentially sought to break down the component parts of the incident to understand what happened (this was perhaps counter-intuitive because as detectives, we had pieced together the various bits of evidence) (see Hall et al, 2009), an approach that was possibly self-defeating in the long term.

However, another way of exploring the issues in the SLI's findings is from a complexity theory perspective, which argues that the MPS is an example of a complex adaptive system (CAS) comprising a series of sub-complex adaptive systems; it is fractal in nature (see Case and Haines, Chapter Six). The MPS is, then, also nested within the wider systems of 'London': local and central government and all their embedded agencies and tasks; and the criminal justice system, with its internal systems of defence and prosecution, victim support, courts service and many others. So, given its nested nature, how does an organisation of this size and internal complexity, which is open to the demands of its wider environment, tackle the issues identified by the Lawrence case? Moreover, in taking a realist perspective on complexity, how does it avoid the more dysfunctional aspects of chaos while undergoing necessary change and adaptation?

CAS are deterministic in nature (see Pycroft, Chapter One), and the finding of the public inquiry was that it is the consequence of the IR of the MPS that the investigation into the murder of Stephen Lawrence developed in the way that it did. Despite the acceptance of IR officially by the MPS (although IR was not a direct recommendation of the SLI), it is claimed, and backed with some evidence, that little has seemed to be achieved since (Green, 2010; Adams, 2013; Okereke, 2013; Peachey, 2013; Stone, 2013). It is argued here that the Lawrence murder and the subsequent inquiry significantly perturbed the CAS that is the MPS and took it to the edge of chaos. If it had remained there much more would have been achieved. The problem is that some politicians, managers and informal leaders often seek equilibrium through controls and negative feedback, and so the attractor (see Jennings, Chapter Two) in this case became the continuing day-to-day needs of the organisation rather than justice for the victims or their families. Critical incident approaches are intended to provide an opportunity 'to reflect upon the incident, critically assess the incident, and engage with issues involved in the incident's occurrence as well as question beliefs, attitudes and behavior' (Thompson, 2011, p 4), but the linear, reductionist nature of this approach means that, in effect, it actually sought to bring the MPS back from the edge of chaos, albeit with more learning and, hence, adaptation than appears to have been achieved. The problems that arise from this are, first, a phase space trajectory (see Jennings, Chapter Two) leading back to equilibrium, where, second, the organisation then becomes 'locked in' (see later) precisely because of its sensitivity to initial conditions (eg IR).

So, a key question that this chapter considers is whether complexity thinking is a better basis for strategic MPS reforms and adaptation than the critical incident solution of nearly 15 years ago, and whether it will help to solve some key dilemmas. The critical incident approach and the training and innovations that followed from it were based on the principles of cognitive dissonance? This approach was reflected in the catchphrase of the time 'Let's nick some racists' (who were, of course, always other people), so the rationale was that if you were arresting people for racism, you cannot be acting, yourself, in a bigoted prejudiced manner (Hall et al, 2009); that is, when you are behaving in one way, it is very difficult to be thinking in another way. Or, you cannot continue to be institutionally racist once you have been told that that is what you are; or, in other words, you cannot be 'unwitting, ignorant, thoughtless and stereotypical' (as SLI para 6.34 found) when you have been given the knowledge (Hall et al, 2009). But recent arguments on the 20th anniversary of Stephen's racist murder suggests that both these hypotheses were wrong: they (that is, the police) just did not get it, that is, they did not understand IR and, hence, did not understand the solutions (see Caless, 2011, p 90). Inaction or rejection, the continuation of the apparently unwitting, must be wilful, it is now suggested. The police, it is claimed, just have not learnt enough from the pain of the SLI experiences (Morris, 2005; Adams, 2013; Alibai–Brown, 2013; Okereke, 2013; Peachey, 2013). This is not to argue that critical incident thinking is unhelpful, most especially, in preventing such incidents developing and practising decision-making. Can complexity thinking provide a better route to help solve these dilemmas about IR in particular, and possibly more generally?

The Metropolitan Police Service as a complex adaptive system

Complexity thinking, when studying systems that are open to their environment, is interested in the relationships between several CAS and the knowledge flows between them, their co-evolution, contexts and environment, and organisations adapting and learning (Laihonen, 2005; Serena, 2011; Thompson, 2011). Policing is argued here to be a knowledge-intense environment where much of the work is self- or small group organised in support of a broad strategic direction, but where immediate direct supervision at the time of activity is rare.

This chapter specifically focuses on the adaptive nature of CAS, a concept most recently developed by the US army in learning from the Iraq War, but which has a long military and organisational theory history (Murray, 2011; Serena, 2011). Adaptation is about knowledge, and its acquisition, interpretation, elucidation, integration, dissemination and, hence, learning.

Another source of complexity thinking in relation to the MPS is about complex systems and output measurement (see, eg, Mike Ledwidge [2013, p 40] and Jake Chapman's [2003] influential book *System failure* for the Demos think tank, both of which consider complex adaptive public services and the government's overemphasis on specific output measures). The context for CAS involves government – direct intervention and localism – and the Mayor for London, and, elsewhere, Police and Crime Commissioners (PCCs), Criminal Justice System (CJS) legislation, the confrontational nature of the courts as a means of testing evidence and the requirements of disclosure. The police also work with: Prison Services; Probation and Offender Management Services (see Lewis, Chapter Eleven, and also Pycroft, Chapter Ten); Victims Services; and Social Services, where there is an emphasis on vulnerable children for example (see Hassett and Stevens, Chapter Five). There are also a variety of CAS embedded within the MPS and the overall police organisation, for example: response teams, who answer 999 calls; neighbourhood teams, who deal with community issues; canteens (the much-derided 'canteen culture' of which there are many varieties); the Police Federation, which represents police officers up to the rank of Chief Inspector; specialist teams for intelligence, murder, drugs, forensic science and counter-terrorism; management teams at borough and force-wide levels; the Superintendents Association; and the Association of Chief Police Officers (ACPO). In the case study, for example, all these interacted with victims' families, support groups, and Members of Parliament (MPs), which were nested within a wider black and minority ethnic (BME) community, a yet wider concerned community, the media and, eventually, the international community (at one stage, Nelson Mandela became involved; see Hall et al, 2009).

When considering the sheer complexity of policing, Reiner (2012, p 36) helpfully describes the issues as the 'complexity of interactions between macro structures and individual actions, and between structural and cultural processes'. Likewise, Serena (2011), in considering the military, identifies tasks, inputs and outputs, and intensive knowledge collection, transfer and integration, for all the CAS; the same is true for policing. He identifies contexts for each as well as a wider environment; in times of crisis, all these CAS have to learn, adapt and change. Williamson Murray (2011), in his book *Military adaptation in war*, subtitles it *Fear of change*. It is also interesting to note that the task array of the new National Crime Agency (NCA) includes the words 'serious, organised, and *complex* crime' in its emerging blueprint for the way forward (National Crime Agency, 2013, emphasis added). However, there is no definition of complex in the blueprint.

Another view of the CAS in policing might be explored through criminal investigations, for example, murder or counter-terrorism specialist squads, which are themselves CAS. In one investigation and related operations, the author accessed or cooperated with the following disciplines or concepts: administration (public, local, central government, academic), banking, biology, chemistry, civil service, demographics, DNA, education, ethics (professional, individual, legal), finance/accountancy, forensic science, fingerprints, fibres, geography, history, law, local/regional/national government, logistics, logic, medicine, metallurgy, military doctrine, nursing, philosophy, politics, public health, public sector, public duty, social sciences and services, socio-biology, voluntary sector, and, of course, intelligence-led and all other forms and categories of policing. Each of these disciplines has their own CAS, knowledge flows, collection, integration and learning. To what extent are multidisciplinary teams the answer to leaders' dilemmas or the complexities, crises and crucibles for police leadership in the 21st century? One answer might be that they are parts of the nested system that make up policing in its broadest sense. Hence, adaptation itself becomes extremely complicated. Thompson (2011) argues that systems thinking would aid that process.

Complexity thinking might also be aided by Rittel's (1972) formulation of 'wicked problems', that is, those where the solution gives rise to further problems (for a further discussion of this, see Grieve et al, 2007; Alison and Crego, 2008). Therefore any solution, whether based on cognitive dissonance, critical incidents or complexity thinking, was going to be difficult.

The Stephen Lawrence Public Inquiry

The case study is part of a continuing effort to understand the wider governance, political, policy, broader strategic, tactical, operational, ethical and community issues in policing in the late 20th and early 21st centuries. It considers the London MPS response to the final report and conclusion, and the Home Secretary's Action Plan in response to the SLI (1997–99) (Home Office, 1999; Hall et al, 2009, pp 99–143). Stephen was murdered by racists in 1993 and his parents Neville and Doreen Lawrence led a campaign to obtain justice when the police and CJS failed to successfully prosecute his killers. An internal police review of the investigation was flawed and incomplete but was initially relied upon to challenge the perspectives of the campaigners (TSO, 1999, pp 195–207). Two men were finally convicted of Stephen's murder in 2012.

The Labour government that came to power in 1997 created a public inquiry under a High Court Judge, Sir William Macpherson, and three advisers (a bishop, a doctor [Richard Stone; see Stone, 2013] and a retired police officer), which had a wide-ranging interpretation of their terms of reference and sat for 18 months. They were asked to inquire into the lessons to be learned for the investigation and prosecution of racist-motivated crime (TSO, 1999, p 6). They went far beyond that to look at the reality of being of a BME background in England and Wales in the late 20th century. They looked at many agencies and institutions. The major, most-publicised finding was that the police, and the MPS in particular, were guilty of IR, Hearing a vast array of witnesses and sitting at six sites in England, their conclusions and 70 complex interacting recommendations included the finding of IR against the entire MPS organisation and related that to other policing services and other agencies, in addition to findings of incompetence, failed leadership, insensitivity to the needs of victims and families, lack of community confidence, and a failure to investigate adequately. Significantly, there were no direct recommendations in respect of the finding of IR; although it was argued – unhelpfully because it was confusing and increased complexity in this author's view – that all the recommendations did apply to IR.

One of several constant parallel refrains heard across the country at the public inquiry Part Two sessions was about the disproportionate unaccountable use of stop-and-search tactics against BME male youths as examples of widespread IR (TSO, 1999, Recommendations 60–3; Home Office, 1999, p 31). There was universal disgust and outrage across all political parties, and statements from all party leaders and the media were unanimous (at that time) in their demands for widespread change.

The context was further complicated by the emergence of a series of cases and causes of argued probable relevance to the findings of the public inquiry, including the death of a young man in West London (Ricky Reel), other kinds of racist incidents and attacks, two later unexplained deaths (the McGowan cousins in West Mercia) and allegations about police stop and search nationwide. These figured in the wider consideration of, first, the public inquiry, and then the commentators and politicians once the report, largely about the murder, but drawing a wider picture of racism in policing and society, was published.

The author was present for most of Part One of the Public Inquiry and for nearly all of Part Two and much thought and ink, publically and privately, has been expended about the SLI over the last 15 years, which has resulted in very mixed feelings and a lack of clarity, probably because of trying to simultaneously hold two conflicting views, which have produced emergent outcomes that would appear to have returned the system of the MPS from the edge of chaos following the inquiry back to equilibrium. The two conflicting views are: first, that a lot has been done but that a lot remains to be done; and, second – with this chapter being written on the 20th anniversary of 22 April 1993, when Stephen's racist murder occurred – that it feels to some as if very little has been done and that some of what was done has been undone, and, further, that some senior and junior officers, commentators, officials, and many politicians have just become more adept at talking about the problems, without actually solving them (see Adams, 2013; Muir and Dodd, 2013; but see especially Peachey [2013] and Travis [2011], who explore differing perspectives of the issues). This situation can be argued to be the perturbation of a CAS at the edge of chaos and returning to equilibrium or stability, as opposed to true learning and adaptation. It might also be seen as an example of maladaptation: adapting in the wrong way (for a military version, see Serena, 2011, p 22, n 62).

To help understand the dynamics of state change in the MPS, it is useful to use a model developed by Sydow, Schreyögg and Koch (2009, p 691) to advance a dynamical framework of organisational path dependence, at the core of which they:

> Identify self-reinforcing processes as drivers that are likely to accumulate in a specific path of action. These inherent

self-reinforcing dynamics that eventually lead to an irreversible state of total inflexibility or lock in are seen as becoming increasingly systemic forces beyond the control of an individual actor. In other words the individual actor becomes entrapped in the system's dynamics.

They argue that this path dependence has four general properties and three phases. The properties are: first, outcomes are unpredictable/indeterminate; second, several outcomes are possible and history selects from among the alternatives; third, as the actors are entrapped, shifting to another option is not possible; and, fourth, the path lock leads to inferior and suboptimal solutions.

In phase one of the model (the pre-formation phase), there is a broad scope of action and multiple interactions, and any apparently random event can unintentionally set off a self-reinforcing process. Within the MPS, the dynamics of IR are products of this process of 'order for free' (see Pycroft, Chapter One). As soon as the dynamics of self-reinforcement occur, the system comes close to bifurcation, or a critical juncture – the murder of Stephen Lawrence and the subsequent inquiry is an example of this. Sydow et al (2009) argue that the development of this path is embedded within other developments and that history matters (remember CAS are historical in nature), but that path dependence is not deterministic from the beginning; rather, there is a tapering process that possibly ends in lock-in.

Phase two of the model (the formation phase) sees the gradual emergence of an organisational path in response to the trigger of the critical juncture in phase one. A critical incidents approach would argue for the importance of responses based upon a utility calculus of increasing returns; however, Sydow et al (2009) also argue for the importance of taking account of other non-cognitive processes within organisations, such as emotional reactions, implicit theories and political processes, among others. Eventually, in phase two, a dominant solution emerges in the form of recursive action patterns, as with those established by the SLI.

Phase three (the lock-in phase) requires that a preferred action pattern (ie the recommendations of the SLI) gets deeply embedded and replicated in organisational practice, which becomes its ontological structure, with some variability at the visible level. Therefore, locked in does not equate with complete rigidity, but the state of equilibrium of the system can be either optimal or suboptimal for the organisation and its wider environs. However, it is generally agreed that locked-in and robust systems are difficult to change. The sensitivity to initial conditions, that is, the order for free that brought about the consequences of the investigation of the murder of Stephen Lawrence and the actions taken, may paradoxically have led to an at least partially unchanged and ontological structure of IR.

The SLI was initially about the incompetent police investigation into what became known as hate crime but, in fact, was specifically a racist murder. In examining the context and causes, it went into wider aspects of diversity and community relations, including the finding of IR. In fairness, despite some exceptions (eg the Pilkington case), the UK has become an international leader on the investigation of hate crime and its transparency (including that of ministers and their willingness to let increased reporting be seen as positive) and is widely admired (see, eg, the OSCE [Organisation for Security and Cooperation in Europe] minutes, cross-government hate crime programme and cyber hate crime progress [Hall, 2005, 2013]). The real issue, however, is that greater change and adaptation might have taken place if the deterministic nature of IR within the MPS had been understood, possibly using complexity thinking, which would have helped prevent the return to equilibrium in many of the nested MPS systems, and thus the whole system, and the long-term problems of the failure to address all the issues and the fear of change.

There were also intellectual and practical developments in policing hate crimes in the areas of critical incidents management, independent advice from non-police officers, community impact assessment and family liaison, which were then applied much more widely in policing, including in murder investigations, community engagement and, indeed, counter-terrorism (Alison and Crego, 2008). This is sometimes used – wrongly in this author's view – as an overarching positive, an answer to all the SLI recommendations and the other wider diversity concerns of BME/gender retention, recruitment and promotion that are again wrongly and illogically seen as secondary to the original objective of remedying incompetent investigations. This fails to take into account Home Secretary Jack Straw's original open terms of reference, and the SLI's interpretation of them (for a recent discussion, see Stone, 2013, p 19).

There is some other evidence of the current relevance of this case study. There are other very current pieces of evidence besides Morris, Burden and Weekes (2004), who revisited some of the issues five years after the SLI report. Their well-meaning and not very forceful report concluded that a blockage to the SLI reforms might have come from a 'permafrost layer' of middle managers. This is an interesting concept, and perhaps a version of a system returning to equilibrium, or a complex *non*-adaptive system. Graham Smith's later report on the development of some of these issues of a possible 'permafrost' in Greater Manchester Police (Smith et al, 2012) was necessarily quite selective. There is much agreement with Graham Smith's findings that efforts to improve the lot of BME staff were being thwarted by existing systems, themselves perhaps evidence of continuing failure to understand and address IR.

There are more pieces in the jigsaw, as evidenced by, first, a forthcoming report from Dr Nathan Hall and others (including this author) for the Hate Crime Independent Advisory Group on the status of the Stephen Lawrence recommendations 15 years later (also, care is being taken not to hijack the 20th anniversary from Mrs Lawrence). It makes for hugely uncomfortable and worrying reading and is causing some consternation in some places in government – principally by sometimes pointing to other areas of public policymaking, besides the police. Second, the views of Mrs Lawrence, which were expressed for a TV programme on Tuesday 16 April 2013 (available on catch-up), made very uncomfortable viewing. Finally, SLI panel member Dr Richard Stone's (2013) flawed (but good in parts) book, *Hidden stories of the Stephen Lawrence Inquiry*, brings together some striking evidence from the transcripts of the SLI, despite the claims of a bizarre Home Office conspiracy theory to protect the police (which this author would refute) (Stone, 2013, pp 6, 7, 52). What all of these findings demonstrate is the need to understand that the whole system has to learn and adapt, and, on this basis, a great deal is yet to done, and some of what has been done needs to be redone.

It is the contention of this chapter that the preceding evidence is indicative of a need for more radical steps at the end of a continuum of solutions to perturb the MPS. This would move it out of the culture of negative controls and equilibrium. Possibly, the solution might be a complete rethink of stop and search, or possibly introducing some positive actions to increase the numbers of BME members of the police service (see Travis, 2011; Peachey, 2013; Muir and Dodd, 2013).[1] However, perturbing the system is not without considerable risks (hence the appeal of equilibrium) and may possibly lead to a further complex, confused and probably hurtful debate at a time when the environment for the police is about changes in governance, wages cuts, cuts in staff and morale influenced by government and media criticism. Many people did not understand IR 15 years ago and it is doubtful that they will understand radical steps now (Caless, 2011, p 90). Also, a very few members of the Black Police Association are argued (eg by Green, 2010) to sometimes be pursuing their own career agendas ahead of the public good; that could add to more division over positive action.

An earlier recognition of the extreme dimensions of this crisis, and a greater emphasis on complexity (although I am not arguing that there was no consideration of complexity at all over the last 15 years, just that its role in CAS and learning, change and adaptation were not seen as significant; for complexity in decision-making, both individually and organisationally, in policing critical incidents, see Alison and Crego, 2008), might have avoided the greatest continuing criticisms (for examples, see Travis, 2011; Muir and Dodd, 2013). However, it would probably not have mitigated the IR finding at the time of publication.

What might have provided an opportunity to have avoided the need to rely on the failed internal review and provided recognition of the investigative and strategic dimensions of Stephen's murder would have been what is now called a 'big data' approach and which would have explored the cumulative experience of nationwide hate crimes and the role of families and their impacts on communities before the public inquiry sat. This might have eased the challenges that the SLI subsequently presented for the organisation, and also aided our understanding of the dynamics of open CAS. Also, this would then have allowed for an earlier response, with a strategy that did not seek to challenge the evidence, and thus might also have limited the organisational damage. However, the purpose here is not to go back before or during the SLI, but to see if there are aspects of complexity thinking that might have been more effective than the strategy to deal with the findings and recommendations that was adopted.

Analysis

As already stated, the foundations of cognitive dissonance as a change agent developed into the approach known as critical incident training. Essentially, this is a psychological theory applied to an organisational-wide problem. Grieve (in Newburn and Neyroud, 2008, pp 70–1; see also Hall et al, 2009, pp 120–1) explores and defines critical incidents as 'any incidents where the effectiveness of the police response is likely to have a significant impact on the confidence of the victim, their family and/or the community'. This is a prime example of impact, consequences and likelihood. What was not clear was how the learning from critical incident management could be translated into organisational adaptation.

Critical incidents management thinking and training was used in a linear and reductionist fashion, seeking to reduce and understand the component parts of the incident (to be clear and transparent, this author was a leading part of the process which made that decision).

Despite this reductionist approach, Thompson (2011) argues that critical incidents thinking is sensitive to complexity thinking through an analysis of open systems because, like critical incidents, opens systems are so interrelated and interdependent that any change in one component brings about changes and adaptations in the whole system (an example of path dependency).

Support for the wider relevance of adaptation also comes from the significant leadership thinker Heifetz (1994, pp 125–30). He has a situational leadership model for exercising authority in crises, which he divides into two categories: technical and adaptive (interestingly for the definition of critical incidents just cited and derived from the SLI, he deals with racism). Technical situations are those where the procedures and policies have been devised already and creative leadership is only required to look for variations and extensions on what already exists. In other words, no paradigm shift is required. On the other hand, adaptive situations are where known methods and procedures will not suffice.

The argument is that known methods and procedures post-SLI do not suffice, but, of course, this chapter's analysis is necessarily selective in its assessment of a variety of SLI recommendations; in reality, some were more successful than others and examples have been chosen from each of those categories. Table 7.1 uses 29 out of 70 recommendations and one finding from the main body of the report.

Table 7.1: Stephen Lawrence Inquiry recommendations compared with cognitive dissonance-based and possible complexity applications

SLI (1999) Recommendations	Actions taken pre-/post-report based in part on cognitive dissonance and critical incidents?	Possible alternative actions using complexity thinking	Notes
Double jeopardy rule. New evidence not available to an earlier acquittal could lead to retrial. Rec: 38	Legislation passed. Encouraged further investigation	Was challenged through the CJS and its multiple CAS before successful implementation tactically and operationally	Successful implementation and prosecution. CJS is a contextual CAS
Family Liaison Officers. Recs: 23–28 (see Grieve, 2009, pp 118–19)	Considerable deployment of officers and training. Considered by many to be successful	This was primarily about knowledge flows in interacting CAS. Although community and independent advisers were used, greater emphasis on interacting CAS internal and external to policing might have led to greater success as change agents	A core part of the cognitive dissonance strategy, while widely praised, did not lead to wider understanding of IR within policing. Subject to some continuing criticism
Independent and Community Involvement in Policing. Recs: 7, 8, 50, 51 (see Azah, 2009; Brathwaite, 2009)	Strategic and local Independent Advisory Groups set up	Could have led to even deeper, more sophisticated understanding of the way multiple pressure and interest groups acted as CAS	Led to greater transparency and confidence
Hate Crimes Definition and Investigation. Recs: 32–44 (see Hall, 2005, 2013)	Cross-government Hate Crime Project and Independent Advisory Group. Multiparty, ACPO and departmental support	Again, earlier understanding of CAS would have produced earlier results by showing how different CAS were tackling the problem in different ways, and using differing knowledge flows in their interaction with other CAS internally and externally	Still some reporting issues 15 years after the SLI report. Part of joined-up government thinking but some years late. Particularly effective and thoughtful CPS activity

Table 7.1 (cont)

SLI (1999) Recommendations	Actions taken pre-/post-report based in part on cognitive dissonance and critical incidents?	Possible alternative actions using complexity thinking	Notes
Joined-up police leadership at the scenes and subsequently of major crimes and incidents. Recs: 20, 21	Critical incident training for all police. Cognitive dissonance fundamental to Strategic Management of Critical Incident Training (SMoCIT) for senior officers	Although CAS came to be considered later (eg Chapman, 2003), greater analysis of the interaction might have improved the learning. For example, differentiating between different nested CAS and their knowledge flows and learning	Less effective at lower ranks. Recently criticised as defensive
Stop and Search. Recs: 60–63	Major changes to Counter Terrorism Stop and Search, albeit over a decade after SLI. Less changes in general crime stop and search. Failure of attempts to control through documentation due to bureaucracy and inefficient IT	One of the major issues at the heart of continuing allegations of IR. Open systems and attractor theory helps here	Current issue 2013 (see {sense?})
IR that is unwitting, ignorant, thoughtless and stereotypical policies and practices in policing (SLI para 6.43)	No direct recommendation. Addressed through cognitive dissonance	Although critical incident thinking attempted to address this using Chapman (2003), it was only partially successful. Adaptation did not take place. Greater emphasis on knowledge flows, integration and adaptation, and learning through multiple CAS would have helped	Was not helped by the absence of a direct recommendation. Confusion over which of the recommendations applied directly to this finding

Conclusions

Specific areas of criticism in the SLI were IR, leadership, apologies (or lack of them), intelligence failures, family liaison criticisms, early efforts at investigation (now called 'the golden hour', based on trauma surgery), general incompetence and allegations of corruption. There were other parallel cases (eg McGowan, Menson, Reel; see Hall, 2005, 2013; Hall et al, 2009). In some of these areas of criticism, improvements have taken place.

On the 10th anniversary of the SLI Report, the MPS published an account of what it had achieved, and, interestingly, there was no mention of IR (MPS, 2009). This raises an intriguing question as to whether, on the basis of a critical incident orthodoxy, the MPS believes that it is not institutionally racist because it is now aware that it was, so that possibility is no longer tenable. There are good things in the 20-year aftermath of the SLI. Transparency about the nature of the problems, hate crime investigations and statistics, some improved collaborative relations with the community, independent advisory groups (IAGs), leadership by government ministers and ACPO, improvement in homicide investigation, hate crime investigation in London, methods of community engagement, improved representation of BME communities in the MPS, recognition by many families of the hard work and dedication of family liaison officers, some aspects of critical incident management, international recognition (OSCE), cyber hate crime developments, proactive engagement about hate crimes with communities; all these amounted to a huge cultural shift. There were also the six legacies outlined by Hall et al (2009): cultural, governance, political, legal, intelligence and international. These are effective to a greater or lesser extent.

The problem remains, however, that this is not seen as enough in some significant areas on the 20th anniversary of Stephen's racist murder (Travis, 2011; Adams, 2013; Alibai-Brown, 2013; Muir and Dodd, 2013; Okereke, 2013; Peachey, 2013; Stone, 2013). Part of this is due to the fact that cognitive dissonance theory, which is about individuals, was applied to an entire organisation. Complexity thinking would have broken down the MPS as an organisation (a macro-CAS) and its contexts and environment into other sub-CAS, and their issues could then have been addressed in a systematic fashion. The 'permafrost' layer identified by Morris, Burden and Weekes (2004) might also then have been tackled.

Thompson (2011) goes further and argues that all critical incidents are amenable to open systems analysis. So, a synthesis of critical indents and complexity thinking is possible. However, as someone, a serving officer, said to the author the other day: "the principles of policing are quite simple, it is their application that is complex"; and, of course, any fool can complicate the issues. However, there are other ways of looking at the fear of change and return to equilibrium besides the dominant narrative of police failure.

Note

[1] Editor's note: at the time of writing, the MPS Assistant Commissioner, Simon Byrne, in an interview with the *Guardian Newspaper* (Byrne, 2003, p 1), has said that they have discussed with the government a change in race relations legislation to allow for positive discrimination in recruitment, based upon the model of Northern Ireland, where, for example, one catholic is recruited for every protestant.

References

Adams, T. (2013) 'Time hasn't been much of a healer', interview with Doreen Lawrence, *UK Observer*, 21 April, New Review section, pp 8–10.

Alibai-Brown, Y. (2013) 'Twenty years after Lawrence, it's taboo to talk racism', *UK Independent*, 22 April, p 17.

Alison, L.J. and Crego, J. (2008) *Policing critical incidents: leadership and critical incident management*, Cullompton: Willan.

Azah, J. (2009) 'Independent advice, operational policing and the Stephen Lawrence Inquiry', in N. Hall, J. Grieve and S. Savage (eds) *Policing and the legacy of Lawrence*, Cullompton: Willan.

Brathwaite, J. (2009) 'Police engagement with communities post Lawrence', in N. Hall, J. Grieve and S. Savage (eds) *Policing and the legacy of Lawrence*, Cullompton: Willan.

Byrne, S. (2013) 'Met police in talks over law change to allow positive discrimination', 2 June. Available at: http://www.theguardian.com/uk/2013/jun/02/met-police-law-positive-discrimination

Caless, B. (2011) *Policing at the top*, Bristol: The Policy Press.

Chapman, J. (2003) *System failure*, London: Demos.

Green, D.G. (2010) 'Time to arrest the grievance culture', *London Daily Telegraph*, 10 February, p 23.

Grieve, J. (2009) 'Practical cop things to do?', in N. Hall, J. Grieve and S. Savage (eds) *Policing and the legacy of Lawrence*, Cullompton: Willan.

Grieve, J., Griffiths, W. and Crego, J. (2007) 'Critical incident management', in T. Newburn and T. Williamson (eds) *Handbook of investigation*, Devon: Willan.

Hall, N. (2005) *Hate crime*, Devon: Willan.

Hall, N. (2013) *Hate crime* (2nd edn), Devon: Willan.

Hall, N., Grieve, J. and Savage, S. (eds) (2009) *Policing and the legacy of Lawrence*, Cullompton: Willan.

Heifetz, R.A. (1994) *Leadership without easy answers*, Harvard, MA: Belknap Harvard University Press.

Home Office (1999) *Stephen Lawrence Inquiry: Home Secretary's action plan*, London: TSO.

Laihonen, H. (2005) 'Knowledge flows in complex systems. Relevance to knowledge intensive organisations', Frontiers of eBusiness Research, pp 359–69. Available at: http://tut-fi.academia.edu/HarriLaihonen (accessed 16 January 2014).

Ledwidge, M. (2013) 'Why it has all gone wrong within our public services. An open letter', *Guardian Newspapers*, 27 March, p 40.

Morris, W., Burden, A. and Weekes, A. (2004) *The report of the Morris Inquiry. An independent inquiry for professional standards and employment matters within the Metropolitan Police*, London: MPA.

MPS (Metropolitan Police Service) (2009) *Stephen Lawrence Inquiry report – ten years on*, London: MPA.

Muir, H. and Dodd, V. (2013) 'Still institutionally racist, say black officers', *Guardian Newspaper*, 22 April, p 9.

Murray, W. (2011) *Military adaptation in war. Fear of Change*, Cambridge: Cambridge University Press.

National Crime Agency (2013) Terms of Reference. Press, 2 February, London Home Office.

Newburn, T. and Neyroud, P. (2008) *Dictionary of policing*, Devon: Willan.

Okereke, K. (2013) 'My cousin was killed in a racist attack....', *Guardian Newspaper*, 22 April, G2 section, p 10 (and others).

Peachey, P. (2013) 'Black officers must enter police at senior levels to combat racism', *Independent Newspaper*, 22 April, p 9.

Reiner, R. (2012) 'Political economy and criminology: the return of the repressed', in S. Hall and S. Winlow (eds) *New directions in criminological theory*, London: Routledge.

Rittel, H. (1972) *On the planning crisis: systems analysis of the first and second generations* (reprint no 107), Berkeley, CA: University of California.

Serena, C. (2011) *A revolution in military adaptation. The US army in the Iraq War*, Washington, DC: Georgetown University Press.

Smith, G., Johnson, H. and Roberts, C. (2012) *Disproportionality in police professional standards. An investigation of internally raised misconduct proceedings in Greater Manchester Police with additional statistical analyses of West Midlands Police and British Transport Police data: and statistical analyses of counter-corruption data in the three services*, Manchester: University Of Manchester.

Stone, R. (2013) *Hidden stories of the Stephen Lawrence Inquiry. Personal reflections*, Bristol: The Policy Press.

Sydow, J., Schreyögg, G. and Koch, J. (2009) 'Organizational path dependence: opening the black box', *Academy of Management Review*, vol 34, no 4, pp 689–709.

Thompson, D.D.P. (2011) 'Using the open systems perspective to understand critical incidents', *Journal of Critical Incidence Analysis*. Available at: http://jcia.aciajj.org/files/2012/02/Thompson-1.pdf (accessed 16 May 2013).

Travis, A. (2011) 'White male culture dominates police, says equality review', *Guardian Newspaper*, 8 April, p 10.

TSO (The Stationery Office) (1999) The Stephen Lawrence Inquiry Report, Cm 4262-1, London: Home Office.

EIGHT

Intersecting contexts of oppression within complex public systems

Charmaine McPherson and Elizabeth McGibbon

This chapter is a theoretical discussion developed by two PhD-prepared nursing professors. Our thinking is embedded in more than 55 years of mental health nursing practice and academic experience. Many of these years were spent working with children, youth, adults, families and communities in crisis – those who bump into the most pointy edges of life and society. We have walked along with street youth, domestic violence survivors, refugees, young offenders, women preparing for criminal proceedings and people who misuse substances. We have worked and volunteered in community-based non-profit organisations, hospitals, emergency services, community mental health clinics, provincial and federal governments, and the World Health Organization. We have worked primarily in Canada, but have also been touched by the most vulnerable in communities in Mexico, Cuba and India. We have extensive backgrounds in the application of social sciences to health issues.

Our theoretical standpoint is that of critical feminist theory based in realist ontology/epistemology and complexity science, and we use an intersectionality lens to draw this thread through our discussion. Our strong practice and academic backgrounds ground our thinking in interrogating oppressions and their intersections and public system complexity as they relate to criminal justice. In our academic and practice work, we focus on the social determinants of health (SDH). The primary factors that shape the well-being of individuals, families, communities and nations are not medical treatments or lifestyle choices, but rather the living conditions they experience (Mikkonen and Raphael, 2010). These factors are known as the SDH: employment and working conditions; income and its equitable distribution; education and early childhood development; housing and food security; age; gender; and race. The SDH are also related to the extent to which citizens are 'provided with the physical, social, and personal resources to identify and achieve personal aspirations, satisfy needs, and cope with the environment' (Raphael, 2009, p 56). According to the World Health Organization (2008, p 1), the SDH are important markers of inequalities in health and well-being:

> The poor health of the poor … is caused by the unequal distribution of power, income, goods, and services, globally and nationally, the consequent unfairness in the immediate, visible circumstances of peoples' lives – their access to health care, schools, and education, their conditions of work and leisure, their homes, communities, towns, or cities – and their chances of leading a flourishing life.

These social determinants form the foundation for our discussion. The overall focus of the chapter is on a broader exploration of intersectionality, complexity and the dynamics of oppression. We examine how complexity science might be used to better understand the conflating relationships among the SDH and well-being, social/ public service access and oppression related to identities such as race, gender and age. It is argued that our analytical gaze should be at the macro-systems level, with emphasis on the unjust structural policy and practice factors that contribute to the development and maintenance of systemic oppression for people in situations of vulnerability. Complexity science is used in combination with intersectionality theory to specifically interrogate equity issues, such as exclusion from services. This exclusion arises from entrenched structural oppression based on 'the isms', such as racism, sexism and ageism. The term 'isms' originated in feminist theory and it is used to capture the broad scope of discriminatory practices and policies related to identities such as age, culture, ethnicity, gender, race, sexual orientation, religious affiliation and social class, to name a few. These 'isms' lead to oppression, where some populations are systematically denied appropriate access to key health and social services.

Complexity science helps to explain the chaotic synergy at play across multiple contextual, situational and identity factors, which often amounts to system-based oppression. We discuss the complex theoretical challenges associated with translating these multidimensional issues into informed social policy and practice. A case study arising from youth criminal justice work is used to apply our integrated theoretical perspective and to further explicate policy and practice implications. The chapter concludes with key areas that require further debate to support public system strengthening to ameliorate inequities related to oppression.

Linking structural oppression to inequities in overall well-being

This section introduces the links among the structural or systemic determinants of well-being and systemic oppression. When individuals and families enter the 'system', be it navigating the criminal justice system or the mental health care system, for example, they also enter the historical structural and public policy contexts that developed and sustained these systems. Public policymakers, practitioners, researchers and educators all share the tendency to isolate these two worlds, as if the structural context is somehow isolated from the ways that people's everyday lives unfold. One of the ways to mitigate this short-sighted approach is to actively engage in a consistent focus on the structural determinants of well-being. Here, 'structural' refers to the economic, social and political structures of society and the moral and cultural systems that underpin them (McGibbon et al, 2013). It is well known that such structures create inequities that persistently disadvantage some people and, at the same time, create and support advantage for others – all along the lines of human rights-based areas such as race, social class, gender, age, religious affiliation, sexuality and age, to name several. These structurally created inequities mean that social injustice is actively maintained by institutional systems such as the criminal justice system. For example, in Canada, 80% of imprisoned women are incarcerated for poverty-related offences; 90% of aboriginal women and 82% of all women in Canadian prisons are survivors of incest, rape or physical assault; and the number of women in prison has increased by 200% in the past 15 years (Canadian Association of Elizabeth Fry Societies, 2008). Also, in Canada, aboriginal peoples' unjust experiences with the criminal justice system have been documented by the Canadian Criminal Justice Association (CCJA, 2000):

• aboriginal offenders are more than twice as likely to be incarcerated than non-aboriginal offenders;
• aboriginal peoples who are accused of a crime are more likely to be denied bail, and more likely to be charged with multiple offenses, and often for crimes against the system;
• more time is spent in pre-trial detention by aboriginal peoples;

- aboriginal clients, especially in northern communities where the court party flies in the day of the hearing, spend less time with their lawyers;
- because court schedules in remote areas are poorly planned, judges may have limited time to spend in the community;
- aboriginal elders, who are also spiritual leaders, are not given the same status as prison priests and chaplains; and
- aboriginal peoples often plead guilty because they are intimidated by the court and simply want to get the proceedings over with.

These statistics point to persistent evidence of the social injustice that is embedded in societal systems – often referred to as oppression. It is very difficult to explore oppression because it is a complex process, rather than a discrete event. Ideas about domination, power and discrimination are interconnected, and there are many different and synergistic kinds of oppression (McGibbon and Etowa, 2009). A cycle of oppression (McGibbon et al, 2008) can be seen in practice settings and in policy decision-making. For example, consider health and social care access for people and families who receive supplementary income from the state (ie social assistance or welfare recipients). Starting with biased information about social assistance recipients, practitioners may develop a stereotype, such as the commonly held belief that people receiving assistance are lazy. In fact, the reasons for unemployment among social assistance recipients are multiple and complex. These stereotyped views of clients mean that practitioners may be missing important contexts related to income, transportation and access to employment and child care when they are developing case management plans or making referrals. Stereotypes can lead us to think in a particular way that demonstrates prejudice. If we believe that people receiving assistance are lazy, we may think that they do not really want to work. Then, when we *act* in a particular way, based on our prejudice, we are participating in discrimination. When we treat people on social assistance disrespectfully during an intake assessment, we are actively discriminating. In this way, we are contributing to a lack of full access to competent and compassionate care.

When our discriminatory actions are supported by systemic power within the health or social system – for example, when substandard intake assessments are not challenged by administration – oppression is the result. The cycle of oppression perpetuates a policymaking that supports social injustice. It is important to note that biased information, stereotyping, prejudice, discrimination and oppression often happen without the perpetrators noticing or acknowledging the problem.

The resulting social injustice is evidenced in poorer health and social outcomes for a growing number of citizens worldwide.

The mental, physical and spiritual suffering caused by oppression is not inevitable. However, its perpetuation is well entrenched in public policy and in the mechanisms for distribution of the necessities of life, including the health, social and legal systems, which purport to alleviate this suffering. These processes are core causes of increasing inequities in health and social outcomes across the life course. Although there is a substantial literature about power and oppression, analysis of the explicit links between social structures and the well-being of citizens has only recently garnered sustained national and international attention (Navarro, 2007). Unfortunately, policymakers and others have progressed at a snail's pace since 18th-century physician Rudolf Virchow's famous claim: 'All diseases have two causes – one pathological and the other political.' Virchow, an anthropologist and a medical doctor, presaged modern-day struggles with the explicit and consistent identification of the structural, rather than individual, behaviour-based causes of health and social problems.

Understanding the issue using intersectionality theory

The concept of oppression does not lend itself to practical application, which is one reason why it has taken so long to make explicit linkages between the processes of oppression and their impact on well-being. This section makes some of these linkages and makes paths to social action more clear through the use of an intersectionality lens for tackling socially determined health inequities.

Intersectionality theory focuses on systemic power and details the interaction of oppressions related to 'the isms' (Collins, 1990; Calliste and Dei, 2000). These forms of discrimination, and hence oppression, in society do not operate independently of each other. Rather, they interact in a complex manner that intensifies oppression. Descriptors of oppression, such as *intersecting* and *interlocking*, bring the discussion beyond additive models, which fail to stress the centrality of power and privilege (Collins, 1990). An intersectionality framework is used to describe the interwoven influences of identities such as gender, sexual orientation, race, ethnicity, disability and age on experiences of injustice (James, 1996; Calliste and Dei, 2000). Feminist intersectionality frameworks emphasise:

an understanding of the many circumstances that combine with discriminatory social practices to produce and sustain inequity and exclusion. Intersectional feminist frameworks look at how systems of discrimination such as colonialism and globalization can impact the combination of a person's social or economic status, race, class, gender, and sexuality. (Canadian Research Institute for the Advancement of Women, 2006, p 7)

Intersectionality is beginning to be explicitly incorporated into discussions about the SDH and women's health research (McGibbon and Etowa, 2007; Hankivsky and Christoffersen, 2008; Hankivsky et al, 2009; McGibbon and Etowa, 2009; Hankivsky and Cormier, 2011), and primary health care renewal (McPherson and McGibbon, 2010). Figure 8.1 builds on earlier work (McGibbon, 2007, 2009; McPherson and McGibbon, 2010) in an effort to design a practical model that allows for multiple intersections, including, but not limited to, 'the isms'. Although feminist theory's concept of intersectionality is key in understanding the health impacts of oppression, it falls somewhat short when one considers how 'the isms', the SDH and geography all combine in a deadly synergy for oppressed peoples. These three

Figure 8.1: Intersections of the social determinants of health

Intersections of
SOCIAL DETERMINANTS
OF HEALTH (SDH)
Early childhood development
Education
Employment and working
  conditions
Food security
Health care services
Housing security
Income and its equitable
  distribution
Self-determination
Social exclusion
Social safety nets

Intersections of
IDENTITY as an SDH
(the "isms")
Age
Culture
(Dis)ability
Ethnicity
Gender
Immigrant
Race
Sexual
  orientation
Social class
Spirituality
...

**Synergies
of SDH**

Intersections of GEOGRAPHY as an SDH
Rural, remote, fly-in
East, West, North, South
Segregation and ghettoization
Unfair geographic access to public services
Lack of public transportation (or funds)
Environmental patterns: weather, pollution,
  dispersion, toxin location ...

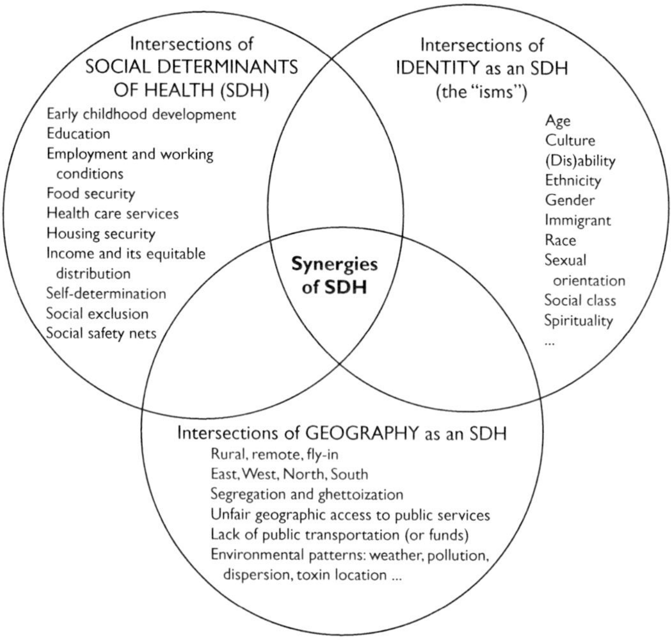

Source: Adapted from McGibbon (2009)

areas must be woven together to enrich an understanding of paths for policy and civil society action to reduce health inequities: (1) the SDH as laid out in the Toronto Charter (Raphael, 2009), and as revised by Mikkonen and Raphael (2010); (2) identity and 'the isms' (eg racism, sexism, classism) as SDH; and (3) geography as an SDH.

There has already been a merging of the first two areas (the SDH and 'the isms') because some of 'the isms' are sometimes referred to as SDH (eg race/racism and gender/sexism). However, all of 'the isms' are also determinants of health and well-being. The geographic or spatial contexts of oppression, including lack of access to services in rural areas and the persistent location of toxic waste sites close to communities of colour, introduce another layer of complexity (McGibbon, 2009). When we consider the spatial contexts of oppression along with the SDH and 'the isms', what we have, ultimately, are intersections of intersections. Taken together, the intersecting areas create a powerful synergy of oppression that is very difficult to disentangle in terms of its policy base and its impact on everyday life. Grace-Edward Galabuzi (2001, p 7), a Canadian scholar, provides a clear example of how these SDH create a synergy of disadvantage for racialised families and communities in Canada:

> The racialisation of poverty is increasingly manifest in urban centres where racialised groups are concentrated, and in the emergence of racial enclaves and a growing racial underclass. This process is intensifying in increasingly racially segregated neighbourhoods. In an increasingly segregated housing market, racialised groups are relegated to substandard, marginal, and often overpriced housing. The growing social inequalities act as social determinants of health and well-being, with higher health risks, barriers to social services, and increased contact with the criminal justice system.

Galabuzi's example illustrates that, taken together, the SDH, identity as an SDH and geography as an SDH create a complex system of disadvantage that public systems and public policy are ill-equipped to tackle. Even the concept of cross-sectoral children's policy intervention has had difficulty gaining a foothold in public policy (McPherson et al, 2006).

Blending intersectionality and complexity science to understand and address issues of oppression

This section builds on the preceding discussion and our previous work (McPherson and McGibbon, 2010; McGibbon and McPherson, 2011) to describe how intersectionality theory can be applied in tandem with complexity theory to better understand and support the amelioration of inequities in the SDH as a root cause of oppression. We explore the ways that this theoretical bridging can further our understanding of how oppression, such as economic segregation and social marginalisation – known precursors to contact with the criminal justice system (Galabuzi, 2001) – functions in individuals' lives and reveals itself within front-line services. Although significantly challenging, it is imperative that these ideas also be situated within the context of complex public service systems.

Complexity science, or the study of complex adaptive systems, has its roots in physics, mathematics and biology. It has now expanded into organisational and systems of organisations issues and it is highly multi- and inter-disciplinary. It has appeal across a number of disciplines that seek to answer questions about living, changing systems. As this book testifies, complexity science is not a unified theory, it is a collection of theories and constructs that have conceptual integrity among themselves (Begun et al, 2003). 'The messy, open systems of complexity science are immensely different from the closed, well-behaved systems that were the original focus of systems science' (Begun et al, 2003, p 255). In viewing public services as *complex adaptive systems*, the *complex* portion implies diversity – a wide variety of elements. *Adaptive* suggests the capacity to change and to learn from experience. In complex adaptive systems theory, the *systems* refer to elements that are independent agents. These agents are located within a densely connected interacting web and the agents act based on local knowledge and conditions (Begun et al, 2003).

The machine metaphor (Morgan, 1997) for organisational systems has not resulted in effective research and practice. Further, in terms of health care as a huge complex social system, Begun and colleagues (2003, p 254) argue that 'linkage, coordination, rationalization, and vertical and horizontal integration have failed to advance health care delivery to acceptable levels of satisfaction for both internal and external stakeholders'. They suggest that thoughtful consideration of health care and similar organisations within the health care *system* would be better facilitated by application of the metaphor of the system as a living organism, rather than the system as a machine. A similar argument could be made for the broader public service system, inclusive of those services associated with criminal justice work. Traditional systems theory (such as Senge, 1990) has its origins in explaining the behaviour of non-living systems, such as machinery. Complex adaptive systems theory reformulates our view of a system as it attempts to explain how living systems work.

Other contributions to this book discuss the 'Butterfly Effect', explaining that the non-linear dynamic systems approach views the world as comprised of a series of interacting systems, where change in any part of those systems can change the context for all of the other elements. They note that the interrelated nature of these systems can work from the genetic and cellular foundations of life through to the 'whole systems' of individuals, society and the state, thus having profound implications for our understanding of cause and effect. This discussion moves beyond language of general systems theory (such as Senge, 1990) to complexity science. We focus primarily on the public system component (as a social system) of a whole-systems approach, suggesting that the public system itself is a complex adaptive system.

The application of complexity science to health and social sciences is not new. Byrne (1998) developed an introductory text for the application of complexity theory to the social sciences. Begun, Zimmerman and Dooley (2003) examined health care organisations through a complex adaptive systems lens, and Matlow et al (2006) used complexity science to examine coordination of care for complex paediatric patients. Systems thinking has also been used by the World Health Organization in considering system strengthening (De Savigny and Adam, 2009). Notably, Paley (2007) argued that many of the recent applications of complexity theory and complex systems to health service delivery in the health care literature were exaggerated claims. Although he agreed that complexity concepts could be extended to systems and structures in health care organisations, he suggested that many authors misunderstood some of the concepts associated with complexity thinking and made unfounded expansive claims. Paley contended that the application of complexity science to public organisations, such as health care organisations, should be used modestly at this stage in the development of complexity science. However, we argue here that it is time to use complexity science when analysing public system issues because of the very complex nature of these systems.

Byrne (1998, p 118) used complexity science in his discussion of the complex character of health and illness:

> The social account given by epidemiology is simply the result of the aggregate of such individual cases. We can

go beyond this to a complex account of the genesis of individual cases ... in terms of diet, housing conditions and ethnicity. This is much better but it is not enough. For a salutogenic account we have to get beyond mere complex causation. We have to think of the interaction of the system levels.

Byrne (1998) started to touch upon some of the early concepts that we further develop here. We use intersectionality in tandem with complexity science to identify the problematic at the macro-systems level. Our gaze is upon structural oppressions across time within the public service system. A complexity theory approach, one that views the public service system as a complex adaptive system, holds great promise for unpacking the complexities inherent in health and well-being inequities. We emphasise the theoretical consistencies between feminist intersectionality theory and a complex adaptive systems perspective, where both constructs integrate the language of multiple perspectives and the ways that these perspectives are intimately linked to systemic structures (McGibbon and McPherson, 2011).

Some portions of the public service system, such as health care and social service organisations, are ideal settings for the application of complexity science because of the diversity of organisational forms and often unpredictable interactions among these evolving and interdependent organisations. Public service organisations are a human affair. They are social systems that are built by humans, run by humans and made for humans. Unlike the cause-and-effect linearity of the physical sciences, the public service system has contexts and histories that are crucial to any analysis and synthesis of the system, or to an individual's experience within that system. Any interrogation of complex systems should bring context to the fore.

Complexity theory, taken in combination with an intersectionality lens, and, in this chapter, within a criminal justice and public service system application, brings people's individual contexts to the fore within the broader context of public services. Public services include individual practitioners, such as social workers or nurses, and how they work inter-professionally, cross-sectorally and inter-organisationally within a broader complex and eclectic web called the public service system. The public service system can also be examined from local, regional, national and global contexts. We have argued that structural oppression 'for some' is built into the system at any or all of these junctures. Without complexity science, we would lose the essential nature of context (eg past/present, individually/organisationally, locally/ globally) and the synergy of the various intersections in the analysis.

Figure 8.2 brings this thinking together in a single graphic, using intersectionality in tandem with complexity science to identify the contextual and non-linear nature of the interrelated, overlapping and synergistic elements of structural oppression.

Figure 8.2: Intersecting contexts of oppression within complex public systems

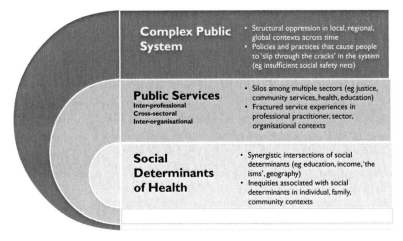

Local, regional, national and global systems of inequity are inextricably linked and cannot be ameliorated without an analytic focus on how these systems act together in a complex web that coalesces to produce growing social inequities (McGibbon and McPherson, 2011). Although feminist intersectionality theory allows us to envision the ways that oppressions come together to compound people's struggles within the criminal justice system, it may be argued that intersectionality theory alone falls somewhat short of describing the interactions within this web of larger systems, particularly the health and social service systems. For example, many youth involved in the criminal justice system have had extensive relationships with mental health, education, child welfare and family social welfare services, to name a few. Many of these youth have experienced a lifetime of fractured service experiences as they were pushed and pulled in and out of inadequate and siloed services that did not work effectively across organisational, professional or sectoral boundaries. It is not difficult to see how structural oppression develops and becomes deeply rooted such that it transcends time barriers in such problematic structures. Further, these fractured experiences become one more intersecting piece in the previously described 'intersections of intersections' for the youth, their families and their communities.

Begun et al (2003) outlined four common features of complex adaptive systems. They exhibit: (1) a dynamic state with constant interacting forces; (2) relationships that are massively entangled; (3) emergent, self-organising behaviour with extensive communication among agents that can spread norms; and (4) a robust adaptation mechanism and an ability to alter themselves in response to feedback, which helps them to survive a variety of environmental conditions. They added two propositions arising from chaos theory (Gleick, 1987) that are particularly relevant as social scientists apply complexity science: (1) 'small, seemingly inconsequential events, perturbations, or changes can potentially lead to profound, large scale change'; and (2) 'what appears to be random may in fact have an underlying orderliness to it' (Begun et al, 2003, p 258). Consider the seemingly small-scale and inconsequential processes surrounding cross-sectoral inter-professional relationship development and maintenance in running a multi-agency young offender programme. However, the relational impacts on a core team and those young offenders with whom the team works may be profound and large-scale. Cross-sectoral and inter-professional relationships, with all their randomness and unpredictability, when examined through a complexity lens, do have an element of underlying orderliness to them: these professional relationships are based on simple humanistic principles of trust, honesty, support and so forth. Such virtues are often ignored and even actively undermined in the public service arena, which helps to explain why inter-professional practice development is advancing so slowly (Registered Nurses' Association of Ontario, 2013).

Complexity theory suggests that a simple pattern of interaction can create a huge number of potential outcomes that may have relevance for societal well-being. Synergistic events such as simple socialisation and engagement across organisational lines have been reported to support the development of trust, understanding and responsiveness among practitioners across multiple sectors, professions and organisations (McPherson, 2008).

Wallace (2007) outlined five characteristics of complex public service change. He suggested that complex change is: (1) large-scale; (2) componential; (3) systematic; (4) differentially impacting; and (5) contextually dependent. Wallace, Fertig and Schneller (2007) noted that the health and education sectors – sectors in which young offenders often initially bump into the public system – as the largest and most complex public services, offer the most potent insights into the complexity of change and strategies for dealing with it. Further, in complex adaptive systems, renewal and long-term viability requires what complexity science calls *destruction*: a transformative breaking down of the old so that change can emerge. It is interesting to consider Wallace's characteristics for public service change to garner insights into the complexity of public system change, which is routinely thwarted in a general resistance to system change in and of itself (Casebeer, 2007; De Savigny and Adam, 2009).

In terms of public system change to alleviate inequities, inter-organisational networks, as a newer and emerging organisational form of the later 20th century, have been proposed to ameliorate the fractured nature of many of our public services, especially for high-need children, youth and their families (McPherson, 2008). Lamothe and Denis (2007) discussed networks of integrated services in health care as an emerging new organisational form and suggested that a social science-informed approach to understanding complex public service change could be insightful. They identified the need to pay attention to micro-level (individual/single organisational level) as well as macro-level (broader or supra-system level) contextual dynamics: 'If networks of integrated services are to become institutionalized new organizational forms, they will be the emergent product of the interactive dynamics occurring at all levels of this specific context' (Lamothe and Denis, 2007, p 71). Networks of integrated services amount to a complex change that expresses many of the characteristics identified within a complexity science frame.

Using complexity logic, if the provision of cross-sectoral public services for young offenders may be conceptualised as a complex adaptive system, then inter-organisational and cross-sectoral collaboration must be seen as a dynamic characteristic of that system. Collaboration can then be expected to manifest itself in diverse and creative ways and would not be an equilibrium state. Collaboration would be an emergent quality of various aspects of the system and would show itself differently at different points in time. This analysis sits apart from the rather static models of cross-sectoral and inter-professional collaboration that were posited in the 1980s and 1990s (Registered Nurses' Association of Ontario, 2013).

In working with people within the criminal justice system, practitioners are actually working across multiple systems, historically as well as currently, with their footprints of past system contacts still visible. System (and practitioner) flexibility is crucial to success, especially in terms of inter-professional and cross-sectoral action, yet our patriarchal public systems are typically rigidly controlled and antagonistic. Complexity science may help us to better understand the dynamics at play where these two conditions coexist – the need for flexibility and rigidity. 'Attempts to rigidly control a complex system can increase problems and unintended consequences' (Matlow et al, 2006, p 86), as individuals 'work around' these controls. Consideration of these issues within a complexity frame with the backdrop of intersectionality is crucial to a more realistic analysis of the possibilities for public system change to ameliorate structural oppression. This analysis informs social safety net strengthening measures with a focus on cross-sectoral and interprofessional prevention and early intervention services and supports for people who might ultimately come into contact with the criminal justice system.

Pulling it all together: case study

This chapter contributes to a relatively new discussion aimed at using intersectionality and complexity theory to better analyse and synthesise the synergistic interplay of various contexts that contribute to structural oppression. The case study that follows (Box 8.1) is an application of the concepts discussed here within a youth criminal justice context. This is a real case that occurred in Nova Scotia, Canada in 2004. The described events and circumstances highlight the complexities at play across numerous individual/family, service and broader public system contexts for this young offender.

Box 8.1: The Nunn Commission of Inquiry, *Spiraling out of control: lessons learned from a boy in trouble*

The Nunn Commission of Inquiry was a landmark public inquiry into Canada's youth criminal justice system. On 29 June 2005, the Nova Scotia provincial government appointed retired Supreme Court Justice Merlin Nunn to head a public inquiry into the circumstances surrounding the release of a youth offender who was convicted under the Canadian Youth Criminal Justice Act 2002 (YCJA) as the result of a fatal car crash. Commissioner Nunn submitted his report on 5 December 2006.

On 12 October 2004, a tragic motor vehicle incident occurred that called into question the effectiveness of the youth criminal justice system. Theresa McEvoy was killed when a young person hit her vehicle at an intersection. The youth was under the influence of illegal substances and was driving a stolen car during a police chase when he hit her vehicle. She was a 52-year-old teacher's assistant and mother of three. What made the incident all the more disturbing was the fact that the youth had a history of contact with the criminal justice system and had just been mistakenly released from custody two days before the fatal incident. The 16-year-old had been released from jail despite having 38 outstanding criminal charges pending against him.

The Commission convened on 29 June 2005, with the chief goal of developing recommendations to strengthen the youth justice system to prevent similar tragedies from occurring in the future. Over 31 days of testimony, Commissioner Nunn heard from 47 witnesses, including the families of those most closely impacted by the incident, policing agencies, government and court officials, educational officials, and the legal establishment.

The final report, entitled *Spiraling out of control: lessons learned from a boy in trouble* (Nunn, 2006), was released on 5 December 2006. The report tabled 34 recommendations in the areas of youth justice administration and accountability, youth crime legislation, and prevention of youth crime. The Commissioner's findings focused much attention on the limitations of the YCJA, which was cited as one of the primary factors leading to this tragedy. Recommendation examples include:

- lobby federal government to remove time limits for sentencing a young person to a community programme like an attendance centre;
- advocate for making public protection one of the primary goals of the federal YCJA;
- the YCJA to include conduct that could endanger public safety;
- advocate for changes to the YCJA to require youth to continue court-ordered behaviour, even after a 'responsible person' is no longer willing or able to provide supervision; and
- advocate for changes to the YCJA to remove the need for a new bail hearing if the person previously designated for supervising the youth outside custody is no longer providing that supervision.

Additionally, there were some recommendations that focused on making public system improvements in responding to 'at risk' children and youth in Nova Scotia. Since the release of the report, the government of Nova Scotia has been relying on its recommendations in the development of new strategies and initiatives, including crime prevention programmes and services aimed at helping children and youth reach their potential.

One context to consider in this case is the justice service system, where a 16-year-old boy was mistakenly released from custody and then became involved in the fatal police chase. The Nunn Commission initially examined the case from a broad service system perspective, which considered federal and provincial legislation, policies and procedures. The recommendations were a beginning attempt to mirror the complex nature of many child and youth issues that can involve multiple service professionals, sectors and partners, including family, community and public services. Early intervention for 'at risk' children and youth as a crime prevention strategy was also included in the Commission's report, but to a lesser extent.

In addition to the immediate tragedy, the circumstances surrounding the young person's life and activities and his involvement in the Nova Scotia justice system must be considered:

> Before January 2004, he had no criminal record. From that time to October 12, 2004, he committed crimes that resulted in 38 separate charges. He was arrested 6 times and appeared in court 11 times. All this took place by the time he was only 16 years old. What is the social and family background of this young person whose actions caused so much tragedy?… What contributed to his spiral into conflict with the law? (Nunn, 2006, p 52)

Using Figure 8.2, if we were to back things up and consider the intersections of the social determinants of health/well-being surrounding this boy and his family before the tragic incident, we must ask: 'Why is it that a 16-year-old boy ended up with 38 criminal charges pending against him in the first place?' An analysis that uses an intersectionality lens in individual/family/community contexts fosters a deeper understanding of this boy's persistent struggles.

The Commission's report (Nunn, 2006) outlined the boy's life in intimate detail over two chapters, with a focus on his early family life, his schooling, his involvement with the Department of Community Services and his conflicts with the law. A portrait of family struggles through divorce, remarriage, multiple relocations, financial hardship, drug use and familial conflict, anger and violence was painted. Many social determinants intersected to create an almost insurmountable situation for this boy. These struggles can be further analysed in the context of his contact with multiple public services, such as:

- education services (early and ongoing behavioural difficulties, school transfers, withdrawal from school);
- health services (contact with family doctors and paediatrician for behavioural issues and diagnosis of Attention Deficit Hyperactivity Disorder (ADHD), medication for ADHD, counselling in mental health services);
- community/social services (multiple requests for support from child protection services by mother, family counselling, parenting skills support, requests for acute voluntary placement intervention, voluntary placement in several public residential facilities/group homes for youth at risk); and
- justice services (regional police services, regional police youth court liaison, Restorative Justice Program, youth justice court system).

With this analysis, it becomes clear how the stage was set for 'criminal activity' and that intervening was indeed a difficult and multilayered process in this boy's life. The sheer complexity of the youth's story is further deepened because it unfolds within the broader complex public service system. The Commission reported that this boy was someone who did not 'slip through the cracks' because of his ongoing involvement in multiple services that were designed to meet multiple needs. However, the existence of services and the boy's (and his family's) contact with the services does not mean that his individual needs were met or that particular programme/service goals were achieved. Based on the ultimate outcomes, one might argue that he was indeed a boy who 'slipped through the cracks' of many services and the Nova Scotia youth criminal justice system, despite many and varied attempts to engage with him and his family.

Where were the built-in structural oppressions that impacted on this boy and, ultimately, resulted in the loss of Ms McEvoy's life? Did his family's involvement with child protection and the Department of Community Services impact the way in which medical and mental health services were delivered? Did this history impact his educational opportunities? How was he likely systematically eliminated from typical youth sports and other extra-curricular opportunities? How was he profiled when he entered his final long-term group home setting? How do we as a society perceive and then deal with young people who come into conflict with the law? This type of analysis may better point the way to broader public system strengthening and reform – one that is linked with people in their family and community contexts, which are, in turn, nested in a complex public system context. Changing one aspect of the system impacts others, not necessarily in a cause-and-effect fashion, but because of the diversity of organisational forms and often unpredictable interactions among these evolving and interdependent organisations. The public service system is a complex adaptive system. As mentioned earlier, unlike the cause-and-effect linearity of the physical sciences, the public service system has contexts and histories that are crucial to any analysis and synthesis of the system, or to an individual's experience within that system. Any interrogation of complex systems should bring context to the fore.

Issues for continued debate

There is an increasing awareness within the scientific community of the need to deal with the complex dimension of public social systems. One must question whether or not this view is shared by public system professional practitioners, decision-makers and politicians. There is clearly need for further analysis, synthesis and debate on many of the issues raised in this chapter. The debate may be continued by considering the following:

- Poverty is a clear precursor to contact with the criminal justice system. What social and economic structures/policies are perpetuating this societal injustice? What is the qualitative and quantitative relationship between the SDH and youth contact with the criminal justice system?
- The psychiatrisation of childhood oppression is often linked to failed service provision. Why do a disproportionately large number of male inmates have a childhood diagnosis of conduct disorder that has followed them for most of their lives?
- How does the criminal justice system operate to perpetuate oppression related to 'the isms'? How is the criminal justice system a vehicle for creating and sustaining societal oppression?
- There is a need for further debate about how the criminal justice system consistently enacts colonial oppression of indigenous peoples, both men and women. What are the public policy precursors to the creation of inequities in criminal justice outcomes for indigenous peoples? How does modern-day colonialism continue to be consistently enacted in the treatment of indigenous peoples within and outside the criminal justice system?
- In what ways is the criminal justice system (eg system policies and practices, as well as practices at the 'front lines') racialised?
- Attempting to fit complexity theory into our current Western understanding of social systems may not be most helpful. There needs

to be debate about whether or not there is a need to fundamentally change the way that we conceptualise and organise our public systems using a complexity science lens.

• Subjectivity and context dependency are key elements in understanding complex public systems. How do we develop service and system analysis techniques that put subjectivity and context dependency at the fore?

We hope to stimulate a debate about how intersectionality theory and complexity theory are natural antecedents to inform public policy to address SDH inequities and oppression. These ideas need to be integrated into a new synthesis of our understanding of the multidimensionality and context-specific nature of complex public social systems. There needs to be a greater interrogation of the system as human beings experience it. Finally, a fundamental acceptance of the non-linearity of such complex systems, with their irregularities and intersections, is required. These understandings and actions are needed in order to create a public system that does not naturally and systematically create further inequities and vulnerabilities for the most disadvantaged.

References

Begun, J.W., Zimmerman, B. and Dooley, K. (2003) 'Health care organizations as complex adaptive systems', in S.M. Mick and M. Wyttenbach (eds) *Advances in health care organization theory*, San Francisco, CA: Jossey-Bass, pp 253–88.

Byrne, D. (1998) *Complexity science and the social sciences: an introduction*, London: Routledge.

Calliste, A. and Dei, G.S. (2000) *Anti-racist feminism: critical race & gender studies*, Halifax, NS: Fernwood publishing.

Canadian Association of Elizabeth Fry Societies (2008) *Mission statement*, Ottawa, ON: Author.

Canadian Research Institute for the Advancement of Women (2006) *Intersectional feminist frameworks – an emerging vision*, Ottawa, ON: University of Ottawa. Available at: http://www.criaw-icref.ca/intersectional-feminist-frameworks-emerging-vision

Casebeer, A. (2007) 'Learning to navigate the noise of change: lessons from complex health systems contexts', in M. Wallace, M. Fertig and E. Schneller (eds) *Managing change in the public services*, Toronto, ON: John Wiley & Sons Canada, pp 193–211.

CCJA (Canadian Criminal Justice Association) (2000) 'Aboriginal peoples and the criminal justice system', *Bulletin of the CCJA*, 15 May.

Collins, P.H. (1990) *Black feminist thought: knowledge, consciousness & the politics of empowerment*, Boston, MA: Unwin Hyman.

De Savigny, D. and Adam, T. (eds) (2009) *Systems thinking for health systems strengthening*, Geneva: Alliance for Health Policy & Systems Research and World Health Organization.

Galabuzi, G.-E. (2001) *Canada's creeping economic apartheid: the economic segregation and social marginalization of racialised groups*, Toronto, ON: CSJ Foundation for Research and Education. Available at: http://www.socialjustice.org/pdfs/economicapartheid.pdf

Gleick, J. (1987) *Chaos: making a new science*, New York, NY: Penguin.

Hankivsky, O. and Christoffersen, A. (2008) 'Intersectionality and the determinants of health: a Canadian perspective', *Critical Public Health*, vol 18, no 3, pp 271–83.

Hankivsky, O. and Cormier, R. (2011) 'Intersectionality and public policy: some lessons from existing models', *Political Research Quarterly*, vol 64, no 1, pp 217–29.

Hankivsky, O., Cormier, R. and De Merich, D. (2009) *Intersectionality: moving women's health research and policy forward*, Vancouver, BC: Women's Health Research Network.

James, C. (1996) *Experiencing difference*, Toronto, ON: Brunswick Books.

Lamothe, L. and Denis, J.-L. (2007) 'The emergence of new organizational forms: networks of integrated services in health care', in M. Wallace, M. Fertig and E. Schneller (eds) *Managing change in the public services*, Toronto, ON: John Wiley & Sons Canada, pp 57–74.

Matlow, A.G., Wright, J.G., Zimmerman, B., Thomson, K. and Valente, M. (2006) 'How can the principles of complexity science be applied to improve the coordination of care for complex pediatric patients?', *Quality and Safety in Health Care*, vol 15, no 2, pp 85–8.

McGibbon, E. (2007) 'Mixed methods designs for applied health inequities research', paper presented at the Third International Congress of Qualitative Inquiry, University of Illinois, Urbana, Illinois, May.

McGibbon, E. (2009) 'Health and health care: a human rights perspective', in D. Raphael (ed) *The social determinants of health* (2nd edn), Toronto, ON: Canadian Scholar's Press, pp 319–39.

McGibbon, E. and Etowa, J. (2007) 'Health inequities & the social determinants of health: spatial contexts of oppression', invited keynote presentation, Nova Scotia Health Research Foundation Health Geomatics Conference, Halifax, NS, October.

McGibbon, E. and Etowa, J. (2009) *Anti-racist health care practice*, Toronto, ON: Canadian Scholar's Press.

McGibbon, E. and McPherson, C. (2011) 'Applying intersectionality & complexity theory to address the social determinants of women's health', *Women's Health and Urban Life*, vol 10, no 1 (Special Issue), pp 59–86.

McGibbon, E., Etowa, J. and McPherson, C. (2008) 'Health care access as a social determinant of health', *Canadian Nurse*, vol 104, no 7, pp 22–7.

McGibbon, E., Waldren, I. and Jackson, J. (2013) 'The social determinants of cardiovascular health: time for a focus on racism', *Diversity and Equality in Health and Care*, vol 10, no 3, pp 139–42.

McPherson (2008) 'Child health networks: a case study of network development, evolution and sustainability', unpublished doctoral dissertation, McMaster University, Hamilton, ON.

McPherson, C. and McGibbon, C. (2010) 'Addressing the determinants of child mental health: intersectionality as a guide to primary health care renewal', *Canadian Journal of Nursing Research*, vol 42, no 3, pp 50–64.

McPherson, C., Popp, J. and Lindstrom, R. (2006) 'Reexamining the paradox of structure: a child health network perspective', *Healthcare Papers*, vol 7, no 2, pp 46–52.

Mikkonen, J. and Raphael, D. (2010) *The social determinants of health: the Canadian facts*, Toronto, ON: York University School of Health Policy and Management. Available at: http://www.thecanadianfacts.org/

Morgan, G. (1997) *Images of organization* (2nd edn), Thousand Oaks, VA: Sage.

Morris W. (2005) *The case for change*, London: Metropolitan Police Authority.

Navarro, V. (2007) 'Neoliberalism as class ideology: or the political cause of the growth of inequalities', *International Journal of Health Services*, vol 37, no 1, pp 47–62.

Nunn, D.M. (2006) *Spiraling out of control: lessons learned from a boy in trouble. Report of the Nunn Commission of Inquiry*, Halifax, NS: Province of Nova Scotia. Available at: http://novascotia.ca/just/nunn_commission/_docs/Report_Nunn_Final.pdf

Paley, J. (2007) 'Complex adaptive systems and nursing', *Nursing Inquiry*, vol 14, pp 233–42.

Raphael, D. (ed) (2009) *Social determinants of health* (2nd edn), Toronto, ON: Canadian Scholar's Press.

Registered Nurses' Association of Ontario (2013) *Developing and sustaining interprofessional health care: optimizing patient, organizational, and systems outcomes. Best practice guideline*, Toronto, ON: Author.

Senge, P. (1990) *The fifth discipline: the art and practice of the learning organization*, New York, NY: Doubleday.

Wallace, M. (2007) 'Coping with complex and programmatic public service change', in M. Wallace, M. Fertig and E. Schneller (eds) *Managing change in the public services*, Toronto, ON: John Wiley & Sons Canada, pp 13–35.

Wallace, M., Fertig, M. and Schneller, E. (2007) 'Managing public service change or coping with its complexity?', in M. Wallace, M. Fertig and E. Schneller (eds) *Managing change in the public services*, Toronto, ON: John Wiley & Sons Canada, pp 1–10.

World Health Organization (WHO) (2008) *Closing the gap in a generation: Health equity through action on the social determinants of health*, Commission on Social Determinants of Health Report, Geneva: WHO.

NINE

Complexity theory, trans-disciplinary working and reflective practice

Fiona McDermott

In this chapter, the argument will be made from a realist perspective that it is at the level of *practice/intervention* that the interconnectedness and interdependency of systems are revealed with particular clarity, confronting practitioners with the reality of what complexity is and means, and its potentially overwhelming impact. In this chapter, the argument is made that the task for human service workers at the service delivery level is to deconstruct complexity, both to make action possible and to enable creative and innovative responses to problems. In particular, the focus of an interdisciplinary team might be on disentangling knowledge, values and interests in order to find common ground for action. A model of reflection-on/in-practice is described, which utilises the interaction of the team itself as a source of insight and the location where the team members' hypotheses for determining actions are shared and examined. The argument for a 'new' type of human service provider, one who is a specialist or expert in working across systems, will be considered with reference to the kind of training that might be required. David Byrne's (1998, 2009) arguments for a realist (post-positivist) perspective on researching complexity will be examined, allied with the work of Pawson and Tilley (1997, 2004).

The real world of the practitioner

Let us begin this discussion of the relationships among complexity theory, interdisciplinary working and reflective practice by considering a fairly typical scenario confronting a social worker in a multidisciplinary health team working in a hospital rehabilitation ward:

Case example: Mrs Li

Mrs Li is a 76-year-old woman of Asian background with English as a second language. She was admitted to hospital for rehabilitation following a fall resulting in a fractured neck of femur (hip); she has a past history of emphysema and a prior stroke. She was unable to walk and has a nasogastric tube that she has forcibly removed herself several times, likely due to confusion. She is heavily reliant on her husband and has limited insight into the level of her own care needs and the impact on her husband. Mrs Li has been on dialysis for the past 16 years. Her main carer is her husband, who is 78 years old and undergoing treatment for cancer. He drives but had a recent car accident that he attributed to stress. Mrs Li wants to return home and her husband also wants her to return home.

Early in the admission, members of the treating team presume that the patient will go to a nursing home. The social worker feels torn as there is pressure to encourage the carer to make a decision at a time when he is unwell and the patient is placing pressure on him to take her home. The social worker is concerned to balance the needs of the patient and carer and to take the role of advocate within the team. The social worker has also expressed anxiety as she will be the person most likely to have to inform the patient and carer of the team recommendation if it is to not return home.

Clearly, this is a complex and complicated situation facing the social worker and the multidisciplinary team, embedded in the 'real' world. As Wolf-Branigin (2013, p xi) comments, it well illustrates the context in which practitioners operate, which he characterises as comprising 'a swirl of data'. The social worker is simultaneously a member of an interdisciplinary team, a member of an organisation and in a relationship with the patient and with the patient's carer. Multiple systems coincide: the client–worker system; the social worker–team system; the team–hospital system; and the social worker–team–hospital–community system. It is a situation where outcomes are uncertain and decisions unclear.

Health service practitioners, like other human service practitioners, are front-line workers who constantly grapple with the tension between individual patient/client needs and the demands and resource limitations of health, social, legal and economic systems. The organisation (in this case, a hospital) comprises the location where the practitioners interact and share information and 'in which the options, decisions, and eventual emergent behaviours emerge' (Wolf-Branigin, 2009, p 118). One activity in which this tension is most significantly to the fore is that sketched in the case example regarding discharge planning for patients (often elderly and/or experiencing a range of chronic complaints) in sub-acute settings where, although their health conditions have stabilised, their continuing fragility requires careful assessment and planning for their rehabilitation and accommodation within community settings.

Complexity, health systems and risk

The health system, then, provides an illustration of what complexity means at the practice level, where social workers (and all health professionals) are faced with determining the 'right' interventions for individual patients amid the 'swirl of data' surrounding them. For example, the complexity of a health problem might be conceptualised in relation to: the illness or disease itself (eg its symptoms, incidence, prevalence, etc); the patient and their family (beliefs about treatment, adherence to treatment, family conflict, etc); the social worker (their accessibility, methods of intervening, etc); the organisational system (the health care team, the team dynamics, disciplinary expertise, etc); the hospital or health care system (eg resources, availability of treatment, care options, etc); health policies (eg health insurance, admission and discharge policies, etc); and the social context (availability of social support, patient's socio-economic status, etc) (Campbell et al, 2007; see also Newhouse and Spring, 2010).

Complicating and adding to these systemic factors is consideration of risk and the health professionals' duty of care towards vulnerable patients, who may, among other health issues, demonstrate limitations in their cognitive capacities for self-determination (Brindle and Holmes, 2005; Atwal, McIntyre and Wiggett, 2012; Denson, Winefield and Beilby, 2012). The generalist, constructivist, perspective that underpins this chapter alerts us to recognising that constructions of risk create a key element informing the decision-making of all stakeholders to the discharge plan.

Each stakeholder may hold different and perhaps conflicting understandings or constructions of the risks involved in discharging a patient, whether their destination be to their own home, a nursing home or other institution. Clarke (2000, p 85) notes:

> practitioners may emphasise the physical domains of risk identification, such as the risk of self-harm or the risk of falling. People with dementia, however, may emphasise biographical domains of risk such as the loss of self-identity,

and family carers may emphasise interpersonal domains such as the loss of a life partner.

There may be little agreement about what the term 'risk' actually means (Stanford, 2010; Phipps et al, 2011; see also Jennings, Chapter Two), but, as McLaughlin (2007, p 1265) points out, risk minimisation constitutes a central theme in much social policy, underpinning notions of regulation and security (Stanford, 2010). Working in contexts permeated by a 'rhetoric of risk' (Stanford, 2010, p 1067) impacts in a potentially coercive way on health professionals', carers' and patients' perceptions and actions, influencing and perhaps constraining what they believe may be in the patient's 'best interests' and simultaneously limiting the patient's freedom to exert his or her own preferences. Their role in risk appraisal thus comprises a combination of objective 'real world' considerations and their own perceptions of risk. As Atwal et al (2012, p 381) point out: 'At the centre of the discharge process is the management of risk, which involves … healthcare professionals managing perceived dangers and determining some dangers are seen as presenting risks while others are not'. Health professionals may fear the blame that may accrue where risks remain unidentified or uncontrolled. Indeed, Stanford (2010, p 1074) argues strongly that social workers may find themselves taking a defensive approach to practice because of the 'overwhelming fear generated by a preoccupation with safety and security as opposed to need'.

In both the UK and Australia (Atwal et al, 2012; Denson et al, 2012), statutory authorities exist that are charged with appointing guardians to make decisions where patients suffer from intellectual impairment, mental disorders, brain injuries, physical disabilities and/or dementia that preclude their capacity to make reasonable decisions about lifestyle, financial or legal matters. While recourse to guardianship may distance the decision-makers from ongoing responsibility for the patient's life, as Denson et al (2012) point out, the journey towards a decision to request appointment of a guardian involves arriving at a compromise over values and beliefs about safety and autonomy, which may well differ among key stakeholders. They are faced with challenging questions to solve: 'What is the risk to be managed?'; 'Who creates the risk and who is subject to it?'; and 'Who defines and controls the risk?' (Phipps et al, 2011, p 279).

For example, in regard to Mrs Li: the physiotherapist may be concerned about the patient's propensity to fall and injure herself should she go home; the social worker may place greater emphasis not on risk, but rather on the patient's right to autonomy and independence;

the carer may be concerned about the pressure on him to monitor the patient's health while being anxious about risks to his own emotional well-being; the patient herself may be currently assessed as having moderate rather than severe dementia and, hence, believe that she should be able to express her freedom to choose where she wishes to live; and the neuropsychologist may believe that the patient's dementia is likely to worsen and, hence, admission to a facility is warranted sooner rather than later. In light of all these ethical and systems-based contingencies, it is clear that both the interventions and the contexts of health service provision are synonymous with complexity.

How to think about complex situations

Complexity theory is concerned with the intersection of systems – individuals (patients), organisations (health treating teams) and institutions (hospitals) – a concern that has been a prevailing analytical focus in classical sociology. The development of complexity theory, characterised by a range of sometimes divergent traditions and approaches, has initiated a rethinking of the concept of system (Byrne, 1989, 2009; Walby, 2003, p 3), within not just sociology, but also many other fields, indicative of its trans-disciplinary relevance. Complexity theory is explanatory theory that explains the changing construction of different systems identified and studied within the natural, biological and social sciences disciplines, which extends our understanding of the world and the way it works (Green and McDermott, 2010). Importantly, complexity theory identifies two interrelated features of systems: the system as self-organising, and the non-linear co-evolution of complex systems adapting to rather than impacting on each other. These changing contexts also constitute the environment for each system.

As we have noted, in the health and social care fields, interventions take place within systems and subsystems that are both mutually independent and interdependent, operating at individual (micro), organisational (meso) and whole-systems (macro) levels. From a realist perspective, context remains central, referring not just to location, but to the interaction of those systems of interpersonal and social relations, biology, technology, and so on. It is the ensuing complexity that generates degrees of uncertainty. Importantly, however, complexity is also associated with patterning (Pawson and Tilley, 2004; Ling, 2012). These patterns comprise those intended and unintended consequences occurring in many and variegated forms. The task (eg of the discharge planning team) is to decipher the configuration of attributes or patterns that produce outcomes (for Mrs Li). In this sense, the intervention (the discharge plan) is context-dependent, with the processes and outcomes being shaped by the particular ways in which systems and subsystems interact.

While systems theory may have been subject to criticism that it proposes a reductive perspective, 'new' systems theory, as revealed in complexity theory, challenges this. The notion of emergence conceptualises linkages at different levels among individuals, structures and systems. Each level coexists and is linked, but elements at each level require specific analysis. For example, sick individuals being treated together may constitute a hospital ward, but both individual and ward would be analysed in distinction from one another, highlighting agency–structure interdependencies, so often a focus of sociologists such as Giddens (1979).

Complexity theory revises the concept of system to grasp the 'unstable and dynamic processes of change' (Walby, 2003, p 17), proposing that changes in complex systems are not unidirectional, but mutually effecting, as such systems co-evolve and adapt to a changing context while simultaneously creating that context. For Byrne (1998, 2009), complexity theory and realism can be comparable, for both recognise the distinctive significance of human agency in social systems and the intersections of social systems with natural ecologies. While the establishment of universal laws of causality may not be possible – with outcomes being the product of multiple causes in interaction and in context – research may enable us to discover what works in particular contexts and, thus, transfer this discovery to other similar contexts. It is the contribution of complexity theory as explanatory theory that enables generalisations to be made. As Pawson and Tilley (2004, p 17) note, a realist approach steers a path between making universal claims about what works and focusing on the particulars of specific measures in specific places relating to specific stakeholders.

Complexity and risk

While complexity theory offers a new and challenging understanding of systems, it is also on a collision course with practices of risk management. Social workers are often seen as 'risk assessors' responsible for identifying and controlling hazards to society (McLaughlin, 2007; Phipps et al, 2011). The task of assessing and thereby presumably averting, or at best managing, risk is essentially a task charged with controlling future events. To attempt to control future events can mean ignoring the pervasiveness of uncertainty and what complexity theory tells us about the capacity for systems to themselves change and adapt. As McLaughlin (2007, p 1265) points out:

> [p]rocedural attempts to reduce uncertainty, especially in a climate in which a concern with risk minimisation is all pervasive ... [may lead] ... to a situation in which there is little room for professional discretion, as failure to follow the correct procedure can leave the worker vulnerable.

In addition, as Stanford (2010, p 1074) points out, a focus on avoiding risk may mean that workers' decisions regarding clients are driven more by concerns with safety (their client's and their own fears of being blamed for adverse outcomes) than with the client's needs. While clients deemed 'high risk' may be subject to restrictions and control (eg Mrs Li may be placed in a nursing home against her wishes), those deemed 'low risk' may be denied services despite their apparent need (eg Mrs Li may be allowed to return to her home with minimal supports or services).

What to do about complexity: the transdisciplinary perspective

Godeman (2008, p 628) notes that transdisciplinary practice 'deals with problems from outside academia which can only be solved through cooperation between academics and practitioners'. Other characteristics of a transdisciplinary perspective – boundary-crossing, orientation to real-life problems, a participatory nature and aiming to develop practical solutions that contribute to the solution of socially-relevant questions – speak clearly to the practitioners' tasks. Pawson and Tilley (2004, p 3), in their account of 'Realist evaluation', emphasise the nature of social programmes as:

> Interventions ... inserted into existing social systems that are thought to underpin and account for present problems. Changes in patterns of behaviour, events or conditions are then generated by bringing fresh inputs to that system in the hope of disturbing and re-balancing it.

As Pawson and Tilley (2004, p 4) note, an intervention is the outcome of many decisions and many decision makers – 'the active engagement of individuals' (Pawson and Tilley, 2004, p 5). Very importantly, in relation to complexity theory, social programmes (or hospital discharge planning) are constantly pushing the adaptation of the many systems involved (family, team, hospital, community) and, thus, are always subject to unanticipated events and unintended consequences. However, simultaneously, the programme or plan arrived at is emergent and self-transformational, changing the very conditions that made it possible in the first place. As Pawson and Tilley (2004, p 9) comment: 'All interventions involve multiple perturbations of pre-existing regularities in behaviours, events or social conditions, leading to the creation of many new regularities'.

As we have noted, in most health settings, an interdisciplinary team of health professionals makes decisions regarding an individual patient's treatment, with the proposition being that such teamwork improves patient outcomes (Newhouse and Spring, 2010, p 309), as the different professions focus their interventions on different aspects of a patient's health needs. As Newhouse and Spring (2010, p 315) comment: 'If patient-centered care is a real goal, and better outcomes result from interdisciplinary practice, then the only rational choice is for multiple disciplines to work together'.

Given that social workers in hospital and many other human service contexts are working with teams comprising others with similar and different perspectives, values, beliefs and purposes, it is likely that the patient's situation under consideration can be investigated in a plurality of ways, and understanding may emerge out of different kinds of knowledge and theorising. As such, this activity lends itself to a trans-disciplinary approach (Russell, 2010, p 38). The trans-disciplinary approach strives to grasp the complexity of a problem, taking into account the diverse perceptions of problems, making links between abstract and case-specific knowledge, and developing descriptive, normative and practical knowledge for the common interest (Hadorn et al, 2010, p 1; see also Fenwick, 2012, p 142; Higginbotham, Albrecht, and Connor, 2001; Plsek and Greenhalgh, 2001; Horlick-Jones and Sime, 2004). Central to developing an interdisciplinary approach to problem-solving is the integration of discipline-specific and practice knowledge. Hadorn, Pohl and Bammer (2010, pp 13–16) identify five core concepts in an interdisciplinary approach to research (which resonate simultaneously with practice contexts) that facilitate trans-disciplinary integration. These are:

1. Shared systems-based thinking, whereby the whole and the parts of a problem are considered in relation to one another by the team.
2. Attention to problem-framing and boundary-setting so that limitations to the scope of the problem addressed are set by the team.

3. Attention to values: these are identified by the team and reflected in the nature of the boundaries set. In the example of Mrs Li, high on the agenda for decision-makers would be analysis by the team of the way risk is to be constructed and understood.

4. Understanding of ignorance and uncertainty: the systems perspective and the boundary-setting initiated facilitate the team's recognition of areas about which nothing may yet be known, or what is known is recognised as partial.

5. Understanding the nature of collaborations: collaboration rests on the team's capacity to harness difference – in ideas, values, understanding, interests and personalities – such that difference enhances rather than destroys collaboration.

Problem-solving in a trans-disciplinary team depends on the extent to which those involved contribute their knowledge and information to the discussion. The more unshared knowledge, that is, (disciplinary) knowledge that is not known to all, is included in the debate, the more comprehensive will be the solution to the problem (Godeman, 2008, p 631). Work is collaborative, requiring self-examination through cycles of self-reflection, and is based on hypothesis generation rather than testing and continuing critical analysis (Wolf-Branigin, 2013, p 7). Importantly, however, issues of power and influence within the team require analysis, and no more so than when questions of risk and its assessment are on the agenda.

How does the multidisciplinary team problem-solve

As was noted earlier, the integration of perspectives across disciplines is vital to the multidisciplinary team's capacity to problem-solve. Godeman (2008, pp 629–38) draws attention to the practicalities of achieving integration, noting that the following factors significantly influence the integration process. First, in order to reach understanding, specialist knowledge needs to be exchanged. With the exchange of specialist knowledge, a common knowledge base is created. This supports the establishment of a shared frame of reference that forms the basis of a group mental model for approaching the problem. Godeman (2008, p 637) comments: 'These [factors] are complemented by the effects of the group situation itself and the capacity of the group to tackle the group process in a reflexive manner' (see also Newhouse and Spring, 2010; Fenwick, 2012, p 150).

As interventions or treatment strategies are built up from a number of components that act both independently and interdependently, the intervention itself may be more accurately thought of as a complex system brought into existence by the health team. As Shiell et al (2008, p 1281) comment:

> the complex systems approach makes us consider the wider ramifications of intervening and to be aware of the interaction that occurs between components of the intervention as well as between the intervention and the context in which it is implemented.

For example, in the case of discharge planning, constructions of risk play a vital role in constraining and enabling decision-making by all health care stakeholders. Indeed, the act of defining risk is, as Phipps et al (2011, p 278) note, an exercise in power, favouring the beliefs and values of those who define and assess it.

The challenge, then, for collaboration between health service providers is to act purposefully in order to bring about the changes and directions that they hypothesise will achieve their proposed goals. This is not primarily a theoretical or academic exercise, for, as Godeman (2008, p 629) notes, it may be 'a project that brings academic cultures into question and discipline-based outlooks into confrontation'. Rather, it is one embedded in the 'real world'. Situations such as that posed by the case example of Mrs Li may mean that the trans-disciplinary team fields questions for itself, similar to those proposed by Pawson and Tilley (2004, p 21) for realist evaluators:

- What do we need to know in formulating discharge plans in this situation? In the case of Mrs Li, the issue of how different stakeholders understand and recognise risk factors would be critical to know.
- What are likely to be the key decisions in implementing this plan?
- Would it work for this patient?
- Are we likely to need to adapt the plan over time?
- How can we track the outcome of the plan over time?
- How can we track the plan and keep it on track?

Trans-disciplinary working

Lawrence and Despres (2004, p 401) point out that trans-disciplinary approaches require a shift in thinking, concepts and methods, moving from 'disciplinary divisions (which search for the unity of knowledge) to collaborative deconstruction (which seeks coherence)'. As Newhouse and Spring (2010, p 313) note, this requires major shifts in philosophy within disciplines: 'The challenge is that the professions need to learn to communicate, understand each others' language, ideally develop a shared language, and learn to coordinate their actions as a team' (Newhouse and Spring, 2010, p 315). Thus, the task for human service workers at the service delivery level may be to deconstruct complexity, both to make action possible and to enable creative and innovative responses to problems. In particular, the focus of an interdisciplinary team might be on disentangling knowledge, values and interests in order to find common ground for action. Indeed, what emerges from the interaction of the team itself is a source of insight for reflection-on-practice and reflection-in-practice. Together, practitioners might ask: 'What is it that we are observing?'; 'How are we observing?'; 'What do we know?'; and 'What do we know because of our observations?' (Wolf-Branigin, 2009, p 122).

This suggests adoption of a process of 'thinking through' the discharge plan a patient will have to travel, cognisant of the critical nature of the context and the priority on patient safety, and sensitive to the likelihood that each plan may differ in its development and delivery. Pawson and Tilley (2004) offer the metaphor of the 'highway code' as a way of assisting evaluators to 'think through' their programme. Again, this translates well to the discharge planning team. The highway code alerts them to the problems that they might expect to confront and some of the safest measures to deal with these issues: 'the highway-code does not tell you how to drive but how to survive the journey by knowing when, where and for what to keep your eyes peeled' (Pawson and Tilley, 2004, p 21).

A model of reflection-in/on-practice

As we have discussed, complexity theory tells us that systems evolve and interact in often unpredictable ways. However, understood from within a realist perspective, social actors are alerted to the centrality of context and the patterning characterising that context. While the practice of reflexivity by itself cannot deliver either certainty or control, utilising strategies that focus on reducing what the actors might identify as key uncertainties may do so. Practitioners require a capacity to make sense of what is relevant, for example, how a particular intervention works within the dynamics of this particular setting and this particular context. Practitioners delivering complex interventions such as devising a discharge plan for Mrs Li are in a position to learn and adapt, to reflexively seek to make sense of the systems in which they are acting, perhaps changing how they work as they increase their understanding of the consequences of their actions. Indeed, their behaviour will be shaped by how they reflect upon these systems and adapt their behaviour in light of this experience.

This requires them to structure their reflections-in/on-practice by asking questions such as those proposed by Ling (2012, p 84): 'How do these factors (eg Mrs Li's cognitive decline, Mr Li's ill-health) interact with each other?' and 'How might these interactions change over time, and to what extent are they amenable to intentional change?' Ling (2012, p 85) comments:

> Rather than seeing an intervention as a fixed sequence of activities, organised in linear form, capable of being duplicated and repeated ... an intervention [includes] a process of reflection and adaptation as the characteristics of the complex systems become more apparent to practitioners.

Practitioners can then be 'held to account for their intelligent adaptation rather than slavishly adhering to a set of instructions' (Ling, 2012, p 85).

The discharge planning multidisciplinary team's reflections might begin with recognition of the importance of identifying, exposing and reducing the uncertainties that challenge them, for example: 'How quickly will Mrs Li's cognitive capacities decline?'; 'In what ways do Mr Li's health problems interfere with his abilities to provide care for her?'; 'How available and appropriate are the resources in the community for supporting the couple?'; and 'How well does the team communicate?'

The team might collaborate by sharing what Ling (2012, p 87) describes as 'contribution stories', which aim to surface and outline how those involved in the intervention understand the causal pathways connecting the intervention to its intended outcomes. The purpose of sharing 'contribution stories' is to capture the narratives of practitioners, assisting them to describe how their activities can produce intended and unintended outcomes. This is an exercise in outlining and exploring their thinking about how different aspects of a proposed intervention interact with each other and with other systems, an exercise that might enable the identification of key uncertainties associated with the intervention – those anticipated causal linkages for which there may be limited evidence or even ignorance.

'Contribution stories' are drawn from those more abstract and perhaps rarely evoked 'theories of change' (Ling, 2012) that practitioners hold, and which explain (to the practitioner) how he or she connects resources and actions to outcomes. Articulating these 'theories of change' provides a starting point for reflection. As the team listens to its members' analysis of the case, the contribution stories and theories of change that motivate members, a plan emerges. The uncertainties and areas of ignorance, ambiguity or limited evidence are surfaced. Hypotheses are generated about likely outcomes, perhaps with reference to the patterns discernible in other similar cases. Once put in place, the discharge plan for Mrs Li, conceptualised as the construction of a system, will be revisited as it starts to emerge and evolve within this particular context. Ongoing and future reflections might address four questions:

1. How is (or did) the team working together?
2. What might (or could) have happened to Mrs Li had the plan/system not been put in place?
3. How does (or did) the plan/system contribute to achieving the goals intended for Mrs Li?
4. Might there be (or have been) other or different ways of achieving these goals?

A 'new' human service practitioner?

Complexity theory offers a new and very different view of the world, but, arguably, a view that accords closely with the 'lived experience' of many practitioners who daily face the 'swirl of data' as they attempt to act strategically, ethically and purposefully in their clients' interests. Not only does complexity theory explain the world more closely in line with our experiences of the world, but it simultaneously challenges us to think about how our professional knowledge bases have traditionally prepared us to practice. Indeed, complexity theory highlights the limitations of traditional discipline-specific knowledge, suggesting that new models of professional practice are required. Currently, there are international efforts to advance inter-professional education (eg the World Health Organization's Framework for Action on Interprofessional Education and Collaborative Practice: http:/www.who.int/hrh/nursing_midwifery/en/). The purpose of the World Health Organization's Framework is to provide policymakers with a broad understanding of how inter-professional education and collaborative practice might work in a global context. The Framework proposes an agenda that 'includes developing supportive management practices; changing the culture and attitudes of health care workers; identifying and supporting champions; revising curricula; and enacting legislation to eliminate barriers to collaborative practice' (Newhouse and Spring, 2010, p 310).

Interestingly, Cooper, Braye and Geyer (2004) propose that complexity theory itself can provide a theoretical framework to underpin professional education. As such, with its explanation of the emergent, uncertain, diverse and self-organising characteristics of systems, it poses a clear alternative to the 'orderly linear framework' (Cooper et al, 2004, p 182) that dominates professional training in the health and social care fields. These authors conclude that 'a complexity framework can provide the scaffolding on which to build IPE [interprofessional education]' (Cooper et al, 2004, p 187).

Eight years on, Fenwick (2012) argues for professionals to learn about collaboration both *in* and *for* practice, that is, to use complexity science both to explain and to educate (Fenwick, 2012, p 143). The teaching of complexity principles in curricula can provide insight about complex systems of practice and a new awareness of the possibilities for action (Fenwick, 2012, p 149). Reporting on a study of a 'complexity-infused curriculum' by McMurtry in 2007, Fenwick (2012, p 150) notes that participants learned to manage difference and diversity rather than seeking harmony and consensus in their inter-professional practice, while also 'learning to make explicit the important disciplinary distinctions among their very different epistemologies, material practices and identities' (Fenwick, 2012, p 150). These abilities, as we noted earlier, are essential to achieving the integration identified as central to trans-disciplinary practice.

The contribution of complexity theory as a theoretical foundation for practice suggests the emergence of a 'new' type of human service provider: one who is a specialist or expert in working across and within systems. In the health field, the kind of training that might be required would include such things as: shared education and assessment tasks with other student health professionals, for example, doctors, physiotherapists and social workers; the provision of opportunities to develop and share analytical frameworks for addressing ethical issues in practice, especially in relation to matters of risk, autonomy and patient safety; training in coping and working with unpredictability and uncertainty; and skills in reflective practice, especially in relation to reflective practice within teams. The kinds of knowledge and skills that social workers (and other health professionals) require when practising in contexts characterised as unpredictable and uncertain (complex) are: an understanding of complex systems and complexity theory (see Sanger and Giddings, 2012); capacities to work across disciplinary boundaries in light of understanding something of the nature of complex systems and what they 'look like' at the practice level; arriving at an understanding of intervention strategies themselves as systems (non-linear, emergent, self-organising), and what this means in terms of the potential to predict and control outcomes; skills in critical reflection-on/in-practice in order to recognise the interpersonal elements in team encounters and make the contest over values, knowledge and interests itself a focus for analysis; and capacities to engage in divergent and creative thinking in order to provide the flexibility essential for the dynamic and adaptive system-in-the-making that is itself the intervention.

Newhouse and Spring (2010, p 311) contribute to this discussion by proposing the adoption of the Evidence Based Behavioral Practice (EBBP) model, which supports evidence-based shared decision-making on inter-professional health teams. This model is purposefully interdisciplinary, relying on an ecological framework as its conceptual foundation. From an ecological perspective, the EBBP posits that in order to promote change, one must influence multiple 'levels', which include the interpersonal, organisational, community and public policy.

Conclusion

Complexity theory assists human service providers to understand and name the problems, challenges and struggles their clients face. Simultaneously, it also provides mental models and strategies for working collaboratively and purposefully across disciplinary divides, and in partnership with service users, to bring about change and enhanced quality of life. As Wolf-Branigin (2009, p 124) comments: '[a]pplying complexity is about developing our knowledge, skills, and ability to understand the interconnectedness and exigencies present within our clients' systems'. Practice contexts characterised by risk discourses, such as those in the health and criminal justice fields, further challenge service providers and service recipients to recognise the ways in which their actions may be constrained, alerting them to the need to find solutions that maximise the freedom of all stakeholders and minimise the potential for coercion, with its implications for defensive rather than needs-driven interventions. Above all, the implications of complexity theory for the development of social policies that draw from contemporary understanding of the nature of systems, and the uncertainty, adaptation and contingency that characterise them, demand consideration.

Practitioners working in the 'real' world encounter first hand and on a daily basis the implications and meaning of complexity. In this chapter, we have chosen an example of a health team planning the discharge of a frail and elderly patient to explore how the insights of complexity theory might inform their actions. The interaction of systems operating at individual (micro), organisational (meso) and whole-systems (macro) levels confronts them. Their accountability in relation to discourses and policies of risk, and the different discipline-specific knowledge they bring to their work, further compound the task. Importantly, however, their collaboration, despite their different perspectives and understanding, presents opportunities to resource and enrich the team's deliberations as they work towards arriving at the 'best possible' plan for the patient. A model of reflection-in/on-practice, derived from an understanding of complexity theory, has been described, providing guidance to their collaborative work. Such a model suggests that the insights of complexity theory and the realities of contemporary practice demand a 'new' human service practitioner: one whose training and practice is shaped by complexity theory, whose focus is not limited by disciplinary boundaries, and whose expertise lies in a capacity to work across and within systems.

References

Atwal, A., McIntyre, A., and Wiggett, C. (2012) 'Risks with older adults in acute care settings: UK occupational therapists' and physiotherapists' perceptions of risks associated with discharge and professional practice', *Scandinavian Journal of Caring Sciences*, doi: 10.1111/scs.2012.26.issue_2/issuetoc, pp 381-93.

Brindle, N. and Holmes, J. (2005) 'Capacity and coercion: dilemmas in the discharge of older people with dementia from general hospital settings', *Age and Ageing*, vol 34, pp 16–20.

Byrne, D. (1998) *Complexity theory and the social sciences: an introduction*, London: Routledge.

Byrne, D. (2009) 'Working within a complexity frame of reference – the potential of "integrated methods" for understanding transformation in complex social systems', contribution towards the CFSC Consortium's paper for UNAIDS on expanding the monitoring and evaluation of Social Change Communication for HIV/AIDS prevention, July.

Campbell, N.E., Murray, E., Darbyshire, J., Emery, J., Farmer, A., Griffiths, F., Guthrie, B., Lester, H., Wilson, P. and Kinmouth, A.L. (2007) 'Designing and evaluating complex interventions to improve health care', *British Medical Journal*, vol 334, no 7591, pp 455–9.

Clarke, C.L. (2000) 'Risk: constructing care and care environments in dementia', *Health, Risk & Society*, vol 2, no 1, pp 83–93.

Cooper, H., Braye, S. and Geyer, R. (2004) 'Complexity and interprofessional education', *Learning in Health & Social Care*, vol 3, no 4, pp 179–89.

Denson, L.A., Winefield, H.R. and Beilby, J.J. (2012) 'Discharge-planning for long-term care needs: the values and priorities of older people, their younger relatives and health professionals', *Scandinavian Journal of Caring Science*, doi: 10.1111/j.1471-6712.2012.00987.x

Fenwick, T. (2012) 'Complexity science and professional learning for collaboration: a critical reconsideration of possibilities and limitations', *Journal of Education and Work*, vol 25, no 1, pp 142–62.

Giddens, A. (1979) *Central problems in social theory*, Berkeley, CA: University of California Press.

Godeman, J. (2008) 'Knowledge integration: a key challenge for transdisciplinary cooperation', *Environmental Education Research*, vol 14, no 6, pp 625–41.

Green, D. and McDermott, F. (2010) 'Social work from inside and between complex systems: perspectives on person-in-environment for today's social work', *British Journal of Social Work*, vol 40, no 8, pp 1–17.

Hadorn, G.H., Pohl, C. and Bammer, G. (2010) 'Solving problems through transdisciplinary research', in J. Frodeman, J. Thompson Klein and C. Mitcham (eds) *The Oxford handbook of interdisciplinarity*, New York, NY: Oxford University Press.

Higginbotham, N., Albrecht, G. and Connor, L. (2001) *Health social science: a transdisciplinary and complexity perspective*, Melbourne: OUP.

Horlick-Jones, T. and Sime, J. (2004) 'Living on the border: knowledge, risk and transdisciplinarity', *Futures*, vol 36, pp 441–56.

Lawrence, L. and Despres, C. (2004) 'Futures of transdisciplinarity', *Futures*, vol 36, pp 397-405.

Ling, T. (2012) 'Evaluating complex and unfolding interventions in real time', *Evaluation*, vol 18, no 1, pp 79–91.

McLaughlin, K. (2007) 'Regulation and risk in social work: the General Social Care Council and the Social Care Register in context', *British Journal of Social Work*, vol 37, pp 1263–77.

Newhouse, R.P. and Spring, B. (2010) 'Interdisciplinary evidence-based practice: moving from silos to synergy', *Nursing Outlook*, vol 58, pp 309–17.

Pawson, R. and Tilley, N. (1997) *Realist evaluation*, New York, NY: Sage.

Pawson, R. and Tilley, N. (2004) 'Realist evaluation'. Available at: www.communitymatters.com.au/RE_chapter.pdf

Phipps, D.L., Noyce, P.R., Walshe, K., Parker, D. and Ashcroft, D.M. (2011) 'Risk-based regulation of healthcare professionals: what are the implications for pharmacists?', *Health, Risk & Society*, vol 13, no 3, pp 277–92.

Plsek, P.E and Greenhalgh, T. (2001) 'The challenge of complexity in health care', *British Medical Journal*, vol 323, pp 625–8.

Russell, J.Y. (2010) 'A philosophical framework for an open and critical transdisciplinary inquiry', in V.A. Brown, J.A. Harris and J.Y. Russell (eds) *Tackling wicked problems through the transdisciplinary imagination*, Earthscan Books: London.

Sanger, M. and Giddings, M.M. (2012) 'Teaching note: a simple approach to complexity theory', *Journal of Social Work Education*, vol 48, no 2, pp 369–75.

Shiell, A., Hawe, P. and Gold, L. (2008) 'Complex interventions or complex systems? Implications for health economic evaluation', *British Medical Journal*, vol 336, pp 1281–1283 (June), doi: 10.1136/ bmj.39569.510521.AD

Stanford, S. (2010) '"Speaking back" to fear: responding to the moral dilemmas of risk in social work practice', *British Journal of Social Work*, vol 40, pp 1065–80.

Walby, S. (2003) 'Complexity theory, globalisation and diversity', paper presented to conference of the British Sociological Association, University of York, April.

Wolf-Branigin, M. (2009) 'Applying complexity and emergence in social work education', *Journal of Social Work Education*, vol 28, no 2, pp 115–27.

Wolf-Branigin, M. (2013) *Using complexity theory for research and program evaluation*, New York, NY: OUP.

TEN

Probation practice and creativity in England and Wales: a complex systems analysis

Aaron Pycroft

Introduction

The Probation Service in England and Wales occupies a unique role in the delivery of criminal justice, with probation staff having multiple roles, including being agents of public protection and enforcement, as well as promoters of rehabilitation and looking after the needs of the victims of crime. To fulfil these roles, the Probation Service has always worked across boundaries and, as argued by Gough (2010, p 21), this position 'has made effective working relationships essential with sentencers, police and prison officers, and a whole host of organisations in the voluntary and community sector'. This chapter will explore the changing nature of probation practice in England and Wales through a critical analysis of the multiple and complex roles of practitioners, and examine whether it is possible for practitioners to maintain these roles in a state of 'superposition' (see later) or whether they are, in fact, contradictory giving rise to unintended and damaging consequences. This analysis of the work of the Probation Service will identify three levels of system, which are complex and adaptive in nature (while acknowledging from a realist and general complexity perspective that all complex systems are nested (fractal) in nature, and that the boundaries of any system are unclear, and also that any system or subsystem has influence beyond what the boundaries may be): the policy system, the organisational system of the probation trust and the individual practitioner–probationer[1] relationship. In this discussion, I want to explore the creative and novel solutions that can be found at 'the edge of chaos' through engaging in necessary, just and virtuous[2] relationships with probationers, which draw upon a realist understanding of the relationships between determinism, order for free and emergence. A key focus for the chapter is that some of the tools and concepts and ways of working that are already familiar in criminal justice and social work are sensitive to working with complexity. In that sense, this approach represents an evolution rather than a revolution.

The policy context

The 2010 establishment of the Conservative–Liberal Democrat Coalition government in the UK has seen the beginnings of changes in social work, child protection and probation practice after the centrally driven national service framework approach of the New Labour governments (1997–2010). In part, these changes have been brought about (it has been argued) due to the need to address significant economic and financial problems, but also due to concerns about the efficiency of the centralism and target culture of the New Labour years. Changes in social work were instigated following the publication of the Munro Review (Department of Education, 2011): the Probation Service in England and Wales is going through a process of significant change that is seeing the monopoly of that service being broken up to provide opportunities for a wider range of agencies to become involved in offender rehabilitation on 'a payment by results (PBR) basis' (Ministry of Justice, 2013). There is much debate about PBR and its efficacy in criminal justice (see, eg, Fox and Albertson, 2011), but it is perhaps indicative of the fact that the government has realised that outputs are rarely proportional to inputs and, from their point of view, it is much better to offload the risk onto other agencies, who can also take the blame and cuts in funding if their approaches do not work, meaning that the government can keep its reputation intact.

Within criminal justice, the priority for the government is a reduction in reoffending and serious further offences (SFO) by those already convicted of a crime. The Offender Management Model (OMM) (NOMS, 2006, p 8) argues that:

> for many – perhaps most – offenders, the relationship with the correctional services is rather … complex. It often involves consecutive, and sometimes concurrent phases and sentences, each of which brings with it a change in the legal context, and often in the physical and organisational ones too.

This model, which is still extant, is designed to provide a single, universal, core, end-to-end process that transcends the contributions of the main providers and, crucially, identifies a tiered structure (see Table 10.1), which determines that resources follow the potential risk, so that the higher the risk, the higher the resources allocated to that particular 'offender'.

Table 10.1: Tiering of offenders under the Offender Management Model

Tier	Offender Profile	Role of Offender Manager
1	Medium- or low-risk harm cases Low likelihood of reoffending cases Low intervention cases requiring monitoring of risk factors only Compliant offenders who are well-motivated to complete the sentence Offenders who present no manageability problems Cases in which punishment is or has become the main objective	Punish
2	Rehabilitation cases in which the focus of work is on the offender's situation Rehabilitation cases with less complex intervention plans Reasonably motivated, reasonably compliant offenders Medium or low risk of harm Resettlement/reintegration cases where practical help is the intervention approach	Punish and help
3	Medium/high likelihood of reoffending cases with multi-factor intervention plans Medium risk of harm cases Cases with personal change as the primary objective Cases requiring high levels of integrative work Cases in which mishandling would have significant organisational consequences Vulnerable offenders	Punish and help and change
4	High and very high risk of serious harm cases – public protection priorities Cases requiring the highest level of skill, qualification and organisational authority Cases requiring unusual or exceptional resource allocation Cases requiring very high levels of inter-agency work High local and national priority cases (prolific and/or persistent offenders)	Punish and help and change and control

Source: NOMS (2006)

Despite the aspiration to provide a range of interventions (particularly at the highest level), in practice, there is a hegemonic approach to risk and risk aversion (see particularly Case and Haines, Chapter Six; see also Hassett and Stevens, Chapter Five) that sees probation officer activity being reduced to control, surveillance and defensible decision-making (see Gough, 2010, 2012). With regard to reoffending, this is self-defeating, with the evidence suggesting that the majority of SFOs are committed by those designated as lower-tier offenders (see Nash and Williams, 2008; Craissati and Sindall, 2009). A complexity perspective tells us that this happens because the higher-tier offenders attract the resources and legislative responses (such as Multi Agency Public Protection Arrangements (MAPPA)) and duty to comply by key organisations (see Clift, 2010, 2012), meaning that lower-tier offenders who are typified by complex and multiple medical, psychological and social needs receive a relative lack of attention, leading to 'order for free' (see Pycroft, Chapter One; see also Grieve, Chapter Seven).

So, while on the surface the changes to probation practice being instigated by the current government may be more promising through a perturbation of the system, a complexity perspective argues that they will, in fact, either exacerbate those failures or, at best, maintain the status quo. This is because of the existence of power laws (see Hassett and Stevens, Chapter Five) and the reality that highly deterministic systems will always replace the 'heavy end' (for a discussion in relation to alcohol problems, see also Holder, 1999) because of 'order for free' at the 'lower end'. It may be appropriate, for example, to focus resources on the most 'dangerous' offenders if they were being incentivised to change, but actually quite the opposite happens, with relatively routine, systemic, monitoring, surveillance and bureaucratic work carried out by the most qualified practitioners. Also, the government is planning that all prisoners (even very short-term ones) receive 12 months' probation (Ministry of Justice, 2013); again, these will be given to market providers, so the same problems apply because of an increase in complexity.

Protecting the public from high-risk offenders is, of course, important and the evidence does suggest that engaging creatively with high-risk offenders can indeed bring about changes (see Maden, 2007). However, we need to understand the determinism of the system and develop approaches that, in practice, do not differentiate between ideals of risk management on the one hand, and rehabilitative ideals on the other. Having good, well-run interventions delivered by highly qualified and motivated staff at the lower-tier level is itself good risk management and crime prevention and will save money in the longer term.

Also, with regard to PBR and multiplicity and complexity of need, how is a successful result determined, should, for example, a probation officer view the fact that a secure tenancy or employment is indicative of progress despite still being convicted for the use of illicit substances? Additionally, the evidence suggests that the consequences of the current arrangements of PBR will inevitably lead to organisational 'gaming of the system' through being 'creative' with outcomes, which might, in part, involve refusing to work with more complex cases, or creaming off less serious cases (see Maynard et al, 2011) and offloading and up-tariffing to the Probation Service to offload the risk (see Jennings and Pycroft, 2012). A report by the Institute for Government (Gash et al, 2013) provides clear evidence of the ways in which this happens across social policy areas where delivery is made by market providers. With the plans for criminal justice, the 'market providers' will inevitably have to cut costs as there will be delays in when payments are made (see Maynard et al, 2011) (and the government has not decided how these funding mechanisms will work).

Organisational complexity

One of the commonalities for organisations and professionals involved in these systems is that they have come to focus primarily on information flows to aid in the practice of risk assessment. Recent developments in information theory and complexity theory show us that information flows are essential in human services, but that we need to understand that 'Knowledge is not a "thing," or a system, but an ephemeral, active process of relating' (Snowden, 2002, p 5) that cannot be stored, controlled or managed.

It has been observed by Max Weber that the only kind of power that we know of is bureaucratic power (MacIntyre, 2011), and this is evident in the narrow positivist, reductionist and essentially static approaches to information flow to be found in probation and other public services. This is typified by a practitioner either sitting behind a computer in an office (with respect to social work, see, eg, the Department for Education, 2011; for probation, see House of Commons Justice Committee, 2011), or when talking with service users, or probationers being entirely systems-driven. For example, in an article for the *Guardian* newspaper, Lowe (2013) cites a study by Hilary Cottom of 'what social workers spend their time doing':

> Spending time alongside social workers, such as Ryan, who works with Ella's son Tom, we saw that 86% of time

is system driven – filling in forms for accountability and discussing them with colleagues. Most shockingly, even the 14% of time spent face to face with a family member is not developmental. The dialogue between Ryan and Tom is dictated by the forms and their need for data and information. This squeezes out any possibility of the sort of conversation that might be needed to develop a supportive relationship as a first step in fostering change.

These bureaucratic approaches fail to understand the need to creatively engage with self-organising processes (see Wolf-Branigin, Chapter Four), which, in themselves, provide a means for the organisation to better achieve its aims in its responsibilities to society and the state.

In Table 10.2, the key features of the mechanistic/bureaucratic systems developed during the 'what works' era are outlined. From a complex systems perspective, the centralised, monolithic approach of the 'what works' era demonstrates a drive towards equilibrium and consequent systemic failures primarily through the imposition of negative control mechanisms. The table also summarises the impact, advantages and possibilities that an application of complexity theory has for probation practice. The move towards strengths-based approaches and also desistance strategies is already under way in probation (see Lewis, Chapter Eleven; see also Case and Haines, Chapter Six); however, there is a danger of using this in a reductionist manner by, for example, arguing that all that is required is to ensure housing and employment to reduce reoffending. My argument is that a whole-systems approach recognises a whole range of bio-psychosocial and deterministic factors that can lead to offending and reoffending. I would, for example, use my own practice experience of working with people who have substance misuse problems for whom the provision of a house or a job, or inclusion back into their families, do not in themselves necessarily prevent relapse, or further offending.

Organisational creativity: a case study[3]

There are some good examples of organisational creativity, but which, by definition – and their proximity to the edge of chaos, and the drive to equilibrium through negative control mechanisms – tend to be short-lived. For example, the Unified Adolescent Team (UAT) was an innovative project set up in 2002 to work with adolescents between the ages of 12 and 20 as a small multidisciplinary team designed to work creatively with young people who have the most severe and complex

Table 10.2: Comparing paradigms

Newtonian-Cartesian paradigm *Essentially mechanistic*	Influence on probation practice ('what works' era)	Complexity science paradigm *Essentially dynamic/self-organising*	Potential for influence on probation practice (post-'what works')
Positivist methodology	Reductionist, RCT, experimental design, reduce background noise leading to poor outcomes	Mixed methods, quantitative/qualitative, exploration of background noise	Cumulative gains, higher-order potential
Linear	Dosage principle	Non-linear	Whole-systems (case management) approach at reasonable level of system abstraction
Controllable	Manually based enforceable didactic programmes/priority on programme integrity	Uncontrollable	Work with group process, build professional relationship
Centralised	Creation of National Probation Service – contestability	Networked providers	Mutual cooperation between agencies
Hierarchical	Targets for compliance and completion of orders and programmes and crime reduction	Non-hierarchical	Democratic organisation, locally agreed targets based on local populations
Limited connectivity	In-house, narrowly focused psychological programmes	Highly connected	Social networks, recovery memes
Uniformity	Accredited programmes appeal to rationalist science	Diversity	Heterodox interventions (including faith-based), self-organised criticality

Table 10.2: (cont)

Newtonian-Cartesian paradigm *Essentially mechanistic*	Influence on probation practice ('what works' era)	Complexity science paradigm *Essentially dynamic/self-organising*	Potential for influence on probation practice (post-'what works')
Cause and effect	Correct dosage = desired outcome	Effect and effect	Importance of practitioner characteristics
Predictable	Actuarial risk assessment tools (ie OASys and OGRS)	Unpredictable	Combined clinical and actuarial assessment
Reductionist	Narrow focus on cognitive-behavioural psychology	Holistic	Building human/social capital, developing desistance strategies
Objective explanation	Rational choice	Subjective and objective explanation	Emergent outcomes
Entity-focused	Crime reduction	Process-focused	Desistance/incentives
Correlation	Criminogenic need, sequencing interventions	Patterning /fractals/self-similarity	Matrix of needs, path dependency, probationer-led interventions
Highly preclusive	Resources follow risk	Highly inclusive	Power laws
System in equilibrium	Negative feedback and lack of embeddedness	System on the 'edge of chaos'	Positive feedback and embeddedness
Attractors are cyclical, fixed point, spiral	Limitation of activity and phase space activity	Strange	Multiple influences and phase space activity
Ethics	Utilitarian/deontological justifies use of coercion	Virtue ethics	Human flourishing as outcome of justice

Source: Adapted from McMillan and Carlisle (2003).
Notes: RCT = randomised controlled trial; OASys = offender assessment system; OGRS = offender group reconviction scale

needs. It is an example of how teams can work effectively when freed from control structures to meet cross-cutting needs across the whole system. The UAT had the following referral criteria, with all of the five criteria needing to be met for the UAT to work with the individual:

1. Aged between 12th and 20th birthday.
2. Demonstrating a significant degree of psychological disturbance relating to adolescent development or serious mental illness.
3. High-risk behaviours, including some of the following: repeated self-harm, lawbreaking, drug and alcohol abuse, excessive dangerous behaviour.
4. Social instability – unstable home placements.
5. A significant history of inconsistent education.

This service brought together professionals from Child and Adolescent Mental Health Services (CAMHS), children's services, educational psychology and youth offending organisations into a single team and was (as far as we know) unique in the focus that it took. The UAT was relatively resource-heavy and focused on a small number of cases (approximately 40 new cases per annum), which was perceived as financially unsustainable in the longer term (it was incorporated into wider service provision in 2010). At the inception of the UAT, the intention was to provide an accessible and useful service that might engage in effective relationships with young people who had previously found it impossible to engage in a process of therapeutic change, and, importantly, to give consistency and stability to the young person by mirroring the advice, support and clinical supervision given to other professionals and their support structures in 'parent' agencies. Also, collaborative relationship-building with senior managers in all the relevant agencies was fundamental as they understood the disproportionate clinical risks and budgetary impact coming from a small number of young people with complex needs. The same small number of children were known to all of the key agencies, and there was a sense among all of those agencies that they could do something better for the cases through a collaborative service. As a consequence of these insights, the UAT was recognised as a service that would frequently need to work outside of the usual frameworks and bureaucratic constraints that were put upon other teams. Collaborative work between agencies underpinned the ethos of the clinical work that followed and despite the autonomy given, collective responsibility was assured, with inter-agency management and oversight being explicitly observed and ongoing for the full eight years of the project.

This example demonstrates the importance of the organisational aspects of working in systems and the need for creativity and novel solutions that are found at the edge of chaos, which is planned and organised, not unordered. Furthermore, our research on this project (using a phenomenological methodology) (Pycroft et al, 2013) demonstrated the efficacy of these approaches in bringing self-organisation to people who were in crisis and out of control. This was achieved by the service users through developing new helping relationships with the UAT workers, which enabled them to build new lives. Importantly, this service delivery was not distorted by the attractors of competition and profit *or* an overriding concern with risk and risk aversion; rather, the UAT recognised the importance of precisely taking risks to gain results for those concerned and of mutual and democratic working.

Practitioner creativity

When a probationer or service user presents with a multiplicity of need, complexity theory shows us the importance of thinking in a non-linear and non-reductionist way. If we take a crude reductionist approach as defined by the use of simplistic risk assessment tools (such as OASys) that seek to identify that which is 'criminogenic' so as to 'prioritise' and 'sequence' interventions, then the loss of 'background noise' cuts out important and relevant aspects of their life, leaving a useless abstracted model. Also, there is an issue for practitioners when we assume that our implicit model of the world – whether it is, for example, cognitive, behavioural, theistic, psychodynamic, humanist (or any of the many variations of) – is a true reflection of reality, but which, in fact, can be another example of epistemic fallacy (see Pycroft, Chapter One). This presents us with the problem of the ways in which our tacit skills and assumptions, the sense we make of the situation, and our methodological training and rigour may well distort the task at hand. This point is nicely illustrated by the 'outcome equivalence paradox' in substance misuse treatment (see Orford, 2008), which shows that very different (but well-run) interventions (such as motivational enhancement therapy, cognitive-behavioural therapy, 12-step facilitation, social and behavioural network therapy) have very similar outcomes; there is no superior approach but neither is there any advantage in matching people to specific interventions. This equivalence seems to extend to criminal justice interventions for substance misuse as well (see evidence from the Drug Treatment Outcome Research Study[4]). From my own practice experience, it was also evidenced by the fact that service users saw no problem in accessing, for example, a cognitive-behavioural therapy programme during the day and Alcoholics Anonymous meetings in the evening.

So, what can explain this outcome equivalence? As a realist, I accept that in working with complex issues such as addiction, there are core principles of working that take into account the dynamic and evolutionary nature of the problems upon which effective, good, ethical and just approaches are based; it is not a case of anything works (and with respect to substance misuse, for example, punishment does not work; see Miller, 2006). Significant progress has been made in identifying core processes of change in relation to addiction and how these relate to bio-psychosocial components. The key psychological processes are motivation and self-efficacy, which can be acquired without recourse to formal interventions (see Arrigo and Wiliams, Chapter Twelve), but when people present for services, the key ingredients are the ways in which those services are delivered. Orford's (2008) explanation for the outcome equivalence paradox is based upon the characteristics of those providing the services, with all the evidence suggesting the importance of open, listening, trusting and empathic professional relationships (see Pycroft, 2010, 2012).

This evidence presents a series of problems for service delivery, which case management models have been developed to try and address: addressing multiplicity of need; assessment (Universal or specialist?); determining which agencies should be involved (Generic or specialist?); knowing where to start (Who is the lead agency?); prioritising resources (Who pays?); and determining what constitutes a good outcome (Who decides?). A key problem is that the more fragmented the service delivery with mechanisms of control and accountability, then the more fragmented the information flow. To address the complexity of these problems, there does need to be a diverse range of responses. Ashby's Law of Requisite Variety,[5] for example, recognises the importance of diversity to survive in the ecological/evolutionary environment; likewise, with organisations, if they over-focus on one-size-fits-all models, then they stagnate and are ineffective. However, from a realist perspective, increased diversity also increases complexity, and therefore, to an extent, it is important to try and reduce some of the complexity to a reasonable level of abstraction so that it can be worked with (see McDermott, Chapter Nine).

In Figure 10.1, I am attempting to examine the relationships between multiple needs that are examples covering a bio-psychosocial perspective where it is not possible to reduce those elements (themselves, fractal in nature) to linear relationships of cause and effect in time and space.

This model indicates the importance of the severity of the problems (depth), the number of variables involved, the system robustness and its energy across the arrow of time. This model is also indicative of entropy in the sense that loss of energy leads to increasing complexity and dissipation of the system and might also approximate to the 'rock bottom' metaphor of 12-step programmes. However, importantly, we know that this is not a one-way process and that with the correct supports, people can become fully functioning members of society, and so the arrow goes both ways in Figure 10.1.[6] It is my contention that in working with multiple needs, the language of strange attractors (sometimes called chaotic attractors) becomes useful. A strange attractor is one in which we can see patterns and regularities in the phase space (see Jennings, Chapter Two), but, in fact, the system never follows the

Figure 10.1: Multiple needs and their approximation to a strange attractor

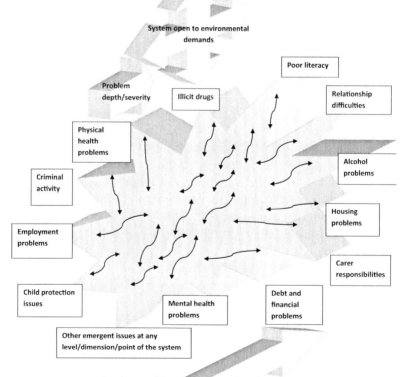

System open to environmental demands

Poor literacy

Problem depth/severity

Illicit drugs

Relationship difficulties

Physical health problems

Alcohol problems

Criminal activity

Housing problems

Employment problems

Carer responsibilities

Child protection issues

Mental health problems

Debt and financial problems

Other emergent issues at any level/dimension/point of the system

The robustness of the system across time/sensitivity to initial conditions same trajectory through the phase space. This chaotic motion is one of both expansion and contraction and operates in more than one dimension; there is order and control, although each order parameter is affected by the behaviour of other order parameters (Guastello and Liebovitch, 2009). These attractors are prone to bifurcate, which is a pattern of instability in which the system becomes increasingly chaotic (complex) by accessing new types of dynamical states; this is not cause and effect, but effect and effect, the fact that outcomes have further knock-on effects. In considering Figure 10.1, the system as a whole is a strange attractor, which is drawing in two or more points from the wider system. It is important to remember that each of the subsystems is also fractal in nature (ie it is a system in its own right, comprised of further subsystems) and that each system may itself be a strange attractor or an attractor such as fixed point, cyclical and so on (see Jennings, Chapter Two). What we are challenged with is a consideration of the ways in which each part of the system, motivation and self-efficacy can be developed, and in a way that influences the whole system.

Challenges for probation staff

It is interesting to consider the current models that are used in probation practice and their sensitivity to complexity. A realist perspective on interventions would seek to develop the ideas of core processes of behavioural change, and self-efficacy and motivation have been integral to probation work through, for example, the application of the Cycle of Change (DiClemente and Prochaska, 1998).

From a complexity perspective, motivation and self-efficacy are examples of self-similarity that have the capacity to affect every level of an individual's behaviour precisely because they are not static, but vary from situation to situation; it is this variability that also makes them an important resource to work with. Self-efficacy is defined by Bandura (1977) as situational confidence and the belief on the part of an individual that they can cope with a situation that is of high risk to them in terms of engaging in unwanted behaviour. Self-efficacy is linked with ideas of positive feedback loops, building confidence and reducing the risk of relapse. Motivation is complex, and would appear to be situationally determined and linked to the reward chemistry of our brains; it is not a simple matter of will power and the rational choice model of making the wrong choices.

With regard to the Cycle of Change, there are a number of problems, including that the Cycle is only one part of a complex three-part meta-model also comprising processes and levels of change (the Transtheoretical Model of Intentional Behavioural Change [TTM]) that most practitioners are not aware of; additionally, it is doubtful whether, in practice, the model is used as intended by its authors. The strengths and weaknesses of the TTM are well documented (see West, 2006), but what I want to focus on is the third part of the model, the levels of change, which is an attempt to integrate into this model the reality of potentially interrelated, mutually reinforcing multiple problem areas. Importantly, DiClemente and Prochaska (1998, p 4) say that:

> the model recognizes that changing any one problem area is usually complicated by other problems that interfere with or facilitate the process of change. The concept of levels of change incorporates the realization that individuals are in different stages of change with respect to problem areas.

The levels of change identified in the TTM range from the most 'superficial' to the most 'profound' and are:

1. Symptom/situational, where the primary concern is to change (usually a single) behaviour (such as excessive drinking) and its antecedents.
2. Maladaptive cognitions, which are the automatic or unconscious thoughts that maintain behaviour.
3. Interpersonal conflicts, which are a major cause of relapse in substance misuse.
4. Family/systems problems, which can lead to relapse, domestic violence, homelessness and so on.
5. Intrapersonal conflicts, which refer to internal conflicts that are long-standing and entrenched to the degree that an individual's behaviour may be bound up with their sense of identity, as in addict, alcoholic or offender.

The levels of change have received the least attention in the model, with most practitioners only aware of the stages of change, for which motivational interviewing (Miller and Rollnick, 2002) has developed as an important adjunct.

An important question, then, becomes how can levels of changes-type models/thinking be incorporated into criminal justice practice in a way that avoids the excessive reductionism and engineering of the 'what works' era? The key challenge for probation staff is to embrace rather than try to ignore complexity. Also, what is often described as chaotic behaviour is, in fact, highly ordered, but any efforts at restricting, challenging and changing the system through the use of coercive power is often counterproductive through bringing about system bifurcation and an increase in system complexity. For example, within the three-part model of the TTM, there is explicit recognition of the importance of biological, psychological and social/environment factors that need to be addressed to bring about behavioural change, and that any one cannot be viewed in isolation. The problem with criminal justice interventions is that they tend to amplify existing problems by bringing about or making worse, for example, housing problems, relationships, employment, substance misuse and mental health problems (see Social Exclusion Unit, 2002). The outcome equivalence paradox demonstrates the need for probation staff to work in a state of superposition (and they are the only criminal justice system professionals who can do this through having access to all parts of the criminal justice system) across, between and through boundaries (this also supports the arguments of McDermott, Chapter Nine). It is also essential that the government changes its current planned changes to criminal justice to allow the most qualified and experienced staff to work at all levels of the system.

I am borrowing the adjective 'superposition' from quantum mechanics and using it as a metaphor. In quantum mechanics the smallest subatomic components exist as both waves and particles simultaneously (see Bartollas, Chapter Thirteen) until they are observed, at which point, they become one or the other (this is known as wave collapse). To extend the metaphor into probation practice, there is the problem of the probation officer adopting a particular role to meet the demands of different agencies, whether that is the court, rehab centre or the victim for example. What the evidence demonstrates from research on case management processes (Partridge, 2004) is the need for consistency, integrity, sensitivity and adaptability. In other words, the probation officer has their own distinct role, distinct skills and distinct knowledge base that operate at the level of the whole system; this whole-system approach is an example of a higher-order solution to the problems of fragmentation, which should not be reduced to control and surveillance.

The flow of information is key to this process, not simply to manage risk or to breach a community order for non-compliance for example, but as a key component of desistance from crime or recovery from addiction. The way we manage this information is fundamentally important, and Snowden (2002, p 6) outlines three heuristics that change the way we think about this knowledge. First, knowledge can only be volunteered, it cannot be conscripted; therefore, realistically, I can only know whether someone has complied with a process or a quality standard. In probation practice, we seem to be only training/ employing people to manage the process of dealing with high-risk offenders, and, even then, at the most basic level. Second, we can always know more than we can tell, and we will always tell more than we can write down. What I can say quite quickly will take a long time to write down, and any reflective writing is only at a level of abstraction of a greater or lesser degree from the original thought. Reflective knowledge (see McDermott, Chapter Nine) is of high value, but also involves a loss of control over its subsequent use. Also, written files and notes on probationers are important, but equally important is the worker who understands the context in which they were written. Third, we only know what we know when we need to know it; human knowledge is embedded, contextual and triggered by circumstance, and to ask someone what they know is to ask a meaningless question in a meaningless context.

Because of these challenges to gaining, understanding and acting upon information related to individual circumstances the human relationship becomes more, not less important. Within this relationship there needs to be an understanding that change takes time, is cumulative but also sensitive to initial conditions so that relapse is the norm rather than the exception.

The key relationships that lead to desistance from crime require higher-order solutions in probation practice, which involve clear parameters to intervention based upon policy and organisational procedures, and which involves the use of state-sanctioned coercion. However, within this framework, and building upon tools already in use, it is possible to engage in improved working and outcomes for the probationer and the organisation. The models and processes outlined are sensitive to a complexity application, and precisely through the acquisition of key characteristics that allow for an embracing of complexity. For the individual practitioner, this will require the understanding and practice of virtue ethics (see Arrigo and Williams, Chapter Twelve; see also Pycroft, 2012), which allows for the probationer's own understanding of their own adaptation to their evolutionary and complex environment to bring about change.

By engaging in consultations/key work sessions and so on at the edge of chaos, the practitioner is taking risks to solve problems (see Innes, 2004; Innes et al, 2005). Innes and colleagues identify a number of processes occurring within these settings, which include: processes of co-evolution, whereby each person in the consultation is a complex adaptive system with a history that informs their discussion, but which changes both of their views over time; distributed control, whereby rule-based complexity is utilised to bring about and develop good outcomes rather than trying to impose them (this is very similar to motivational interviewing), but accepting that what emerges may be unpredictable; a recognition that within non-linear systems, outputs/outcomes are not necessarily proportional to inputs, and chance remarks/conversations can be as important as formal consultations; and a recognition that each consultation is different despite there being the same people involved, which can be fairly predictable, and there are times when we need to think more creatively to generate free-flowing discussion.

These kinds of strategies work best when based upon ethical and just interventions that are recognised at all levels of the system. When problems/issues arise in other parts of the system, it is imperative that the probation officer work with their probationers to understand these processes and, where necessary, to advocate for them to managers as well as other agencies in a way that is obvious to the probationer. I can provide two examples to demonstrate problems with reductionist approaches and the efficacy of sowing seeds to demonstrate emergent outcomes.

In the past, I managed a community detox and aftercare centre. The centre as a system was partially closed as there was not free entry into the building; a member of staff had to open the door to let people in. There was much discussion about whether we should be regularly drug-testing people to 'be sure' whether they were clean or not. My argument was that this was not necessary as if there were any problems with drug use, then it would emerge during the course of therapeutic groupwork and challenge from other residents; in this sense, any relapse and discussion thereof becomes part of, rather than separate from, the therapeutic process. This process was entirely dependent upon knowing people, their patterns and behaviours on a daily basis. I argued that drug-testing meant that the technology would become the attractor, that is, it would impact upon relationships and staff would become lazy in this respect. I lost the argument and drug-testing was implemented; the consequences of which were that, first, evasion strategies became more sophisticated and, second, there was a clear reliance on testing as a *first* port of call rather than engaging with individuals on a personal level. It is not, of course, that these things are mutually exclusive, just that in our busy working lives, our default position is overly reductionist rather than engaging with a reasonable level of complexity.

The second point about sowing seeds and emergent outcomes (of a positive kind) is a recognition that we cannot expect people to know, understand and find a solution now, irrespective of what intervention strategy is used (this is also a challenge to PBR – 'What timescales determine a good outcome?'). So, a simple example from my own practice involves talking to someone we can call Adrian. Adrian was in his late 20s and had an alcohol problem that was getting progressively worse and leading to loss of housing and experiencing other problems. On the basis of ongoing one-to-one work, I raised the issue with Adrian of whether he had been sexually abused as a child, he thought about it and stated that he had not been abused. Adrian eventually left the programme, but I saw him in the street a couple of years later; we got chatting and he was doing relatively ok, had found himself some accommodation and his drinking had reduced. On meeting him, *I* could not at that time remember the specifics of his case, but clearly our conversation had been of significance to *him* because his words to me were "Do you remember that you asked me whether I had been abused as a child? Well, actually, I was, and I got some help with this and its really helping me get sorted."

These effective approaches are in contrast to the features of the 'what works' approach and particularly the use of time-limited, didactic-style cognitive-behavioural therapy programmes, which had a good fit with the need for a more managerial agenda in probation work. Unfortunately for managers, but fortunately for the rest of us, our life, its influences and the capacity to change is far more diverse. Also, complexity theory helps us to understand the issue of scaling or scalability, which 'refers to a system or network's ability to accommodate growth capacity without harming the system or network' (Wolf-Branigin, 2013, p 24). In the case of probation practice, the 'what works' initiatives were based on pilot studies that demonstrated treatment effect. However, once these programmes were rolled out nationally, the treatment effect was lost (Merrington and Stanley, 2004), demonstrating an issue related to scale, and supporting my key argument that you cannot industrialise human relationships. This has fundamental implications for the training, development and supervision of probation officers, who require a very unique set of skills and theoretical underpinning. It is ultimately self-defeating to rely on the reductionist and utilitarian marketplace to provide these, and the state needs to ensure that professional qualifications and opportunities for development that meet these needs are in place.

Conclusion

Despite the heralding of radical changes to the Probation Service in England and Wales that promise to bring more diversity and effectiveness to addressing the problems of crime, a complexity perspective suggests that this approach will simply run into similar problems to those experienced during the preceding 'what works' era. These problems will include problems associated with the existence of power laws and, consequently, a wrong focus on the wrong end of the system, which makes the system highly deterministic, and thus self-defeating in its outcomes. Rather, I would argue for developing the strengths that the Probation Service has always had in its state of superposition and the ability to cross organisational boundaries, and recognising the importance of highly qualified staff working with all groups in the system. It is not that more agencies should not be involved and, as I have argued, a diversity of problems requires a diversity of responses, but there is a limit to this and there needs to be a reasonable level of abstraction from the whole to make this not just manageable, but also meaningful and effective for the courts, victims, probationers and wider society. This is also supported by the overwhelming and incontrovertible evidence of the importance of constructive and ethical professional relationships in restoring individuals to full citizenship. Criminal justice in England and Wales has an opportunity to bring about innovation based upon practical and theoretical resources that are already in existence for the benefit of society, victims and probationers and it is illogical and unethical that, in many cases, they choose to ignore what is available to them.

Notes

[1] There is current confusion/debate as to what people on probation in England and Wales should be called. My concern is with regard to the relationship with the Court Order and the Probation Service, so I am using 'probationer' to reflect a virtuous relationship or a probationary period that would ideally leads to assuming full rights in the community, that is, full citizenship.

[2] I am referring to the virtue ethics tradition, which is concerned with:

> the virtues themselves, motives and moral character, moral education, moral wisdom or discernment, friendship and family relationships, a deep concept of happiness, the role of the emotions in our moral life and the fundamentally important questions of what sort of person I should be and how we should live. (see: http://plato.stanford.edu/entries/ethics-virtue/)

For a full discussion, see Arrigo and Williams (Chapter Twelve) and Pycroft (2012).

[3] This section is adapted from Pycroft et al (2013).

[4] See: http://www.dtors.org.uk

[5] See: http://pespmc1.vub.ac.be/ASHBBOOK.html

[6] Also the work on dissipative structures of Ilya Prigogene (see: http://www.nobelprize.org/nobel_prizes/chemistry/laureates/1977/prigogine-autobio.html), which is seen as bridging the natural and social sciences through challenging the irreversibility and entropy model of thermodynamics and the Newtonian model, is important here (see Bartollas, Chapter Thirteen).

References

Bandura, A. (1977) 'Self efficacy: Toward a unifying theory of behavioural change', *Psychological Review*, vol 84, no 2, pp 191–215.

Clift, S. (2010) 'Working together to manage the risk of serious harm', in A. Pycroft and D. Gough (eds) *Multi-agency working in criminal justice: care and control in contemporary correctional practice*, Bristol: The Policy Press, pp 95–110.

Clift, S. (2012) 'Risk, assessment and the practice of actuarial criminal justice', in A. Pycroft and S. Clift (eds) *Risk and rehabilitation: management and treatment of substance misuse and mental health problems in the criminal justice system*, Bristol: The Policy Press, pp 21–64.

Craissati, J. and Sindall, O. (2009) 'Serious further offenses: an exploration of risk and typologies', *Probation Journal*, vol 56, no 1, pp 9–27.

Department for Education (2011) *The Munro Review of child protection: final report: a child-centred system*, London: HMSO.

DiClemente, C. and Prochaska, J. (1998) 'Toward a comprehensive, transtheoretical model of change: Stages of change and addictive behaviors', in W.R. Miller and N. Heather (eds) *Treating addictive behaviors* (2nd edn), New York, NY: Plenum Press, pp 3–24.

Fox, F. and Albertson, K. (2011) 'Payment by results and social impact bonds in the criminal justice sector: new challenges for the concept of evidence based policy?', *Criminology and Criminal Justice*, vol 11, no 5, pp 395–413.

Gash, T., Panchamia, N., Sims, S. and Hotson, L. (2013) *Making public service markets work: professionalising government's approach to commissioning and market stewardship*, London: Institute for Government.

Gough, D. (2010) 'Multi-agency working in corrections: cooperation and competition in probation practice', in A. Pycroft and D. Gough (eds) *Multi-agency working in criminal justice: care and control in contemporary correctional practice*, Bristol: The Policy Press, pp 21–34.

Gough, D. (2012) 'Risk and rehabilitation: a fusion of concepts?', in A. Pycroft and S. Clift (eds) *Risk and rehabilitation: management and treatment of substance misuse and mental health problems in the criminal justice system*, Bristol: The Policy Press, pp 65–86.

Guastello, S. and Liebovitch, L. (2009) 'Introduction to nonlinear dynamics and complexity' in S. Guastello, M. Koopmans and D. Pincus (eds) *Chaos and complexity in psychology: the theory of nonlinear dynamical systems*, Cambridge: Cambridge University Press, pp 1–40.

Holder, H. (1999) *Alcohol and the community: a systems approach to prevention*, Cambridge: Cambridge University Press.

House of Commons Justice Committee (2011) 'The role of the probation service', 8th Report. Available at: http://www.publications. parliament.uk/pa/cm201012/cmselect/cmjust/519/519i.pdf

Innes, A. (2004) 'Complexity and the consultation', in A. Holt (ed) *Complexity for clinicians*, Oxford: Radcliffe, pp 37–47.

Innes, A., Campion, P. and Griffiths, F. (2005) 'Complex consultations and the "edge of chaos"', *British Journal of General Practice*, vol 55, no 510, pp 47–52.

Jennings, P. and Pycroft, A. (2012) 'The numbers game: a systems perspective on risk', in A. Pycroft and S. Clift (eds) *Risk and rehabilitation: management and treatment of substance misuse and mental health problems in the criminal justice system*, Bristol: The Policy Press, pp 7–20.

Lowe, T. (2013) 'Payment by results – a "dangerous idiocy" that makes staff tell lies: management based on outcomes makes good people do the wrong thing – and those most in need get a much poorer service'. Available at: http://www.guardian.co.uk/local-government-network/2013/feb/01/payment-results-staff-fictions (accessed 22 May 2013).

MacIntyre, A. (2011) *After virtue* (3rd edn), London: Bloomsbury.

Maden, A. (2007) *Treating violence: a guide to risk management in mental health*, Oxford: Oxford University Press.

Maynard, A., Street, A. and Hunter, R. (2011) 'Using "payment by results" to fund the treatment of dependent drug users – proceed with care!', *Addiction*, vol 106, pp 1725–9.

Merrington, S. and Stanley, S. (2004) '"What works?": revisiting the evidence in England and Wales', *Probation Journal*, vol 54, no 7, pp 7–20.

Miller, W. (2006) 'Motivational factors in addictive behaviors', in W. Miller and K. Carroll (eds) *Rethinking substance abuse: what the science shows and what we should do about it*, New York, NY: Guilford Press, pp 134–52.

Miller, W. and Rollnick, S. (2002) *Motivational interviewing: preparing people for change* (2nd edn), New York, NY: Guilford Press.

Ministry of Justice (2013) *Transforming rehabilitation, a revolution in the way we manage offenders. Consultation paper CP1/2013*, London: The Stationary Office.

Nash, M. and Williams, A. (2008) *The anatomy of serious further offending*, Oxford: Oxford University Press.

NOMS (National Offender Management Service) (2006) 'The NOMS Offender Management Model'. Available at: http://www.swmprobation.gov.uk/wp-content/uploads/2013/03/offender_management_model_1.pdf (accessed 7 June 2013).

Orford, J. (2008) 'Asking the right questions in the right way: the need for a shift in research on psychological treatments for addiction', *Addiction*, vol 103, pp 875–85.

Partridge, S. (2004) *Examining case management models for community sentences*, London: Home Office.

Pycroft, A. (2010) *Understanding and working with substance misusers*, London: Sage.

Pycroft, A. (2012) 'Relationship and rehabilitation in a post-"what works" era', in A. Pycroft and S. Clift (eds) *Risk and rehabilitation: management and treatment of substance misuse and mental health problems in the criminal justice system*, Bristol: The Policy Press, pp 175–94.

Pycroft, A., Wallis, A., Bigg, J. and Webster, G. (2013) 'Participation, engagement, and change: a study of tservice users of the Unified Adolescent Team', *British Journal of Social Work* vol 1-18, doi:10.1093/bjsw/bct089.

Snowden, D. (2002) *Complex acts of knowing – paradox and descriptive self awareness*, Basingstoke: IBM UK.

Social Exclusion Unit (2002) *Reducing re-offending by ex-prisoners*, London: HMSO.

West, R. (2006) *Theory of addiction*, Oxford: Blackwell Publishing.

Wolf-Branigin, M. (2013) *Using complexity theory for research and program evaluation*, Oxford: Oxford University Press.

ELEVEN

Responding to domestic abuse: multi-agented systems, probation programmes and emergent outcomes

Sarah Lewis

The new domestic abuse (DA) programme 'Building Better Relationships' (BBR) has recently been implemented within Probation Trusts in England and Wales, witnessing a shift from the feminist psycho-educational Duluth model (eg as featured in the Integrated Domestic Abuse Programme [IDAP]) to a more strengths-based approach. In this chapter, I aim to demonstrate how complexity theory can be valuable within the context of DA interventions and contribute to significant advancements and developments within probation practice and other rehabilitative settings. I intend to provide a critique of the BBR programme in light of complexity, reflecting upon past theoretical orientations to DA interventions and highlighting possible emergent outcomes in the future. It will be argued that while BBR has made some significant progression from recent theoretical discussions, considering DA programmes from a complexity perspective can aid further development for the future. I argue for the efficacy of applying complexity theory to DA interventions within probation practice, recognising the importance of taking a whole-systems approach in protecting women and families from violence. I will take a realist perspective to knowledge, accepting that knowledge is partially known, socially constructed and is given meaning through human interaction and interpretation. Social reality therefore incorporates a number of levels, from individual to societal, and it is believed that this post-positivist perspective is appropriate when discussing the inherent determinism and non-linearity of domestic violence.

At the heart of the Duluth model has been the issue of gender equality, and the move to the BBR programme is not without controversy. It is interesting, for example, to consider the statement by Strid, Armstrong and Walby (2008, p 29) that:

> Gender equality as a term is not often used in UK policy documents on gender based violence.… Gender is never present in legislation … in the few gender based violence policy documents where gender equality is explicitly either a means or an end, gender equality is rarely the end goal of policy.

Clearly, the focus for the probation service is a reduction in reoffending rather than gender equality, but the consequences of this might well be significant. Strid et al (2008) go on to highlight the awkwardness of the relationship between gender-based violence and gender equality, so gender-based violence becomes 'domestic violence' and is framed as an issue of crime and justice. They make the highly pertinent point that the focus on gender equality can become 'lost', with the presumption that everyone 'else' is addressing gender, when, in fact, no one is (Strid et al, 2008). When considering the changes to probation practice, it is recognised that there is a need for a strengths-based approach, but it is also argued that we cannot lose sight of the fact that domestic violence *is* gender-based violence. As we see the development of desistance-based approaches that emphasise the accumulation of social and human capital in probation practice, we should also remember that perpetrators of domestic violence are generally in a relationship, do have accommodation and can reside with their victim, that is, domestic violence is both complex and unique.

Since the implementation of Duluth-based accredited programmes (eg IDAP) within probation and prisons in 2003, a number of issues have been highlighted within its evaluation. These include problems such as high waiting lists and staff turnover (Bilby and Hatcher, 2004), the lack of focus upon the individual and inflexibility within the programme (Eadie and Knight, 2002; Rees and Rivett, 2005; Morran et al, 2011), and problems associated with high attrition (see Jewell and Wormith, 2010). Further to this, evidence for the effectiveness of such programmes has been varied, limited and methodologically problematic (Babcock et al, 2004), with a somewhat narrowing focus upon patriarchy and 'power and control' (Dutton and Corvo, 2007). In light of these problems, discussions of a new rolling DA programme was placed onto the rehabilitative agenda with the hope to design a DA programme that was flexible, contemporary and responsive to the needs of those participating in it, with a focus upon evaluation (Weatherstone, nd). In response to this, BBR was designed to retain the integrated approach that operated under IDAP while taking a more individualistic approach that was responsive to desistance research. Taking a more holistic view of DA, BBR has continued to utilise Dutton's (1995) Nested Ecological Approach, though has supplemented this with the General Aggression Model to take into account a wider range of factors relating to aggression to support a more individualistic approach. In response to these significant changes with probation DA interventions and the complexities associated with DA, complexity theory can be applied in order to evaluate this new programme, considering the assumption of homogeneity, multi-agented systems, whole systems and co-adaptation. Using these aspects of complexity to evaluate BBR on a theoretical and practical level, it will end by discussing ways in which complexity can be reduced through non-bureaucratic working relationships.

Challenging the assumption of homogeneity

Homogeneity within the context of DA intervention assumes that those that participate within a DA rehabilitative intervention or programme are similar to one another and commit DA against their partner for similar reasons. However, it is becoming increasingly recognised that DA perpetrators are more heterogeneous than previously believed (Jeglic et al, 2012) and, in light of this, BBR has embraced a more individualistic programme that is designed to suit individual need. When focusing in on individual risk factors, the literature is broad and varied, drawing upon emotional (Dutton, 1995), social (Maiuro et al, 1986), bio-social (Soler et al, 2010), psychological (Ross and Babcock, 2009) and attitudinal factors (Stith et al, 2004), as well as a number of findings relevant to substance use (Murphy et al, 2005) and empathy (Schweinle and Ickes, 2007). It is argued that this diverse range of factors is indicative of the fact that DA perpetrators are themselves complex adaptive systems that comprise DA. From a complex systems perspective, this not only highlights the possibility of risk factors influencing one another (eg attachment styles impacting upon levels of empathy), but may also signify additional bidirectional and dynamical risk factors that *emerge* when such variables interact with one another. An understanding of the nature of emergence (in the technical sense of the output/outcomes being dependent upon the interaction effects of all the known and unknown variables: see Pycroft, Chapter One) within a rehabilitative context makes the ability to create a responsive and individualised approach challenging at both a theoretical and operational level (Gadd, 2004). While this highlights the difficult task within interventions, it illustrates the importance of an approach that identifies and understands the individual within their context, as one part of the whole system.

Within the literature, Babcock (2009) highlights the importance of focusing upon identified strengths instead of weaknesses/deficits, which are foundational to a 'blaming and shaming' culture that has been associated with programme delivery (Johnson and Sullivan, 2008) in the 'what works' era of probation practice in the UK. The traditional Duluth-based interventions have been criticised for such an approach and the new BBR programme shows some advancements in light of such criticism, focusing upon a more strength-based approach that helps to nurture potential protective factors that exist within the lives of DA perpetrators. Within the context of complexity theory, a strength-based approach that focuses upon the range of protective factors instead of a narrow positivistic approach that focuses on cognitive deficits could be seen as a vehicle to provide positive feedback loops that can drive change through positive reinforcement.

It is proposed that what is essentially an ecological 'person in context' approach embraces diversity for the purpose of being responsive to the needs of the perpetrator participating within the programme precisely to promote desistance from crime. Different responses to programmes may arise from the causal roots of an individual's DA, whether that be an insecure attachment , poor socialisation or psychopathological characteristics, which, in turn, may be further complicated by, for example, gender patterns (Kelly and Johnson, 2008), substance misuse (Humpreys et al, 2005) and learning disability (McMurran, 2002). Holtzworth-Munroe, Meehan, Herron, Rehman and Stuart (2003) highlight from their research that perpetrators with particular problems work more effectively within some kinds of interventions than others. Such an observation again emphasises the complex nature of DA perpetrators and their crimes and suggests that DA interventions need to shift to a more differentiated approach whereupon flexibility and diversity are embedded within its structure (Fisher, 2011). Fisher (2011) argues that in order to achieve this, a greater understanding of the complexities that underlie DA perpetrators is needed to explore what elements of a programme are successful for specific typologies under specific conditions. When considering the diverse range of factors that contribute to DA, we also need to fully appreciate the complexities of its causality, its inherent determinism (see Pycroft, Chapter One) and the need to grasp the non-linear nature of outcomes from intervention. If we fail to understand this, then this will significantly limit our development of rehabilitative interventions within probation practice.

When taking a more individualistic view of DA, Fisher (2011) argues that it is the case not simply of exploring an individual's problems and complex needs, but recognising that each problem and/or need may vary in breadth and depth. In order to effectively respond to this challenge, the connectivity between agents (eg programme tutor and probationer) within a subsystem (like probation) and between subsystems is significant. Mitleton-Kelly (2003) highlights that connectivity can vary over time in relation to density, intensity and quality, and the degree of connectivity impacts upon this relational network. Therefore, an effective transfer of knowledge and information relevant to the DA perpetrator that feeds back both between and within 'the system' in the future through collaboration and communication is important. On a practical level, it is questioned how such an approach can be successfully actualised in light of complexity. What happens, for example, if there is a conflict of needs within a group, how might a practitioner manage this differentiated approach? In respect to gender inequality, O'Cinneide (2002) and Strid et al (2008), respectively, ask two questions that I believe are relevant to this issue: 'Will there be a dilution to the lowest common denominator, losing expertise and focus?'; and 'Are the differences sufficiently great that they are best addressed with separate remedies?' Consequentially, if DA perpetrators are as complex as suggested, how can individual need be met within a group context and how can this be successfully achieved in order to reduce the risk of reoffending in the future and meet the need of the victim and public?

It is also argued that BBR may in some ways become more homogeneous in respect to style and content. This may be more familiar to practitioners with a 'general offending' or person-centred background and a similar predicament may exist whereupon intervention approaches are becoming standardised without considering the differences that exist between offender groups on a broader level. Therefore, it is suggested that we consider not only the heterogeneity of 'the individual', but also the differences between offending groups on a contextual level, reflecting upon how rehabilitative interventions will differ depending upon the client group. Gelles (2001) highlights how the standardisation of treatment programmes since the 'what works' agenda has prematurely taken place before we know what works, for which men and under what circumstances. Polaschek (2010) similarly comments that instead of focusing upon 'what works', it is now more appropriate, in light of the issues of homogeneity, to be addressing 'what to provide, for whom'.[1] This could provide a possible answer to what makes DA perpetrators in the community different or a 'special' case. DA perpetrators are in the unique position of possibly living with the victim (NOMS, 2010a), with the potential for abuse to reoccur in the long term (Mullender and Burton, 2001a, 2001b), a scenario that may not be the case in many general offending or sexual offending groups. With this in mind, it is not sufficient to only consider the individualistic factors associated with the perpetrator, but to consider where BBR may become more homogeneous and in what ways DA perpetrators can be differentiated from other offending groups.

Bennett and Williams (2001) acknowledge that treatment effectiveness can be measured through a number of ways, including behaviour, attitude, reoffending rates or completions. Research relevant to the success of DA interventions has been complicated by methodological flaws and has focused upon linear outcomes, which not only has encouraged a 'one-size-fits-all' approach, but also does not take into account the complexities of human behaviour (Mair, 2004). With the intended payment by results initiative of the Conservative government, it is likely that this approach will continue to dominate the correctional climate; yet, there are a number of questions that arise from such an approach (see also Pycroft, Chapter Ten). First, how can 'success' or 'effectiveness' be conceptualised and how is it being operationalised within probation practice? Westmarland and Kelly (2012) discuss DA intervention programmes within social care and highlight that while there is an ongoing debate surrounding the efficacy of DA programmes internationally, part of this disagreement stems from a failure to consider a broad range of potential outcomes or to consider the notion of 'success' broadly enough. When considering the complexity associated with DA perpetrators and their individualistic needs, Jewell and Wormith (2010) highlight an interesting finding which suggested that the theoretical orientation of a treatment programme was important for 'different' DA perpetrators with respect to levels of attrition (which have previously been linked to recidivism). More specifically, they found that men who were more educated and court-mandated were more likely to complete feminist psycho-educational programmes then men who were not educated or court-mandated. Also, older men attended cognitive-behavioural programmes more readily than younger men. When examining BBR, I have concerns as to: first, whether 'high attrition rates' have been associated with IDAP as opposed to more complex problems lying under the surface that may be linked to the perpetrator; and, second, with a focus on evaluation (as promised within the limited BBR literature available; Weatherstone, nd), whether these evaluations would be sufficient enough based upon the complexity of DA and rehabilitative interventions in general. In light of the desistance literature, the journey away from crime not only is a rocky and challenging road, but has been described by Glaser (1964) and supported by Maruna (2004) as a 'zig-zag' pattern, depicting a moving in and out of criminal activity prior to sustained desistance. With this in mind, it is unrealistic to assume: first, that any programme outcome is accurately measurable based upon the dynamics of criminal activity (it is, in fact, to some extent, unknowable); and, second, that such a positive 'outcome' will immediately follow a particular intervention. A cumulative effect is far more reasonable to assume, which appreciates the layers of interaction that exist for the DA perpetrator. Such a predicament as this does not rest easy in light of the possible victims that could be harmed as a result of a 'relapse' per se; this highlights the very reason why DA interventions need to be coordinated, integrated (Shepard et al, 2002) and interconnected. As Babcock et al (2004) rightly highlight, treatment is only one component of a coordinated community response to DA and it cannot address the complex dynamics of DA in itself, with Wolfe and Jaffe (1999) arguing for investment within preventive strategies as well as rehabilitative.

Bowen and Gilchrist (2004) evaluated DA offender programmes and concluded from their work that motivation to change, programme integrity and therapeutic factors were important, as well as psychological variables, stating that a more 'multifaceted evaluation' was needed in order to successfully capture a true picture of rehabilitative outcomes. This would provide a number of benefits within probation practice and interventions, particularly during this time of uncertainty and with the implementation of BBR on the horizon. Discovering the elements within an intervention that can lead to more positive outcomes will allow for continuous improvement and development, and encourage innovation and creativity. In order to gain a clearer picture of this murky reality, a multifaceted and differentiated approach within analysis is welcomed in response to the shift towards the heterogeneity of programmes in the future. While it is important to provide a holistic programme within DA interventions, it will be interesting to discover to what extent evaluation is holistic within the BBR agenda.

Multi-agented systems and a whole-systems perspective

An integrated and multi-agency approach is not new to DA interventions and has been a key aspect of current DA probation interventions that utilise the Duluth model (Pence and Shepard, 1988). From a complexity perspective, Morin (2006) argues that an understanding of the whole system, or indeed its individual parts, must always be limited (see McDermott, Chapter Nine). Within the context of DA programmes, it is important to understand and acknowledge the 'subsystems' that make up the knowable whole system (see Figure 11.1).

Subsystems operate within a larger system, so, for example, any given programme is made up of individuals who, in themselves, constitute complex adaptive systems, the requirements of the programme constitute a subsystem and so on. These human systems can be broken down further into their constitutive range of bio-psychosocial systems or broadened out to include other criminal justice agencies, such as social services, the police and statutory or voluntary organisations. Each part within the system interacts with their own environment and with one another, at different times, to different degrees, at different levels and within different contexts. Each also brings information that informs the relevant part of the system of perpetrator risk, and these perspectives differ and evolve over time through the interaction of each part. For example, the victim may interact with both the perpetrator and Women Safety Workers (WSWs)[2] (whose role is to support and communicate with the partners of those offenders on the group), but may also receive support outside the 'subsystem' of probation through voluntary agencies such as Women's Aid. While Women's Aid may not have a direct interaction with probation on a specific occasion, emergent outcomes from the victim's interaction will lead to adaptations for all agents that interact with the victim. Similarly, interactions may occur between the police and perpetrator as a result of a domestic call-out, and, consequentially, contact with probation will take place. Such information is vital for the WSWs and probation as a whole in order to provide a sound risk management structure that protects the victim/partner. While Figure 11.1 only outlines the probation subsystem, layers of interactions and parallel processes that take place, embedded within and between other processes, it highlights a rich and complex network of interconnectedness, which operates within the potential for far-reaching ripple effects.

When considering DA interventions, a complex systems perspective highlights the importance of recognising the openness of the system, so while we may intend for certain interactions (eg between the programme tutor and perpetrator) to impact upon positive changes in offending behaviour, there are also changes that may negatively or positively impact upon the goals of these agents and other people involved in the system. To illustrate, Yalom (1995) describes how a group 'climate' can be highly influential within the context of an intervention, with Koslowski and Ilgen (2006, p 78) discussing the interaction of groups operating as complex dynamical systems that 'develop as members interact over time and evolve and adapt as situational demands unfold'. Having witnessed mental models or schemata in operation myself as a programme facilitator, these can later develop into a group where decision norms are constructed, providing either a catalyst for change (through positive feedback loops) or a hostile 'climate' that inhibits change and promotes anti-social collusion. For example, one or more anti-social group members may interact with the 'perpetrator' during a group session, and these interactions may lead to negative consequences that cause the programme tutor to focus more upon group management than the intervention itself. As a result of such negative emergent outcomes (or attractors; see Pycroft, Chapter One; Wolf Branigin, Chapter Four; see also Jennings, Chapter Two), treatment managers, offender managers, programme managers and possibly WSWs may initiate interactions with one another in order to fulfil their risk management role. Gaining an insight into each part of the subsystem, as well as considering emergent outcomes between agents, can broaden one's understanding of the capacity of dynamical structures that exist within one small part of the system and lead to changes in the behaviour of the whole system. An understanding of this path dependency, which is a defining feature of complex adaptive systems (see Pycroft, Chapter One), allows for insight into emergent outcomes and also provides a basis to take action to deliver successful interventions.

Due to the environmental demands operating around a system, and the ways in which a system adapts to meet those demands, it is argued that outcomes can never be truly predicted or ultimately controlled (Heylighan et al, 2007). This means that within the context of probation and criminal justice interventions, the relationships between these multi-agented parts are of great significance, for victim support and protection, crime prevention, and also desistance from crime. This is believed to lead to not only a greater appreciation of the different perspectives within the system, but also greater communication and an increased likelihood of positive outcomes. Within a mixed economy of criminal justice interventions, I agree with Hague and Malos (1998) that developing a common understanding and value of complementary approaches can, in turn, lead to a greater flow of information between agents, subsystems and whole systems. Such a coordinated response has been found to contribute towards significantly lower rates of reoffending within the context of DA perpetrators (Shepard and Pence, 1999; Shepard et al, 2002), and, as Morran et al (2011) concludes from Gondolf's (2002) contributions, 'the system matters'. Within this 'system', both new approaches and consistent research are recommended by Morran et al (2011), a notion that has previously been supported by Babcock et al (2004), who appreciate the importance of including researchers within a coordinated response in order to assess progress and continuously develop DA interventions for the future, providing, in essence, a 'learning' culture within DA interventions. In light of these arguments, it is felt that the development of a new programme could have consequentially led to a consideration of the whole system, as Gondolf (2002) recommends. BBR has retained an integrated approach within DA interventions and this has been recognised as important; however, within this current climate of competition, there was an opportunity for innovation that was not fully appreciated or seized. In light of the shift to greater private and voluntary involvement in the future, it is vital that communication continues to flow between and within the system and that discussions of system development take place with the collaborative involvement of the practitioner.

The Duluth model outlines the importance of DA and, consequentially, DA interventions to embrace a nested ecological model, which considers four levels: the ontogenetic (individual), the microsystem (including intimate relationships), the exosystem (including social structure) and the macrosystem (including broad attitudes and beliefs regarding DA). Interactions, similar to those of subsystems within a larger 'system', provide feedback that either inhibits or encourages change. With respect to complexity theory, the Duluth model is a useful example of how a rehabilitative intervention can take a whole-systems approach. While BBR has focused more heavily upon ontogenetic variables, it is argued that the complexity of the systems of DA have, consequentially, been shifted out of view with the loss of a whole-system perspective. While a greater focus upon individual factors is responsive to the literature associated with a strength-based approach, this does not mean that other parts of the system should be forgotten. In relation to DA, if the context in which DA operates is overlooked and knowledge of societal risk factors are ignored at the expense of the ontogenetic, it is argued that the system may be threatened and probation's response to DA interventions may not meet its potential in address DA recidivism within our society. While an examination of the power of patriarchy may not be as evident in BBR as it was in IDAP, by looking through the lens of complexity theory and by targeting each level of 'the system', probation staff will be able to address offending behaviour and respond to the anti-social attitudes and beliefs associated with power and control that exist on a broader level within rehabilitation. Pycroft (2010) argues in connection with whole systems that the end goal is not to create a perfect system, but to produce a system by which learning can take place and adaptation is possible. A disjointed system, Fisher

Figure 11.1: The 'whole system' context of domestic abuse intervention within probation practice

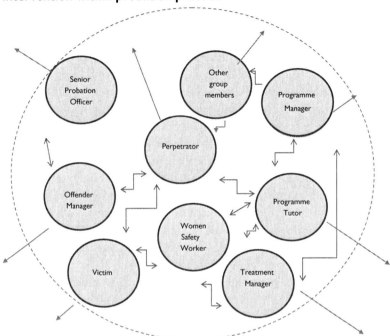

(2011) argues, not only leaves gaps in action and a lack of confidence in the system, but ultimately does not protect the victim. Relating this to DA interventions, there are concerns that if the ontogenetic wave is overemphasised and the macrosystem is forgotten, this may not only prevent learning to emerge and be acted upon, which is vital within the development of DA interventions, but will create a disjointed system that leaves the victims of DA vulnerable.

Adaptation and co-evolution within the system

When considering the relationship between practitioner and probationer and other system members, adaptation and co-evolution of agents is believed to take place both implicitly and explicitly. Sedgwick (2001) discusses how a therapeutic relationship is a dialectical process which transforms both parties whereupon both facilitator and perpetrator co-evolve through simultaneous adaptation (Mitleton-Kelly, 2003). Iliffe and Steed (2000) found from their research that within a therapeutic context, not only do therapists experience varying degrees of burnout, but adaptations were made in relation to their own levels of trust and security. This work was both cited and developed within

Bailey, Buchbinder and Eisikovits's (2011) work, which focused upon male social workers who provided services for male perpetrators of DA within a social work context. From their small-scale research, Bailey et al (2011) found that male practitioners went through a reconstruction of their sense of self, both professionally and personally. From their research, they describe a period of adaptation as tensions between work and private life became more conscious for the workers. Once this 'stage of confusion and anxiety' faded in time, practitioners reported the development of coping mechanisms that allowed them to separate their self from those they worked with and develop their own self-acceptance. Lehmann and Simmons (2009) suggest that facilitators can even mirror some other characteristics of group members through unnecessary controls, being inflexible with rules and demonstrating a more punitive approach that is not congruent to a therapeutic environment.

Within the context of probation practice, Petrillo (2007) examined female probation officers and their experiences of working with high-risk probationers. With respect to DA perpetrators, she discussed the struggle over power within a supervisory relationship. Petrillo's (2007) work highlights how role conflict between enforcement and rehabilitation can create a number of emergent outcomes, which includes the need for male perpetrators of DA to attempt to control a supervision session that is being facilitated by a female officer. Similarly, within a group environment or one-to-one session, the feelings of being manipulated or controlled by a DA perpetrator that emerge are familiar to any programme facilitator or, indeed, probation officer. In operational terms, it is essential that staff are supported and given the opportunity to explore their own values, identities and belief systems, as these not only impact upon their rehabilitative work (see Morran, 2008; Day and Ward, 2010), but could also have a negative impact on their lives. The importance of a belief in offender change has been cited consistently within recent literature dedicated to the working relationship (Lewis, forthcoming [a] and [b]), and if this belief is threatened or not preserved within rehabilitative work, emergent outcomes that are linked to recidivism are believed to be more likely (see Lewis, forthcoming [a] and [b]).

This highlights a key issue for probation practice with respect to tutors of DA programmes accessing regular psychological and supervisory support. Regular supervision for tutors and continual opportunities for open communication are important for effective team functioning and the therapeutic bonds (or lack thereof) between themselves and the probationers. While supervision does hold an evaluative value through video-monitoring, it is argued that a greater focus upon the psycho-dynamical variables and belief systems of the practitioners is required. In comparison, less attention has been given to those offender managers that work with DA perpetrators within supervision or alongside a DA-related specified activity. Investing in positive engagement strategies and good working relationships that are believed to promote change is admirable, but systems need to be effectively managed in order for specific psychological support to be provided for all practitioners within probation. The impact of DA work upon correctional staff can be significant and long-lasting, and the probation service has a responsibility to provide a variety of supportive measures that meet the emotional needs of those that work with this client group. In the same way that DA perpetrators are not homogenous, neither are those that work with DA day in and day out. In light of this, a differentiated approach with respect to support is required that meets the needs of practitioners and minimises the impact that such work can have on those that work within this field.

As highlighted earlier, facilitators can and do 'adapt', and these adaptations can be perceived and understood in a number of ways. For instance, Newman and Nutley (2003) made the observation that during the managerialisation of probation and subsequent transfer of 'the relationship' to those working in programmes, probation staff that had worked within a social work model continued to utilise their working relationships within their practice to facilitate and support change even though this was at conflict with the changes within probation. When applying this to DA interventions, it is questioned whether, irrespective of the abandonment of the Duluth model within interventions, practitioners will continue to facilitate interventions that are congruent with their own positionality and belief systems, which may support the feminist perspective. It is also important to note here that practitioners themselves are complex adaptive systems and, therefore, while open to adaptations within the environment in which they work, can also be subject to positive and negative feedback loops that either encourage or prevent change. In connection with this, Halleck (1971) found that therapists construct their role on the ideological stance that reflects both the moral and political world that exists within society, suggesting how the broader environment can mould and shape those that work with DA perpetrators. While adaptation will take place, it is argued that a number of variables, including practitioners' positionality, may impact upon the implementation of BBR programmes and either promote such changes or inhibit new initiatives. It is therefore important that during the BBR implementation, the programme is seen to be legitimate, and a genuine 'buy in' by practitioners takes place. If this does not occur, resistance from staff, programme non-compliance and programme drift may be emergent outcomes.

Ross, Polaschek and Ward (2008) summarise the point clearly:

> Systemic policies often dictate therapist workloads, access to supervision and professional development, levels of training and so on. Thus 'the system' has a key role in determining whether a therapist will have the capacity to approach a therapeutic alliance with the necessary optimism, enthusiasm and commitment. (Ross et al, 2008, p 9)

Reducing complexity through non-bureaucratic relationships

When considering DA and DA programmes from a whole-systems perspective, it seems clear that there is a high level of complexity, and a reduction in this complexity is worth considering. Positive working relationships both between and within systems would not only increase the flow of information and improve communication, but support a coordinated and holistic approach to DA. The quality of the relationship between agents will determine the level of success within an intervention as it is now generally accepted that a working relationship between probationer and practitioner can be a 'vehicle for change' (Copsey, 2011) and lead to positive outcomes. Safran, Samstag, Muran and Stevens (2001) acknowledge that different patterns can exist within a therapeutic alliance and, it turn, can alter different change processes and outcomes. Further to this, such interactions have been described as a 'complex relational web' (Weaver, 2012) or an 'intricate web of inter-relationships' (Mitleton-Kelly, 2003), which is defined and constructed in reference to the social environment. Depending upon the quality of the relationship, Weaver (2012) argues that outcomes such as trust and mutual concern or, conversely, domination and fear can emerge from a positive or negative relationship, respectively. From my own recent research endeavours while working within probation, these findings are congruent with those of Weaver (2012). When considering positive working relationships within probation practice, probationers discussed how an increased belief in self, feelings of acceptance and mutual respect, and honesty towards their probation supervisor emerged both during and after their relationship with probation practitioners (Lewis, forthcoming [b]). Negative relationships were also explored within the research and emergent outcomes including rejection, anxiety and blame were discussed by probationers. It is therefore argued that the 'climate' that exists within a group room (or one-to-one session) is congruent with change, and is not, as Mitleton-Kelly (2003) states, inhibited or blocked by over complicated bureaucracy and procedures. In order to promote change, practitioners should aim to operate on the edge of chaos, working far from equilibrium (see Pycroft, Chapter Ten) in order to encourage positive feedback loops and reinforce pro-social behaviour. Based upon the standardised approach to date within rehabilitative programmes in general, it is questioned how prepared the probation service is to free itself from the rigid approaches adopted thus far so that innovation and creativity can be embraced.

In order to reduce complexity and increase flow through working relationships, it is therefore important to review the manualisation of interventions in the future. MacLeod (1999) states that the quality of a therapeutic relationship is of greater significance (involving important aspects such as the co-construction of empathy) than the techniques themselves; a notion supported by Norcross (2002), who reported that specific techniques only accounted for 15% of positive outcomes, compared to 30% attributed to the therapeutic relationship. These findings have a number of implications for probation practice and support the rationale of focusing upon engagement skills, 'the relationship' and reflective practice through the new initiatives that have been founded by the Offender Engagement Programme in light of emerging research. Creating rigid manuals that are operationalised using terms such as 'programme integrity' creates a standard by which each tutor can be observed, but reduces the ability to be responsive to the probationer participating in the programme and limits therapeutic artistry (Mann, 2009). Marshall and Burton (2010) argue that an over-manualised treatment can be restrictive and discourage a full recognition of the unique features of an individual. As cited by Marshall and Burton (2010), Fisher (2008) discovered that greater manual adherence led, in fact, to a less effective treatment within the context of DA interventions and that a more psychotherapeutic approach showed greater promise. In support of this notion, Rivett and Rees (2008) agree that a strict manualised approach limits the ability of a programme to consider the heterogeneity of DA perpetrators in changing their thoughts and behaviour. While it would seem that the BBR programme has recognised the importance of the therapeutic relationship within DA interventions, it is argued that this lacks sufficient depth and exploration in light of its importance and does not reflect a focus on 'the relationship' adequately within its training.

There seems to be an assumption within the literature (and, consequently, within the BBR literature) that when 'the relationship' is discussed, we are all clear on what this 'looks like' and make the assumption that practitioners all experience it and know how it can be achieved within practice. Therefore, as recommended by Mann (2009), practitioners need to be trained in both therapeutic skills as well as programme content. Further to this, consistent and meaningful support needs to be established for practitioners to enable them to continuously build and reflect upon their skills and knowledge in order to produce mindful practitioners that possess skills that are congruent to facilitating change. In isolation, however, skills training and the continuous development of these skills is not enough. If the facilitator is considered as a whole, their beliefs, values and characteristics (and the interaction of these) have a significant role in how respected and legitimate a practitioner is perceived to be by DA perpetrators. A system that supports the exploration of values and promotes mindful and reflective practitioners may not only reduce complexity, but also allow for interventions to be facilitated effectively within probation practice. This represents a radical departure from some current practices within probation (such as the assessment of 'manual adherence'), which may be uncomfortable for those who seek control and order and liberating for those that enjoy the idea of working on the edge of chaos.

To draw some conclusions about the current poor outcomes relating to DA interventions to date, I purpose that this may be not only due to the narrow conceptualisation of success, as discussed earlier, but also because the whole system is not mobilised. Key performance indicators such as compliance and completion, as well as the audit process, can become a type of attractor (see Jennings and Pycroft, 2012, ch 13 ; see also Jennings, Chapter Two), which can distort the therapeutic value of the programme and not provide the desirable outcome despite a whole range of controls. In fact, these controls may even be a form of negative feedback driving the programme towards equilibrium and stability. To move forward, Zimmerman (1996) proposes the replacement of firm boundaries within a traditional organisation with more flexible bonds to allow for an open system that is based upon trust instead of control. By encouraging positive feedback loops of communication throughout 'the system', Zimmerman (1996) proposed the use of chaotic management strategies to encourage staff autonomy and power to develop their potential (edge of chaos; see Pycroft, Chapter Ten).

Therapeutic relationships can also be considered in relation to coercion within rehabilitation. An assumption that generally exists within a therapeutic context is the aspect of motivation. If an individual is ready and willing to change, then they may decide to embark upon some form of therapy to assist them in making such changes. Within probation, this is not always the case and, in some senses, correctional interventions are already at a disadvantage due to the reality of what is in effect quasi-coercion.[3] As McNeill (2013) rightly highlights, this can be considered a moral problem within the realms of rehabilitation as, ultimately, they are programmes of compliance and therefore enforceable. It is becoming increasingly recognised that in order for an offender to desist from crime, the probationer needs to take part in their own rehabilitation through collaborative working and active participation (Rex, 1999).

Within BBR, progress has been made with respect to the practice of coercion, whereby probationers are asked to sign the 'conditions of success' in order to attend a programme. These 'conditions' include the fundamental ground rules around engaging with the programme, such as playing an active, supportive, respectful and open role within the group. It is highlighted to the individual prior to signing that while they have the 'choice' to refuse such conditions, if this is their decision, then the order is returned to court. A number of group members, when faced with this decision, do highlight that, really, 'I have no choice', and it is questioned whether this is just disguised coercion. This concept of quasi-coercive treatment has been welcomed by some (Stevens, 2012); however, research has suggested that coercion has little impact upon outcomes in itself (Day et al, 2004), but that it is more about *how* the offender perceives this coercion. Building upon intrinsic motivation has been seen to decrease perceived coercion (Wild et al, 2001), as well as offender 'buy-in' to the programme (Day et al, 2004). Day et al (2004) stated that the therapeutic relationship and skills of the practitioner can be used to inhibit the effects of coercion and reduce complexity through engagement and collaborative working. To some extent, coercion may be necessary within the work of interventions and, instead, a glance towards legitimacy may inhibit the effects of coercion as it exists currently. If a perpetrator can effectively 'buy in' to such an intervention, whether it is optional or not no longer becomes an issue. As Pycroft (2012, p 184) summarises:

> The issue, then, is not simply about coercion or non-coercion, but the way in which the rehabilitative relationship is configured, the ways in which particular personal characteristics are expressed within different settings and the degree to which they are seen as legitimate.

With respect to the BBR programme, pre-group sessions have been increased (from one to two) in order to prepare DA perpetrators for programme work and build motivation, to develop the therapeutic relationship between facilitator and probationer, and to promote legitimacy. To develop this further, it is argued that a collaborative response between systems will smooth out complexity as well as build upon the legitimacy of the programme, with multiple agent 'buy-in' and an overall more cohesive system.

Conclusion

Applying complexity theory to DA interventions is useful in order to gain a greater understanding of DA and draw some conclusions as to how such knowledge can be practically applied in the future within DA interventions. There is no simple solution to DA and in light of current probation initiatives, this leaves programmes in a difficult and ever-challenging position. In order to progress within the realm of DA interventions and rehabilitation, further continuous research needs to be integrated within a flexible programme that is established on the premise of becoming the first *learning* programme of its kind. A programme that is able to evolve, shape and adapt (working on the edge of chaos), as well as flexibly meet the needs of perpetrators, victims and society as a whole. Fluid communication, good working relationships and substantive legitimacy are important for such an approach to be successful in addressing DA effectively within our communities. The importance of the relationship and need to create flexibility through reducing bureaucracy through the de-manualisation of programmes is vital within and between systems and this may be achieved through effective and thorough training and support that is responsive and suitable to the needs of the practitioner.

While an individualistic, differentiated approach is welcomed, societal aspects that are characteristic of DA should not be ignored as a result of this shift. It has been argued that if the movement towards more ontogenetic ways of working accelerates, these themes may be diluted, with further consequences to practice. A whole-system approach should therefore be embraced within DA interventions in order for a coordinated and collaborative response to be actualised through interconnectivity and feedback processes. It is reasonable to argue that, in some ways, BBR has been innovative within its approach to DA and has addressed a number of the problems associated with Duluth-based interventions; however, the context and structures within which BBR is situated may potentially constrain and inhibit its efficacy. It will be interesting to observe how the BBR programme is evaluated in the future and whether it will address evaluation with as much rigour as it has promised. At this stage, it is tentatively argued that BBR does not sufficiently respond to the complexities of DA within programme and system development in order to achieve long-term success in addressing DA within our communities. More work is encouraged that embraces a complexity perspective and draws upon the knowledge and insights that can emerge from such an approach. It is appreciated that this holds many challenges, but with one in four women experiencing DA during their lifetime (Home Office, 2013), these challenges are worth overcoming.

Notes

[1] Although, in the past, this has become a process of matching individuals to particular interventions, which is not supported by the research evidence (see Pycroft, Chapter Ten).

[2] Once BBR is implemented, WSWs will be renamed Partner Link Workers.

[3] Offenders may 'consent' as an alternative to a more punitive sanction such as prison.

References

Babcock, J. (2009) 'Foreward', in P. Lehmann and C.A. Simmons (eds) *Strengths-based batterer intervention: a new paradigm for ending family violence*, New York, NY: Springer.

Babcock, J.C., Green, C.E. and Robie, C. (2004) 'Does batterers' treatment work? A meta-analytic review of domestic violence treatment', *Clinical Psychology Review*, vol 23, pp 1023–53.

Bailey, B., Buchbinder, E. and Eisikovits, Z. (2011) 'Male social workers working with those that batter: dilemmas in gender identity'. *Journal of Interpersonal violence*, vol 26, no 9, pp 1741–62.

Bennett, L. and Williams, O. (2001) 'Controversies and recent students for batterer program effectiveness', Applied Research Forum, National Electronic Network on Violence Against Women. Available at: http://xa.yimg.com/kq/groups/20981664/1106805941/name/Q.+Controversies+%26+Recent+Studies+of+BIP+Effectiveness.pdf

Bilby, C. and Hatcher, R. (2004) *Early stages in the implementation of the Integrated Domestic Abuse Project*, Home Office Online Report 29/04, London: Home Office.

Bowen, E. and Gilchrist, E.A. (2004) 'Comprehensive evaluation: a holistic approach in evaluating domestic violence perpetrator programs', *International Journal of Offender Therapy and Comparative Criminology*, vol 48, no 2, pp 215–34.

Copsey, M. (2011) *The offender engagement programme, an overview from programme director, Martin Copsey*. Retrieved from http://www. essexprobationtrust.org.uk/doc/The_Offender_Engagement_ Programme_Overview_July_11.pdf

Day, A. and Ward, T. (2010) 'Rehabilitation as a value-laden process', *International Journal of Offender Therapy and Comparative Criminology*, vol 54, no 3, pp 289–306.

Day, A., Tucker, K. and Howells, K. (2004) 'Coerced offender rehabilitation – a defensible practice?', *Psychology, Crime and Law*, vol 10, no 3, pp 259–69.

Dutton, D.G. (1995) 'Male abusiveness in intimate relationships', *Clinical Psychology Review*, vol 15, pp 567–81.

Dutton, D.G. and Corvo, K. (2007) 'The Duluth model: a data-impervious paradigm and a failed strategy', *Aggression and Violence*, vol 12, pp 658–67.

Eadie, T. and Knight, C. (2002) 'Domestic violence programmes: reflections on the shift from independent to statutory provision', *The Howard Journal*, vol 41, no 2, pp 167–81.

Fisher, A. (2008) 'Re-visioning male violence: men of courage', paper presented at the First Provincial Conference on Male Sexual Victimization, Toronto, Ontario, March.

Fisher, E. (2011) 'Perpetrators on domestic violence: co-ordinating responses to complex needs', *Irish Probation Journal*, vol 8, pp 124–40.

Gadd, D. (2004) 'Evidence-led policy or policy-led evidence? Cognitive behavioural programmes for men who are violent towards women', *Criminology and Criminal Justice*, vol 4, no 2, pp 173–97.

Gelles, R. (2001) 'Standards for programs for men who batter? Not yet', in R. Geffner and A. Rosenbaum (eds) *Domestic violence offenders: current interventions, research and implications for policies and standards*, New York, NY: Howarth Press.

Glaser, D. (1964) *Effectiveness of a prison and parole system*, Indianapolis, IN: Bobbs-Merrill.

Gondolf, E.W. (2002) *Batterer intervention systems. Issues, outcomes and recommendations*, London: Sage.

Hague, G. and Malos, E. (1998) 'Inter-agency approaches to domestic violence and the role of social services', *British Journal of Social Work*, vol 280, pp 369–86.

Halleck, S.L. (1971) *The politics of therapy*, San Francisco, CA: Jossey-Bass.

Heylighan, F., Cilliers, P. and Gershenson, C. (2007) 'Philosophy and complexity', in J. Bogg and R. Geyer (eds) *Complexity, science and society*, Oxford: Radcliffe.

Holtzworth-Munroe, A., Meehan, C., Herron, K., Rehman, U. and Stuart, G.L. (2003) 'Do subtypes of maritally violent men continue to differ over time?', *Journal of Consulting and Clinical Psychology*, vol 71, pp 728–40.

Home Office (2013) 'Ending violence against women and girls in the UK'. Available at: https://www.gov.uk/government/policies/ending-violence-against-women-and-girls-in-the-uk

Humpreys, C., Regan, L., River, D. and Thiara, R.K. (2005) 'Domestic violence and substance use: tackling complexity', *British Journal of Social Work*, vol 35, pp 1303–20.

Iliffe, G. and Steed, L. (2000) 'Exploring the counsellor's experience of working with perpetrators and survivors of domestic violence', *Journal of Interpersonal Violence*, vol 15, pp 393–412.

Jeglic, E.L., Maile, C. and Calkins-Mercado, C. (2012) 'Treatment of offender populations: implications for risk management and community reintegration', in L. Gideon and H.-E. Sung (eds) *Rethinking corrections: rehabilitation, re-entry and reintegration*, London: Sage.

Jennings, P. and Pycroft, A. (2012) 'The numbers game: A systems perspective on risk', in A. Pycroft and S. Clift (eds) *Risk and rehabilitation: management and treatment of substance misuse and mental health problems in the criminal justice system*, Bristol: Policy Press.

Jewell, L.M. and Wormith, J.M. (2010) 'Variables associated with attrition from domestic violence treatment programs targeting male batterers: a meta-analysis', *Criminal Justice and Behavior*, vol 37, pp 1086–113.

Johnson, S.P. and Sullivan, C.M. (2008) 'How child protection workers support or further victimize battered mothers', *Affilia*, vol 23, no 3, pp 242–57.

Kelly, J.B. and Johnson, M.P. (2008) 'Differentiation among types of intimate partner violence: research update and implications for interventions', *Family Court Review*, vol 46, no 3, pp 476–99.

Koslowski, S.W. and Ilgen, D.R. (2006) 'Enhancing the effectiveness of work groups and teams', *Psychological Science in the Public Interest*, vol 7, no 3, pp 77–124.

Lehmann, P. and Simmons, C.A. (2009) 'The state of batterer intervention programs: an analytic discussion', in P. Lehmann and C.A. Simmons (eds) *Strengths-based batterer intervention: a new paradigm in ending family violence*, New York, NY: Springer.

Lewis, S. (forthcoming [a]) 'Learning from success and failure: deconstructing the working relationship within probation practice and exploring its impact, using a collaborative approach', *Probation Journal*.

Lewis, S. (forthcoming [b]) 'Exploring positive working relationships in light of the aims of probation, using a collaborative approach', *Probation Journal*.

Mair, G. (2004) 'Introduction: what works and what matters', in G. Mair (ed) *What matters in probation*, Cullompton: Willan Publishing, pp 1–11.

Maiuro, R.D., Cahn, T.S. and Vitaliano, P.P. (1986) 'Assertiveness deficits and hostility in domestically violent men', *Violence and Victims*, vol 1, no 4, pp 279–89.

Mann, R. (2009) 'Sex offender treatment: the case for manualisation', *Journal of Sexual Aggression*, vol 15, no 2, pp 121–31.

Marshall, W.L. and Burton, D.L. (2010) 'The importance of group processes in offender treatment', *Aggression and Violence Behavior*, vol 15, pp 141–9.

Maruna, S. (2001) *Making good: how ex-convicts reform and rebuild their lives*, Washington, DC: American Psychological Association.

McLeod, J. (1999) 'A narrative social constructivist approach to therapeutic empathy', *Counselling Psychology Quarterly*, vol 12, no 4, pp 377–94.

McMurran, M. (2002) 'Assessing and changing motivation to offend', in W.M. Cox and E. Klinger (eds) *Motivating people for change: a handbook of motivational counselling*, Chichester: Wiley.

McNeill, F. (2013) 'When punishment is rehabilitation', in G. Bruinsma and D. Weisburd (eds) *The Springer encyclopaedia of criminology and criminal justice*, Springer.

Mitleton-Kelly, E. (2003) 'Ten principles of complexity and enabling infrastructure. Complex systems and evolutionary perspectives on organisations: the application of complexity theory to organisations', Complexity Research Programme, London School of Economics. Available at: http://www.psych.lse.ac.uk/complexity/PDFiles/publication/Ten_principles_of_complexity_enabling_infrastructure.pdf

Morin, E. (2006) 'Restricted complexity, general complexity', paper presented at the Colloquium 'Intelligence de la complexité: épistémologie et pragmatique', Cerisy-La-Salle, France, 26 June (translated from the French by Carlos Gershenson).

Morran, D. (2008) 'Firing up and burning out: the personal and professional impact of working in domestic violence programmes', *Probation Journal*, vol 55, no 2, pp 139–52.

Morran, D., Wolf-Light, P., Andrew, M. and Macrae, R. (2011) 'Re-education or recovery? Re-thinking some aspects of domestic violence perpetrator programmes', *Probation Journal*, vol 58, no 1, pp 23–36.

Mullender, A. and Burton, S. (2001a) *Reducing domestic violence… What works? Perpetrator programmes*, Home Office Briefing Note, London: Home Office.

Mullender, A. and Burton, S. (2001b) 'Good practice with perpetrators of Domestic Violence', *Probation Journal*, vol 48, no 4, pp 260–8. doi: 10.1177/026455050104800403

Murphy, C.M., Winters, J., O'Farrell, T.J., Fals-Stewart, W. and Murphy, M. (2005) 'Alcohol consumption and intimate partner violence by alcoholic men: comparing violent and nonviolent conflicts', *Psychology of Addictive Behaviors*, vol 19, pp 35–42.

Newman, J. and Nutley, S. (2003) 'Transforming the probation service: 'what works', organisational change and professional identity', *Policy and Politics*, vol 31, no 4, pp 547–63.

NOMS (National Offender Management Service) (2010) *What works with domestic violence offenders?*, London: Ministry of Justice.

Norcross, J.C. (2002) *Psychotherapy relationships that work*, New York, NY: Oxford University Press.

O'Cinneide, C. (2002) *A single equality body: lessons from abroad*, Manchester: Equal Opportunities Commission, Commission for Racial Equality and Disability Rights Commission.

Pence, E. and Shepard, M. (1988) 'Integrating theory and practice: the challenge of the Battered Women's Movement', in K. Yllo and M. Bogarde (eds) *Feminist perspective on wife abuse*, Beverly Hills, CA: Sage.

Petrillo, M. (2007) 'Power struggle: gender issues for female probation officers in the supervision of high risk offenders', *Probation Journal*, vol 54, no 4, pp 394–406.

Polaschek, D.L.L. (2010) 'Rehabilitating violent offenders', in J. Brown and E. Campbell (eds) *Handbook of forensic psychology: theory, assessment, research and practice*, Cambridge: Cambridge University Press, pp 441–52.

Pycroft, A. (2010) *Understanding and working with substance misusers*, London: Sage.

Pycroft, A. (2012) 'Rehabilitation in a post what works era: the possibilities of co-mimethical virtue', in A. Pycroft and S. Clift (eds) *Risk and rehabilitation: the management and treatment of substance misuse and mental health in the criminal justice system*, Bristol: The Policy Press.

Rees, A. and Rivet, M. (2005) 'Let a hundred flowers bloom, let a hundred schools of thought contend', *Probation Journal*, vol 52, no 3, pp 277–88.

Rex, S. (1999) 'Desistance from crime: experience of probation', *Howard Journal of Criminal Justice*, vol 38, no 4, pp 366–83.

Rivett, M. and Rees, A. (2008) *Addressing offender behaviour: Context, practice and values*, Devon: Willan.

Ross, E.C., Polaschek, D.L.L. and Ward, T. (2008) 'The therapeutic alliance: a theoretical revision for offender rehabilitation', *Aggression and Violent Behaviour*, vol 13, pp 462–80.

Ross, J.M. and Babcock, J.C. (2009) 'Proactive and reactive violence among intimate partner violent men diagnosed with antisocial and borderline personality disorder', *Journal of Family Violence*, vol 24, pp 607–17.

Safran, J.D., Samstag, L.W., Muran, C. and Stevens, C. (2001) 'Repairing alliance ruptures', *Psychotherapy*, vol 38, no 4, pp 406–12.

Schweinle, W. and Ickes, W. (2007) 'The role of men's critical/rejecting overattribution bias, affect and attentional disengagement in marital aggression', *Journal of Social and Clinical Psychology*, vol 26, no 2, pp 173–98.

Sedgwick, D. (2001) *Introduction to Jungian psychotherapy: the therapeutic relationship*, New York, NY: Taylor & Francis.

Shepard, M. and Pence, E. (eds) (1999) *Coordinating community response to domestic violence: lessons from Duluth and beyond*, Thousand Oaks, CA: Sage.

Shepard, M.F., Falk, D.R. and Elliott, B.A. (2002) 'Enhancing coordinated community responses to reduce recidivism in cases of domestic violence', *Journal of Interpersonal Violence*, vol 17, no 5, pp 551–69.

Soler, H., Vinayak, P. and Quadagno, D. (2010) 'Biosocial aspects of domestic violence', *Psychoneuroendocrinology*, vol 25, no 7, pp 721–39.

Stevens, A. (2012) 'The ethics and effectiveness of coerced treatment for people who use drugs', *Human Rights and Drugs*, vol 2, no 1, pp 7–16.

Stith, S.M., Smith, D.B., Penn, C., Ward, D. and Tritt, D. (2004) 'Intimate partner physical abuse perpetration and victimization risk factors: a meta-analytic review', *Journal of Aggression and Violent Behavior*, vol 10, pp 65–98.

Strid, S., Armstrong, J. and Walby, S. (2008) *Report analysing intersectionality in gender equality policies for the United Kingdom and the EU*, QUING Project, Vienna: Institute for Human Sciences (IWM). Available at: http://www.quing.eu/files/results/ir_uk.pdf

Weatherstone, P. (nd) 'New direction in NOMS: domestic abuse programmes', Rehabilitation Service Group, Ministry of Justice. Available at: http://www.cepprobation.org/uploaded_files/Pres%20 STARR%20Par%20Weatherstone.pdf

Weaver, B. (2012) 'The relational context of desistance: some implications and opportunities for social policy', *Social Policy and Administration*, vol 46, no 4, pp 395–412.

Westmarland, N. and Kelly, L. (2012) 'Why extending measurements of "success" in domestic violence perpetrator programmes matters for social work', *British Journal of Social Work*, vol 43, no 6, pp 1092–1110..

Wild, T.C., Newton-Taylor, B., Ogborne, A.C., Mann, R., Erickson, P. and Macdonald, S. (2001) 'Attitudes towards compulsory substance abuse treatment: a comparison of the public, counsellors, probationer and judges' views', *Drugs: Education, Prevention and Policy*, vol 8, pp 33–45.

Wolfe, D.A. and Jaffe, P.G. (1999) 'Emerging strategies in the prevention of domestic violence', *Domestic Violence and Children*, vol 9, no 3, pp 133–44.

Yalom, I.D. (1995) *The theory and practice of group psychotherapy* (4th edn), New York, NY: Basic Books.

Zimmerman, B. (1996) 'The art, science of managing changeability. Lessons from chaos to complexity theories', keynote presentation at the Order and Chaos Conference, Grenfield College, Memorial University, Newfoundland, Canada.

TWELVE

Complexity, law and ethics: on drug addiction, natural recovery and the diagnostics of psychological jurisprudence

Bruce Arrigo and Christopher Williams

Introduction: the complexity of drug addiction

According to most experts, successful drug addiction intervention and substance abuse recovery necessarily *requires* the use of external constraints and, in some cases, even exogenous forms of coercion (Morgan and Lizke, 2007; Barlow, 2010; Walker, 2010). What this means, then, is that any subsequent manifestation of disorder (ie decompensation, relapse or dependency-seeking) will necessitate further system control from outside the disorganised and disruptive self. This is a self whose patterns of behaviour are deemed too unpredictable, too chaotic, to warrant the freedom to be (Williams and Arrigo, 2002, 2007, forthcoming). But, what if the above-stated theoretical claims and the science that has been used to test and measure them were flawed? What if the mobilisation and activation of human social capital (eg from a complexity perspective, the addict's possible self-organisation) *required* perturbations of disorder, disequilibrium and instability to make this natural recovery more fully realisable? Moreover, what normative framework regarding ontology (ie the 'laws' of being) might exist to support this alternative approach to drug addiction and natural recovery? How, and in what ways, might this framework and approach suggest an emergent and radicalised jurisprudence: one that advances a collectivist agenda in overcoming system control and regulation by way of externalities or formal intervention (eg mandated in-patient medication treatment, structured out-patient rehabilitation programming)?

This chapter critically probes the under-examined relationship between substance abuse and spontaneous self-healing. To situate the critique, two streams of philosophical analysis will be presented and integrated. In particular, selected insights from the science of complexity studies (non-linear dynamical systems theory) and the diagnostics of psychological jurisprudence (PJ) will be described. The relevancies of these insights will be fitted to the necessity of exogenous system-based policy reform. These reforms will emphasise changes in substance abuse, mental health and criminal justice theory and science for and about human social capital.

The human project: the science of complexity, adaptability and self-organisation

The evolving science of dynamical systems theory has, from its inception, been inspired by the 'inherent creativity', 'spontaneous appearance of novel structures' and 'autonomous adaptation to a changing environment' (Heylighen, 2001, p 253) that characterises and unifies the diverse phenomena it studies. This science, then, focuses on the study of system non-linearity and complexity. One of a series of interrelated principles defining such systems, *self-organisation*, describes a process by which structures or patterns appear without impositions from external agents (eg Ashby, 1962; Prigogine and Stengers, 1984). Indeed, one of the most fundamental features of self-organising systems (as distinguished from mechanistic systems) is the process by which order is generated, namely, pattern formation occurs through repeated interactions *within* the system. The self-organising process is thus internal to the system, rather than dependent upon intervention from exogenous influences. In other words, '[t]he pattern is an emergent property of the system, rather than a property imposed on the system by an external ordering influence' (Camazine et al, 2003, p 8).

Of particular interest for present purposes is this self-organising feature of living systems – including, at least hypothetically, human systems of a biological, psychological and/or social nature. The ways in which the behavioural patterns of those systems can exhibit emergent order in a largely autonomous fashion following periods of disorder potentially contradicts our intuitive suppositions concerning the need for and utility of outside manipulation. As Heylighen (2001, p 254) suggested of our perception of organised phenomena, 'we tend to assume that someone or something must have arranged the components in that particular order'.

The fundamental instability of dynamical systems, combined with their capacity for self-organisation, enables them to adapt – sometimes spontaneously – to environmental changes. Self-organising systems are, in this respect, creative systems. The emergence of novel dynamics and higher levels of organisation in living systems following (indeed, because of) the presence of disorder means that these systems are not simply driven into deeper and deeper levels of disorder, as might typify a 'closed' system (see, eg, Bruzzo and Vimal, 2007). Distinguished instead by an 'open' relationship with the environment, non-linear dynamical systems exhibit a tendency to form new, more adaptive structures and more functional patterns of behaviour than that which had previously characterised the system.

As Ashby (1962) and others have since proposed, dynamical systems such as living organisms tend always towards a state of equilibrium. Perturbations can destabilise such systems, initiating a process of reorganisation and thus propelling them towards more adaptive states of equilibrium. Dynamic, self-organising systems are, in this respect, characteristically resilient, capable of assimilating noise and utilising perturbations for adaptive or restorative purposes. Environmental pressures of sufficient magnitude can promote disorder and thus trigger the self-organisation process, facilitating the long-term fitness of the system by prodding adaptive self-change. In short, external demands or pressures result in internal changes within the system that produce a series of restorative adaptations in the interest of systemic equilibrium.

It is significant to note that, unlike linear systems, non-linear dynamical systems can have a range of possible 'solutions'; that is, a range of possible adaptive outcomes that serve the interests of restoring a functional relationship with the external world. In other words, 'there is a range of stable configurations into which the system may settle' and, importantly, 'there is no *a priori* way to decide which solution is the "right" one' (Heylighen, 2001, p 270). This characteristic of non-linear dynamical systems contributes to their unpredictability and promotes their distinctive creativity. The stability (or orderly configuration) resulting from self-organising processes will, though unpredictable, be suited to the particular demands of the system's present circumstances. We might read this to mean that the uniqueness of a particular non-linear dynamical system and its prevailing circumstances largely precludes the imposition of predetermined behavioural patterns and outcomes. No defined outcome or adaptive process intended to generate that outcome will necessarily be effective for any given system. By their nature, self-organising systems require creative freedom and a variety of possible relationships with their environment to successfully adapt and maintain a healthy system–environment relationship that promotes stability and growth.

These basic features or principles of self-organising dynamical systems can, at least analogously, aid our understanding of many human behavioural outcomes. Research in the area of addiction studies, for instance, continues to uncover recovery dynamics similar to those associated with self-organisation in non-linear dynamical systems (eg Klingemann and Sobell, 2007). Variously described as 'self-change', 'natural recovery' or 'spontaneous remission', an increasing wealth of literature suggests that for some people, some of the time, recovery from gambling (Toneatto et al, 2008), smoking (Doran et al, 2006), eating disorders (Polivy, 2007), criminality (Takala, 2007) and other addiction- and dependence-based disorders can occur without formal intervention or professional assistance (eg Edwards and Babor, 2012). Recent empirical support for this claim in the substance abuse literature, for example, reports natural recovery rates as high as 73% (Schutte et al, 2006) and 66% (Rumpf et al, 2009), respectively. Thus, as Klingemann et al (2009, p 1510) concluded, 'self-change is a major pathway to recovery and … [it] may provide a rich source of information on mechanisms of behavior change in general'.

Conceptually, 'self-change' or 'natural recovery' suggests that some persons enduring addiction- or dependence-based problems successfully navigate the path of recovery through autonomously devised and implemented strategies of resolution. Much akin to our assumption that organisation (particularly following disorder) necessitates external ordering influence, the popular image of the addict is one of a lack or loss of control, necessitating therapeutic guidance or imposed – perhaps mandatory – treatment. As research on the self-organising dynamics of non-linear systems has challenged the first of these assumptions, research on self-change and natural recovery continues to challenge the latter. Not only are many within the substance-dependent population not powerless (in the sense that 12-Step programmes conceive of powerlessness), but formal treatment-based intervention may be unnecessary, insufficient and even counterproductive (eg Walters, 2000a, 2000b).

As critical influences from the environment often instigate self-change in non-linear dynamical systems, many cases of natural recovery appear to be preceded by one or more triggering events, the occurrence (or endurance) of which signals the need to initiate a transformative process. A variety of perturbations (eg family or job concerns, legal problems, feelings of losing control over oneself) can serve as critical events, and subsequent periods of disorder may be sufficient to instigate a process of reorganisation to better meet environmental demands. Self-initiated, autonomous desistance from unhealthy drug use (and modifications of unhealthy behavioural patterns in general) can give rise to a complexity of organisation that is better able to withstand future perturbations than that which is artificially organised from without. As is the case with non-linear dynamical systems more generally, adaptive change in populations of substance-dependent persons may require the creative freedom to navigate a variety of 'attractors'. In the science of complexity, attractors constitute a range of possible adaptive outcomes (eg low-risk drug or alcohol use) into which a system settles (Williams and Arrigo, 2007), rather than complete abstinence, as required by some treatment programmes (eg Cohen et al, 2007; see also Jennings, Chapter Two; Wolf-Branigin, Chapter Four; Pycroft, Chapter Ten).

Psychological jurisprudence: the diagnostics of drug treatment and the conditions of spontaneous recovery

PJ is a radical philosophical perspective and a dynamic critique of human social capital (Arrigo, 2004; Arrigo et al, 2011), rooted in the continental rather than analytic tradition (Arrigo, 2012). This is a tradition that rejects excessive reliance on empiricism or scientism as the only basis to explain phenomena, emphasises historicism (eg the importance of languages and codes, space and time, contexts and settings) as a way to account for the vagaries of possible experience, identifies prospects for human social change (ie transformation) as rooted in consciousness and its emancipation, and recognises the socio-cultural embeddedness of knowledge, experience and reality (eg Hardie-Bick and Lippens, 2011). Human social capital refers to the social person, to the self in society, being human and doing humanness differently. This difference consists of growing incipient and adaptive intra-psychic, interpersonal, institutional and communal forms of human social relating, and it (this difference) emerges from being/doing human social relating ever-more humanistically (Sartre, 1956; Fromm, 1994 [1941]), virtuously (Levinas, 2004) and productively (Marx, 1964; Deleuze, 1983). This is being/doing that, under sufficient and necessary non-linear dynamical systems conditions, mobilises and harnesses will in the service of power (Nietzsche, 1968). Power refers to the unleashing of latent possibilities in being (eg *doing* drug treatment, relapse and recovery differently) and the marshalling of untapped potentialities in becoming (eg *embodying* drug treatment, relapse and recovery differently). It is in this way, then, that PJ represents an assessment of the forces – whether symbolic, linguistic, material and/or cultural in their essential compositions – that aesthetically, epistemologically, ethically and ontologically bind and check (that govern authoritatively) the willing of human social capital as difference (Arrigo, 2012). Presently, the interdependent, mutually supporting and co-productive operation of these whole-system forces establishes harm-generating conditions that domesticate (constrain) and discipline (coerce) the self in society (Arrigo, 2010, 2011a). These conditions capture the social person as *shadow*: the traces of being and/ or of becoming (Arrigo and Milovanovic, 2009). This being and/or becoming is less than what is or could be imagined (intra-psychically, in consciousness), less than what is or could be spoken (interpersonally, in shared histories), less than what is or could be inhabited (institutionally, in lived and/or embodied practices), and less than what is or could be replicated (communally, in the artefacts of a culture).

When expressions of the social person as shadow are collectively taken to be healthy and normative dimensions of human social progress, then the *society of captives* is made more imminent (Arrigo, 2013a). This is captivity that renders being otherwise, as lacking in consciousness (ie doing/embodying drug treatment, relapse and recovery differently is made inconceivable or unimaginable). This is captivity that renders being otherwise, as deferred in texts (ie the developing narratives of self-healing, self-change, self-adaptation or self-organisation are made incomprehensible or indescribable). This is captivity that renders being otherwise, as absent in systems of thought and in bodies of knowledge (ie the theory and science of human social capital as difference, addiction studies and spontaneous recovery are made un-presentable or uninhabitable) (eg Arrigo and Takahashi, 2006; Kimberly and McLellan, 2006; Williams and Arrigo, 2007).

Overcoming PJ's diagnosis of captivity requires a re-engagement with the madness that it (the society of captives) nurtures, the citizenship that it (the shadow) erodes and the human social justice that both imprison (ie difference as freedom constrained and coerced, reduced and repressed) (Arrigo and Williams, 2009). A reconsideration of this sort necessarily specifies how risk (ie the freedom to be/become) is managed such that identities (ie doing/embodying humanness differently) are recursively marginalised for and about one and all (Arrigo, 2011a). The enduring manifestation of this state of affairs is the harm of captivity (Arrigo, 2012), the crime of social dis-ease (Arrigo, 2013a, 2013b). These considerations draw attention to the theory, method and praxis of PJ and they are reviewed in brief in the following.

As theory, PJ indicates that captivity extends not only to the kept, but also to their keepers, regulators and watchers (Arrigo et al, 2011; Arrigo and Davidson, 2013). The kept encompass all those who aesthetically, epistemologically, ethically and ontologically are confined (ie domesticated and disciplined). The keepers or jailers of the kept include all those who utilise techniques and rely on mechanisms that discipline and domesticate difference (ie that impose constraints on and/or exercise coercion over risk). The regulators of the kept consist of all those who educate for and about captivity, administrate over captivity's maintenance, and govern and/or legislate on behalf of captivity's normalisation. The watchers of the kept are composed of all those who uncritically observe or sadomasochistically depend upon captivity's harm-generating dynamics (ie the punitive general public, the corrections industry).

The harms emanating from the society of captives are existential (the imprisonment of individual and collectivist consciousness), social (the bondage of sameness reproduced interpersonally, institutionally and/or communally) and corporeal (the confinement of embodied subjectivity, of human/social capital) in their essential compositions and effects. They (these harms) consist of limits on being, constraints on one's humanity and denials of becoming, coercions of one's humanity (Arrigo and Milovanovic, 2009). Sustaining this captivity – an imprisonment that is totalising in its reductions and repressions – is madness for one and all (Arrigo et al, 2011). Indeed, under conditions of totalising confinement, the society of captives transmutates into the captivity of society (Arrigo, 2013a).

The manifestation of this captivity – of human social capital constrained by and coerced through excessive investments in risk management practices that reduce/repress difference to sameness – reifies the risk society (Bauman, 1998; Beck, 2009). The risk society normalises bad faith (ie self-deception and 'escaping' from freedom's burden) (Sartre, 1956) and false consciousness (Marx, 1964) (ie the hegemony of othering difference, the reification of fetishising sameness) (Arrigo and Bersot, 2014). Risk management is maintained through the forces that bind and check human social capital. As previously stated, these forces include symbolic, linguistic, material and cultural influences. The interactive, interconnected and interdependent intensities and flows of these influences co-produce the social person's reality, and they are the domesticating and disciplining contexts from within which the social person makes meaning, discerns choice, reaches judgment and undertakes action (eg contemplates doing drug recovery differently, contemplates embodying drug recovery differently). Presently, the co-production of these intensities and flows supports captivity conditions (eg being human through compulsory forms of drug treatment) and nurtures captivity's ubiquity (eg doing humanness through mandated forms of recovery vis-à-vis drug and other specialty courts). Thus, will in the service of power is neither mobilised nor harnessed. The society of captives and the captivity of society inexhaustibly prevail.

As method, PJ considers the question of citizenship – of restoring it and of revolutionising it – guided by PJ's Aristotelian-derived (Aristotle, 1976) normative theory (Arrigo et al, 2011). This theory of being holds that the embodied practice of excellence (or of living virtuously, generatively and mindfully) is dynamic, it evolves. Doing human flourishing (ie excellence in being and in citizenship), then, is about cultivating non-linear and emergent habits of character for, by and about one and all. These evolving habits of character – when imagined (ie symbolic realm), spoken (ie linguistic realm), lived (ie material realm) and reproduced (ie cultural realm) – have the nearest power to unleash latent human social capital, to release us from the forces that bind and check, and to overcome the madness that replicates (indeed, celebrates) the shadows of the social person. These shadows are no more than aesthetical, epistemological, ethical and ontological traces of who we could be or could become uniquely, collectively and interdependently (Arrigo, 2013b).

Thus, on the diagnostics of drug treatment and the conditions of spontaneous recovery, PJ questions how and for whom limit-setting constraints (ie reductions in being through risk management) and denial-imposing coercions (ie repressions in becoming through risk management) mobilise the doing of human social capital as difference. Consistent with this method of analysis, Arrigo (forthcoming[a]) has commented on the social person as shadow and the system-sustaining captivity that binds and checks various other citizen groups and/or collectives. Indeed, as he summarily noted:

> when psychiatrically disordered convicts are placed in long-term disciplinary isolation, how and for whom does this practice exhibit courage, compassion, and generosity? When criminally adjudicated sex offenders are subsequently subjected to protracted civil commitment followed by multiple forms of communal inspection and monitoring, how and for whom is dignity affirmed, stigma averted, and healing advanced? When cognitively impaired juveniles are waived to the adult system, found competent to stand trial, and sentenced and punished accordingly, what version of nobility is celebrated and on whom is this goodness bestowed? (Arrigo, 2013a, p 27)

Overcoming the presence of harm-generating flows and intensities requires both will and way (Williams and Arrigo, forthcoming). We contend that PJ's virtue-based philosophy of being – of doing citizenship ever-more humanistically, adaptively and excellently – is a protean antidote to the criminological shadow (Arrigo and Williams, 2009) and to the harm of social dis-ease (Arrigo, 2011b; Arrigo and Bersot, 2014).

As praxis, PJ affirms the interactive, mutually supporting and interrelated link between *thinking about* (ie theorizing) and *doing* (being for and about) social justice (ie the flourishing of human social capital) (Williams and Arrigo, forthcoming). Theory and action are inseparable from and interconnected to this change-oriented enterprise. The project in question is the social person's evolution: the self in society as transforming, as becoming other than being (Levinas, 2004; Arrigo, 2013b). Harnessing and residing within this untapped potential for change (ie of embodying ever more so the ethic of individual well-being, communal good and societal accord) begins as an exercise in critique (ie the solution).

This Aristotelian-based critique considers *how* the virtues of individual responsibility and societal accountability cohabit justice (Arrigo et al, 2011). An assessment of this cohabitation is necessary as it provides a key mutuality from within which to explore the potential of becoming, of managing risk differently and of human social capital as dynamically virtuous and productive freedom. Thus, embodying habits of character (virtues) excellently is an existential, social and corporeal excursion into becoming otherwise (Deleuze, 1983) in and through the SOCIUS (SOCIETY + I + US) (Deleuze and Guattari, 1987). This undertaking is an ongoing journey in schizo-analysis (ie de-territorialisation and re-territorialisation) for a people yet to be (Deleuze and Guattari, 1987). Advancing efforts that further actualise this more complete flourishing or mutating self-excellence (the in-process subject) is a praxis response to captivity, risk management, the shadow and the forces, flows and intensities that support them all.

As praxis strategy, cultivating transforming habits of character entails critical reflexivity or mindfulness (Bourdieu and Wacquant, 1992). Mindfulness is about de-territorialising (disassembling, decoding and demystifying) the images, texts, practices and cultural representations of that which sustains the harms of reduction and/or repression for the kept, as well as for their keepers, regulators and watchers (Arrigo and Milovanovic, 2009). This praxis strategy is about *overcoming* how we think about and do social justice through the shadows and traces of the social person, through the bondage of captivity, and through the totalising constraints and coercive harms that both (ie the society of captives and the criminological shadow) co-produce. Thus, on the diagnostics of drug treatment and the conditions of spontaneous recovery, PJ as normative praxis advances therapeutic interventions and prescriptions that re-territorialise. These are reconfigurations of human social capital that honour, dignify and affirm the harnessing of potentiality's becoming, as other than being (eg the social person as *embodying* drug treatment, relapse and recovery differently). When justice is cohabited as such, then the social person's symbolic, linguistic, material and cultural emancipation is made that much more realisable.

Integrating the science of complexity and the diagnostics of psychological jurisprudence: the case of drug dependency

Figure 12.1 visually depicts the harm-generating conditions that sustain captivity and the shadow with respect to the human social problem of drug dependency and natural recovery for, by and about one and all. The figure also integrates the previously specified insights regarding the science of complexity into the analysis as a way of demonstrating how spontaneous order is consistent with overcoming the diagnostics of PJ. The figure reflects the interdependent, mutually supporting and co-productive forces or spheres of influence that situate the social person. In this instance, several prevailing aesthetical (symbolic), epistemological (linguistic), ethical (material) and ontological (cultural) flows and intensities are presented. These are the flows and intensities within which the recovering substance abuser takes up residence (dwells) and out of which this self in society (this human social capital hailed as addict) makes meaning, discerns choice, reaches judgment and undertakes action.

The fluctuating intensities and influencing flows of the aesthetic realm currently symbolise the doing/embodying of difference mostly as lacking in individual and collectivist consciousness. Put another way, the captivity of bad faith (ie the hegemony of othering difference) and false consciousness (ie the reification of fetishising sameness) normalise as healthy only circumscribed images of drug addiction, dependency or the criminal substance user. The internalised dominance of these portraits helps to make representations of the self in society that include the *doing* of drug treatment, relapse and recovery differently and the *embodying* of drug treatment, relapse and recovery differently largely inconceivable. Overcoming this captivity – an imprisonment whose madness is totalising for, by and about one and all – requires the summoning of will (generative mindfulness) in the service of power (ie mobilising dynamic possibility in being; harnessing transforming potentiality in becoming). Consistent with the science of complexity, *existential self-organisation* is the recognition that the reconstitution (re-territorialisation, reassemblage, resuscitation) of the social person necessitates the retrieval, consumption and circulation of images that capture a different aesthetic. These images symbolise the 'self in society', 'humanness', 'treatment', 'relapse', 'desistance', 'recovery' and so on as other than the fragments and partialities of human social capital that harmfully domesticate and discipline, constrain and coerce, reduce and repress consciousness (Arrigo and Milovanovic, 2009). Instead, the ensuing symbolisations *image craft* the heart of freedom (Cornell, 1998); this is the ongoing life-affirming pursuit of being/doing happiness, flourishing or excellence another way.

Figure 12.1: Psychological jurisprudence, drug addiction and natural recovery: the society of captives, the criminological shadow and spontaneous order

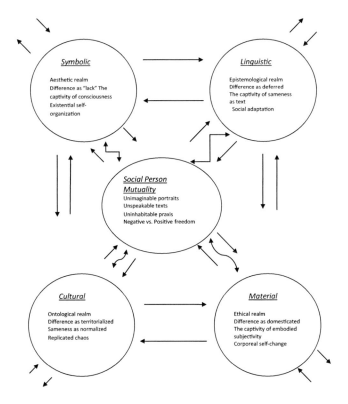

Source: Adapted from Arrigo et al (2011, p 164)

The fluctuating intensities and influencing flows of the epistemological realm currently manifest as absent or deferred the story of difference and render as present and evident the story of sameness. When the story of sameness (in individual and collectivist consciousness) is spoken and/or written, it becomes a shared history, an animated text. As a narrative for, by and about human social capital, the privileging or materialising of this text renders mostly as silent the more dynamic, non-linear and transformative narratives of self-healing. Indeed, organic recovery by way of the complex adaptive system that the human social project constitutes is deemed incomprehensible or, even more disturbing, indescribable (eg Williams and Arrigo, 2002; Arrigo, 2004). This is the bondage of sameness reproduced *ad infinitum* and *ad nauseam* interpersonally, institutionally and/or communally (Arrigo, 2013a). Overcoming these harm-generating/intensifying stories of captivity necessitates an animated text for, by and about the dynamic and yet-to-be-written flourishing of citizenship. These narratives of doing humanness differently, productively and excellently extol the journeying of a people yet to be. *Social adaptation*, then, is the complex systems theory counterpoint to social stagnation. The former is the self in society as fluid, in-process, unscripted and departing (ie moving towards the unwritten, untold, unusual and ever-more unencumbered embodiments of being). The latter is the self in society operating under equilibrium conditions, status quo dynamics, linear movements, predictable patterns and closure trajectories. Embarking on the knowledge-generating excursion of social adaptation – and the emergent networks of interaction that follow from it – is a revolution of human social capital in the making (Deleuze, 1983; Arrigo et al, 2011).

The fluctuating intensities and influencing flows of the ethical realm currently exercise dominion over difference and govern the management of risk (addiction and dependency, relapse and recovery), through bodies of knowledge and systems of thought that domesticate and discipline human social capital. When the stories of sameness are reproduced and the narratives of difference are limited and/ or denied, then the animated texts for, by and about both become lived histories, embodied truths. When the social person inhabits these truths, then captivity is corporealised and normalised (Arrigo, 2013a, 2013b). Indeed, this captivity is harm's embodied subjectivity. The manifestation and maintenance of this imprisonment engenders docility in thinking about and doing human social justice differently as praxis (Arrigo, 2011a). This is difference constrained by and coerced through exogenous system-sustaining mechanisms of efficiency (drug and mental health courts, institutional treatments) and techniques of utility (threat assessment protocols, drug kits and pre-packaged programming). When risk's replacement or alternative bodies of knowledge are reduced and repressed, then they (being and becoming as transformative) are made uninhabitable in systems of thought. This is the theory and science of human social capital, drug addiction and spontaneous recovery as an absent or un-presentable body of knowledge. Overcoming corporealisations such as these is an exercise in sustained critique (Arrigo, 2012). The reflexive work of *self-change* – of working through from within rather than from without – is about the revolution of the mind, self and other, and society. This is the SOCIUS re-corporealised (Deleuze, 1983). When the social person, as an evolving and becoming other (Deleuze and Guattari, 1987), is ever-more dynamic and productive in its embodying of human social capital, then justice is cohabited differently. This cohabitation is mutating self in society, excellence mobilised, and harnessed as freedoms awaiting release.

The fluctuating intensities and influencing flows of the ontological realm culturalise the images (aesthetic realm), texts (epistemological realm) and practices (ethical realm) that authoritatively govern the social person. This is the reproduction of human social capital – of difference territorialised and sameness normalised – as a consumable, mass-marketed commodity. Indeed, the industries of chemical dependency, substance abuse treatment and managed recovery are manifold (eg Kimberly and McLellan, 2006). Continued reliance on and excessive investments in such prescriptive remedies as methadone clinics, detoxification facilities, prison-based rehabilitation services, corporate employee assistance programming (EAP), drug-testing labs and so on legitimise as healthy and acceptable imposed order, external constraints, institutional mandates and forced compliance (ie coercion).

These commercialised artefacts of culture manage risk and, with it, reduce and repress doing/embodying difference to an existential, social and corporeal jurisprudence that sets limits to, restricts choice and action by, and exerts control over dynamic and transformative human social capital (Arrigo, 2011a). When these harm-generating intensities and flows are culturalised, then their captivity-intensifying and shadow-building tendencies extend to and from the kept, as well as to and from their keepers, regulators and watchers. This harm is negative freedom (Fromm, 1994 [1941]): the reproduction and dissemination of the pseudo-self whose uncritical dependence on mechanisms and techniques of escape distances the social person from doing and embodying humanness ever-more uniquely, interdependently, excellently and productively. Overcoming negative freedom is an invitation to re-ontologise the social person positively. This is difference:

not as lacking in consciousness; not as deferred or, worse, silenced in drug treatment manuals, policies and procedures; and not as an absent body of knowledge or an uninhabitable system of human science or social thought. *Replicated chaos* is the complex systems science response to negative freedom. This is the self in society as dwelling ever-more virtuously (eg courageously, compassionately, generously, nobly) within unpredictability, spontaneity, randomness, instability, contingency and uncertainty. This is the social person as settling within iterative orderly disorder (the strangeness of being/becoming) another way (Arrigo and Milovanovic, 2009; Arrigo et al, 2011). Residing within this habitus (Bourdieu, 1990) – always and already positional, relational and provisional – is an evolving journey for a people yet to be (Deleuze and Guattari, 1987).

Drug addiction, treatment and recovery: substance abuse, mental health and criminal justice system policy reform

Although admittedly provisional, the proposed integration of complexity science coupled with the diagnostics of PJ poses some interesting, if not provocative, questions for consideration on the matter of drug addiction and system reform. As a general proposition, these queries address the dynamics of power (the images that dominate consciousness for and about difference), politics (the narratives that postpone or silence the incipient and adaptive stories of being and becoming), privilege (the bodies of thought that territorialise human social capital) and their harm-reinforcing cultural replications. Collectively, these are the conditions that sustain the society of captives thesis and the criminological shadow.

With respect to the problematic status of drug addiction and natural recovery – especially by way of institutional and community-based treatments, interventions and services – changes in substance abuse, mental health and criminal justice practice are most assuredly needed. At issue is the social person – whether as drug user or abuser; correctional specialist or assessment expert; in-patient counsellor or out-patient therapist; family member, enabler or friend. In short, drug addiction, treatment and recovery implicate all those who aesthetically, epistemologically, ethically and ontologically are captivated by equilibrium conditions, status quo dynamics, linear movements, predictable patterns and closure trajectories. These are the 'point attractors' of the society of captives: the complex systems dynamics that finalise being (Bahktin, 1982) and foreclose becoming (Deleuze,

1983). As such, we contend that policy prescription necessarily begins as a reconsideration of theory, science and their interdependencies, including their bodies of knowledge and systems of thought, which therefore govern the drug addiction, treatment and recovery industry.

The theory of science: on the being of policy

Based on the science of complexity and the diagnostics of PJ, human social capital, in image, through text and by way of practice, is currently, and problematically, *experimentalised* as an object of inquiry. Stated otherwise, difference is separated from the parts to which it is connected and from which it takes up residence, makes meaning and undertakes choice and action. However, the 'doing' of restoration requires the work of schizo-analysis (ie de-territorialisation). Thus, for example, it is not enough to engage in restorative justice (Strang and Braithwaite, 2001), therapeutic jurisprudence (Wexler and Winick, 2003) or victim–offender mediation and conflict resolution (Umbreit, 2012) as policy prescription for drug addiction. Instead, PJ's reflexive mindfulness begins as a diagnosis about the social person. This diagnosis emphasises an assessment of the interconnected, mutually supporting and co-productive whole-system forces into which the social person is inserted and out of which the self in society does humanness. Put simply, then, what are the limits and denials, constraints and coercions, reductions and repressions that are normalised by the cultural reproduction of the previously mentioned, industry-driven practices? Moreover, even when undertaken in a different way, how and to what extent does reliance on these policy prescriptions advance flourishing excellence for, by and about one and all? This is the excellence of risk as existentially self-organising, socially adapting, corporeally changing and non-linearly replicating. This is the overcoming – the theory of science journey – that awaits development with respect to the being of criminal justice, mental health and substance abuse system policy reform.

The science of theory: on the becoming of policy

Based on the science of complexity and the diagnostics of PJ, human social capital, in image, through text and by way of practice is currently, and problematically, *hypothesised* as a fully retrievable, dissectible and therefore knowable phenomenon. Its properties include foundational realities, universal laws and absolute truths that are discoverable. But this perspective requires a particular type of empiricism in order for the theory to logically cohere (eg DiCristina, 1995; Crewe, 2013). Among others, these empirics include the following positivist claims:

- If it cannot be measured, it does not exist.
- If it cannot be counted, it does not have significance.
- If it cannot be isolated or disaggregated, it contains confounds or biases.
- If it cannot be categorised or compartmentalised, it suffers from validity and/or reliability threats.

However, these empirics fail to account for PJ's theory of human social capital. This theory acknowledges that the embodying of transformation requires the work of schizo-analysis (ie re-territorialisation). Thus, and by way of illustration, it is not enough to inhabit drug recovery, crime desistance or psychiatric health differently as policy prescription (Arrigo and Milovanovic, 2009; Arrigo et al, 2011). Instead, corporealisations such as these must be impermanent, flexible, loose and mutable because all embodiments are susceptible to industry dynamics and normalisation flows. Indeed, inhabiting and harnessing difference ever-more courageously, generously, benevolently, compassionately and so on necessitates system openness: iterative movement towards the untapped, strange and uncertain (rather than finite, familiar and definite) potential of human social capital. This is the overcoming – the science of theory journey – that awaits development with respect to the becoming of criminal justice, mental health and substance abuse system policy reform.

Conclusion

This chapter examined the delicate relationship between substance abuse and natural recovery informed by the science of complexity studies and the diagnostics of PJ. At issue was whether effective healing and restoration necessitated external forms of constraint and/or coercion or whether they required periodic bouts of predictably unpredictable system disruption and disorganisation. To address this matter, the non-linear dynamical systems concepts of adaptation and self-organisation were described, and the whole-system conditions (ie intra-psychic, interpersonal, institutional and communal) that bind, check and therefore govern human social capital were delineated. Currently, these conditions reductively and repressively limit and/or deny being human and doing humanness another way (ie differently). This difference is the social person otherwise evolving virtuously and productively through incipient images, narratives, practices and cultural reproductions of dynamic human social relating. As was argued, when these more organic, mutable and self-regulating conditions are mobilised and activated (ie willed), then the power that they unleash and harness includes prospects for greater flourishing in being and becoming for, by and about one and all. Thus, growing this metamorphosis in addiction studies – and in the dependency-seeking literature more generally – warranted additional explanation and further amplification.

Along these justificatory lines, the concepts of existential self-organisation, social adaptation, corporeal self-change and replicated chaos were tentatively discussed. When integrated with the underlying normative framework of PJ, these dynamical systems notions suggested a departure in how difference could be conceived of in consciousness, spoken of and/or transcribed in histories, embodied within organisational practices, and reproduced through the everyday artefacts of a given (sub)culture. Indeed, as theorised, the fluctuating intensities and influencing flows emanating from these disordered, unstable and chaotic perturbations help to make spontaneous order more fully realisable. The jurisprudence of this ontology advances a quality of citizenship and excellence (ie virtue) that dignifies and affirms, ever more so, being human (the humanness of being a recovering addict), and that celebrates and honours, ever more so, becoming otherwise than being (the humanness of transforming/evolving in being). The substance abuse, mental health and criminal justice system policy reforms that follow from this proposed radicalising of human social capital dramatically reframe the theory and science of drug addiction, treatment and recovery.

Given the preceding commentary, it should come as no small surprise that the science of complexity and the diagnostics of PJ are in agreement on the matter of the most significant 'industry' at stake with respect to drug addiction and spontaneous order. In short, the only commerce worth investing in is human social capital done dynamically and embodied transformatively. This is the mass-marketing of the social person's ingenuity (image-conjuring), creativity (text-telling) and novelty (body-making), including the cultural representations and artefacts of each. The non-linear, unstable and strange whole-system perturbations necessary for the productivity of this industry to spontaneously emerge, mutate, assemble, dissipate and/or reorganise is a revolution in the making. This is critical addiction studies as a journey in being human and becoming human differently as well. The drug policy prescription that grows this agenda in research and education anticipates its own release. What is at stake is the unleashing and channelling of will in the service of power. Given present conditions, the prescriptive remedy as proposed and developed throughout this chapter suggests that deferring, forestalling or foreclosing this difference is both captivity-generating and harm-sustaining. In either case, doing/ embodying human social capital reductively and/or repressively is simply unsupportable.

References

Aristotle (1976) *Ethics* (trans J.A.K. Thomson), New York, NY: Penguin.

Arrigo, B.A. (ed) (2004) *Psychological jurisprudence: critical explorations in law, crime, and society*, Albany, NY: SUNY Press.

Arrigo, B.A. (2010) 'De/reconstructing critical psychological jurisprudence: strategies of resistance and struggles for justice', *International Journal of Law in Context*, vol 6, no 4, pp 363–96.

Arrigo, B.A. (2011a) 'Madness, citizenship, and social justice: on the ethics of the shadow and the ultramodern', *Law and Literature*, vol 23, no 3, pp 405–41.

Arrigo, B.A. (2011b) 'Guest editorial: forensic psychiatry and clinical criminology: on risk, captivity, and harm', *International Journal of Offender Therapy and Comparative Criminology*, vol 55, no 3, pp 347–9.

Arrigo, B.A. (2012) 'The ultramodern condition: on the phenomenology of the shadow as transgression', *Human Studies: A Journal for Philosophy and the Social Sciences*, vol 35, no 3, pp 429–45.

Arrigo, B.A. (2013a) 'Managing risk and marginalizing identities: on the society of captives thesis and the harm of social dis-ease', *International Journal of Offender Therapy and Comparative Criminology*, vol 57, no 6, 672–93.

Arrigo, B.A. (2013b) 'Recognizing and transforming madness, citizenship, and social justice: toward the revolution in risk management and the overcoming of captivity', *International Journal of Offender therapy and Comparative Criminology*, vol 57, no 6, 712–19.

Arrigo, B.A. and Bersot, H.Y. (2014) 'Introduction: recognizing and transforming international crime and justice studies', in B.A. Arrigo and H.Y. Bersot (eds) *The Routledge handbook of international crime and justice studies*, London: Taylor and Francis, pp 1–5.

Arrigo, B.A. and Davidson, L. (2013) 'Managing risk and marginalizing identities: on captivity and citizenship', *International Journal of Offender Therapy and Comparative Criminology*, vol 57, no 6 (Special Issue), pp 663–5.

Arrigo, B.A. and Milovanovic, D. (2009) *Revolution in penology: rethinking the society of captives*, New York, NY: Rowman and Littlefield.

Arrigo, B.A. and Takahashi, Y. (2006) 'Recommunalization of the disenfranchised: a theoretical and critical criminological inquiry',. *Theoretical Criminology:An International Journal*, vol 10, no 3, pp 307–36.

Arrigo, B.A. and Williams, C.R. (2009) 'Existentialism and the criminology of the shadow', in R. Lippens and D. Crewe (eds) *Existentialist criminology*, Cullompton: Routledge-Cavendish, pp 222–48.

Arrigo, B.A., Bersot, H.Y. and B.G. Sellers (2011) *The ethics of total confinement: a critique of madness, citizenship, and social justice*, New York, NY: Oxford University Press.

Ashby, W.R. (1962) 'Principles of the self-organizing system', in H. Von Foerster and G.W. Zopf Jr (eds) *Principles of self-organization: transactions of the University of Illinois symposium*, London: Pergamon Press, pp 255–78.

Bakhtin, M. (1982) *The dialogic imagination: four essays*, Austin, TX: University of Texas Press.

Barlow, J. (ed) (2010) *Substance misuse: the implications of research, policy and practice*, London: Jessica-Kingsley Pub.

Bauman, Z. (1998) *Globalization: the human consequences*, Oxford: Blackwell.

Beck, U. (2009) *World at risk*, Cambridge: Polity Press.

Bourdieu, P. (1990) *The logic of practice*, Stanford, CA: Stanford University Press.

Bourdieu, P. and Wacquant, J.D. (1992) *An invitation to reflexive sociology*, Chicago, IL, and London: University of Chicago Press.

Bruzzo, A. and Vimal, R. (2007) 'Self: an adaptive pressure arising from self-organization, chaotic dynamics, and neural Darwinism', *Journal of Integrative Neuroscience*, vol 6, no 4, pp 541–66.

Camazine, S., Deneubourg, J., Franks, N., Sneyd, J., Theraula, G. and Bonabeau, E. (2003) *Self-organization in biological systems*, Princeton, NJ: Princeton University Press.

Cohen, E., Feinn, R., Arias, A. and Kranzler, H. (2007) 'Alcohol treatment utilization: findings from the National Epidemiological Survey on Alcohol and Related Conditions', *Drug and Alcohol Dependence*, vol 86, pp 214–21.

Cornell, D. (1998) *At the heart of freedom: feminism, sex, and equality*, Princeton, NJ: Princeton University Press.

Crewe, D. (2013) *Becoming criminal: the socio-cultural origins of law, transgression, and deviance*, London: Palgrave Macmillan.

Deleuze, G. (1983) *Nietzsche and philosophy*, New York, NY: Columbia University Press.

Deleuze, G. and Guattari, F. (1987) *A thousand plateaus*, Minneapolis, MN: University of Minnesota Press.

DiCristina, B. (1995) *Method in criminology: a philosophical primer*, Albany, NY: Harrow & Heston.

Doran, C., Valenti, L., Robinson, M., Britt, H. and Mattick, R. (2006) 'Smoking status of Australian general practice patients and their attempts to quit', *Addictive Behavior*, vol 31, pp 758–66.

Edwards, G. and Babor, T.F. (eds) (2012) *Addiction and the making of professional careers*, New Brunswick, NJ: Transaction Publishers.

Fromm, E. (1994 [1941]) *Escape from freedom*, New York, NY: Henry Holt & Company.

Hardie-Bick, J. and Lippens, R. (eds) (2011) *Crime, governance, and existential predicaments*, London: Palgrave Macmillan.

Heylighen, F. (2001) 'The science of self-organization and adaptivity', in L.D. Kiel (ed) *The encyclopedia of life support systems*, Oxford: Eolss Publishers, pp 253–80.

Kimberly, J.A. and McLellan, A.T. (2006) 'The business of addiction treatment: a research agenda', *Journal of Substance Abuse Treatment*, vol 31, no 3, pp 213–19.

Klingemann, H. and Sobell, L. (eds) (2007) *Promoting self-change from addictive behaviors: practical implications for policy, prevention, and treatment*, New York, NY: Springer.

Klingemann, H., Sobell, M. and Sobell, L. (2009) 'Continuities and changes in self-change research', *Addiction*, vol 105, pp 1510–18.

Levinas, E. (2004) *Otherwise than being*, Pittsburgh, PA: Duquesne University Press.

Marx, K. (1964) *The economic and philosophical manuscripts of 1844*, New York, NY: International Publishers.

Morgan, O.J. and Lizke, C.H. (eds) (2007) *Family interventions in substance abuse: current best practices*, New York, NY: Routledge.

Nietzsche, F.W. (1968) *The will to power* (new edn) (ed Walter Kaufmann), New York, NY: Vintage Books.

Polivy, J. (2007) 'The natural course and outcome of eating disorders and obesity', in H. Klingemann and L. Sobell (eds) *Promoting self-change from addictive behaviors: practical implications for policy, prevention, and treatment*, New York, NY: Springer, pp 119–26.

Prigogine, I. and Stengers, I. (1984) *Order out of chaos*, New York, NY: Bantam Books.

Rumpf, H.J., Bischof, G., Hapke, U., Meyer, C. and John, U. (2009) 'Remission from alcohol dependence without formal help: current status of the research', *Sucht*, vol 55, pp 75–85.

Sartre, J.P. (1956) *Being and nothingness: an essay on phenomenological ontology*, New York, NY: Philosophical Library Press.

Schutte, K.K., Moos, R.H. and Brennan, P.L. (2006) 'Predictors of untreated remission from late-life drinking problems', *Journal of Studies on Alcohol*, vol 67, pp 354–62.

Strang, H. and Braithwaite, J. (eds) (2001) *Restorative justice and civil society*, Cambridge: Cambridge University Press.

Takala, J. (2007) 'Spontaneous desistance from crime'. in H. Klingemann and L. Sobell (eds) *Promoting self-change from addictive behaviors: practical implications for policy, prevention, and treatment*, New York, NY: Springer, pp 127–37.

Toneatto, T., Cunningham, J., Hodgins, D., Adams, M., Turner, N. and Koski-Jannes, A. (2008) 'Recovery from problem gambling without formal treatment', *Addiction Research and Theory*, vol 16, pp 111–20.

Umbreit, M.S. (2012) *Victim offender mediation: conflict resolution and restitution*, National Institute of Corrections, Federal Bureau of Prisons, Rockville, MD: BiblioGov.

Walker, S. (2010) *Sense and nonsense about crime, drugs, and communities: a policy guide* (7th edn), Belmont, CA: Wadsworth.

Walters, G.D. (2000a) 'Associate editor's editorial: should we be treating substance-abusing offenders?', *International Journal of Offender Therapy and Comparative Criminology*, vol 44, no 5, pp 525–31.

Walters, G.D. (2000b) 'Spontaneous remission from alcohol, tobacco, and other drug abuse: seeking quantitative answers to qualitative questions', *American Journal of Drug and Alcohol Abuse*, vol 26, pp 443–60.

Wexler, D.B. and Winick, B.J. (eds) (2003) *Judging in a therapeutic key: therapeutic jurisprudence and the courts*, Durham, NC: Carolina Academic Press.

Williams, C. and Arrigo, B. (2002) *Law, psychology, and justice: chaos theory and the new (dis)order*, New York, NY: SUNY Press.

Williams, C.R. and Arrigo, B.A. (2007) 'Drug-taking behavior, compulsory treatment, and desistance: implications of self-organization and natural recovery for policy and practice', *Journal of Offender Rehabilitation*, vol 46, nos 1/2, pp 57–80.

Williams, C.R. and Arrigo, B.A. (forthcoming) 'Compassion, suffering, and human flourishing: toward a moral and jurisprudential psychology of social justice', in C.V. Johnson, H. Friedman, J. Diaz, B. Nastasi and Z. Franco (eds) *The Praeger handbook for social justice and psychology*, Westport, CT: Praeger.

THIRTEEN

Constituting the system: radical developments in post-Newtonian society

Clemens Bartollas

> Human consciousness, the human soul, the human mind, human subjective feelings have been a matter of concern not only for philosophers and theologians, but recently also for neuroscientists, physicists and others. (Reinis et al, 2005, p 1)

Introduction

This chapter makes two arguments. First, there are deep homologies between sociological and criminological inquiry into the nature of reality, non-linear causality and quantum theory. In particular, I argue that there is a homologous synergy between the Copenhagen Interpretation of quantum mechanics and constructionist approaches to philosophy, sociology and criminology. This chapter intends to discuss the usefulness of quantum theory to criminology, not in a reductionist mathematical manner, but through an examination of factors that lead to novel developments and solutions in criminological and sociological theory and practice from a constructivist (post-positivist/postmodernist) perspective.

The second argument is articulated by Polkinghorne (2007) and others that one of the consequences of the triumphalism of the model of classical mechanics developed since Newton has been a separation of spiritual faith on the one hand, and what is perceived to be 'reason' on the other. It is worth making the point that the uncertainty of quantum mechanics has challenged that triumphalism and that spiritual and theological inquiry makes a significant contribution to our understanding of justice, ethics and what is humane. Just as there have been eminent physicists such as Faraday, Maxell and Klein who are committed Christians, so are there currently figures such as Peter Hodgson (see Hodgson, 2005) who see no contradiction between faith and reason. In fact, both are committed to an understanding of reality and our places and influence within that reality. This chapter is written in the spirit of rational inquiry, and the growing understanding that the relationships between people, 'reality' and its 'causes' is much stronger than we could have thought; in the words of Nils Bohr, 'Anyone who is not shocked by quantum mechanics has not understood it' (cited by Gribben, 1994) because this theory argues that knowledge (observer effect), matter and reality are totally constitutive of each other.

Quantum mechanics is considered one of the most profound scientific development of the 20th century (Kleppner and Jackson, 2000). Quantum mechanics drives and shapes the modern world, as it makes possible everything from washing machines to computers, from mobile phones to nuclear weapons (Kumar, 2008, p xiii). It can be argued that the spectacular advances in biology, chemistry and medicine, as well as nearly every other science, could not have been able to occur without the tools that quantum mechanics made possible (Kleppner and Jackson, 2000). Kleppner and Jackson went on to say: 'Without quantum mechanics there would be no global economy to speak of, because the electronics revolution that brought us the computer is a child of quantum mechanics' (p 893). And they go on: 'So is the photonics revolution that brought us the Information Age. The creation of quantum physics has transformed our world, bringing with it all the benefits – and the risks – or a scientific revolution' (Kleppner and Jackson, 2000, p 893).

Quantum mechanics has been applied to quantum consciousness, contending that the human mind is a macroscopic quantum process (Hameroff, 2007, pp 1035–45). Also, quantum physics has been applied to a neurophysical model of mind–brain interaction (Schwartz et al, 2004). Quantum mechanics have been utilised in complex systems of modelling, such as quantum econophysics, which provides contributions to system sciences such as complex systems modelling. In exploring the frontiers of mind–body medicine, Deepak Chopra discusses quantum healing, which he considers to be a promising new area of medicine (Chopra, 1989).

A quantum view of the world for criminological theory is fitting because it provides a more fluid, complex and realistic understanding of human behaviour than is contained in positivistic explanations of criminality. Nor is quantum mechanics caught in a simplistic understanding of human behaviour that does not begin to capture why individuals do what they do. In addition, the quantum view emphasises human agency and responsibility, explores the possibilities of living in a quantum community and can be applied to new schools of criminology, such as peacemaking, feminist criminology and constitutive criminology.

The early advances of quantum mechanics, however, created fierce debates as it challenged Albert Einstein's special theory of relativity. Einstein contended that quantum theorists described a world not of certainty, but of fundamental indeterminism in which all we could ever know were the outcomes of our observations rather than some fundamental truth or order (Overman, 1966, p 75). Einstein remarked: 'It was as if the ground had been pulled from under one, with no firm foundation to be seen anywhere, upon which one could have built' (Kumar, 2008, p 1).

The Copenhagen Interpretation of quantum mechanics

From 1924 to 1927, several physicists, including Niels Bohr, Werner Heisenberg and Max Born, developed what became known as the Copenhagen Interpretation. It should be stated that there is no definitive statement of the Copenhagen Interpretation. Nonetheless, there are several basic principles that are usually accepted as being part of this interpretation (see Hodgson, 2005):

1. The indefinable nature of the particle–wave duality, which represents a central tenet of quantum mechanics. The basic subatomic properties (originally called quanta, but now called photons) exist in a state of superposition whereby they are both wave (momentum) and particle (position) simultaneously until they are observed, at which point there is 'wave collapse', meaning that they settle into being either a wave *or* a particle.
2. Heisenberg's uncertainty principle that it is not possible to know the value of all the properties of the system at the same time (you cannot measure both momentum and position). In a paper in 1927, Heisenberg gave a succinct statement of the 'uncertainty rule': 'The more precisely the position is determined, the less precisely the momentum is known in this instant, and vice versa' (Heisenberg, 1927, p 1). This relation has profound implications for such fundamental notions as causality and the determination of the future behaviour of an atomic particle.
3. The principle of quantum inseparability, which vividly shows the interconnected nature of all reality and, in many ways, is the most fascinating and surprising finding to emerge from the quantum worldview. The key to this surprise is the word 'local'.

Locality means that a body at location A that intends to act on a second body at location B must traverse the intervening distance. The velocity of this intervention, as Einstein argued, must be no greater than the speed of light. But quantum theory does not regard the bodies at A and B as separate objects, but continues to view them as a single entity. That is, quantum inseparability is based on the assumption that the bodies at A and B are interconnected to such a degree that they function as one unit.

The quantum connection is immediate, intimate, unmediated, unmitigated and invisible. The confidence of physicists that the quantum world might be tied together by non-local influences increased with John Stewart Bill's experiment on quantum inseparability in 1964 and increased even more with the later experiments by Freedman and Clauser (1972).

4. The quantum mechanical description of large systems will closely approximate the description provided by classical physics (the world we experience). However, the choices that observers make within that system will have a profound effect upon the system being acted upon.

Fundamentally, the quantum view denies the classical mechanical approach (see Pycroft, Chapter One; Jennings, Chapter Two) by arguing that a simple causative model is unable to explain the complexity and the multidimensional nature of human behaviour. A linear approach, such as assumed by positivism, suggests that X causes Y, which causes Z, which, in turn, causes something else. However, according to the post-positivistic model found in quantum mechanics, this form of logic ignores the complexity of mind and reality. In the words of Schwartz et al (2005, p 8): 'Quantum theory thereby converts science's concept of us from that of a mechanical automaton, whose conscious choices are mere cogs in a gigantic mechanical machine, to that of agents whose conscious free choices affect the physically described world'.

Another development in this area of understanding is the importance of inner experiences in perceiving external reality; this has been explained by David Bohm (1980) (one of the pioneers in the development of quantum theory). He proposes that the *implicate*, or internal, order is where reality is created for the *explicate*, or external, order. He illustrates this through the dye drop which is placed in a liquid such as glycerine encased between two glass cylinders. In rotating the outer cylinder slowly, the dye drop threads out into the liquid. The dye seems to totally disappear after a number of turns of the cylinder. Bohm then questions what would happen if the cylinder were rotated backwards the same number of turns that it was rotated forwards. He responds that the drop would reconstitute itself, indicating that the random state has been an internal, or implicit, order rather than one of disorder. He argues that what we think of as randomness is an indefinitely high degree of order. When it revolves into a form that can be recognised, such as the drop of dye, it becomes 'explicate', external or observable (Bohm, 2002).

What Bohm is suggesting is that the tangible reality of our everyday life is a type of illusion or hologram. It is not that the snow is not piled up in front of the door, but if you look at the snow from a holographic viewpoint, you perceive a different view of the snow, a different reality. Underlying this tangible external reality is a deeper order of existence. It is like a small piece of holographic film that gives birth to a complete hologram. This deeper level of reality is what Bohm calls the implicate, or 'enfolded', order (the unobserved internal thread binding reality). Our present level of understanding physical existence is the explicate, or 'unfolded', order (the external tangible world you can touch, feel, taste and smell) (Bohm, 2002).

Bohm is contending that what appears to be a stable, visible and audible world is an illusion. What you believe you see is the explicate, or unfolded, order of things; it is like watching a child being born, but the conception of the child is an underlying order that is the origin of the physical reality of life. The conception is implicate, or enfolded, harbouring our present reality, much as the DNA in the nucleus of the cells harbours potential life and directs the nature of the cells' unfolding. Thus, Bohm concludes that all tangible substance and movement are illusory because they emerge from a more primary order of the universe, which he called the holomovement (Bohm, 1980). Furthermore, the insight that reality is interconnected is used by post-positivist theories to develop a new vision of social relations and community. The Newtonian or mechanistic society views human beings as living machines or automatons. This antiquated worldview sees the basic building blocks of the universe as isolated and impenetrable atoms bouncing around in space and colliding with each other like tiny billiard balls. These isolated, separate and interchangeable parts in the world confront each other in pursuit of their own self-interest. The Newtonian view of the universe is that of entropy – everything is moving towards disorder – but the Quantum paradigm sees a much different relationship between order and disorder. It contends that humans can join together to achieve a society in which order and disorder are united in such a way as to realise a dimension of human existence that philosophers, theologians, utopians, visionaries and social scientists have dreamed up, but that human societies have been unable to realise.

Ilya Prigogine, the 1977 Nobel prize-winner in chemistry, adds to this with his theory of dissipative structures, which may be the missing link between living systems and the larger universe in which they arose. This theory explains 'irreversible processes' in nature: the movement towards higher and higher orders of life. It also solves the riddle of how living things have been running uphill in a universe that is supposedly running down (Prigogine and Staggers, 1984).

His term for open systems is 'dissipative structures'. Their form or structure is maintained by a continuous consumption, or dissipation, of energy. Energy moves through and, at the same time, forms the dissipative structure. These structures can be described as highly organised but always in process (flowing movement). He realised that a major factor that distinguishes living, open systems from closed systems, such as machines, is a far-from equilibrium environment, which is an environment of high energy and the influx of new chemicals. This environment is 'chaotic' in a different way from a 'thingless' soup of entropy and equilibrium, because it is chaotic with competing energy and chemical fluctuations. It is this instability that is the key to transformation. Accordingly, the dissipation of energy creates the potential for sudden reordering. Living systems are able to appear and evolve in this environment (Prigogine and Staggers, 1984).

The significance of Prigogine's dissipative structures theories is that they replace the pessimism of the increasing entropy of the Newtonian world with a positive conclusion. They contend that the world is organic, surprising, adaptive and alive. This dynamic, ever-changing system is presently poised at the edge of chaos; but it has always been at the edge of chaos when the greatest changes have taken place both in the physical and social worlds.

Chaos theory adds that complex systems, especially in nature, have acquired the ability to bring order and disorder into balance. The edge of chaos is this balancing point, and, according to M. Mitchell Waldrop:

> Is where new ideas and innovative genotypes are forever nibbling away at the edges of the status quo, and where even the most entrenched old guard will eventually be overthrown. The edge of chaos is where centuries of slavery and segregation suddenly gave way to the civil rights movement of the 1950s and 1960s, where seventy years of Soviet communism suddenly give way to political turmoil and ferment; where eons of evolutionary stability

suddenly give way to wholesale species transformation. The edge of chaos is the constantly shifting battle zone between stagnation and anarchy, the one place where a complex system can be spontaneous, adaptive, and alive. (Waldrop, 1992, p 12)

Quantum mechanics, societal change and criminological theories

A post-positivist worldview grounds the individual in the world beyond self and contends that we are all interconnected by constant and flowing exchange through the choices that we make (for a discussion on neural networks, see Pycroft, Chapter Ten). We are all part of a continuum, despite the apparent separate lists of things, interconnected by subatomic particles forming a holographic fabric. Everything is made of this senseless fabric until we make choices in the system.

Quantum theory is commonly seen as a theory in process and sharing many of the assumptions of chaos theory and complexity theory. The connections between these theories, as demonstrated by the contributions to this book, have implications for the ethics and administration of the justice and other public systems in contemporary society.

An example of this is in the application to organisational administration and policy analysis. According to Overman, chaos administration evokes the images of dissipative structure, self-organisation and dynamic complexity. Quantum administration, in turn, proposes a new logic of complementarity, constructionism, as well as participatory collusion in management and organisation. The quantum methods apply Heisenberg's principle of indeterminism and Born's rules of probabilistic interpretation. The metaphors and methods of chaos and quantum theory can be applied to management issues such as budgeting and performance appraisal (Overman, 1996, pp 75–89).

Danah Zohar and Ian Marshall contend that a quantum society offers a 'more responsive, less hierarchical society – a more natural society'. They perceive the quantum society as 'a free-form dance company each member a soloist in his or her own right but moving creativity in harmony with the others' (Zohar and Marshall, 1994, p 21). This society, which Zohar and Marshall see as emerging, has a number of promising features. It will be holistic in its movement beyond Newtonian competition, conflict and confrontation, and its pursuit of new dynamic interaction structures. It will get beyond the individual–collective dichotomy found in extreme individualism and extreme collectivism. It will be plural in that the Newtonian notion of one truth, one way of doing things and one expression of reality will give way to a more pluralistic vision. This emerging post–Newtonian society will also be responsive to all it citizens. Finally, it will be established on spirituality and will place greater emphasis on questions relating to the purpose and direction of society, the dimensions of its underlying, interconnected reality, and the source of its roots, system of values and moral foundation (Zohar and Marshall, 1994, pp 29–32).

The soul of humans, continued Zohar, cries out for 'some sense of fellow feeling with something beyond ourselves' (Zohar, 1990, p 128). Quantum physics' understanding of relationships is based on intimacy, in that we influence each other. We are able to:

> get inside each other and change each other from what within in such a way that 'I' and 'you' become a 'we.' This 'we' that we experience is not just 'I' and 'you'; it is a new thing in itself, a new reality. (Zohar, 1990, p 128)

A post-positivist understanding sees community as an extension of neither individualism nor collectivism. The intrinsic nature of community, according to a post-positivist's view, denies the notion that individuals profit by serving themselves or that individuals can only define themselves through a collective movement. Fostering community does not require participants to lose themselves, but to join with others to become more than themselves. A true post-positivist community is not based on power relations, social class or social status. It avoids perceiving some individuals as more desirable than others, for it recognises that all individuals, regardless of their backgrounds, have something to contribute to the vitality of community life. Post-Newtonian communities thrive on finding ways to celebrate diversity while finding creative unity in differences. Indeed, the true meaning of equality would be realised.

The spirit of both local and global communities in a post-positivist society must be based on covenant rather than contract. A community based on covenant is more receptive to compromise and negotiation, is able to mitigate the harmfulness of conflict when it arises, and avoids setting one group in opposition to another. Covenant promotes harmony and cooperation. It becomes easier to be a caretaker of souls in this setting than in those arranged by formal, legal or bureaucratic contracts (Zohar and Marshall, 1994, pp 37–8).

First, although the movement in theories of crime is towards integrated theory, the quantum mechanics paradigm moves beyond positivism in suggesting that a simple causative model is unable to explain the complexity and the multidimensional nature of human behaviour. According to quantum theorists, the simplistic Newtonian mechanistic model leads to other erroneous assumptions: a cause-and-effect approach, a reductionistic approach and a linear approach. A cause-and-effect approach assumes both that human behaviour is predictable and that it can be fixed. A reductionistic approach proposes that analysis of the parts is all that is needed for understanding why social or scientific phenomena take place. A linear approach suggests that X causes Y, which causes Z, which, in turn, causes something else. However, according to the positivist paradigm, this form of logic ignores the complexity of mind and reality.

For example, in 1994, four Midwestern teenagers decided to take a Bronco belonging to one of their parents and run away to Canada. The Bronco broke down in a neighbouring state, and they realised that they would need to steal another car. They stopped a woman, who thought that the Bronco with lights on top was a police vehicle. One of the teenagers approached the woman and pretended to be a police officer. She demanded to see identification. He returned to the Bronco and instructed one of his companions to take a .22 rifle that they had brought along and shoot her. The 15-year-old youth, who had committed no more serious acts than vandalism, complied. He shot her once, broke the window and stabbed her 31 times.

All the theories of delinquency and crime fall far short of explaining this youth's violent behaviour. He certainly came from an inadequate family background. He had been sexually abused by his natural father at the age of two and physically assaulted by an adoptive father at the age of 15. His mother had been married eight times and appeared to fail in a number of ways to fulfil his emotional needs. He also did poorly in school and had failed twice. He had some history of drug abuse, and it can be argued that he was peer-dependent. He was particularly fearful of the youth who had instructed him to shoot the woman. Yet, in working with this youth, it became abundantly clear that what took place that night – so much out of context with what had come before – emerged from the totality of all his experiences, frustrations, inadequacies and unmet needs.

Second, quantum theory places an importance on human agency. It suggests not only that humans have free will and are responsible, but that they can very much shape the reality of their lives. Positivism, in contrast, contends that individuals, both juveniles and adults, are determined and are limited by biological and constitutional individual factors, structural social factors in their lives, their processing of events, and the economic exploitations they face.

The fact is that individuals do not always create a life of dignity and responsibility. As one who testified in death penalty cases for 30 years (always on the defence), I am much aware of the harm, pain and death that individuals can inflict on others. In one recent case in which I declined involvement, a serial murderer had killed 11 women, some of whom still had parts of their bodies in his house.

If we choose to harm others, then we have no right to live in society. We are choosing not to be part of the quantum community. We must be isolated to prevent our harming others. These facilities must be humane, in which the staff treat inmates with dignity and respect. For those who want to improve themselves, these facilities must provide opportunities for self-growth.

Third, the post-Newtonian paradigm presents a much more fluid and involving self than is found in the Newtonian notion of a personal identity that is fixed, definite and unchanging through time. The quantum view sees the self as changing and open to the possibility of emergence at every moment. It is free, not determined. The natural state of the self is flow, harmony and cooperation with other living things.

In contrast, positivism tends to present a unidimensional and mechanistic understanding of both non-offenders and offenders. They are perceived as either good or bad, violators or non-violators, violent or non-violent, peer-oriented or loners, socialised or unsocialised, and achievers or non-achievers. Personality structure is fixed by biological traits, by fulfilment of psychological needs or by environmental conditions. There is little room for surprise or the unexpected, for loyalty in one context and disloyalty in others, and for both group commitment and extreme narcissism.

Fourth, much like the complex interrelationships of things in the material world, the social world is also best defined as the multidimensional web of interrelationships that tend to take on relatively pervasive patterns over time. These various dimensions can be seen in personality and behaviour patterns, family relationships, and patterns of community, economy, ideology and policy. Each of these systems and subsystems must borrow resources from other systems and subsystems to pursue their own self-construction.

The quality of this web of interrelationships will greatly affect what takes place in adolescents' and adults' lives. Youth and adults who have a troubled web of interrelationships will tend to exhibit a number of problematic behaviours. The more disruptive these relationships are, the post-Newtonian approach would add, the more likely it is that these youths will adopt pervasive and undesirable patterns over time. Disruptive social relationships also lack the ability to borrow enriching resources from other systems and subsystems that would facilitate healing and integration in youths' lives.

Fifth, self-generating and reproductive systems rely on resources from external sources to survive. Since no person and no system of social organisation is born with all these needs met, the human adaptive capacities seek out ways in which to meet those needs and acquire the necessary resources. Once that is accomplished, the system tends to reproduce itself on the basis of the specific inputs and outputs. For example, youth gangs have developed and endured through the process of providing several resources for their members, including self-esteem, economy, safety, solidarity, tensions, recognition and political organisation. The new paradigm explains the existence and persistence of delinquency by the process of acquiring and exchanging necessary resources to preserve and reproduce the means by which those needs are met.

Sixth, the key to understanding the emergence and persistence of delinquency and criminal behaviour involves examining how behaviours and circumstances come to be defined as delinquent in the first place. Crime, of course, is relative to the norms, values and culture of the group that define it. Similarly, what are the circumstances in which those behaviours are delinquent and under what circumstances are they not? For example, some behaviours are acceptable for adults but not for children. What influences those definitions and how does delinquency become reproduced once it is identified as a problem? The answer to these questions reveals that delinquency is a multidimensional social construct that is not considered a social problem until enough people collectively act as if it is a social problem.

Seventh, quantum theory has room for change and transformation. It is reluctant to condemn a person for events that they have done because of their human capacity to transform themselves. What is the translation of this? Should persons who have committed dastardly murders be forgiven simply because they feel that they are a new person? Who can or will verify or concur with this changed status? The fact is that differing assessment and risk assessment tools, whether actuarial or clinical, have proven extremely inadequate in verifying rehabilitation in a person.

Quantum theory, religious belief and radical criminology

Harold Pepinsky and Richard Quinney's (1991) edited reader, titled *Criminology as peacemaking*, developed the peacemaking approach in criminology, drawing on three peacemaking traditions (religious and humanistic, feminist, and critical traditions). Pepinsky and Quinney write that the whole of the American criminal justice system is predicated on the continuance of violence and oppression (as seen in the prison system), war (as seen in the 'war on crime' and the 'war on drugs'), and the failure to account for how the larger social system contributes to the problem of crime (as seen in the failure to reduce poverty in society) (Pepinsky and Quinney, 1991). This also concurs with constitutive criminology, which is a postmodernist-influenced theory developed by Stuart Henry and Dragon Milovanovic in which crime is conceived as an integral part of the overall production of society and co-produces human agents and the cultural and social structures they create (Henry and Milovanovic, 1996). This theory defines crime as 'the harm resulting from humans investing energy in a harm producing relations of power that denies or diminishes those subject to this investment, their own humanity'. From this perspective, a criminal is viewed as an 'excessive investor' while the criminal is known as a 'recovering subject' (Henry and Milovanovic, 1996, p 3). Henry and Milovanovic believe that society can reduce the frequency of harm through reducing the capacity of excessive investors to dominate and dehumanise others and, at the same time, trying to accomplish a social transformation.

For peacemaking criminology, this transformation is linked to the understanding that crime is connected to suffering and that to end crime, we must end suffering. This means that poverty, racism, sexism, alienation, abuse within families, harassment and all other forms of suffering must be dealt with if crime is to be reduced. For example, the aim of feminist theories is to seek social justice, pointing out that the Newtonian system is a mechanistic system that has treated humans as machines and that has promoted a patriarchal and racist society. Both women and minority ethnic groups experience discrimination and the lack of power in this society. Zinn's (1980) *A people's history of the United States* aptly portrays how in the US, this Newtonian society has served the powerful and people of privilege, against those who lack power and privilege. It is the latter who have been denied social justice, and women, especially, are challenging their status and roles of the past and are demanding more equality and power in the present.

Additionally, peacemaking criminology holds that the state itself perpetuates crime (and violence) through repressive policies of social control such as the death penalty, lengthy prison sentences for offenders and the criminalisation of non-violent drug offences. Peacemaking criminology further asserts that the focus on individual offenders has been at the neglect of certain institutional arrangements in society that contribute to our high crime rate, and that criminology should concern itself with promoting a greater amount of social equity across social class lines. Lastly, peacemaking criminology argues that the most significant change to be made by the criminal justice system is to move away from *criminal* justice to *restorative* justice (Pepinsky and Qunney, 1991).

Peacemaking criminology is certainly not mainstream criminology. It is not positivist in its orientation and is not obsessed with detailed statistical analyses of the cause of criminal behaviour. This is not to say that peacemaking criminology is not interested in the causes of crime; rather, it approaches the aetiology issue through non-traditional means. For example, in giving a summary of the basis of peacemaking criminology, Pepinsky and Quinney (1991, pp 3–4) tries to capture how the key issues of this approach can be framed, which includes the following: the thought of the Western rational mode is conditional, limiting knowledge to what is already known; the truth of reality is emptiness and, ultimately, all that is real is beyond human conception; each life is a spiritual journey into the unknown and the unknowable, beyond the egocentric self; human existence is characterised by suffering, crime is suffering and the sources of suffering are within each of us; through love and compassion, beyond the egocentric self, we can end suffering and live in peace, personally and collectively; the ending of suffering can be attained through a quieting of the mind and an opening of the heart to being aware; crime can be ended only with the ending of suffering, only when there is peace – through the love and compassion found in awareness; and understanding, service and justice all flow naturally from love and compassion, from mindful attention to the reality of all that is, here and now (Pepinsky and Quinney, 1991).

These understandings are also, for example, becoming more evident in the explorations of the relationships between complexity theory and Eastern philosophy (Byrne [1998] cites the work of Hayles; for examples, see also Ma and Osula, 2011).

The relationship between quantum physics and theology has been examined by John Polkinghorne (2007). Also, according to Hodgson (an eminent physicist), the essential presuppositions of science that matter is good, rational, orderly and open to the human mind are all to be found in the Old Testament (Hodgson, 2007). The relationship between quantum theory and theology is developed further by Diarmuid O'Murchu (1997), who establishes the following principles:

1. Life is sustained by a creative energy, fundamentally benign in nature, with a tendency to manifest and express itself in movement, rhythm and pattern. Creation is sustained by a superhuman, pulsating restlessness; a type of resource vibrating throughout time and eternity.

2. Wholeness, which is largely un-manifest and dynamic (not static), is the wellspring of possibility. In seeking to understand life, we believe that the whole is always greater than the sum of the parts; paradoxically, the whole is contained in each part, yet no whole is complete in itself.

3. Evolution is underpinned by a deep unfolding structure characterised by design and purpose, necessitating an unceasing interplay of order and disorder, randomness and creativity.

4. The expanding horizon of divine belonging is the context in which revelation takes place; all creatures are invited to respond, to engage in the co-creative task of being and becoming. All life forms have unique roles in this process, the primary focus of which is creation itself rather than formal religion.

5. Because the capacity to relate is itself the primary divine energy, impregnating creation, we humans need authentic ecclesial and sacramental experiences to explore and articulate our innate vocation to people in relationship.

6. Ultimate meaning is embedded in story, not in facts. All particular religious stories belong to a larger story, which includes but also transcends the specific religious traditions of any one historical or cultural epoch. All sacred texts are attempts at articulating ultimate truth and archetypal value approximations that require fresh interpretation with each new cultural epoch.

7. Redemption is a divine–human process of befriending those elements of our experience that threaten our security and integrity, rather than one of rescue by an external, divine agent.

8. Structural and systematic sin abound in our world, often provoking people to behave immorally. To integrate the global shadows, we need fresh moral and ethical guidelines to address the structural and systemic sinfulness of our times. The foundation of these guidelines is as much a political as a religious duty.

9. Because we are primarily beneficiaries of light (and not of darkness), and our final destiny – both here and eternally – is that of enlightenment, we all need those sacred moments of ritualistic/

sacramental space, serving as heightened encounters with the sustaining mystery that unfolds us.

10. The concepts of beginning and end, along with theological notions of resurrection and reincarnation, are invoked as dominant myths to help us humans make sense of the infinite destiny in our infinite universe.

11. Extinction and transformation, the evolutionary equivalents of Calvary and resurrection, are central coordinates of cosmic and planetary evolution. Their interplay at this historical moment – our 'kairos' – provides the primary focus for the praxis of the quantum theologian.

12. Love is an interdependent life force, a spectrum of possibility, ranging from its ultimate divine grandeur to its particularity in subatomic interaction. It is the origin and goal of our search for meaning.

Conclusion

One of the major foci of this chapter is to inquire about the usefulness of quantum theory to provide a paradigm shift to criminological theory and practice. Using the Copenhagen Interpretation of quantum mechanics, this chapter delineated several approaches derived from the assumptions of quantum mechanics, and postulated that they can be helpful in developing a post-positivist approach to criminological theory. In this constructionist (post-positivistic/postmodern) perspective, criminological theory and practice is not limited by the unidimensional, deterministic and mechanistic model found in Newtonian science.

The other foci of this chapter pertain to the triumph of Newtonian science, which led to a separation of spiritual faith on the one hand, and what was perceived to be reason on the other hand. It is my argument that the uncertainty of quantum mechanics has challenged this sense of triumphalism and that spiritual and theological inquiry make a significant contribution to our understanding of justice, ethics and what is humane. For example, peacemaking criminology, as Pepinsky and Quinney have proposed, is based on the belief that each person has a spiritual journey into the unknown, and through love and compassion, we can end suffering and live in peace, personally and collectively. They go on to say that understanding, service and justice all flow from love and compassion, from mindful attention to the reality of all that is here and now (Pepinsky and Quinney, 1991).

References

Bohm, D. (1980) *Wholeness and the implicate order*, London, Boston, and Henley: Routledge & Kegan Paul.

Bohm, D. (2002) *Wholeness and the implicate order*, New York. Routledge.

Byrne, D. (1998) *Complexity theory and the social sciences: an introduction*, London: Routledge.

Chopra, D. (1989) *Quantum healing: exploring the frontiers of mind/body medicine*, New York, NY: Bantam.

Freedman, S.J. and Clauser, J.F. (1972) 'The physics of the Einstein Podolsky Rosen Paradox', *Foundations of Physics*, vol 7, pp. 893–8.

Gribben, J. (1994) *In search of Schrödinger cat: quantum physics and reality*, New York, NY: Bantam Books.

Hameroff, S.R. (2007) 'The brain is both neurocomputer & quantum computer', *Cognitive Science*, vol 31, pp 1035-45

Henry, S. and Milovanovic, D. (1996) *Constitutive criminology: beyond postmodernism*, Los Angeles: Sage.

Heisenberg, W. (1927) 'Quantum Mechanics: The Uncertainty Principle' ['Über den anschulichen Inhalt der quantentheoretischen Kinematik und Mechanik'], *Z. Phys*, vol 43, no 3–4, pp 172–98.

Hodgson, P.E. (2005) *Theology and modern physics*, Ashgate Science and Religious Series.

Kleppner, D. and Jackson, R. (2000) 'One hundred years of quantum physics', *Science, New Series*, vol 289, no 5481, pp 893–8.

Kumar, M. (2008) *Quantum: Einstein, Bohr and the great debate about the nature of reality*, New York: W.W. Norton & Company.

Ma, A.M.J. and Osula, B. (2011) 'The Tao of complex adaptive systems (CAS)', *Chinese Management Studies*, vol 5, no 1, pp 94–110.

O'Murchu, D. (1997) *Quantum theology*, New York, NY: Crossroad Publishing Company.

Overman, E.S. (1996) 'The new science of management: chaos and quantum theory and method', *Journal of Public Administration: Research and Theory*, vol 6, pp 75–9.

Pepinsky, H.E. and Quinney, R. (eds) (1991) *Criminology as peacemaking*, Bloomington, IN: Indiana University Press.

Polkinghorne, J. (2007) *Quantum physics & theology*, New Haven, CT: Yale University.

Prigogine, L. and Staggers, I. (1984) *Order out of chaos: man's new dialogue with nature*, New York, NY: Bantam Books.

Reinis, S., Holub, R. and Smrz, P. (2005) 'A quantum hypothesis of brain function and consciousness', *Ceskoslovenka Fyziologie*, vol 54, pp 26–31.

Schwartz, J.M., Stapp, H.P. and Beauregard, M. (2004) 'Quantum theory in neuroscience and psychology: a neurophysical model of mind/brain interaction', *Phil. Trans Royal Society*, vol 360, pp 1309–927.

Waldrop, M.M. (1992) *Complexity*, New York, NY: Simon and Schuster.

Zinn, H. (1980) *A people's history of the United States*, Harper Collins.

Zohar, D. (1990) *The quantum self: human nature and consciousness defined by the new physics*, New York, NY: William Morrow.

Zohar, D. and Marshall, I. (1994) *The quantum society: mind, physics, and a new social vision*, New York, NY: William Morrow and Company, Inc.

Conclusion

Clemens Bartollas and Aaron Pycroft

In this book, we have focused on developing an understanding of the scope of complexity theory and its application to criminal justice and social work (and beyond). The various chapters, while representing an exposition of some of the defining features of complexity, also demonstrate that these features are given different interpretations or levels of significance depending upon whether you are looking at this from a positivist, post-positivist or constructivist position; and even then, these positions have philosophical and theoretical differences within them. It can appear that the study of complexity is very complex; however, what this book does demonstrate is that differing ontological, epistemological and methodological traditions are open/sensitive to complexity, albeit in ways that tend to fall along the traditional fault lines of the 'natural' and 'social' sciences. However, the very fact that complexity is being studied across the sciences, social sciences and in social theory, and with some broad areas of consensus, should be enough to refute any fundamentalist charges of physics envy/grand theorising on the one hand, or accusations of soft science on the other.

The particular challenge that complexity theory poses involves the application and analysis of whole-systems thinking for our particular theoretical position, and especially in relation to human systems. The universal cosmos is, of course, the ultimate fractal, comprising evolving constituent systems – so much for the nature of galaxies as self-organising systems for example – but what does complexity theory mean for our understanding of human consciousness, the nature of human society and the processes that occur therein? In this sense, the book takes us on a journey from: first, abstract mathematical, mechanical and deterministic concepts in the Platonic, Cartesian and Newtonian tradition(s), and the development of Descartes's 'ghost in the machine' idea to accommodate human consciousness in the clockwork universe; to, second, what would appear to be a more human(e) approach through the Aristotelian, Marxist, existentialist, postmodern tradition(s), focusing on the primacy of human experience, learning and the non-reducibility of evolving and complex human life. It is also important to note that quantum mechanics arises from the positivist tradition but radically changes our understanding (if the Copenhagen Interpretation is correct) of the nature of mind–matter interaction.

As stated in the Introduction, there are no real cut-off points between these different approaches contained within these chapters, with many elements crossing over into the different perspectives. The bulk of the chapters take a post-positivist and realist perspective on the issues, which, from an applied social science point of view, seems to offer good ways of doing research on real social problems (see later), but we would argue that within a complexity framework, each tradition has much to learn from the others, particularly when it involves dealing with human beings. Certainly, I (Pycroft), in terms of thinking through the issues in Chapter Ten, although starting from a realist position and the necessity of incorporating attractor theory, found myself erring closer to constructivist positions about the nature of relationships than I had expected, precisely because good working relationships are constructed, they do not exist *a priori*; complexity theory opens up new and exciting perspectives.

Reading the book as a whole and seeing what has emerged, it is interesting to reflect on the process and the challenges for us as Editors to engage with the differing approaches to complexity. These challenges were apparent in the peer review process, from book proposal through to completed manuscript; the Editors have had lengthy Skype and email discussions with each other and various exchanges with the contributors as well as The Policy Press to try and develop a coherent, meaningful and useful book. We have all been challenged to move out of our own academic/theoretical silos. However, the process has been creative and (we hope) made for a better book precisely because complexity theory requires whole-systems thinking in a way that is fundamentally interdisciplinary, crosses divides and includes the possibility of a rapprochement between the 'natural' and the 'social' sciences and social theory. We would therefore challenge readers, rather than simply focusing on the areas or chapters of the books that resonate with their own studies and viewpoints, to think about the ways in which different traditions have developed and what the relationships between seemingly different approaches might be.

Teaching complexity

How does one teach and do research in the area of complexity theory given that this area of study has only emerged in recent years and contains possibilities for literally hundreds of research topics. Indeed, it would be possible to take each of the chapters in this volume and a groundswell of opportunities for additional research would be found. We are, it can be argued, at the beginning of a major paradigm shift in research in the areas of social work, criminology, public policy and organisational analysis. However, our experience of teaching in criminology, criminal justice, psychology and social work for undergraduates and postgraduates (including for professional qualifications) is positive. Complexity has an intuitive appeal, particularly to practitioners, precisely because it addresses the very issues that they are grappling with and that are highlighted throughout this book. In terms of teaching from the book, there are a variety of opportunities in the various chapters to generate a lively teaching environment. Let us illustrate by a number of examples that could be used to increase and stipulate students' engagement.

Figure c.1: Rethinking relationships between epistemological traditions in relation to complexity

In Figure c.1 (which should also be linked with Figure i.2 in the Introduction), we outline what we see as some of the key features of differing traditions, starting with Plato and Aristotle. Through the lens of complexity theory, we have indicated some possible relationships with different (highly selective and broad) areas of each tradition, but you might want to try and develop this to include other components, either as part of your learning or teaching. Our experience of our own professional and academic backgrounds leads us to ask the following (again, not exhaustive) types of question when thinking about these issues:

1. Are these positions entirely contradictory in the sense that there is one correct narrative that allows us to understand complexity whether from a positivist, post-positivist or constructivist perspective?
2. Or, are these positions existing on a continuum of knowledge and examples of antinomies in so far as we can discover the nature of complexity and reality and arrive at the same robust conclusions but via different methods?
3. Or, are these positions dialectical in nature in so far as what emerges from conflict or dialogue between these different traditions allows us to arrive at useful insights to explain the nature of reality, while understanding that this knowledge will always be relative and never complete?
4. Is it possible that developments in apparently very different traditions can act as feedback loops to inform and develop each other, similar to a neural network approach, with either stronger or weaker links between the ideas or theories, which represent the nodes of the network?

Undoubtedly, your ontological/epistemological position will determine your answer to these questions, but we would also add that whether we are by default a positivist, post-positivist or constructivist, we are all seeking ways to identify and explore regularities in the social lives of which we are part. If we are involved in the endeavours of criminal justice or social work, then we are invariably trying to improve lives, and, again, we would argue that complexity theory enables us to do that through employing new and innovative ideas and techniques; we are able to do this precisely because we stand on the shoulders of giants, but the downside of this is that we tend to work on the basis of orthodoxy. Anything new is always a challenge, in the words of one reviewer for the proposal for this book: "I believe the claim that it would be the first such book. I had no idea there was a community thinking along these lines." This is not a criticism of the reviewer especially, as they went on to make some useful comments about the structure/content of the book, but the challenge for people engaged in the study of complexity is not to develop a complexity silo of their own, where we are just talking to each other, even if from different traditions; fundamentally, our approaches have to demonstrate that complexity can provide accessible insights and solutions into very serious social problems, and it is our contention that this book goes some way towards doing so.

- Using the Introduction and Chapter Ten, have students examine Figures i.1 and i.2 and discuss them in conjunction with Table 10.2, with its comparison of paradigms. You might want to explore their understanding of what a paradigm is, and discuss how the positivism paradigm differs from the post-/non-positivistic paradigms found in complexity theory and how this relates to the traditional fault lines of the natural and social sciences; how do these approaches affect our understanding of society and the problems that we are dealing with?
- Chapter Two provides an opportunity to think about risk approaches in organisations and the ways in which risk can be measured, mitigated and, ultimately, understood. Use basic exercises such as flipping coins or rolling dice to understand the probabilities of certain outcomes and the nature of chance, and whether complexity theory enhances our understanding of the mathematics of chance/ probability in our everyday lives.
- Chapter Three provides an opportunity to discuss what complexity tells us about what the nature of determinism and free will might be. Does this chapter support the view that individuals make wrong choices, or are there forces at work beyond individual control – what are the implications of either and what can/should follow from these understandings in criminal justice and social work?
- In Chapter Four, Alcoholics Anonymous (AA) is mentioned as a complex adaptive system, which, along with other 12-step programmes, has touched the lives of so many people. Important questions are: where is the nature of self-organisation found in this self-help group? Why has it spread worldwide? How is AA different from most government-initiated interventions and how does complexity help us to understand this?
- In Chapter Five, there is the example of Samuel McLaren, who received a sentence of life imprisonment for abduction and sexual assault. The concepts of 'normal accidents' and power laws within complex systems are difficult and contentious and this case provides

an opportunity to discuss ideas of acceptable levels of risk and decision-making about interventions.

- Chapter Six can be used to think about what the purposes and functions of risk assessment should be, and whether the fractal nature of human experience is problematic or provides an opportunity for resolving difficulties? Students can be asked to think about designing a risk assessment tool and what kinds of approach they might take and why?

- In Chapter Seven, the case study of the Stephen Lawrence Inquiry is found. Have students look at the 20-year history of this hate crime murder? What does complexity add to our understanding of institutional racism in terms of understanding 'order for free' and systems becoming 'locked in'? The chapter also provides an opportunity to consider the real organisational paradox of the need for creative solutions but also the need for control.

- In Chapter Eight, the Nunn Commission of Inquiry focused on lessons they learned from a youth in trouble. The goal of this inquiry was to develop recommendations to strengthen the youth justice system. What recommendations would students make to strengthen the youth justice system in their jurisdiction? Also, use the concept of 'intersectionality' to work through the ways in which multiple disadvantages are linked and also exacerbated through current service provision in wider public services.

- In Chapter Nine, there is an account of a hospital ward in which the patient appears to have encountered oppression and abuse. How much of this abuse can be related to the mechanistic approach to Newtonian science that still dominates the medical community? Use this as a case study for reflective practice and the ways in which complexity theory enables practitioners to become 'change agents'.

- In Chapter Ten, there is the conclusion that criminal justice in England and Wales has an opportunity to restore individuals to full citizenship through the use of higher-order and novel solutions to complex problems. Make links between the concept of strange attractors and the ways in which current policies and practices lead to 'unintended' consequences in efforts to rehabilitate people.

- Have your students read Chapter Eleven and ask them to think about the uniqueness of domestic abuse crimes, but perhaps examine them in the light of intersectionality theory. Discuss what the aims of domestic abuse programmes should be, and what the balance should be between punishment and rehabilitation. Importantly, though, what is the role of the practitioner and constructive relationships in this process and, again, how does complexity theory enhance these processes?

- Chapter Twelve provides an opportunity to examine the need to re-engage with the foundational ethics of the work that is being carried out in criminal justice and social work. Is it the case, for example, that the resurgence of interest in virtue ethics re-establishes the fully human character of criminal justice and social work and fits with whole-systems and strengths-based and desistance approaches? If this is the case, what are the key differences and perceived failures of deontological or utilitarian approaches to this work and in what senses can the principle of self-organisation be applied to desistance from problematic behaviour?

- In Chapter Thirteen, peacemaking criminology would represent a good project for the class. Class members could examine the origin and background of this topic. They could evaluate how much potential this concept has for implementation in society. As part of this debate, it could be questioned whether peacemaking criminology is more possible in some societies than others and what this model would look like in terms of the criminal justice system. What are the relationships between 'faith' and 'reason' and why is it important to discuss these issues in relation to criminal justice and social work (eg you could think about the extent to which faith-based organisations deliver major programmes in the criminal justice and social work arenas and are funded by the government to do so), and do quantum perspectives tell us anything new about these age-old debates?

Researching complexity

This book demonstrates that a diverse range of research methodologies is useful for researching theory, from mathematics to agent-based computer modelling through to phenomenology. However, researching complexity favours multidisciplinary and triangulated approaches that seek to comprehensively capture the detail of what it means to be a human in context. So, on the one hand, computer technology allows huge amounts of data to be gathered to identify population and subpopulation patterns, but phenomenology allows an opportunity to identify a personal experience. In this respect, it is important to understand that when we speak of 'system', the 'individual' is a complex adaptive system in their own right. The contexts of criminal justice, social work and other human services are, then, ripe for a complexity perspective to bring new perspectives to old problems, particularly in respect of multi-agency working and organisational creativity, to understand the behaviour of the whole system rather than just a part of it. This involves talking with people from different disciplines, including the 'natural' sciences, engineering, computer science, geography, psychology and so on. Our experience is that once you start to do this – to look for common opportunities for research and scholarship – it provides for rich and rewarding activities.

Useful further resources

All of the contributors to this book have an expertise in complexity in their own fields and we would strongly recommend that you use the references from each chapter to follow up on key readings. Many universities across the world now have complexity research groups or centres and the following are a few useful organisations that have websites and a variety of resources, which can be accessed as follows:

- At the Institute of Criminal Justice Studies (University of Portsmouth), in conjunction with other departments and external organisations, we are developing a network of academics and practitioners who are applying complexity theory in relation to criminal justice and social work and related areas. If you are interested in being a part of this network then you can contact: aaron.pycroft@port.ac.uk
- Cognitive Edge is concerned with management practices and the application of the Cynefin Model, see: http://cognitive-edge.com/
- The Santa Fe Institute (see: http://www.santafe.edu/) is a world-leading multidisciplinary research centre with a range of resources (including the opportunity to do short Massive On Line Courses [MOOCS] in complexity theory).
- The London School of Economics Complexity Research Group. Available at: http://www.psych.lse.ac.uk/complexity/
- The European Complex Systems Society. Available at: http://www.complexssociety.eu/

Index

Note: Page numbers followed by *n* refer to information in a note. Page numbers followed by *fig* and *tab* refer to information which appears only in a figure or a table on that page.

A

abuse *see* child protection practice; domestic abuse and probation programmes; sexual victimisation in childhood
adaptation 170–1, 185, 186
  and domestic abuse programmes 231–4, 238
  and policing since Stephen Lawrence Inquiry 9, 141, 144–6, 147, 151–2, 153–4*tab*
  and reflective practice 192
  and self-organising systems 248–51, 262, 263
  see also complex adaptive systems
age and structural oppression 160, 163
agency
  and structure 29
  see also human agency
agent-based activity
  and complex adaptive systems 86, 93
  and emergence of programmes 81–2, 90, 91
agent-based modelling (ABM) 91
aggression
  and child maltreatment 74
  and child saturation in community 74
  General Aggression Model and domestic abuse 223
  hormones and antisocial behaviour 64
Agnew, R. 71–2, 75
Alcoholics Anonymous (AA) 84, 85, 291
animals and risk 42–3

ANS hyperarousal and criminal behaviour 63*fig*, 65, 69
antisocial behaviour *see* criminal behaviour
Apollo 13 (film) 22
apophenia principle 48
Aristotle 17, 31, 254
Armstrong, J. 221–2
Arrigo, Bruce 254
Ashby, W.R. 249
Ashby's Law of Requisite Variety 209
'Asset' risk assessment tool 117–19
  complexity critique 119–33, 120, 122–3, 126, 129–30
  introduction of AssetPlus 131–2, 133
atomism 19
attachment and criminal behaviour 67–8
attractors 41–55
  and child protection practice 101
  and criminal justice and social work programmes 81, 86, 88, 90
  and recovery from addiction 251
  strange attractors 41, 42, 210–11
Atwal, A. 184
autonomic system (ANS) hyperarousal 63*fig*, 65, 69
Avigad, J. 17

B

Babcock, J. 224, 227, 230
Baby P (Peter Connelly) 100
Bailey, B. 232
Bammer, G. 188–9
Bandura, A. 211

Bar-Yam, Y. 22–3

Bayes' Theorem and quantification of
risk 44–5, 51–3, 90

BBR *see* Building Better
Relationships (BBR)

Beaver, K. 60

Begun, J.W. 166, 167, 170

behaviour *see* human behaviour;
organisational behaviour

'being in itself' and 'being for itself'
35*n*

benefits recipients and oppression 162

Bennett, L. 226

Bentham, Jeremy 20

Berkeley, Bishop (George Berkeley)
17

Bernard, T. 61

Bernstein, P.L. 44

Bhaskar, Roy 29

bifurcation 31, 101, 104, 110, 211

'big data' approach and policing 151

Bill, John Stewart 272

black and minority ethnic (BME)
community
and policing 144–5, 146–7, 150, 155
see also race and ethnicity

Black Police Association 150

'Black Swan' effect 49

'blaming and shaming' policy 224

Bohm, David 272–3

Bohr, Nils 270, 271

Born, Max 271, 275

boundaries and limits
and criminal justice and social work
programmes 81, 87, 88, 90, 91
and postmodernist approach 32
replacement with flexible
boundaries 236
and trans-disciplinary working 188,
189

Bowen, E. 227

Brahe, Tycho 40

brain
dysfunction and criminal behaviour
63*fig*, 64–5, 69, 72, 73, 74
and impact of parenting 67–8, 69
sexual victimisation as cause of 72
dysfunction and parenting quality
74
neural networks 33
and risk analysis 44, 46, 48, 53–4

Braye, S. 194

Buchanan, M. 98

Buchbinder, E. 232

Building Better Relationships (BBR)
programme 221–3, 224, 230–1
and adaptation and co-evolution
233–4, 238
danger of homogenisation 225–7
and evaluation 226, 227, 238–9
and therapeutic relationship 235–6,
237–8

Burden, A. 149–50, 155

bureaucratic approaches 11, 203–4,
234–8

Burton, D.L. 235

Butterfly Effect *see* sensitive
dependence on initial conditions

Byrne, David 4, 17, 18, 29, 30, 31,
100–1, 167–8, 181, 186

Byrne, Simon 156*n*

C

Camazine, S. 248

Camus, Albert 35*n*

Canadian Criminal Justice Association
(CCJA) 161–2

captivity and psychological
jurisprudence 252–3, 256, 258,
260

Cartesian dualism 20, 28, 30, 287

causation
apophenia principle 48
contingent causation 29
and critical realism 30
as inadequate explanation of human
behaviour 12, 277

Cellular Automata 4
and rule-based complexity 26–8,
29, 31

change
models of change and Probation
Service 211–16
public services and complex change
170–1
quantum theory and space for
change 279
self-change and recovery from
addiction 250–6, 259, 263
see also adaptation

chaos and chaos theory 1, 18, 170
bifurcation 31, 211
chaos administration 275

chaotic state of complex systems 82, 83, 91, 93
criminal behaviour and Integrated Systems Theory 71, 74, 75
definition of chaos 40
and mathematical theory 4, 40
Metropolitan Police and Stephen Lawrence Inquiry 142–3
non-linear outcomes from linear tests 128
see also Complex Systems Science and youth justice; 'edge of chaos' position; sensitive dependence on initial conditions
chaotic attractors *see* strange attractors
Chapman, Jake 144
child development
and Integrated Systems Theory risk factors 69–70, 71
and risk of offending 127
child maltreatment and criminal behaviour 73–4
child protection practice 7, 97–111
complexity theory and understanding 97–8, 100–10
case example 102–5
linear approaches 98–100, 102–5, 106–7
child saturation and criminal behaviour 74
Chopra, Deepak 270
Cilliers, Paul 4, 16, 17, 23, 24, 30, 31–3
Clarke, C.L. 183–4
Clauser, J.F. 272
climate as complex adaptive system 107
Climbié, Victoria 100
clockwork universe and positivism 18, 19
Coalition government 200, 202, 213, 226
coercion
and addiction treatment 80, 84, 247, 250
and psychological jurisprudence 252–3, 258–9
domestic abuse programmes 236–7
cognitive dissonance and policing 142, 143, 151, 153–4tab, 155
cohabitation of justice 255, 256

collaboration and trans-disciplinary working 171–2, 189, 193–4, 207–8
colonialism and oppression 176
Colwell, Maria 100
community: post-positivist community 276
community factors/characteristics and criminal behaviour 63fig, 66, 67, 68fig, 72, 74
complex adaptive systems 21–6
and child protection practice 100–10
components and characteristics 85–9, 93, 170
definition 100–1
domestic abuse perpetrators as 23, 228
four states of systems 82–5, 93
human beings as 11–12, 42
innovation, maintenance and evaluation 89–92
as living organisms not machines 166–7, 273
Metropolitan Police Service as 8–9, 142, 144–6, 155
probation practitioners as 11, 233
public services and structural oppression 166, 168–9, 176
social work and criminal justice programmes as 6–7, 79–93, 98, 187–9
complex needs and creativity 204, 207–8, 209–11
complex state of complex systems 82, 83, 93
Complex Systems Science and youth justice 113, 116
critique of Risk Factor Research approach 7–8, 119–30, 132–3
complexity theory 1–2, 15–35
complex and complicated distinction 21–2
definition of complexity 82
mathematical background 4, 15–16, 17, 39–41
research opportunities 288–9
teaching opportunities 288–93
conditional probability 50–3
connectivity *see* interconnectedness
Connelly, Peter 100

Conservative–Liberal Democrat
  Coalition government 200, 202,
  213, 226
constitutive criminology 271, 280
constructivism *see* postmodernism
  (constructivism)
context
  and complex public systems 177
  contingent causation 29
  criminal behaviour and Integrated
    Systems Theory 71
  and knowledge 214
  'person in context' approach and
    domestic abuse 224
  and trans-disciplinary working
    185–6, 191
contingent causation 29
continued antisocial behaviour 62,
  63*fig*, 66, 67, 68
'contribution stories' and reflection
  192–3
Conway, John 128
Cooper, H. 194
Copenhagen Interpretation 12, 269,
  271–5, 283
Cottom, Hilary 203–4
covenant and quantum communities
  276
Cox, P. 102
creativity
  and dynamical self-organising
    systems 249
  and probation practice 11, 199–218
  see also innovation
Crime and Disorder Act (1998)
  116–17
criminal behaviour
  and Integrated Systems Theory
    (IST) 6, 59–75
    examples of complexity and crime
      73–4
    risk factors and criminal behaviour
      6, 61–70, 71–4, 75
  and quantum mechanics 12, 277
  social determinants and
    intersectionality theory 174–6
  see also criminology
criminal justice system
  criminal justice programmes as
    complex adaptive systems 6–7,
    79–93
  and structural oppression

aboriginal peoples in Canada
  161–2
youth justice 169–70, 172–6
  see also policing and complexity
    thinking; Probation Service; youth
    justice
criminology
  developmental criminology 69–70,
    71, 127
  and quantum mechanics 12, 269,
    270–1, 276–83
  resistance to complexity theory 72,
    75
  youth justice
    hegemony of positivism 114–19
    reliance on quantitative measures
      113
critical feminist theory 159, 160
critical incidents approach and
  policing 9, 142–3, 148, 151–2,
  153–4*tab*, 155–6
critical realism 30–1
critical social science 9
Critical Systems Heuristics 87
cross-sectoral working *see*
  multidisciplinary and trans-
  disciplinary working
Cycle of Change 211–12
cyclic state of complex systems 82,
  83, 93

D

'Daemon' intellect and determinism
  19, 20
Day, A. 237
decision-making and Prospect Theory
  53–4
Demos 144
Denis, J.-L. 171
Denson, L.A. 184
Descartes, René 19, 20, 287
desistance theory and probation 204,
  213, 214
  and domestic abuse perpetrators
    222, 226–7, 237
Despres, C. 190
destruction and complex change 171
destructive labelling and criminal
  behaviour 63*fig*, 66–7, 69
determinism 19, 20, 277–8
  and Cellular Automata 28
  and chaos theory 40

see also social determinants of health (SDH)
developmental criminology 69–70, 71, 127
diagnostics of psychological jurisprudence and drug addiction 248, 256–64
DiClemente, C. 212
diet/nutrition and antisocial behaviour 63*fig*, 64–5, 68, 69
disability and structural oppression 163
discharge planning and multidisciplinary response 182–3, 185–6, 190, 192–3, 292
discipline and criminal behaviour 67, 68*fig*
discrimination
  and practitioners' stereotypes 162
  see also institutional racism; structural oppression
disorder and order and quantum mechanics 272–5
dissipative structures and quantum mechanics 274, 275
diversity 209
  homogeneity assumptions
    and domestic abuse programmes 223–7
    and drug treatment 258–9, 262–3
  and postmodernist approach 32
  and trans-disciplinary working 189
domestic abuse and probation programmes 11, 221–39, 292–3
  adaptation and co-evolution 231–4, 238
  difficulty of measuring of outcomes 226–7
  need for individualised approach 11, 223–7, 230, 238
  poor outcomes 11, 222, 226, 236
  reducing complexity 234–8
  and whole-systems perspective 222–3, 227–31, 238
Dooley, K. 167
drug courts in the US 84
Drug Strategy for England 2
drug use and misuse and complexity
  and antisocial behaviour 62, 63*fig*, 64–5, 69

law and ethics and addiction treatment and natural recovery 11–12, 247–64, 293
  and adaptability and self-organisation 248–51, 262, 263
  policy considerations 261–2, 263–4
  and psychological jurisprudence 12, 251–64
  see also substance misuse and complexity
Duluth model domestic abuse programme 221–3, 224, 227, 230, 238
Dunedin Multidisciplinary Health and Development Study 73
Dutton, D.G. 223
dynamic systems 39, 125, 170
  adaptability and self-organisation 248–51, 262
  criminal justice and social work programmes 81
  and quantum mechanics 273–4
  risk assessment and management of sex offenders 103, 104–5, 110
  youth justice
    and intersectionality theory 171–2
    introduction of flexible assessment tool 130–2, 133
    and Risk Factor Research 120, 123–4
  see also non-linear dynamical systems (NDS)
dynamical systems theory 248–51

E

early anti-social behaviour 62, 63*fig*, 65, 66, 67, 68, 73
economic theory: Prospect Theory 53–4
ecosystems and complex adaptive systems 81, 86
  and substance misuse treatment 81, 89–90
'edge of chaos' position 24, 204, 208, 214, 235, 236, 274–5
Einstein, Albert 16, 34*n*, 271, 272
Eisikovits, Z. 232
emergent properties 25, 170, 186
  and child protection practice 101–2, 104

emergent behaviour and programmes 81–2, 87–8
probation work and emergent outcomes 215–16
and domestic abuse programmes 11, 223, 228–9
empiricism and criminology 70, 71, 114
employment problems and criminal behaviour 63*fig*, 66–7, 68, 69
environmental risk factors and antisocial behaviour 73, 74
environmental toxins and antisocial behaviour 63*fig*, 64, 66, 69
enzymes and antisocial behaviour 63*fig*, 64, 69, 73, 74
epigenetics 6
equilibrium state of complex systems 82, 83, 93
  and approach to feedback 87
  dynamical self-organising systems 249
  and Metropolitan Police after Stephen Lawrence Inquiry 142–3, 147–50
  and 'what works' approach 204, 236
ethics
  law and drug addiction and natural recovery 11–12, 247–64, 293
  and postmodernist approach 32
  see also values
ethnicity *see* race and ethnicity
evaluation
  and complex adaptive systems 88
  and criminal justice and social work programmes 91–2
  domestic abuse and probation programmes 226, 227, 238–9
  see also feedback
Every Child Matters (Green Paper) 100
Evidence Based Behavioural Practice (EBBP) model 195
evolution and response to risk 42–3, 49, 54
exclusion from services and structural oppression 9, 160
existential self-organisation 256–7
experimental criminology 114–15

F

Failure of Invariance 53
faith *see* religious beliefs

'false negatives' and 'false positives' 52
family conditions
  and antisocial behaviour 63*fig*, 64, 65–6, 69
  and intersectionality theory 174, 175
  parenting and children's brains 67–8, 69, 72
  child protection and family as complex adaptive system 100–1
  and risk-based approach in youth justice 120, 122
family liaison officers 153*tab*, 155
Farrington, D. 117
feedback
  and complex adaptive systems 87, 170
  and criminal justice and social work programmes 81, 83, 90
  and probation practice 11, 224, 225, 236
  see also evaluation
feminist criminology 271, 280
feminist theory and structural oppression 159, 160
  and intersectionality frameworks 163–4, 169
Fenwick, T. 194
Fertig, M. 170–1
Field-Fisher, T.G. 100
Fisher, A. 235
Fisher, E. 224–5, 230–1
flexibility
  and probation programmes 236, 238
  and youth justice practice 130–2, 133, 171–2
fractal measurement and youth justice 8, 116, 119–24, 129–30, 132, 133
fractal nature of police 142
Franklin, C. 85
free will *see* human agency
Freedman, S.J. 272
frequentism and positivist criminology 71, 114
'frozen watchfulness' in children 98

G

Galabuzi, Grace-Edward 165
Galileo 39–40
gamblers and risk analysis 45, 46
probability and Gambler's Fallacy 48–9, 50

Game of Life (computer game) 128
Gelles, R. 225
gender
    and antisocial behaviour
        and childhood maltreatment 73
        peer victimisation and aggressive
            behaviour 74
        psychiatrisation of childhood
            oppression 176
    gender equality
        and domestic abuse discourse
            221–2, 225
        and post-Newtonian society 280
    probation practitioners and
        adaptation and co-evolution 232
    and structural oppression 9, 160,
        161, 163
General Aggression Model 223
'general' complexity 4, 16–17
general systems theory 2, 6
genes and antisocial behaviour 63*fig*,
    64, 68, 69, 73–4
    and quality of parenting 72, 74
geography and social determinants of
    health 164–5
Gershenson, C. 31–2
Geyer, R. 194
Giddens, A. 186
Gilchrist, E.A. 227
Glaser, D. 226–7
Gödel, Kurt 7, 28, 92
Godeman, J. 187, 189, 190
Gondolf, E.W. 229, 230
Gough, D. 199
grassroots decisions 79, 81, 88
Greenhalgh, T. 21
Grieve, J. 151
Guastello, S. 24

H

Hadorn, G.H. 188–9
Hague, G. 229
Hall, Nathan 150, 155
Halleck, S.L. 233
Hassett, P. 101
Hate Crime Independent Advisory
    Group 150, 153*tab*
hate crimes and policing 149, 155
Hayek, Friedrich 81–2
health and well-being
    inequities and structural oppression
        9, 160, 161–3

and intersectionality theory
    163–77
see also healthcare systems and
    settings
healthcare systems and settings
    and complexity 20–1, 167–8
    interorganisational networks 171
    as living organism 166
    multidisciplinary working and
        responses 181–6, 188–90
    see also health and well-being;
        hospitals
Heifetz, R.A. 152
Heisenberg, Werner 271, 275
Henry, S. 59
Henry, Stuart 280
Herron, K. 224
heterogeneity *see* diversity
Heylighen, F. 20, 31–2, 248, 249
historicism and psychological
    jurisprudence 251
Hodgson, Peter 269–70, 281
holistic approaches *see* whole-systems
    approaches
Holtzworth-Munroe, A. 224
homogeneity assumptions
    and domestic abuse 223–7
    and drug treatment 258–9, 262–3
hormones and antisocial behaviour
    63*fig*, 64, 69
hospitals
    children's unexplained injuries 97,
        98–9, 108
    discharge planning 182–3, 185–6,
        190, 192–3, 292
    see also healthcare systems and
        settings
human agency 291
    and criminal behaviour 62
    and positivism 19–21, 277–8
    and quantum mechanics 272, 276–7
    rejection of free will in Integrated
        Systems Theory 70
    subject and postmodernist approach
        32
    and substance misuse programmes
        80
    see also agent-based activity;
        complex adaptive systems
human behaviour
    and economic theory 53–4
    influences on 39

Probation Service and models for change 211–16
human beings as complex systems 11–12, 42
  response to risk 43–6, 48–55
  see also brain
human social capital and psychological jurisprudence 248, 251–6, 258, 261–2, 263–4

I

identities and 'isms' and structural oppression 9, 160, 161, 163, 164–5, 176
ignorance: acknowledgement of 189
Ilgen, D.R. 228–9
Iliffe, G. 231–2
incentives and regression to the mean 47–8
Incompleteness Theorems 7, 28, 92
individual decisions and emergent behaviour 81–2
individualism and quantum society 275–6
individualistic approach to domestic abuse 11, 223–7, 230, 238
inequities in well-being and structural oppression 9, 160, 161–3
  and intersectionality theory 163–77
information flows and complexity 203–4, 213
initial conditions *see* sensitive dependence on initial conditions
inner experiences and quantum mechanics 272–3
Innes, A. 214
innovation
and dynamical self-organising systems 249
  and edge of chaos position 274–5
  and emergent programmes 83–4, 88, 91
  see also creativity
Institute for Government 203
Institute of Medicine (US) 21
institutional problems 68
institutional racism and policing 8, 141, 142, 143, 146–7, 149, 150, 153–4*tab*, 155, 292
Integrated Domestic Abuse Programme (IDAP) 221, 222, 226
Integrated Systems Theory (IST)

and criminal behaviour 6, 59–75
developmental timeline 69–70, 71
examples of complexity and crime 73–4
levels of analysis 59–60, 61
restatement of theory 67–8
testing of theory 68, 74
unique features 70–2
interconnectedness and complex adaptive systems 79–80, 81, 82–3, 86, 90, 93, 181
domestic abuse and probation programmes 225
and quantum mechanics 271–2, 275
see also social networks
interdisciplinary approaches 1, 59, 70, 74, 166, 287, 288
lacking in criminology 71–2
see also Integrated Systems Theory (IST); multidisciplinary and trans-disciplinary working
International Self-Reported Delinquency Survey 121*tab*
interorganisational networks 171–2
inter-professional practice 170, 171–2, 193–4
intersectionality theory and oppression 9, 163–77, 292
blending with complexity theory 166–72
youth justice case study 172–6
IQ *see* verbal intelligence quota (IQ)
'isms' *see* identities and 'isms'

J

Jackson, R. 270
Jaffe, P.G. 227
Jeffery, C. Ray 59
Jennings, P. 101, 109
Jewell, L.M. 226

K

Kahneman, Daniel 53
Kauffman, Stuart 16, 24
Kelly, L. 226
Kempe, C.H. 98–9, 108
Kepler, Johann 39–40
Kernick, D. 2, 18
Kleppner, D. 270
Klingemann, H. 250
knowledge

as active process 203
knowledge sharing 189
and probation practice 213–14
Koch, J. 147–8
Kozlowski, S.W. 228–9
Kuhn, Thomas 80

L

labelling *see* destructive labelling
Labour governments 116, 146, 200
Laming, H. 100
Lamothe, L. 171
Lanier, M. 59
Laplace, Pierre-Simon 19, 20
law and ethics and drug addiction
    11–12, 247–64, 293
Law of Large Numbers 48, 49, 50
Lawrence, Doreen, Baroness
    Lawrence 146, 150
Lawrence, L. 190
Lawrence, Neville 146
Lawrence, Stephen 141–3, 146–56,
    292
Ledwidge, Mike 144
Lehmann, P. 232
Lewin, K. 59
Liebovitch, L. 24
lifestyle patterns and antisocial
    behaviour 63*fig*, 67
Likert-type ratings scales 120, 121*tab*,
    122
linear approaches 277
    and child protection practice
        98–100, 102–5, 106–7
    Metropolitan Police training and
        management 142
    youth justice and understanding of
        offending 113–14, 115, 116–19
    complexity critique of positivist
        approaches 7–8, 119–30, 132–3
    introduction of non-linear tool
        131–2, 133
    linear statistical analyses 114
Ling, T. 192–3
living conditions *see* social
    determinants of health (SDH)
'locked in' systems 27
    and policing 8, 9, 147–9, 292
logical positivism 30, 80
Lorenz, Edward 18, 40, 124–5, 126,
    127–8
low self-control theory 72

low verbal intelligence quota (IQ)
    and criminal behaviour 63*fig*, 65,
    69
Lowe, T. 203–4

M

McLaren, Samuel 102–5, 109, 110,
    291–2
McLaughlin, K. 184, 187
MacLeod, J. 235
McNeill, F. 237
Macpherson, Sir William 146
Malos, E. 229
mandatory drug treatment
    programmes 80, 84, 247, 250, 253,
    259–60
Mandelbrot, Benoit 119, 122, 125
Mann, R. 236
manual adherence and domestic abuse
    programmes 235, 236
marginalised people *see* structural
    oppression
Marshall, Ian 275–6
Marshall, W.L. 235
Maruna, S. 226–7
materialism 19
mathematics
    and analysis of complex systems 23,
        92
    classical mechanics 39–40
    and background to complexity
        theory 15–16, 17, 39–41
    and chaos 4
    power laws and child protection
        108–9
    and risk analysis 4–6
        conditional probability 50–1
        and 'regression to the mean' 46–7
Matlow, A.G. 167, 172
Maxwell, J. 30–1
mechanisms: social mechanisms 29
mechanistic view of world 39–40,
    273–4, 280
medicine
    and quantum healing 270
    and 'scientific method' 20, 21
Meehan, C. 224
mental illness and antisocial behaviour
    60, 63*fig*, 65, 69
Metropolitan Police Service (MPS)
    and Stephen Lawrence Inquiry
    141–56, 292

as complex adaptive system 8–9, 142, 144–6, 155
Mihata, K. 101–2
Mikkonen, J. 165
Mikulecky, D. 28–9
Mill, John Stuart 20
Miller, J. 59, 61
Miller, J.H. 92
Milovanovic, Dragon 280
mindfulness 255, 261, 283
mind–body dualism 20, 28, 30, 287
Mitchell, M. 82
Mitleton-Kelly, E. 225, 234, 235
modelling and programmes 91, 92
'modelling relation' 28–9
Monoamine oxidase (MAO) and antisocial behaviour 64
  monoamine oxidase A (MAOA) genotype 73, 74
moral panics and overestimation of risk 44
Morin, E. 4, 16–17, 31, 227
Morran, D. 229–30
Morris, W. 149–50, 155
motivation and probation work 209, 211
  and domestic abuse programmes 227, 236–8
multidisciplinary and trans-disciplinary working 10, 21, 181–96
  challenges of 190–1
  collaborative working 171–2, 189, 207–8
    training for collaboration 193–5
  in Probation Service 199, 204, 207–8
    domestic abuse and probation programmes 11, 227–39
  and reflective practice 10, 191–3, 196, 292
  research opportunities 293–4
Munro, E. 2, 97, 200
Muran, C. 234
Murray, H. 59
Murray, Williamson 145

N

National Crime Agency (NCA) 145
National Society for the Prevention of Cruelty to Children (NSPCC) 97

natural recovery 12, 247–8, 250–6, 259
negative freedom and drug treatment 259–60
Nested Ecological Approach 223, 230
networks
  interorganisational networks 171–2
  see also neural network approaches; social networks
neural network approaches 32–3
neurotransmitters and antisocial behaviour 63*fig*, 64, 69, 74
New Labour *see* Labour governments
Newhouse, R.P. 188, 190–1, 195
Newman, J. 233
Newton, Sir Isaac 16, 18, 19, 20
  and mechanistic view of world 39–40, 273–4, 280
  Newtonian separation of faith and reason 269–70, 283
Nietzsche, Friedrich Wilhelm 35*n*
nominalism 17
non-accidental injury (NAI) to children 98–100, 101, 108
non-linear dynamical systems (NDS) 1, 2
  adaptability and self-organisation 248–51, 262
non-linearity 185
  and emergence in social care applications 82
  and fractal measurement 119, 132
  and sensitive dependence on initial conditions 128, 133, 167
  and system-based oppression 9, 177
Norcross, J.C. 235
Nunn Commission of Inquiry (Canada) 172–5, 292
Nutley, S. 233
nutrition *see* diet/nutrition and antisocial behaviour

O

O'Cinneide, C. 225
Offender Engagement Programme 235
Offender Management Model (OMM) 200–1
offending *see* criminal behaviour; Probation Service; youth justice
O'Murchu, Diarmuid 282–3

On Track Youth Lifestyles Survey 120, 121*tab*
open systems 166, 236
  dissipative structures 274, 275
  and policing 152, 155–6
oppression *see* structural oppression
order and disorder and quantum mechanics 272–5
'order for free' systems 8, 24, 25, 27, 82, 149, 202, 292
Orford, J. 209
organisational behaviour 39–55
  organisational creativity in Probation Service 204, 207–8
  quantum administration 275
  and regression to the mean 47–8
  and risk analysis and management 42–55
organised complexity 85
Orientation of Social Support (OSS) 88, 90
outcome equivalence paradox 208–9, 213
outsourcing services *see* 'payment by results'
overestimation of risk 44, 49, 50
Overman, E.S. 275

P

P, Baby (Peter Connelly) 100
Page, S.E. 92
Paley, J. 167
paradigm comparison 204, 205–6*tab*, 291
pareidolia effect 48
parenting
  brain dysfunction and parenting quality 74
  and children's brains 67–8, 69
  genes and parenting quality 72, 74
  and risk of child abuse 98–9
Partner Link Workers *see* Women Safety Workers
path sensitivity *see* sensitive dependence on initial conditions
patterning and outcomes 185–6
Patton, M.Q. 91
Pawson, R. 4, 20, 29–30, 181, 186, 187–8, 190, 191
'payment by results (PBR)' 200, 203, 216, 226

peacemaking criminology 12, 271, 280–3, 293
peer associations and antisocial behaviour 63*fig*, 65–6, 66–7, 68, 69
  and adolescents with intellectual and developmental disabilities 84
  parenting and impact on children's brains 67
peer victimisation and antisocial behaviour 74
  quantum mechanics perspective 277, 278–9
Pepinsky, Harold 280, 281, 283
periodic behaviour 18
'person in context' approach 224
Petrillo, M. 232
phase space and risk 41, 42–3, 48, 49–50
  phase space reduction 52, 53
Phipps, D.L. 190
physical laws and classical mechanics 39–40
Plato/Platonism 17, 19, 29, 31
Plotinus 34*n*
Plsek, P. 21
Pohl, C. 188–9
Polaschek, D.L.L. 225, 234
policing and complexity thinking 141–56
  'big data' approach 151
  Metropolitan Police Service as complex adaptive system 8–9, 142, 144–6, 155
  and Stephen Lawrence inquiry 141–3, 146–56, 292
    adaptation and analysis of police response 9, 141, 144–6, 147, 151–2, 153–4*tab*
    and institutional racism 8, 141, 142, 143, 146–7, 149, 150, 153–4*tab*, 155
Polkinghorne, John 269, 281
positivism 4, 16, 19–21, 39, 80
  Cellula Automata 26–8
  and complex adaptive systems 7
  determinism and human behaviour 277–8
  Integrated Systems Theory 70
  and youth justice 114–19
    critiques of 7–8, 115–16, 119–30, 132–3

Risk Factor Research approach 113–14, 115, 116–19
see also post-positivism (realism)
post-positivism (realism) 16, 17, 28–31, 288
  policing and complexity 142
  postmodernist rejection of 31
  and quantum mechanics 12, 269–83
  and social work and complexity theory 80, 92, 98
  and trans-disciplinary working and reflective practice 10, 181–96, 292
  and youth justice approach 7–8, 113
postmodernism (constructivism) 16, 17, 24, 31–3, 287
  and critical realism 30–1
  and quantum mechanics 269, 283
poverty
  and antisocial behaviour 63*fig*, 66, 176
    social disorganisation and strain on parenting 67–8
  and inequities in health and well-being 160
    racialised factor 165
  see also structural oppression
power
  bureaucratic power 203–4
  systemic power *see* structural oppression
power laws
  and injuries to children 7, 101, 105–6, 107–9
  and probation reforms 202, 217
practitioners
  Probation Service
    adaptation and co-evolution 231–4
    as complex adaptive systems 11, 233
    and creativity 208–11
    reducing bureaucracy and complexity 234–8
  stereotypes and structural oppression 162
  and 'swirl of data' 182, 183
  trans-disciplinary working and reflective practice 10, 181–96, 292
  youth justice and risk assessment tools 122–3, 129–30, 132
pregnancy/prenatal conditions and criminal behaviour 63*fig*, 64, 69

Prigogine, Ilya 274
probability and statistics 43
  Bayes' Theorem and quantification of risk 44–5, 51–3
  conditional probability 50–3
  criminal behaviour and Integrated Systems Theory 70, 75
  frequentism and positivist criminology 114
  Gambler's Fallacy 48–9, 50
  and human approach to risk 45–6, 48–55
  and regression to the mean effect 46–8
  and substance misuse treatment programmes 90
Probation Service 10–11, 199–218
  creative thinking 204, 207–11
  models of change and challenge for practitioners 211–16
    application of complexity 214–16
  Offender Management Model (OMM) 200–1
  policy context and reforms 200–4, 213
    paradigm comparison 204, 205–6*tab*, 291
  superposition of probation officers 213, 217
  see also domestic abuse and probation programmes
problem-framing and problem-solving and trans-disciplinary working 188, 189–90
process and causality 30
Prochaska, J. 212
programme delivery and scientific realism 29–30
proportionality and understanding offending 115
Prospect Theory 53–4
protective factors 62, 71, 75, 224
psychiatrisation of childhood oppression 176
psychological jurisprudence 12, 251–64
psychological support for probation practitioners 232–3
psychological theory *see* cognitive dissonance

public systems
  as complex adaptive systems 166,
    168–9, 176
  and complex change 170–1
  and oppression *see* structural
    oppression
Pycroft, A. 26, 101, 109, 230, 237

Q

qualitative risk assessment and youth
  justice 8, 131–2
quantitative criminology and youth
  justice 8, 113–16
quantum inseparability 271–2
quantum mechanics 32, 33–4, 213,
  269–83, 287
  Copenhagen Interpretation 12, 269,
    271–5, 283
  and criminological theories 12, 269,
    270–1, 276–83
  and religious beliefs 280–3, 293
  Einstein's critique 271
Quinney, Richard 280, 281, 283

R

race and ethnicity
  and discrimination and
    disempowerment 280
  and structural oppression 9, 160,
    161–2, 163, 165, 176
  see also black and minority ethnic
    (BME) community
racism *see* institutional racism
random behaviour 18, 170
  and quantum mechanics 272–3
randomised controlled trials (RCTs)
  20, 21, 114
Raphael, D. 165
realism *see* critical realism; critical
  social science; post-positivism
  (realism)
recovery and drug addiction 12,
  247–8
  and dynamical self-organising
    systems 250–6
  and psychological jurisprudence
    258, 259–60
reductionism 28–9, 31, 34, 114–15,
  277
  and Metropolitan Police 8–9, 142,
    151–2

and probation work strategies
  215–16
and risk-based approach in Youth
  Justice System 113, 116–19, 123
  complexity critique 7–8, 119–30,
    132–3
reductionist approach in Youth Justice
  System 8, 119–24, 129–30, 132,
  133
Rees, A. 235
reflective practice
  probation practitioners 235, 236
  and trans-disciplinary working 10,
    191–3, 196, 292
'regression to the mean' 46–8
Rehman, U. 224
Reiner, R. 145
rejectors 41
relationship problems
  and criminal behaviour 63*fig*, 66–7,
    68, 69
  and strengthening social networks
    89
religious beliefs and quantum
  mechanics 12, 269–70, 276, 280–3,
  293
replicated chaos and negative freedom
  260, 263
resilience
  dynamical self-organising systems
    249
  social networks and complex
    adaptive systems 86–7, 88–9
restorative justice 281
'restricted' complexity 4, 16
risk analysis and management 42–55,
  291–2
  and child protection practice 101,
    105–6, 109–10
  linear focus in management of sex
    offenders 102–5, 106–7
  criminal behaviour risk factors and
    Integrated Systems Theory 6,
    61–70, 71–4, 75
  domestic abuse and complex risk
    factors 223
  drug treatment and psychological
    jurisprudence perspective 255,
    258–9
  miscalculation of risk 43–4, 45,
    48–9, 50, 53–4
  and Probation Service 200–3

Offender Management Model (OMM) 200–1
reductionist approach in Youth Justice System
  fractal measurement as alternative 8, 119–24, 129–30, 133
  replacement with more flexible assessment tool 130–2
  Risk Factor Research (RFR) 7–8, 113–14, 115–16, 116–19, 119–30, 132–3
  risk avoidance strategies 50, 184, 186–7, 202
  risk society and human social capital 253
  and trans-disciplinary working 183–4, 186–7, 189
  see also risk factors
Risk Factor Prevention Paradigm (RFPP) 113, 116, 117
'risk factorology' 117
Rittel, H. 145
Rivett, M. 235
road safety and linear approaches 107
Robinson, M. 60
Rochester Youth Delinquency Survey 121*tab*
Ross, E.C. 234
routine activities
  and antisocial behaviour 63*fig*, 67
  and management of sex offenders 102–3
rule-based complexity and Cellular Automata 26–8, 29, 31

S

Safran, J.D. 234
Samstag, L.W. 234
Santa Fe Institute (SFI) 16, 92
Sayer, Andrew 29
scale and efficacy of interventions 216
Scaled Approach to youth justice 118, 129–30, 131, 132
Schneller, E. 170–1
Schreyögg, G. 147–8
Schwartz, J.M. 33–4, 272
scientific realism *see* positivism; post-positivism (realism)
scientific view of world 19, 20, 107
  Integrated Systems Theory 70, 71
  see also mechanistic view of world; quantum mechanics

SDH *see* social determinants of health (SDH)
Seattle Social Development Project 121*tab*
Sedgwick, D. 231
self-change and recovery from addiction 250–6, 259, 263
self-efficacy and probation work 209, 211
self-help and Alcoholics Anonymous 85
self-organisation
  and complex adaptive systems 11–12, 86–7, 93, 170, 185, 248
  and criminal justice and social work programmes 80, 81, 82, 83, 84, 85, 88
  existential self-organisation 256–7
  law and ethics of drug addiction programmes 12, 247–51, 262, 263, 293
self-organising systems 24, 32, 40
sensitive dependence on initial conditions (Butterfly Effect) 167, 170
  domestic abuse programmes and outcomes 229
  and policing after Stephen Lawrence Inquiry 8–9, 148–9
  and youth justice 8, 116, 124–8, 129–30, 133
Serena, C. 145
sexual orientation and oppression 163
sexual victimisation in childhood 72, 102, 216
shadow and human social capital 252, 254, 256
shared systems-based thinking 188
Shiell, A. 190
Simmons, C.A. 232
simple attractors 41
simple systems 28–9
simulation and testing programmes 91
'Sit Down, Shut Up, and Call an Attorney Curriculum' (US programme) 84
Smale, S. 128
small-world network support 88–9, 90
Smith, Adam 81–2
Smith, Graham 150
Snowden, D. 213–14

social adaptation and human social
capital 258
social capital *see* human social capital
social determinants of health (SDH)
9, 159–60
and intersectionality theory 164–5,
169*fig*, 177
youth justice case study 174–6
social disorganisation 63*fig*, 66–7
social injustice *see* structural
oppression
social innovation schemes 88
social mechanisms 29
social networks
and complex adaptive systems 86–7,
88, 278
and criminal behaviour 278–9
strengthening and substance misuse
treatment 81, 82–3, 88–9, 89–92
see also peer associations and
criminal behaviour
social relations
and causality 29
dynamic qualities 126
and quantum mechanics 273–4,
275–6, 278
and response to risk 44
see also social networks
social work
bureaucratic work load 203–4
child protection practice 7, 97–111
emergence of social work
programmes 79–80
multidisciplinary working and
responses 181–96
social work programmes as complex
adaptive systems 6–7, 79–93, 98,
187–9
see also Probation Service
spatial contexts of oppression 165
spiritual beliefs *see* religious beliefs
spontaneous recovery 12, 247–8,
250–6, 259
Spring, B. 188, 190–1, 195
Stanford, S. 184, 187
statistics
youth justice and linear approaches
114
complexity critique 125–6, 128,
129–30
see also probability and statistics
Steed, L. 231–2

Stephen Lawrence Public Inquiry
141–3, 146–56, 292
and institutional racism 8, 143,
146–7, 149, 150, 153–4*tab*, 155
stereotypes and structural oppression
162
Stevens, C. 234
Stevens, I. 101, 102
Stone, Richard 146, 150
stop and search and BME male
youths 146–7, 150, 154*tab*
strain: perceptions of and antisocial
behaviour 63*fig*, 64, 65, 66, 67, 69
strange attractors 41, 42, 210–11, 292
Straw, Jack 149
Streeter, C.L. 85
strengths-based approaches 204, 222,
224, 230
stress during pregnancy and criminal
behaviour 69
Strid, S. 221–2, 225
structural oppression 159–77
and inequities in well-being 9, 160,
161–3
and intersectionality theory 9,
163–77
youth justice case study 172–6
structure and agency 29
Stuart, G.L. 224
subject and postmodernist approach
32
subjectivity and complex public
systems 177
substance misuse and complexity 21
and criminal justice and social work
programmes 80
mandatory treatment programmes
80, 84, 247, 250, 253
strengthening social networks 81,
82–3, 88–9, 89–92
outcome equivalence paradox
208–9, 213
reductionist strategies 215
see also drug use and misuse and
complexity
suffering and peacemaking
criminology 280, 281
superposition of probation officers
213, 217
Sydow, J. 147–8
synergy of oppression 164–5

systemic approach and systems
  thinking 145, 166–7, 185–6, 195
  and Integrated Systems Theory 71
  see also whole-systems approaches
systemic power *see* structural
  oppression

T

temporal sensitivity 125
  and youth justice assessments 123–4,
  126–7
theology and quantum physics 281–3
therapeutic relationship and domestic
  abuse programmes 234–8, 292–3
Thompson, D.D.P. 142–3, 145, 152,
  155–6
Tilley, N. 4, 20, 29–30, 181, 186,
  187–8, 190, 191
Tillich, P. 35*n*
Toronto Charter 165
trans-disciplinary working *see*
  multidisciplinary and trans-
  disciplinary working
Trans-theoretical Model of
  Intentional Behavioural Change
  (TTM) 211–12
Trimpop, R.M. 46
Tversky, A. 53

U

uncertainty: acknowledgement of 189
uncertainty principle and quantum
  mechanics 271
unexplained injuries to children 97,
  98–100, 101, 108
Unified Adolescent Team (UAT) 204,
  207–8
unintended consequences 2, 86, 91,
  98, 172, 292
United States
  emergence of programmes 79, 84–5
    substance abuse treatment
    programmes 80, 89–92
  hegemony of positivist criminology
  114
utilitarianism 20

V

values
  and quantum society 276

and trans-disciplinary working 189
  see also ethics
verbal intelligence quota (IQ) and
  criminal behaviour 63*fig*, 65, 69
Vila, B. 61
violence 73, 74
  see also aggression; criminal
  behaviour; domestic abuse and
  probation programmes
Virchow, Rudolf 163
virtue ethics
  and probation practice 214
  and psychological jurisprudence 12,
  254–5, 262–3, 293

W

Walby, S. 186, 221–2
Waldrop, M. Mitchell 274–5
Wallace, M. 170–1
Ward, T. 234
Warren, K. 85
weather prediction 40
Weaver, B. 234
Weaver, W. 85
Weber, Max 203
Weckes, A. 149–50, 155
welfare recipients and oppression 162
well-being *see* health and well-being
Westmarland, N. 226
'what works' policy
  'blaming and shaming' 224
  and bureaucracy 204, 205–6*tab*, 216
  and need for individualised
  approach 225
Whitehead, A. 59
whole-systems approaches 2, 287
  assessment and youth justice 131–2
  and complex systems 23
    and emergence of programmes 81
    public systems 167
  and probation services 204
    domestic abuse programmes
    222–3, 227–31, 238
  see also complex adaptive systems;
  Complex Systems Science;
  structural oppression
'wicked problems' 145–6
Williams, O. 226
Wilson, T. 22
Wolf-Branigin, M. 182, 191, 195, 216
Wolfe, D.A. 227
Women Safety Workers (WSWs) 228

Women's Aid 228
World Health Organization 160, 167
  Framework for Action on
    Interprofessional Education and
    Collaborative Practice 193–4
Wormith, J.M. 226

Y

Yalom, I.D. 228
Young, T.R. 125
Youth Audit risk measurement 120,
  121*tab*
youth justice 113–35
  Risk Factor Research (RFR) and
    linear approach 113–14, 115,
    116–19
    complexity critique and alternative
      approach 7–8, 113, 115–16,
      119–33
    structural oppression and
      intersectionality theory 160,
      169–70, 170–6, 292
Youth Justice Board (YJB) 118
Youth Justice System (YJS) and risk-
  based approach 113, 116–19, 123,
  129
Youth Offending Teams (YOTs)
  117–18

Z

Zimmerman, B. 167, 236
Zinn, Howard 280
Zohar, Danah 275–6